AMERICA AND THE WAR OF 1812

65951

AMERICA AND THE WAR OF 1812

EUGENE M. WAIT

Kroshka Books
Commack, New York

Editorial Production:	Susan Boriotti
Office Manager:	Annette Hellinger
Graphics:	Frank Grucci and John T'Lustachowski
Information Editor:	Tatiana Shohov
Book Production:	Donna Dennis, Patrick Davin, Christine Mathosian and Tammy Sauter
Circulation:	Maryanne Schmidt
Marketing/Sales:	Cathy DeGregory

Library of Congress Cataloging-in-Publication Data

Wait, Eugene M.
     America and the War of 1812 / Eugene M. Wait.
         p.   cm.
     Includes bibliographical references (p.   ) and index.
     ISBN 1-56072-644-X
     1. United States--History--1809-1817. 2. United States--History--War of 1812. 3. United States--History--War of 1812--Influence. I. Title.

| E341.W2 | 1999 | 98-51316 |
| 973.5'1--dc21 | | CIP |

Copyright © 1999 by Eugene M. Wait
     Kroshka Books. A division of
     Nova Science Publishers, Inc.
     6080 Jericho Turnpike, Suite 207
     Commack, New York 11725
     Tele. 516-499-3103   Fax 516-499-3146
     e-mail: Novascience@earthlink.net
     e-mail: Novascil@aol.com
     Web Site: http://www.nexusworld.com/nova

All rights reserved. No part of this book may be reproduced, stored in a retrieval system or transmitted in any form or by any means: electronic, electrostatic, magnetic, tape, mechanical photocopying, recording or otherwise without permission from the publishers.

The authors and publisher have taken care in preparation of this book, but make no expressed or implied warranty of any kind and assume no responsibility for any errors or omissions. No liability is assumed for incidental or consequential damages in connection with or arising out of information contained in this book.

This publication is designed to provide accurate and authoritative information with regard to the subject matter covered herein. It is sold with the clear understanding that the publisher is not engaged in rendering legal or any other professional services. If legal or any other expert assistance is required, the services of a competent person should be sought. FROM A DECLARATION OF PARTICIPANTS JOINTLY ADOPTED BY A COMMITTEE OF THE AMERICAN BAR ASSOCIATION AND A COMMITTEE OF PUBLISHERS.

Printed in the United States of America

CHAPTER I

THE JEFFERSONIANS

When Abraham Lincoln was born, the American nation was the world of President Jefferson. Agrarian Thomas Jefferson was a simple man in comparison to his two predecessors, caring for none of the pageantry which had fastened itself upon the presidency. This was attuned with Jefferson's conception that the best government was that which governed least. Jefferson was intent upon economy in government and the paying off the Federal debt. With the control of Congress in his hands, Jefferson proceeded to reverse Federalist policies. He cut the size of the army to a bare outline of its former self and ended all naval construction. This was popular with most voters. He abolished the newly created courts and put Albert Gallatin to work as Secretary of the Treasury administering the public economy in such a manner as to insure the utmost frugality. Gallatin, who had migrated to the United States from Switzerland and had served in Congress as a Jeffersonian Republican, held his office until 1813.

Elected in 1800, the new president also wished to cut taxes with the object of ending all taxes on production in an age before income taxes. His first step was the abolition of the excise tax which had caused so much trouble in the Whiskey Rebellion of the previous decade. This action satisfied Secretary Gallatin immensely since the secretary of the treasury had been caught in that civil conflict against taxes on whiskey production in the backwoods of the west. The direct taxes levied as a result of the naval war between France and the United States were abolished. However, there remained taxes on salt, sugar, tea, and coffee. Jefferson hoped that the tax on salt and sugar could be ended, but the need of he government for some revenue stood in the way of this work.

The most important act of his administration though was his purchase of Louisiana province from France. This purchase, despite its size, was not to be enough. American desires for land to the west and south were to be common throughout Lincoln's life. Settlement was to continue in the Nineteenth Century, past Lincoln's death. In 1803, there were already Americans living in Spanish territory adjacent to the United States. A certain trade existed although not always with the approval of Spanish officialdom, especially back in Spain.

He had made the Louisiana Purchase in the interests of the people, despite his constitutional scruples in doing so being a strict constructionist. With the Mississippi in American hands, the peace necessary for economy in government was ensured. Even more so, he feared that the Louisiana area would fall into British hands, leaving the infant United States at the mercy of the British Empire. Jefferson still feared British influence above all things. Indeed he was a strong exponent of expansion, seeing in the United

States, a great nation in size in the Americas. Americans had a mission of democracy and enlightenment. The question of the constitutionality of the move was met with the realism which all parties followed religiously. The weakened opposition made a formal objection, voting against the purchase as a matter of record, and immediately forgot their opposition in their appreciation of the action as being good business sense. Jefferson was fortunate in having an opposition which was losing ground and which ended praising his administration of public business.

Although the Republican Party had many malcontents who wanted the government jobs which Jefferson was cutting as a result of the new policy of economy in government, Jefferson was able to strengthen the party through other means. He spread the depositing of public funds among many banks creating a wide interest in the Republican cause among the bankers, who were hopeful for more patronage from the government. In the hope of gaining the adherents of Federalism for his party, he was judicious in the granting of public offices to members of the Federalist Party as well as his own party. A realist above all else, Jefferson expected the state governments controlled by Federalists to reciprocate, but Connecticut repulsed all Republican office seekers. It is interesting to note that only Connecticut and Delaware (plus two electoral votes from Maryland) cast their electoral votes against Jefferson in the election of 1804. Jefferson's administration was popular, although a faction of Republicans headed by John Randolph in Congress opposed Jefferson throughout his second administration. [1]

Jefferson had strong views. He expressed beliefs on the international situation early in his Administration to the great Robert R. Livingston, who had been a law partner of John Jay, an assemblyman, a delegate to the Continental Congress and one of the five drafters of the Declaration of Independence with Jefferson, and a chancellor of New York. He was a secretary of foreign affairs and later a minister to France for Jefferson. It was Livingston who would have to play a diplomatic role in the problem of Europe to the Americans before Lincoln was born.

Britain and France were seizing American ships. Jefferson erupted. The new president wrote that "we believe the practice of seizing what is called contraband of war is an abusive practice, not founded in natural right." The war between Britain and France "cannot diminish the rights of the rest of the world remaining at peace. The doctrine that benefit warring nations are monstrous and the rational doctrine is correct that "the wrong which two nations endeavor to inflict upon another, must not infringe on the rights or convenience of those remaining at peace." Contraband is anything that might help each nation or it is nothing. There can be no line between them. All trade is legal or no trade is legal. Neutrals had the right of freedom to trade in Jefferson's view, and their ships could not be searched. This is of great importance but not worth a war. War was not "the most certain means of enforcing them. Those peacetime coercions which are in the power of every nation, if undertaken in concert and in time of peace, are more likely to produce the desired effect." The president was to believe this throughout his eight years in high office. [2]

The war clouds in Europe continually affected the United States, leaving war a mere step away. Jefferson opposed interfering in European affairs and vainly hoped that America's passive neutrality would induce England and France to respect American rights. Great Britain, with its naval power assured by the victory of Trafalgar, continued to attack American shipping. Indeed, the British government became more strict and aggressive. American weakness was taken advantage of by the British. Their frigates stopped American ships off American ports. They seized seamen from ships.

Jefferson's immediate reaction was to strengthen the defenses of the seaports. Congress passed appropriations for this work, but not to build warships. Rather than to declare war on Great Britain, Jefferson undertook a non-importation policy and promoted the Embargo Act, which was passed by Congress on December 22, 1807. It was directed at both sides of the European conflict since both were seizing American ships. The Embargo Act forbade commerce with foreign nations and American exports fell from $110,084,207 in 1807 to $22,430,960. The agrarian interests, loyal to Jefferson, bore the suffering with fortitude, but the manufacturing and trade interests of the North protested strongly and engaged in smuggling. The acts were hurting the American economy.

Enforcing acts passed by Congress caused near-insurrection in New England. Some Federal collectors resigned in the face of public opposition, while others were taken to court. Courts in sympathy with the smugglers refused to find smugglers guilty. The New Englanders felt that the British depredations should be stopped by an American-British alliance. Temporarily cowed by the call for secession in New England and Federalist prophecy of bloodshed, Congress relented and restored trade with all countries except France and Great Britain. [3]

In domestic affairs of the time, there were problems and situations with rising portents in youth for the years ahead. The Van Burens had held slaves but many Jeffersonian Republicans believed that slavery should be abolished, following the example of the vote in the Lower House of New Jersey. Further, they favored universal manhood suffrage. Those who had the vote would be encouraged to acquire property. They felt that state legislatures and private individuals should finance canals, like the now surveyed Delaware and Chesapeake Canal, and public roads. Should Republicans establish banks and land companies, they would provide sixty million dollars in capital for development. They stressed education. Republicans called for common schools, academies, and state universities. The Federalist government would stay out of such endeavors, however. It was not their business it was believed.

A New Jersey creed for Republicans was printed elsewhere in the closing day of the election of 1804. It began with the belief "that God created all men free and equal" and "that all power exists originally with the people, and is by them delegated to their representatives." The people's will when constitutionally expressed, is the supreme law. Minorities could protest and opinion is not punishable by law. Further, Republicans believed that religions should not be established and that religious tests for public office were against reason and liberty. As long as they supported free government they could elect and be elected. A republic is based upon virtue and knowledge. Republicans were for peace and believed all navies and armies led to war. The right to feed a friend was superior to starving an enemy. They favored free trade and opposed regulation. For them, America was an example for the world. [4]

Meanwhile, the young Martin Van Buren, whom Lincoln was to meet decades later, was active in politics. Van Buren was a descendant of Dutchmen who had settled in the New York village of Kinderhook in early times and who had never intermarried with other peoples in the colony and later the state. People in the village were living in the past, with their Dutch heritage, their Dutch language, their Dutch church, and their Dutch marriages. Class lines were important there; the Van Burens with their humble lives still had kinship with the local notables. This was the town into which Martin was born on December 5, 1782.

His amiable father and his capable mother worked hard on the family farm and in their tavern with their six slaves. However, since the father, Abraham Van Buren, was generous with loans of small amounts to his friends, admittedly, the family was always hard pressed. Abraham's wife, Maria, was ambitious for her children and guided them into a practical life. Because Martin grew up to become bright and manly and was civil and deferential, the local gentry favored him. His schoolmaster, David B. Warden, taught him well and Martin Van Buren learned by his experience in school to rein in an ardent disposition and to avoid hastiness and impulsiveness natural in his personality.

Lawyer Francis Sylvester provided the young man with an opportunity to read law and enter politics. While only seventeen, Van Buren played an important part in the nomination of John P. Van Ness to Congress. John was a native of Kinderhook and won the election as a Jeffersonian Republican in the Jeffersonian landslide of 1800. Having married a Washington heiress in the meantime, Van Ness loaned Van Buren travel expenses and a stake to go to New York City and to become Van Ness's clerk. Because of he Van Ness-Burr connection Martin Van Buren was exposed to Burr's blandishment and growing enmity to both Jefferson and Hamilton. Although the clerk was expected to support New York's Aaron Burr, privately he held more independent views. He stayed in Burrite circles for awhile, but only for awhile.

Van Buren observed as Burr worked toward challenging the Jefferson-Clinton power which had pushed the vice-president from center stage in New York. Burr planned to make a coalition of anti-Hamiltonian Federalists and Republican Burrites or stalwarts which could defeat Clinton's New York coalition which Burr thought was fragile and held together solely by patronage. The stalwarts nominated Burr for the governorship and Tammany seconded the move. George Clinton was nominated vice-president and no longer favored Burr at the same caucus which nominated Jefferson for a second term. Van Buren was to vote for Clintonian's Morgan Lewis for New York governor despite strong pressure from the Van Nesses whom he owed an obligation. The voters were mostly on the Clinton side also and the ambitious Burr was routed in his own state. [5]

At this time, there lived sixty miles north of New York City, not too far from Kinderhook, a small boy named William Henry Seward, who was not yet introduced to politics and who knew about slavery. His father Samuel Seward owned a farm and owned African American slaves. There were three slaves and young Harry often felt more at home with them in the kitchen than the family members in the parlor. Seward was later to write that they "had a fund of knowledge about the ways and habits of the Devil, of witches, of ghosts, and of men who had been hanged; and, what was more, they were vivacious and loquacious, as well as affectionate towards me." His parents never spoke anything bad against slavery but also said nothing bad against the slaves they owned. He went to school and often had to fight, but he took to education and was a star pupil. He loved to read and books became a great part of his life. Soon he was to go to college. He was born on May 16, 1801, in this township of Florida, New York.[6]

In slave country, John Caldwell Calhoun had been born on March 18, 1782, in the frontier district of South Carolina, to a father who was an Indian fighter and plantation owner. Despite a difference in temperament between them, but alike in political interest when each were more mature in age, the boy and Patrick Calhoun had the basic view that government should provide "the largest amount of individual liberty as possible under the restrictions necessary to ensure social order." When he was old enough there was no formal schooling in the South Carolinian frontier. His strong minded mother, Martha Calhoun taught him the basics of education. John proved a bright youngster and so his parents sent the boy, at age thirteen, to the Appling, Georgia, school of his brother-in-law, the Reverend Moses Waddel. Shortly after he was embarked on his studies, his father and Mrs. Waddel died so the school was discontinued. In fourteen months on his own as it were, John read the books of the library owned by Waddel, mostly historical, and political science, or geography, before being called home. He worked on the family plantation for five years. He was his own overseer and oft times ploughboy along with the black slaves. Aristocracy had not yet come to the frontier. Calhoun spent a lot of time in hunting and fishing, but never drank, gambled, or joked. He was a South Carolina puritan and later deist. To him life was work and duty.

In 1800, one of his older brothers James Calhoun came to the plantation and suggested he get educated in one of the professions. John Calhoun said he could not afford this. However, if he could be financed and his mother should approve, he was ready to begin the next week. The oldest brother was called from Augusta, Georgia, and they had a family conference. The terms were accepted and Calhoun went to Moses Waddel's new school in Willington in Abbeville County, South Carolina and began a two year preparation for Yale University. Admitted to the junior class in Yale, he sailed through college and went to Litcihfield's law school.

The widow of first cousin Senator John Ewing Calhoun opened social doors for the young John C. Calhoun and he later married her daughter Floride, his second cousin. He studied law for a full year. At Litchfield, he developed a distaste for the law profession and Federalists. He was not accepted socially and learned of the disunion sentiments of Timothy Dwight of Yale and Tapping Reeve of Litchfield. By then, Calhoun was a marked nationalist, a period which lasted for about three decades. Back in Charleston, he studied under William H. De Savssure, a prominent attorney, and was admitted to the bar. He was a success although he disliked being a lawyer. Not long afterwards he became a planter on his own as a result of his wife's dowry. Then he was elected to the state legislature.[7]

Meanwhile, Jefferson was enmeshed with the foreign situation at hand. But he had a dim view of what was needed to face it. His pacifism exerted itself and his great desire for neutrality became an obsession with him. Foreseeing no treat that would necessitate the use of men of warships, and a farmer, Jefferson, with his natural antipathy to the sea and ships, early decided to lay up the seven larger vessels of the U. S. Navy. By December of 1801, he had placed five frigates unmoved, but ready for any possible use, at the Washington navy-yard. This antipathy was itself grounded when the campaigns against North African pirates required their use and that of their additional reinforcements in ships. After victory along the Barbary coast, Jefferson again raised up the ships and relied upon gunboats which were falsely presumed to be useful in protecting the American coast against the British. This remained his policy in his second term also. Nothing was done to effectively present a naval force to protect America from a predatory England and France. Jefferson's beliefs and economic policy prevented this. He wanted a cheap defense and would not consider the possibility of war with either country.[8]

Hamilton and the Federalists found much to disagree with the Jeffersonian Republicans and their economy in government. In their view, Republican zeal for lowering expenditures in government was weakening that institution and the Federalists found fault with lowering revenue by abolishing internal revenue taxes. The opposition had a strong dislike of foreigners and immigrants and deprecated Jefferson's pro-French and anti-British policy. Federalists wished limits on the naturalization of immigrants because they supposedly harmed the nation's sentiments and principle and habits. They brought foreign basis and prejudice with them. Only birth, education, and family of the

Hamiltonian class provided a universal love of country. They forgot that Hamilton was an immigrant.

Federalists sharply criticized Jeffersonians for their attacks upon the judges and for their views on religion and politics. Their judicial actions were endangering the barrier unconstitutionality deposited with the courts. Hamilton's policy charged that the liberals or Jacobins of America believed "that children should not be given religious instruction." This was clearly not the case. They also falsely charged that Jefferson wished to be a dictator, which was irrational because the president wanted less government and not more government. The Republicans were too democratic for the Federalists and the latter feared equality and democratic ideas. Of course there were some extremists like the democratic legislator of Rhode Island who wished to abolish all debt, dues, and demands and wished an equal distribution of property. [9]

In his retirement, former president John Adams, a force to be reckoned with as George III had learned, found fault with the Jefferson Administration, especially with its defense policy and foreign policy. Words were not enough, he knew, America must be armed. Jeffersonian exhortations to European nations would not work. It was no good to tell European rulers to be wise, reasonable, fair, and just because that was what the Americans wanted them to be. Wishes were not enough; they would not work. Adams realized that economic sanctions were self-defeating. Commerce would decline and revenues would fall. Still he did not recede from his faith in his countrymen.

Republican congressmen were taking the line "that the moment you raise a public force you give up your liberty; and therefore there must be neither an army, navy, fortification, a select militia, or even a revenue, because if any of these exist they just be entrusted to the executive authority, establish a system of patronage, and overthrow the Constitution." To Adams this sounded well and good, but it would not protect America from her enemies. He opposed the oft times Jeffersonian remark that a French Revolution was needed in America. This turned him against their ideas of democracy. [10]

Jefferson was eager to reach a peaceful understanding with Great Britain. His chief desire was to achieve the end of impressments and when Rufus King failed, he gave over the task to James Monroe. The president suggested that the two nations reach an accord in this matter by an agreement not formalized in a treaty. This would be a face-saving attainment. Shortly, however, he soon asked for a treaty which would win an American settlement for the United States on impressment, blockades, visiting and searching on the high seas, contraband, and trade with British colonies. This would be the concession of Great Britain on these issues in return for which the United States would return naval deserters and agree on a band of exporting contraband to enemy territory. By asking so much, Jefferson would have had to accept much less and indeed it looked like he would get nothing. Chief minister Henry Addington and his country would not give way, contrary to Washingtonian expectations.

The president might have thought William Pitt's arrival on the British scene in London would mean good tidings for Anglo-American agreement, but he was sadly disappointed. Pitt as prime minister once again was intent upon destroying Napoleon whose desire for territory and power in Europe upset British views of what Europe should be like and offered a threat to Britain. Being for a strict policy, Pitt, although once a friend of the United States, would not budge on the issues facing America and Britain. The British navy continued to impress sailors from ships of neutral powers and Jefferson was upset as were all Americans. In this atmosphere Monroe could do nothing as he headed for Spain to negotiate another agreement. When Pitt died in 1806, his government was reformed, headed by Lord Grenville who was determined to fight Napoleon no matter who got hurt. [11]

While James Monroe expressed the correct American view "that the American flag protected all sailors on American ships, regardless of their national origin, the British complained that they sought only British subjects." It was well known that British sailors needed only to find an American captain to abandon a British ship for an American ship and that witnesses that the subject was an American could be bought to falsely swear that he was know by them to be an American. Half of the new sailors were British born and many of those were deserters from British warships. Since the British sailors were badly treated and ill-paid, they were eager to join the American ship crews where the pay was high and the discipline was comparatively easy. Many thousands of sailors had left British ships.

The root of the problem was lack of American interest in returning deserters, according to British official at a time when England's survival was threatened. However, the British went further than this to assert that "once an Englishman, always an Englishman." In addition many Americans were taken into British vessels on surface evidence and were "flogged into obedience to his Majesty's officers." The result was that sailors deserted in large numbers from British ships. During 1804 an entire British squadron lost enough sailors to be unable to sail forth because of desertion, while the large number of deserters jeered the officers in the streets of Norfolk. [12]

In his lifetime, Uriah Phillips Levy made a difference in the United States Navy, but in 1805 he was a thirteen year old seaman on a merchant ship, the *Rittenhouse*, bound for the United States' ports with a return voyage cargo from London. He was a Jewish lad from Philadelphia where some 3,500 Jews lived, subject to persecution, but in a lesser amount than in most of the world. Two years earlier, Uriah had left home for the seas, which was a happy choice for this adventurous lad. Nearing the American shore, he and his fellow sailors saw a ship coming out of the mist. Captain Moffit looked through his spy glass and saw that it was a French privateer. It was too late to make a run for it and the French crew soon boarded the *Rittenhouse* to take her to Cuba. Once at Santiago on the southeast coast, they sold the ship's cargo and released the ship and its crew, which were soon at the Turk Islands in the Bahamas for a ship load of salt with its ready market in the United States.

On the way back they met with a storm. They did not have enough time to reef all the sails, but might have made it to shore had not the ship begun to leak. Pumps could not do enough, so Moffit ordered the sailors to abandon ship. It was a terrifying night and early morning, but they survived and after days, reached the islands. They slept under the shade of coconut trees. Uriah awoke first and discovered a wrecked brig one mile away. They enjoyed coconuts, fish, and fresh water and after eating were able to repair and sail the brig. At Eleuthara, they filed the brig with pineapple and reached Philadelphia later.

In a latter incident in Levy's life, about 1807, he was imprisoned by a press gang, only to be released sometime later. Before they let him go, Admiral Cochrane offered the young man a lieutenant's commission in the British navy. Levy politely declined the offer and insisted that he be released. This was done. He sailed some more and at the age of nineteen, in 1811, Levy and two friends George Meschurt and Washington Garrison purchased a small schooner. This took all the money he had saved in his youth. The partners named their vessel the *George Washington*. They made a good voyage to the Canary Islands, West Africa, and Cape Verde Islands. Then on January 12, 1812, the first mate Sam Tully stole the ship in the Cape Verde Islands. Levy was put ashore, but found the pair who had done it and seized them as they attempted to assault him with butcher knives; to return to be executed as pirates. They had sunk his ship and spent part of the 2,000 Spanish milled dollars he had had on board. Expenses took some of the rest and the partners recovered half. A sailing captain's life would be exciting and a problem as shown in the early life of Levy. [13]

---

[1] Hickey, Donald R., *The War of 1812: A Forgotten Conflict,*, Urbana, Ill: *University of Illinois Press, 1989, pp. 5ff.*

[2] Whitman, Willson, *Jefferson's Letters*, Eau Claire, Wis: E.M. Hale, n.d., p.206. Quotes on p. 206.

[3] Dudley, William S., *1812*, 1985, pp. 1-2, 23.

[4] Schlesinger, Arthur M. Jr., ed., *History of American Presidential Elections, 1788-1968.* 2 vols., New York: Chelsea House, 1971, I, 174-176.

[5] Niven, J., 1983, pp. 5-10, 15-19.

[6] Taylor, John M., *William Henry Steward: Lincoln's Right Hand*, New York: HarperCollins, 1991, pp. 12-14.

[7] Capers, Gerald Montimer, *John C. Calhoun--Opportunist: A Reappraisal*, Chicago: Quadrangle, 1960, pp. 3-19.

[8] Channing, Edward, *The Jeffersonian System 1801-1811*, New York: Harpers, 1906, pp. 36-37.

[9] Schlesinger, *History*, pp. 160, 177-181.

[10] Smith, Page, *John Adams*, 2 vols., Garden City NY: Doubleday, 1962, II, 1089-1090.

[11] White, P.C.T., *Nation on Trial*, 1965, pp. 17-20, 23-24.

[12] Carr, Albert Z., *The Coming of War: An Account of the Remarkable Events Leading to the War of 1812*, Garden City NY: Doubleday, 1960, pp. 224-225. Quotes on pp. 224, 225.

[13] Felton, Harold W., *Uriah Phillips Levy*, New York: Dodd, Mead, 1978, pp. 15-40.

CHAPTER II

MADISON

In March of 1805, James Madison in Washington DC had written Armstrong in Pairs that the Government would appeal to France for a boundary settlement. He proposed that Spain would cede the Floridas and draw a western boundary line along the Guadalupe or Colorado rivers to their sources, and then a line to the headwaters of the Mississippi or Missouri Rivers. A neutral ground was to be settled upon. He gave Armstrong various alternative neutral zone proposals.

When Armstrong received the letter on May 1, 1806, he met with Talleyrand. Napoleon, who had been dealing with Spain directly and privately, told his minister that Charles IV of Spain would not give up the Floridas. The French Government told Armstrong that Napoleon would intervene with Spain and obtain the Floridas and a good western boundary for the United States whenever the Americans would declare war on England and ally themselves with France. Jefferson rejected the idea and would not yield to the entreaties of Turreau, French minister to the United States. Negotiations broke down. The boundary question remained unsettled until 1819 and no more negotiations were undertaken until after Napoleon's fall. [1]

With the defeat of the Continental allies, England could still stand alone, behind its water walls. The British Government turned to the economic weapon of boycott. On May 16, 1806, Fox had declared a partial blockade of the northern coast of Europe. On November 21, Napoleon retaliated by closing all Europe to British trade. Less than one month later, it was stricter and neutrals had to choose sides. The United States did not want to choose and did not choose. Official America remained neutral. Jefferson was not going to change this for anything. Peace was still his main objective. Our nation was hurt while Napoleon and Britain issued a very large number of licenses to trade with the enemy. Also smuggling was common. [2]

Meanwhile, the British Government nominated Holland and Auckland to treat with the American envoys, beginning on August 27, 1806. Both of these men wanted an Anglo-American understanding or peace but unfortunately this was not achieved. Once again the chief issue was one of impressment. The two Britishers had decided upon a compromise that the London Government would not agree upon, for a temporary end to impressment combined with the right of Britain to stop and search American vessels at sea for deserters. By this means the truth would prevail and protect all American citizens in American ships who were American by naturalization and not merely British deserters. Both sides would make significant concessions, but the British ministers would not ratify the idea. There would be no compromise or concessions at all on this issue.

Still, however, a treaty of compromise was drawn up to cover almost all of the other points of disagreement. Contraband was limited except for provisions; American trade with French colonies was allowed with certain regulations. On the other hand, a neutral could not trade with a blockaded port. And there were other compromises in the sequence of give and take. No sooner was this achieved than Napoleon declared a blockade of the British Isles in his Berlin Decree. On March 3, 1807, Erskine, British minister to America, hurried the newly received treaty, but Jefferson decided that without a satisfactory impressment agreement, the treaty would be unacceptable. In London, the British Government issued orders in council. Neither government would henceforth compromise until it was too late for concessions. The controversy over impressment was the deciding factor. [3]

At a dangerous time in American history, the Jeffersonian Republicans, preferring to rely upon militiamen and privateers, further decreased the number of full time soldiers, halted naval construction, and decommissioned most of the force of frigates. The remaining ships were further reduced by rot and deterioration. America had no navy. Determined on a defense of the coast, Jefferson and then Madison spent a total of 2.8 million dollars on coastal fortifications. Republican policy led to a weak land defense because militiamen were lacking in training and were poorly equipped. Privateers proved to be no match for enemy warships and could protect neither the coast nor commerce. Further the small gunboats that the Administration had built were decommissioned. Jefferson decided that the 1.5 million dollars they had cost to build was a waste because the boats were most costly gun for gun than frigates. By 1809, Jefferson had to decommission those he had built. The idea was a costly failure.

The British Navy blockades raised the ire of the Americans. The two nations also disagreed on international law. Britain favored the idea that French goods could be seized on American ships, while the Americans argued that neutral vessels protected all goods they carried and no other nation had rights to take those products. Both nations believed in theories that benefited them. In the American Civil War, the United States reversed its stand and seized foreign neutral vessels attempting to supply the Confederacy. Lincoln, unborn at this time, established part of the same policy that Britain had followed in the early years of the nineteenth century. [4]

Meanwhile, on April 26, 1806, the British frigate *Lander* sailed into American waters off Sandy Hook. Its captain ordered his cannoneers to fire a shot into a small unarmed vessel, killing a seaman. Everyone in the United States was angered. This was a gross insult to their nation. Jefferson and his Administration protested. The British promised reparations. No sooner was this settled than the *Leopold* attacked the *Cheasapeake*. [5]

On June 22, 1807, the American naval vessel the *Chesapeake* sailed forth into the Atlantic from Norfolk. Ten miles out on the next day, they were hailed and stopped by the British frigate *Leopold*. Commodore James Barron, the American, met with the British officer who showed him British orders to search the *Cheaspeake*. The British demanded that the sailors whom they said had recently deserted H.M.S. *Melampus* and joined American ships in Norfolk harbor. Barron would not hear of that and resisted. The *Leopold* fired for ten minutes and killed three and wounded eighteen U.S. crewmen. Since his guns were not ready, Barron was able to reply with only one shot before surrendering to the search which netted four crewmen. The heavily damaged American ship barely made it home. Because he had been unprepared, Barron was court-martialed. [6]

This incident caused a countrywide cry of anger and demands for war. Citizens of Norfolk exploded and broke the water casks of the entire British squadron in port. The anger even reached Kentucky, far from the scene of the incident and the shipping industry. Kentuckians wanted retaliation and talked of embargo and war. Militia units paraded. Resolutions were adopted. The indignant people of Kentucky wanted some kind of action, perhaps the end of trade and diplomatic relations with Britain.

The response was widespread and clear, crossing party lines, but Jefferson only ordered British warships to leave American waters. He awaited a response from London. Britain's officials paid reparations and returned two of the captured crewmen. The third had died in Halifax hospital and the fourth had been a British subject and already had been hung. Later, Kentucky's legislature passed a law in support of the embargo with sixty-four votes in favor and only one against. Of the western states only Louisiana was against Jeffersonian policies in the matter. [7]

The matter remained vivid in the United States and was talked about for years around the firesides of America. Although Britain recalled Admiral Berkeley who had given the order, the Admiralty treated him so well that it was a fresh spur to negative public opinion in America. Amid the talk of war in Congress and an invasion discussion, the Canadian militia was mobilized in Lower Canada. This sobered some Americans. These people foresaw that the proposed attack would be in force. However, most people probably felt that an American invasion of Canada would be a success. They wrongfully thought that the Canadians were disaffected. [8]

Winfield Scott was a Virginian farmer's son, born on June 13, 1786, near Dinwiddie Courthouse. His father, William Scott, was a respected member of the community. His grandfather, James Scott, was a political refugee from Scotland, having enlisted in the service of Prince Charles Stuart. James was a lawyer. Winfield was educated in the classical tradition. He took a liking for philosophy and decided to become a lawyer. Studying under David Robinson, a good man of high reputation in Richmond, he was provided, as were Robinson's other students of law, with a good preparation for the bar examinations. Robinson was a Federalist while Scott was a Jeffersonian Republican.

The *Chesapeake* incident brought him into action however. Scott left the Robinson law office to join the Virginia militia southwards in Petersburg. He was shortly on the parade ground in a uniform. He showed enough leadership to be placed in command of a squad at Lynnhaven Bay. He was to meet a landing force from British ships off the coast. This was important service for such a young man. Learning that eight unarmed British sailors were ashore to buy provisions, Scott and his men ambushed them and captured all eight. He was to treat them generously, providing for them at his own table. Meanwhile, he had informed his superiors and President Jefferson ordered them released. Soon Scott was able to go back to the law office. Then he obtained a commission as a captain with the help of two congressmen. [9]

Both the English and the French seized American ships and confiscated their cargoes. A tenuous situation became worst with the Berlin Decree. One of the ships, the American *Horizon*, was captured by the English and then released after her cargo was seized. It sailed forth for Lisbon with a British cargo and, when off the coast of France was wrecked, and that portion which was saved was seized by the French and sold. When the news of this reached Jefferson, he suggested an embargo to prevent U. S. trade with anyone, with the hopes of pressure which would succeed in gaining respect from the belligerents. The Senate acted immediately and the House of Representatives passed the embargo with little contemplation. Despite the congressional prompt action, the embargo was not universally popular or universally observed. Indeed there was much trade taking place and an allied amount of political feeling during the four years of the embargo. In Jefferson's last months in office there was greater opposition. [10]

Thomas Jefferson preferred peace to war and was a natural neutral in the European war, but his patience must have been very strained in his second term. Although a close friend of France, he had considered an alliance with Great Britain in the summer of 1805 because of French hostility to the United States. Only the actions of British ships off the coast of the new nation turned him back to his strict preference for neutrality and love for France and its people. However, he would have preferred having British power on the high seas except for the *Chesapeake* ' outrage, which changed his mind. Expecting war, Jefferson thought it would give his nation a chance to acquire Florida and Cuba, which fitted into his expansionist policy. Until this opportunity came, he would undertake an embargo on British products, which it has been seen he did, since it would deny Britain her markets and sources of agricultural production in the United States. This, he thought, would be a solution for the problem at hand rather than war which Jefferson always wished to avoid. His belief was that this would force Britain to her knees, and he launched it in December of 1807.

This policy did nothing to keep Britain and France and their respective allies from seizing 900 American ships in the next five years. The vaunted economic power of the United States did not put enough pressure on the two belligerents to bring them to terms. The embargo hurt the American nation more than the warring powers of Europe. Merchants took advantage of the loopholes in the law and smuggled. The first result, however, was a national depression. [11]

The embargo's effects were ironic. One of the reasons to implement this, Jefferson's biggest mistake, was British impressments, but as a result of the law, American seamen had to leave the nation and find jobs on British warships and merchantmen. Jefferson disputed the British policy on the West Indies carrying trade, but when he shut American ships up in their ports, British businessmen gained this commerce. The British West Indies received a virtual monopoly of supplying Europe with the produce. It made some men rich through smuggling and British traders rich also.

Finally in 1809, Congress changed the law, as we have seen, to end trade only with neutrals. This did not work either, but lasted until the war. The basic premise of Republican policy was false. A weak and divided neutral could not force two powerful nations in an uncompromising war to be just and fair to that neutral, the United States. [12]

On January 6, 1808, Jefferson had written that the embargo was keeping American vessels and seamen at home. Thus saved "is the necessity of making their capture the cause of immediate war; for, if going to England, France was determined to take them, if to any other place, England was to take them." Until the two European nations "return to some sense of moral duty, therefore, we keep within ourselves. This gives time. Time may produce peace in Europe, peace in Europe removes all causes of difference, till another European war; and by that time our debt may be paid, or revenues clear, and out strength increased." Jefferson was involved in a waiting game. He wanted peace above all even when hardpressed. [13]

The Federalists did not see it that way. To the Federalists of New England, Jefferson's embargo was wicked. Because of this Jeffersonian action it was necessary for gentlemen to retreat and save money for the hard times ahead. Judge Wendell of Boston sold his Oliver Street mansion with its garden, orchards, and marble fountains and bought the smaller Gambrel-roof and the Abiel and Sally Holmes moved into the house from the parsonage. By then the Holmes had three children, grandchildren of the judge. It was next

The Difficult War: The Era of the War of 1812

to the grounds of Harvard College and had a flower garden which the parsonage did not have and the house belonged to the family where improvements might be made, without consulting the parish. Wendell saved money and the Holmes moved up in the world. Wendell and other Federalists thought that instead of the embargo, America should be fighting the French who after all were conquering Europe. [14]

Meanwhile, many Americans evaded the law despite strict instructions for enforcement. Ships and custom agents were used by the government, but their work was difficult. The small navy could not be everywhere at once and custom agents often helped the merchants and shippers avoid enforcement. Orders had gone out for captains to seize any boats and ships used by Americans to violate the embargo laws. They were to work with revenue officers. Goods landed on beaches at the edge of borders were to be seized if they were carried across into the United States for sale, contrary to the law. [15]

America might be beset with the effects of war in Europe, but still had influence there. The American Revolution in its broadest sense continued to influence European thought. In some ways it showed the pathway to success to millions of people who sought democracy. Conservatives could predict it would fail, but the people saw its triumph and Thomas Jefferson showed them hope. Europeans might lack the experience of self-government, but in their deepest thoughts shown in later upheavals what Jefferson and Washington stood for had their allegiance also. Free elections, economic opportunity, and self government appealed to them immeasurably. They would not have a government which stifled their best results, but one which would address their problems instead of ruling over them. Of course what were solutions could not be agreed upon, either then or later, but they did not wish to have large and dictatorial European type governments as then existed. Only their lack of experience got in the way of what they wanted.

In America there were beliefs along these lines, but the Americans had the experience along varied lines since the beginnings. Since American opinion was out in the open, unlike that of Europe, it is easier to follow. There were conservatives who looked to a certain aristocracy, which could be one of talents as shown by Alexander Hamilton, an early exponent of governmental and business development which alarmed those who would have rule of the agrarian segment. Thomas Jefferson were for small government which allowed the individual to prosper. Like Europe their solutions were different then and later.

Americans conservatives of a later date were to draw upon both Jefferson and Hamilton for conservative business interests. American liberals were to draw upon Jefferson for liberalism in democratic ideas and upon Hamilton for governmental activities in the market place. The big issues are often different now, but the common thread is over what the government should do and what the individual should do. This is the issue of what should be done and by whom.

Jefferson stood as a symbol and guide to European thinkers and although Washington and Franklin were better known, Jefferson survived to advise many leaders of government and thinking men in his retirement years. After this presidency, prudence could be cast aside. He would openly hate Napoleon for the devastation in burning Europe and advise freedom loving Greeks, Portuguese, Poles, Frenchmen, Spaniards, and Hispanic Americans. He also corresponded with British liberals. [16]

---

[1] Marshall, *Louisiana Acquisition*, pp. 43-45.
[2] Guerard, Albert, *Napoleon I: A Great Life in Brief*, New York: Alfred A. Knopf, 1973, pp. 89-92.

[3] White, *Nation*, pp. 28-40.

[4] Hickey, *War of 1812*, pp. 8-13.

[5] Coggeshall, George, *During Our War with England in the Years 1812, '13, '14 interspersed with Several Naval Battles Between American and British Ships-of-War*, New York: George Coggeshall, 1856, p. lii.

[6] Coles, Harvy L., *The War of 1812, 1965*, pp. 6-7; Dudley, William S. ed., Naval War, *1985, I, 26-28*.

[7] Hammack, James Wallace, Jr., *Kentucky and the Second American Revolution: The War of 1812, 1976*, pp. 3-4; Hickey, War of 1812, p. 17; Abernethy, Thomas Perkins, The South in the New Nation, 1789-1819, Baton Rouge: Louisiana State University Press, 1961, pp. 316ff; Dudley, Naval, I, 20-31, 190.

[8] Babcock, Louis L., *The War of 1812 on the Niagara Frontier*, Buffalo NY: Buffalo Historical Society, 1927, pp. 5ff.

[9] Eisenhower, John S.D., *Agent of Destiny: The Life and Times of General Winfield Scott*, New York: Free Press, 1997, pp. 1-4, 6-10.

[10] Channing, *Jeffersonian*, pp. 210-232.

[11] Sears, Louis Martin, *Jefferson and the Embargo*, Duke University Press, 1927 (Octagon Books reprint of 1966), pp. 3-31, 52=53; Hickey, *War of 1812*, pp. 19-21.

[12] Bruce, William Cabell, *John Randolph of Roanoke, 1773-1833*, New York: G.P. Putnam Sons, 1922, I, 321-322; Hickey, *War of 1812*, pp. 21-24; Ketcham, Ralph, *James Madison: A Biography*, London: Macmillan, 1971, p. 491.

[13] Whitman, *Jefferson's*, pp. 240-241. Quotes on pp. 240-241.

[14] Bowen, Catherine Drinker, *Yankee from Olympus: Justice Holmes and His Family*, Boston: Little, Brown, 1944, pp. 20-22.

[15] Dudley, William S, (ed.), *The Naval War of 1812: A Documentary History*, Washington DC: Naval History Center, 1985, I, 34-36.

[16] Spiller, Robert E., *Literary History of the United States: History*, 3rd ed. rev., London: Macmillan, 1963, pp. 208-210.

CHAPTER III

FRONTIER AMERICA

The kindly nature of Jefferson held high hopes for the Indians, too high, for the short term, for most of the Indians. However his benevolent attitude was a welcome relief for the times. They were on a par with uncivilized whites. Jefferson held the natural state views of the eighteenth century philosophers of the noble bearing of the Indians. In this philosophy, the wild Indians had not been yet corrupted by civilization and thus lived in an ideal world. To them the Indians were nature's noble man. Uncivilized natives could reach the level of the white man. If he was a noble man, the Indians could not be benefited by civilization, but this contradiction was not seen. Others felt that the Indian was the enemy and blocked their way to lands in the West.

If the Indians could be civilized, in Jefferson's words, "humanity enjoins us to teach them agriculture and the domestic arts; to encourage them in that industry which alone can enable them to maintain their place in existence and to prepare them in time for the state and society which to bodily comfort, and to improvement of the mind and morals." Despite this view, Jefferson also took a practical stand on the Indians. Jefferson found land acquisition and settlement to be more important than helping the Indians reach a level of civilization. He would get the Indians in such debt that they would be forced to sell their lands to the settlers. He did not so much want their protection as their removal from lands that the settlers wanted. On this issue of the Indians Jefferson was a mass of contradictions and the poor Indian did not know which way to turn. Many Americans wanted to Christianize the Indians but did not wish to treat them in accord with the principles taught by Jesus. [1]

One tribe had already moved toward civilization-- the Cherokee. Despite this not all was well with the tribe. To the south, the Upper Cherokee Towns were unhappy that the Lower Cherokee Towns with their control of the tribal organization had gotten, for years, almost all of the annuity coming from the national government. They decided to send a deputation of chiefs to place their complaints before President Thomas Jefferson. Early in 1808, they sent a group of chiefs to Washington and talked to officials there. They told Jefferson that the Lower Cherokee Towns chiefs divided up almost all of the annuities among those Indians in the neighborhood. Jefferson listened and then informed them that once the funds were handed over, as they must, to the authorized representatives of the tribe, it was purely a Cherokee decision what to do with the funds. He could only have the Indian agent to suggest redress of these grievances to the other Cherokee chiefs.

Cherokee leader Alexander Saunders suggested to the president that the Indian nation be divided up into two parts. Tracts should be surveyed for farms so that the Cherokees could be farmers on their own private lands. They were to live under American jurisdiction and laws and to become citizens of the United States. He reckoned without the land hunger of the pioneers. Jefferson instructed the agent to explore the possibility of fixing a line between the two groups of Cherokee; but more in touch with the aims of his people, Jefferson bought up the questions of giving lands across the Mississippi to those who still wished to follow the hunt. Those Cherokees who preferred to hunt would give up their lands in the towns.

Unfortunately, the agent, Colonel Return J. Meigs, ignored the idea of the dividing of the lands which was the Indian idea and took up the Jeffersonian idea of the exchange of ideas and the removal to the west to be agreed by the chiefs of the Cherokees, with quiet bribery. Black Fox held a clandestine council and appointed river chiefs to go to Washington to sign a treaty for the exchange of lands. He brought it out at open council to take the people by surprise. The Ridge was indignant and knew he must speak. They had heard the talk of the principal chiefs, he said, but this opinion was not binding, formed in the corner to drag the Cherokees from their country to the dark land of the settling sun.

Ridge resisted this. The people should be consulted before they should leave the land of their forefathers. He suggested they look over the land and decide whether they wished to leave or not for promised lands in the West. At the end of his brief discourse, the natives cheered Major Ridge. Black Fox knew his effort was doomed. Three chiefs were broken including Black Fox. Although later reinstated, Black Fox felt disgraced for life.

Next the council chose a new delegation including Ridge and they headed on to Washington in November of 1808. Ridge was impressed by the unfinished Capitol which was already most imposing to the frontier Indians. They stopped by the War Department where Indian affairs were managed under Henry Dearborn. There was a dual purpose in the delegation. Those from the Lower Towns wished to exchange lands in the east for a wilderness tract on the Arkansas River, while those from the Upper Towns wanted to found an elective government and adopt such laws of the United States which were suited to them.

The Cherokee delegation wrote a word of greeting for Jefferson which was interpreted. In this they expressed their gratitude for his eight years of protection and stated that they had progressed in agriculture and domestic manufactures. Then they drew up papers to Dearborn which he gave to the president in favor of a dividing line and a regular administration of American laws among the Cherokees.

The outgoing president brought up the difficulty of the establishment of government and laws for the Cherokees. He asked who would determine which laws to accept. Each of the Cherokees believed himself equally free; who would set and enforce the laws, Jefferson wondered. He suggested a system of representative government for the Cherokees by majority vote. Meigs should, he suggested, instruct the delegates in American government and law. The president was more interested in the removal proposal for permanent settlement in western lands. Back home, in January of 1809, the Lower Towns decided not to leave for Arkansas and came to the settlement with the Upper Towns and all selected a national council. Thus the future was influenced, and removal was to be left up to Jackson twenty years later; some Indians of the civilized tribes emigrating in between times. [2]

Manuel Lisa had been a resident along the Mississippi, which the Cherokees were destined to cross, when the Louisiana Purchase was made and he decided to remain in the area he knew so well to pursue his fortune. He made a partnership with William Moron and Pierre Menard of Kaskaskia, Illinois, and signed on several veterans of the Lewis and Clark Expedition to form a trading mission to proceed up the Missouri. Lisa and his party made contact with the trapping Crow Indians. Successful in his endeavor in the far west, Lisa returned to St. Louis where he formed the Missouri Fur Trade Company to exploit fur trading possibilities in the trans-Mississippi. Lisa' partners were well-connected including agent for the Western Indians and brigadier general of the militia of the Missouri Territory William Clark, and subagent Rube Lewis, brother of Governor Meriwether Lewis.

Another fur company was founded by an easterner named John Jacob Astor of New York. Astor had experience in the China trade, in which he traded pelts, ginseng root, and silver for tea and silk. He had been purchasing furs from Montreal for this trade, but he decided to lay his claim on the fur trade on the Columbia River, from whence he could sail across the Pacific to Canton. Astor founded his American Fur Company in 1808, later changed its name to the Pacific Fur Company. When the United States Congress passed nonimportation and embargo decrees, the Canadians turned to Astor to supply them with goods for the fur trade around the Great Lakes. Astor agreed on condition that the Michilimackinac Company would buy into his Columbian venture. This way he hoped to assure his company a monopoly on the Columbia River. When the U. S. government relented, the Canadians backed out of the deal, which they had not intended to keep anyway and Astor knew that he was in for a fight.

Hiring clerks and partners from the Canadian companies, Astor sent a ship around the Horn to the Columbia and sent an overland party across the continent in 1810. The shipload of clerks and traders met disaster at the hands of the Indians and the overland party barely reached Astoria in 1812. While Astor's men were making their settlement at the mouth of the Columbia River, other traders were attempting to open up a trade with Santa Fe. Efforts to open up trade with the Spaniards failed and for their part the Astorians had a rough go of it.

Difficult times were also plaguing the settlers between the Mississippi and the Appalachian Mountains. The closing of continental ports by the British blockade and excessive production by the farmers. Prices fell in New Orleans because of the glut from upriver and the lack of opportunities for sale on the continent. Many a farmer reached New Orleans to die of yellow fever or took their scant earnings over the Nachos Trace where they were robbed.

Meanwhile the exhaustive methods of the farmers created the need of new lands. The plains of the Louisiana Purchase did not yet tempt the Americans, but Canada and Spanish Florida did. American seized Baton Rouge and declared that East Florida from the Mississippi to the Perdido River now belonged to the United States. President Madison soon back them up. In all this lies the reasons for western support of war with Great Britain in the next few years. Meanwhile, William Henry Harrison, Governor of Indiana Territory, led the drive for Indian lands, splitting the tribes into factions and by means of liquor gaining the land grants by the Indians.

While James Wilkinson continued as an agent and adviser to the Spanish government on the west--had advised them to fortify the Texas and Florida frontiers against the Americans--, he made contact with his friend Aaron Burr, who had just killed Alexander Hamilton in a duel and had to flee into hiding, and gained him for his conspiracy. They joined with them Englishman Charles Williamson who reported the conspiracy for separating western lands from the American Union to British minister Anthony Merry. Burr made a career of furthering the conspiracies initiated by Wilkinson, making contacts in the western lands. Part of the plan was based upon a war between the United States and Spain and upon the dissatisfaction of the Latin peoples in Louisiana.

Both independent of and dependent on the Burr conspiracy, there was open dissatisfaction with the Union among farmers in the then West. Separationist talk was common in some areas and at various places and where Burr appeared rumors of separationism were sure to spread. The plans of the conspirators were complicated and ill-formed with many informers giving information on them to the government in Washington.

When he learned of Burr's plans, Federalist Alexander Henderson of Wood County, Virginia, a center where conspirator Harman lived, organized a meeting of the people of the county who condemned the conspirators, supporting President Jefferson, and made plans for raising a corps of militia to fight the planned plotter army. This doubtless became known in Washington.

In 1806, President Jefferson called the Cabinet together to discuss the reported plot to separate the West from the Union. After a short session of discussion, Jefferson decided to send orders to the western governor to be on their guard, but it was soon decided to give John Graham, secretary of Orleans Territory and second in position there, who was in Washington at this time, discretionary powers to arrest Burr upon an overt action which made him liable to the charge of treason. Graham was given the commission to become governor of Louisiana in the place of Wilkinson who was implicated and who had recently disobeyed orders.

Due to the lack of evidence which would stand up in court, Burr escaped justice in Kentucky and resumed his plans to found a country composed of Mexico, the Mississippi Valley, and the Ohio Valley. Boats and supplies were collected along the waterways of the West and men were recruited for the army. The state government of Ohio seized much of his force headed down the river for New Orleans where Burr could gain control of Louisiana by a political coup. Before he made it, General Wilkinson betrayed Burr to Jefferson, and prepared to defend Louisiana against Burr's force, Faced with certain defeat, Burr surrendered to the authorities of the territory of Mississippi, escaped, and was arrested to stand trial and to be acquitted, for lack of evidence to prove him guilty. Wilkinson's role received a whitewashing. The general was even more a scoundrel than Burr and it remained to historians to discover just how disloyal Wilkinson really was. [3]

Jefferson, secure at home and nearing the end of his administration, had a new namesake on June 3, 1808, with the birth, in Christian County in Kentucky, of Jefferson Davis, son of Samuel Emory Davis and his wife Jane Cook Davis, eight months before Lincoln was born. Davis' Christian County was in the southwestern part of the young state. Young Davis was also born in a log cabin, but it was larger and had glass windows, brought from Georgia where Samuel E. Davis had been born. Samuel had fought in the Revolutionary War. After three years as a soldier, he formed his own company and soon defended Savannah. When the future president of the Confederacy was born, his parents had already had nine children; the eldest Joseph was to be a great influence upon Jefferson Davis. Both Davis and Lincoln were born Southerners but their paths were soon to part. [4]

The Lincolns came to America seeking opportunity and land for farming. When Samuel Lincoln's father Edward was cut out of his father Richard's will, he lost considerable inheritance and had to struggle. Samuel himself went to Salem, Massachusetts, as an indentured servant. The line to the president's grandfather passed

The Difficult War: The Era of the War of 1812

through Samuel's son Mordecai, who moved to Scituate, and his son Mordecai Jr. who died in Barks County, Pennsylvania, in 1736. Next in line was John Lincoln.

John Lincoln first settled the Shenandoah Valley in Virginia and deeded a 210 acre farm to his son Abraham, who became a captain in the militia and fought against the Cherokees in 1776. This patriot militia officer married Bersheba and sired five children including one Thomas Lincoln. Tom was to be the father of the sixteenth president of the United States. From old frontier to newer frontier, the Lincolns moved to Kentucky in 1782, where the first Abraham bought 5,544 acres. He was land rich. Few people lived in Kentucky and during the war they had a tough time protecting themselves against the Indians. Dangers continued after the conflict and it was in Kentucky that Abraham was killed by a rifle bearing Indian while leaving his field near Long Run community not far from Hughes' Station in May of 1786. Son Mordecai shot one of the Indians whose silver pendant proved a good target for the deadly bullet. [5]

Tom Lincoln was a boy of ten when his father was killed. Since the eldest Mordacai got the farm and large tracts elsewhere, Tom hired out to farmers to support himself. In between his farm work, he learned carpentry and cabinet making and was to work on the dam of Samuel Haycraft Sr. He was a good workman, but he was a wild buck at fighting and best left alone. He did not drank much and was a Separate Baptist of Armenian beliefs. At age nineteen in 1795, he joined the militia and became a soldier to defend the frontier from Indians for a couple of months. Lincoln saved his money, but with his proceeds from Mordecai's sale of family lands, Thomas bought a farm in 1803.

Marrying Nancy Hanks, the Virginia-born daughter of Henry Sparrow and his wife Lucy Shipley Hanks, on June 12, 1806, Tom settled in Elizabethtown in a cabin near the courthouse. The cabin was made of log and was a common construction for time and place. There in his own home, he made cabinets and worked as a carpenter. Nancy bore him a daughter Sarah. He bought another town lot. [6]

For awhile the Lincolns lived on the farm of George Brownfield and in late 1808 moved to his recently purchased 348 1/2 acres of indifferent soil in hilly country on the Big South Fork of Olin's Creek, about two and a half miles from Hodgenville. Why he did not move to his Mill Creek farm, bought in 1803 with its better acreage is unknown. Perhaps he wished to have it rented out while he farmed elsewhere. For his Nolin farm he paid $200 in cash and assumed a small obligation to an earlier owner Richard Mather. They lived in a cabin of logs built from a stand of woods nearby. [7]

Nancy was pregnant and her time came on the Sunday morning of February 12, 1809. Perhaps she had the granny woman or midwife of the community, Aunt Peggy Walters, to help her deliver the boy. Tom was present and put some more wood on the fire and another bearskin over the mother and then walked to the Sparrows. He stopped off at the neighbors. Eleanor Atkinson later recollected that her mother went over to the Lincoln's and helped Thomas with the mother, child, and house for awhile before returning home. The infant boy was named Abraham after his paternal grandfather.

Baby Abe came into a frontier environment. In his place and time the log cabin was common housing and his father was a regular small farmer without slaves or pretensions. Next to the place where the log cabin was located, one can find natural springs, a limestone sinking spring carved of limestone. It had a cool stream and dropped into a basin below hardwood trees. Abe grew up to be like his father in this sylvan farmland. They were farmers who worked hard, but were always ready to stop a spell and talk. Thomas worked hard all of his life at farming and carpentry, while Abraham was to leave the farm at age twenty-two and soon become a lawyer, that development of ambition on the frontier.

There was plenty of wood available for the making of things from a house to utensils. Hunting and fishing provided for the table, as did gathering. The woods were full of blackberries, raspberries, huckleberries, cranberries, and wild strawberries and chestnuts, hickory nuts, and groundnuts. Thomas grew Indian corn on his acreage and when he moved to a more fertile farm, this was the more plentiful, as much as four hundred bushels of corn. [8]

Hardin County, where Abraham was born, was located in the west middle part of Kentucky where the Salt River flowed. In the north and west the land was hilly and thin. There is falter and sandy soils in the center. The rich alluvial soil is in the east and south. Most of the land was in corn and tobacco. Elizabethtown was the county seat on the highway, then a rough creation, from Nashville to Louisville. The county was named after Colonel John Hardin. Long after Lincoln left, the legislature changed its composition and made it a part of Larve County. [9]

The early cabin was primitive with an earth floor and roof of rough slabs kept hold by poles and staves. There was little light. The walls were made of logs and there was a small square opening, with greased paper to let in light. Lincoln's door was fashioned with hinges of wood or of hide for the two long broad slabs. Their fireplace was made of stone and the chimney was made of sticks and clay. Since there was no iron available on the frontier, the bed was made of wood. One end rested on a crotched stick, driven into the ground, and the other end enclosed in the log walls. Rough slats were placed across the frame. [10]

Nancy Lincoln was five feet eight inches tall, of a generally lean body. She was never out of temper and was most affectionate. The calm woman was highly intelligent with a good memory, quick perception, and an almost acute judgment. Spiritually and ideally inclined, she was not materialistic. She had dark hair and bluish green eyes. A stout man of five feet ten inches, Thomas Lincoln weighed 196 pounds. He had dark hair and hazel eyes. he was a man of great strength and courage with an uncommon endurance. In a fight, he usually prevailed. In one encounter his friend put him up against a man named Hardin, who was a successful fighter also. In a long bout Thomas Lincoln won over Hardin without a scratch. The men became good friends after that. Thomas could tell a good story or joke. Abraham was to follow his parents quite well in character and characteristics. [11]

When Lincoln was nominated as president and was pressed for biographical material for the public, he told J. L. Scripps of the Chicago *Tribune*, "Why, Scripps, it is a great piece of folly to attempt to make anything out of me or my early life. It can all be condensed into a single sentence, and that sentence you will find in Gray's Elegy. 'the short and simple annals of the poor.' That's my life, and that's all you or anyone else can make out of it." Scripps later wrote Herndon: "Lincoln seemed to be painfully impressed with the extreme poverty of his early surroundings, and the utter absence of all romantic and heroic elements. He communicated some facts to me concerning his ancestry, which he did not wish to have published then, and which I have never spoken of or alluded to before." [12]

Shortly after Lincoln's birth, Kentucky's leading newspaper included an address by Joseph Coppinger in St. Louis, along the Mississippi, expressing his feelings that France and England had unwarranted policies, greatly unjust toward the young United States. It appeared to Coppinger that "these oppressors of the universe, who had stained every quarter of it with innocent blood, were now discordantly viewed with each other which should deal out to us the greatest measure of wrong." The situation, he believed, was novel in the history of the world. Americans must exert themselves to meet this crises in full justice, coolness, and union.

Jefferson was the required guide for us. Coppinger favored the president' wisdom and moderation. The partisans of liberty found the country poor and oppressed and was now leaving it rich, flourishing, and independent. He would avoid entangling alliances with both France and England. A policy of justice, prudence, and good sense (qualities which the European nations did not have) was the best policy. While seeking the preferred peace, he would prepare for a defensive war in which he Americans would rely upon their militia, a favorite fallacy of the times. Driven from the market of the world, we must cultivate our own markets. God would be on our side if we did not provoke a war which would be a great calamity for our country. We must be educated in the useful arts, trades, and sciences. [13]

With direct trade cut off, American trade through Spanish Florida reached a height of commerce. Goods flowed through Amelia Island and the St. Mary's River which divided Florida from Georgia. Bales of cotton from the slave states and various produce awaited shipment in British ships, which were landing merchandise to be smuggled into the United States. It was more expensive to trade by this means, but this trade was better than none. The American government could not collect duties on these smuggled goods at a time when there was a large deficit. Another negative was that in this trade Americans paid higher prices and were paid less for their cotton and produce. Representative Elisha Porter of Rhode Island complained that their trade made the rich richer and the poor poorer.

As one of the last acts of his Administration, Jefferson had signed the Non-Intercourse Act. This substituted a new policy in the place of a ban on foreign commerce totally. From that act Americans could trade with all nations except Great Britain and France, once again. Further trade could be legally resumed should either nation cease violating American neutral rights. Neither nation took this bait. War needs superseded the benefits of merchants, especially when so much trade was getting through anyway. Despite their bitterness toward the combatants, Americans were unwilling to support their beloved president when it came to money; even though their profits were becoming pinched by the seizures by the combatants. Soon orders went out to American captains to seize illegal privateers, to keep foreign warships out of American territorial waters, and report citizens assisting or supplying armed foreign ships. [14]

Meanwhile, there was a decided opposition to the expected appointment of Albert Gallatin as secretary of state because of his foreign birth. It was well believed that the former secretary of the treasury, was fit for high office. However, some of his friends even felt that he should not receive that high office. William Branch Giles and Samuel Smith had been Gallatin's friends the last twenty years, but they were opposed to Gallatin at this point. Michael Leib joined them in opposition.

A few days before the inaugural, Wilson Cary Nicholas visited Madison to warn the president-elect that there would be serious opposition to Gallatin. There was no other candidate for the high office. Some one suggested that if Robert Smith would be named to the treasury post, his brother Samuel would vote for Gallatin and Samuel accepted the idea, although he knew that Robert was unsuitable for the position. However, Gallatin objected and Robert Smith was named secretary of state instead. It was a political appointment to secure Samuel's support for the upcoming administration. Gallatin would remain at the treasury post. There, he would hold Smith in an open contempt and advise economy spending in that dangerous world. Smith and Gallatin had been friends socially, but this changed. [15]

Meanwhile, in the business world, the situation of corporations under the Constitution was not yet settled. Then on March 15, 1809, the Supreme Court decided that the right to settle cases between citizens of different state also included corporations. The issue had come before the Court when the Bank of the United States sued a Georgia tax collector for property he had seized when it would not pay Georgia taxes. Tax collector Deucaux argued that the Court had no jurisdiction. The corporation was not a private citizen. Further some of the stockholders claimed that there was no federal power to judge in the case. The Court agreed with their argument and it was not until 1844 that it was overturned in the ruling that the corporation belonged to the state which chartered it. [16]

In January of 1809, the British Government instructed their minister at Washington that their two 1807 orders in council would no longer be applied to the United States once they met three conditions. First, that the American officials should remove their embargo type restrictions on Great Britain and leave them in force against France. Second, it should renounce all claims on colonial trade, and agree to the rule of 1756 on such trade. Third, it should allow Great Britain to seize all American ships trading or attempting to trade with French ports or those who acquiesced in French decrees. The Americans agreed to the first and were told that the British would lift its restrictions. Shortly, the British repudiated the agreement and its minister. In March of 1809, Congress raised the embargo against neutral nations. They left the embargo against Great Britain, France, and their dependencies. The American ministers at London and at Paris informed the two Governments of the action. [17]

Then word reached Washington DC through diplomatic channels that George III (or his Government) wished to pay honorable reparations for the British aggression against the *Chesapeake*. The British envoy was able to tell the new administration of James Monroe that the British authorities had relieved the offending officer from his command and would restore the prisoners to their American soil. Madison was very happy to receive this news and the State Department had the correspondence of April published in the various "American newspapers to provide the citizens of the United States with the disposition of the matter which so engaged the people of our nation."

The British minister to the United States, David M. Erskine wrote that the British action afforded "a fair prospect of a complete and cordial understanding, being re-established between the two countries. He also wrote that the British government was determined to send an envoy extraordinary to negotiate a treaty resolving all difficulties between the two nations. If Madison would renew trade relations with the British, George (or his Government) would withdraw the British orders in council so harmful to American trade. Madison thought that this was a good idea. Erskine then gave out the false information that the orders in council would be withdrawn in June. Madison responded with a declaration for renewed trade. [18]

There were celebrations in commercial centers in the United States. In New York City, the Federal Republican Committee recommended that ship owners and masters of vessels should display their colors on the following Monday to honor the American triumph in getting Britain to restore commercial trade. Churches were to rang their bells for a full hour and there was to be a Federal salute of guns three times during the day. The Federalists also celebrated because this would mean peace with Great Britain and the

The Difficult War: The Era of the War of 1812

weakening of French influence in the United States. Three days later, the colors were flown, the bells were rung, and the people cheered. [19]

As a minister to the United States, David M. Erskine was friendly to the Americans and wished an accommodation with the Americans. He was a Whig and had an American wife, both of which turned him toward the Americans in friendship and interest. Canning trusted him to negotiate on three points. First he was authorized. Should both French and British war vessels be excluded from American waters, he could tender reparations on the *Chesapeake* matter. This was done but it was not enough for the British leaders. There were a series of harsh provisions. Secondly and thirdly, Canning offered to recall the orders in council should the Americans repeal its embargo against the British but keep them against the French. Further they should allow British ships to seize American ships carrying on the prohibited trade with France. This was unacceptable. Erskine, by a careful and friendly negotiation managed to arrange a treaty, but Canning repudiated it and ordered Erskine to return to England. Erskine had failed to arrange things in accordance with the wishes of the ministry. [20]

---

[1] Washburn, Wilcomb E., *Handbook of North American Indians: History of Indian-White Relations*, Washington DC: Smithsonian Institute, 1988, pp. 35-36.

[2] Wilkins, Thurman, 1985, pp. 44-51.

[3] Abernethy, *Burr*, pp. 11-79, 84-275.

[4] Strode, Hudson, Jefferson Davis: *American Patriot, 1808-1861*, New York: Harcourt, Brace, 1955, pp. 3-7.

[5] Warren, Louis Austin, *Lincoln's Parentage and Childhood*, New York: Century, 1926, pp. 3-8, 10-11, 13; Barton, William E., *The Paternity of Abraham Lincoln*, New York: George H. Doran, 1920, *passim*; Barton, William E., *The Lineage of Lincoln*, Indianapolis: Bobbs-Merrill, 1919, pp. 29-41.

[6] Warren, *Lincoln's*, pp. 9-54, 56, 59-74, 133-134, 138-140, 159-160, 232-234; Beveridge, Albert J., *Abraham Lincoln, 1809-1858*, 2 vols. Boston: Houghton Mifflin, 1928, I, 12.

[7] Beveridge, I, 23; Warren, *Lincoln's, pp. 54-74, 87, 94-106; Basler, R.P., IV, 70; Booth, Edward Townsend,* Country Life in America as Lived by Ten Presidents of the United States, *New York: Alfred A Knopf, 1947, pp. 193-194.*

[8] Booth, *Country*, pp. 184, 191-196.

[9] Collins, Lewis, *History of Kentucky*, Maysville, Ky: Lewis Collins, 1847, Reprint Lexington, Ky: Henry Clay Press, 1968. p. 335.

[10] Beveridge, *Lincoln*, I, 3.

[11] Hertz, Emanuel, *The Hidden Lincoln*, 1938, pp. 275-276.

[12] Herndon, William H., *Life of Lincoln*, 1930, Angle edition.

[13] *Kentucky Gazette and General Advertiser* (Lexington), March 13, 1809, pp. 1-2.

[14] Adams, Henry, *History of the United States of America During the Administration of James Madison*, New York: Library of America, 1986, pp. 116-118; Dudley ed. *Naval War*, pp. 36. 39. 40-41.

[15] Adams, *Madison*, pp. 9-13.

[16] Ireland, Robert M., "Bank of the United States v. Deucaux," Hall, Kermit L,. *The Oxford Companion to the Supreme Court of the United States*, New York: Oxford University Press, 1992, p. 61.

[17] Updyke, Frank A., *The Diplomacy of the War of 1812*, Baltimore: Johns Hopkins, 1915, pp. 108-110.

[18] *Kentucky Gazette*, May 2, 1809, p. 3.

[19] *Cobbett's Political Register*, XV (January-June 1809), col. 852-854.

[20] Chaining, *Jeffersonian*, pp. 233-236.

CHAPTER IV

THE NATION

On March 4, 1809, the first Madison inaugural was held. It was a great day for Madison, a small and pale man, who was obviously nervous for the occasion. With him was outgoing president, Jefferson was both happy that he could retire at age sixty-six and that his younger friend James Madison was succeeding him to the presidency. They had long been friends and colleagues. They were also long time political allies. Madison was Jefferson's choice for the position and he could not have made a better one. Madison had been the most important founder of the Constitution and during the Washington Administration was the chief congressman in the nation. He was actual founder of the Jeffersonian Republican Party as lieutenant for Jefferson policies and ideas. Politically they were very compatible. During the previous eight years he was secretary of state and chief adviser of Jefferson, and now he was to continue the policies of his chief. [1]

In relation to the new president, Jefferson cherished his friendship and would not intervene with Madison in forwarding with approval applicants who wanted Jefferson to get them a post with the new administration. He knew it was not his to intervene. It was Madison's administration and not his. He expressed himself in a circular in which he said that "the friendship which has long subsisted between the President of the United States and myself, gave me reason to expect, on my retirement from office, that I might often receive applications to interpose with him on behalf of persons desiring appointments. Such an abuse of his dispositions towards me would necessarily lead to the loss of them, and to the transforming me from the character of a friend to that of an unreasonable and troublesome solicitor."

In the process, he did make some suggestions of appointment for a few people who were of value for some specific occasion. In general he stuck to his declaration. The publication of the document did serve its purpose. It kept the solicitations of men who sought office down and protected both he and Madison from their importunities. For as with every administration there were large numbers of applicants for the limited number of federal jobs available. [2]

However, Jefferson did correspond with Madison on various affairs of state, such as the Indian situation of the Cherokees and Chickasaws. Before he left the presidency, he wrote Madison, that he had received information about white intruders moving on their lands. He noted that a letter from General Henry Dearborn, secretary of war, to Colonel Return Jonathan Meigs had directed him to have them ordered off these premises and informed them that if they did not leave, they would be forced out by military force.

"These orders remained still to be given, and they should go to the officer commanding at Highwassee. A very discreet officer should be selected. On the Cherokee lands, Wafford's settlement should not be disturbed as the Indians themselves expect to arrange that with us, and the exchange for lands beyond the Mississippi will furnish a good opportunity." All the intruders on the Chickasaw lands would be removed, except those by Doublehead's reserve which was under Indian title to the white settlers there. In this Jefferson showed his grasp of government and knowledge of what went and was going on in the nation. [3]

Interested in the education of the Indians he wrote that he wanted the government to buy a farm near Detroit for land to erect dormitories for Indian boys and girls to educate them in a school there in English and the household an mechanical arts. It would be for Father Richard who was going to France for aid. The farm was to be cultivated by the Indian lads under the direction of a farmer of proper character. The land would also house a blacksmith and a carpenter. [4]

In April of 1809, there were in London modified orders in council, brought about by pressures created to meet charges. The nations of Spain, Portugal, and Turkey became new allies for the British and trade was opened up there. Alexander Baring used his influence for the giving of concessions to the United States. Thus merchants had strong ties to America and to the English Whigs. Even Canning with his strict views was prepared to allow neutral trade with Germany and the Baltic. He reduced the cost of licenses to trade in Europe. It is ironic that war was so close when the opposing powers would sell the right of trade on a case by case basis. Trade could be allowed by this means, although the denial of the more complete right of trade was bringing the Americans and British close to war. [5]

In the British House of Commons, on May 23rd, Canning stated that Erskine's agreement was not in conformity with his Majesty's wishes. It was beyond the minister's instructions. However, the Government would act to lessen the blow to American merchants and speculators by this reversal of what was supposed to be British policy and which they made arrangements to trade with the British. The merchants had acted in good faith to trade under the Erskine agreement and would be greatly harmed by opening trade once gained and finding that the situation had not changed as they were led to believe by the British minister. The American ships and their cargoes would be allowed to proceed to their destined ports, secure and profitably. Words of this was published as far away as Lexington, Kentucky, in the *Kentucky Gazette*. [6]

In the midst of many columns on the war in Europe and some on the embargo issue in the papers there was concern about the possibility of Indian attacks on the frontier, which after all was not too far from the log cabin where the infant Abraham was the center of attention. The chief topics of conversations outside of farming were the Napoleonic wars and their consequences in America, and horsebreeding and racing. Westerners now added talk of Indian hostilities if the newspapers were any indication. While only a minor part of the Kentucky population read the journals of news, the information found therein was verbally expressed in conversations. Most Americans of that day got their information verbally from those who read and those who had opinions whether they read or not. Kentuckians evolved their interests over in racing, the prime sport of Americans of that day, especially in the state where horses formed the reason for existence of men--Kentucky. Horses racing was to continue to be *the* sport for many decades to come. [7]

Lieutenant Kingsley, commander of the garrison at Bellevue on the banks of the Mississippi, and a Mr. Johnson, United States factor, also at the fort, reported that the Indians were preparing for battle. The army officer had doubted the friendship of these natives for Americans and now he was certain that they would soon attack. Kingsley launched a readiness campaign of his own and prepared to move into the new fort against an estimated two thousand Indians. However, he needed small cannon for his blockhouses, ammunition for them, and two or three accomplished spies or scouts if he was to succeed. He undertook the precaution of burning bonfires at night so that the Indians could not make a night attack without being seen.

On April 12th, Johnson reported that, on the opposite bank of the Mississippi, one could see the entire nation of the Sac. They had been there for ten days, counciling and trading. The Indians told the whites that they were their friends, but Johnson doubted this. The chiefs talked to Kingsley and Johnson. A dancing party of natives came up and asked permission to dance around the fort. Then they rushed up to the open gate and came into the fort, but the soldiers brought up the cannon and the Sacs yelled and left. A certain Jarror told the officers that the Sac planned to take the fort under the guise of talk and trading. These reports added to the concern of the people of the frontier. [8]

There was danger from the slaves as well as Indians for in May of 1809, the newspaper reported that three black slaves owned by a Mr. Chapman of Adair County killed him with the repeated blows of a handspike. They then carried the body with considerable exertions to burn it on a log fire. Authorities apprehended the slaves who confessed to their crime. [9]

Kentuckians were not as interested in the formation of manufacturing as the people of the eastern cities, however, the editors of the *Kentucky Gazette* included the report of the committee of commerce and manufacture of June 21st in the pages of their newspaper for the edification of Kentuckians. Lincoln never saw a factory until considerably later in life. The issue of protectionism through tariffs was an important, difficult, and delicate one in the early years of the Republic. Abraham Lincoln was to take a Whig view of the issue when he reached the time of his majority. The congressmen on the committee managed to make a plan which they believed to have the support of Congress. They tried to undertake a moderate program between the need to withstand foreign competition and the need to prevent monopolies from developing.

Americans had a fear of monopolies even this early. Government monopolies were common in the history of trade of the modern era and Americans naturally opposed them, remembering them as harming American interests when they were colonials, the tea monopoly playing a role in the early revolutionary period of the country. The committee's plan was to raise duties. They worried that such heavily imported items such as salt would leave America in need in case of war interruptions if Americans did not have a salt industry at home. This hit close to home to the Kentuckians as well as other Americans so that they included salt duties as well as tariff barriers in high tariffs. [10]

The people of the western states were even more concerned with the need of transportation and William Eaton suggested from Ashford, Connecticut, that Americans import camels from Northern Africa to provide a means to transport goods. Eaton was traveling, had seen the southern states, and thought that the camel was the answer to Southern problems. Plantations there were located close to navigable streams and lands were vacant in the hills and plains not close to the rivers. He would remedy this situation. Eaton had tried to import camels as a practicable project when he traveled through North Africa. After describing the camels' abilities to go long distance without food and water, he suggested that they would do well in the plains he had seen in the South. He also praised the sheep and mules in Moslem lands. [11]

The American defense was ill-prepared for any armed conflict. Money had been spent for a fleet of gunboats of dubious value in a war. Jefferson's gunboats were unproven and had a short lifespan of about one year. Except for gunboats, the American navy had only a few frigates and sloops. On the bright side, the navy had the best officers and seamen of any navy. In contrast the army was divided into two camps and this internal friction sapped the officers and men of any effectiveness.

Differences evolved around General James Wilkinson, whom Jefferson had long favored and protected. He had recently been acquitted of being a Spanish pensioner of which charge he had been guilty. The past president had also saved the general from courts-martial in his relations with Aaron Burr. Wilksinson had been disloyal to General Anthony Wayne in the nineties and in his turn, the next general down was an opponent. Wade Hampton, that general, felt the utmost contempt for Wilkinson and gathered around him a party of officers who did not like Wilkinson.

When Madison took office, Wilkinson was on his slow way to New Orleans to take charge. Although the situation was momentarily urgent, the general took his time, spending six weeks on the Atlantic coast, stopping at Annapolis, Norfolk, and Charleston. The war scare passed and he left New Orleans for Havana and Pensacola, which he later claimed were vital stops on a special mission for the president. Arriving at New Orleans on April 19, 1809, he had found a body of two thousand recruits.

Almost all of the officers and men sunk in indolence and dissipation. They lacked subordination, discipline, and police. Almost one-third of them were sick. There was no land or water transportation, a scant medical assistance, and few paymasters. The force was ill-supplied. Floods kept Wilkinson from moving his troops to an encampment and they stayed in the city. On June 10th, the general sent his troops to a selected camp below the water level, but kept dry by dikes. More than five hundred of his men were sick from chronic diarrhea, billous or intermittent fevers, and scurry among other illnesses.

Secretary of War Dr. William Eustis wanted to move the troops upriver to a more healthful climate near Fort Adams, but Wilkinson argued that the move upriver would have diseased nine-tenths of the men. This might have been debated, but Wilkinson correctly believed that it would cost twelve thousand dollars and he would not be able to protect New Orleans, from the fort at Natchez. He did not have the money and was prepared to risk his troops to keep the British from New Orleans. Most of his men became sick anyway. Orders came to move and after long delay he did so. Wilkinson lost two hundred and fifty soldiers to death on the march upriver. During the first year 764 troopers died and 167 deserted. Wilkinson was summoned to Washington DC and Wade Hampton succeeded him in command of this disaster. [12]

There was another personal conflict at the time. Jefferson was distressed by the division between Gallatin and Smith. He wrote a friend that he had "learned with great sorrow that circumstances have arisen among our executive counselors which have rendered foes those who once were friends. To them it will be a source of infinite pain and vexation, and therefore chiefly I lament it, for I have a sincere esteem for both parties. To the President it will be really inconvenient; unless we were to believe the newspapers which pretend that Mr. Gallatin will go out." Such an event would create a day of mourning for the nation in Jefferson's viewpoint. He hoped "that the position of both gentlemen will be made so easy as to give no cause for either to withdraw."

Jefferson had consulted with all of the cabinet, but in the present circumstances he deemed it Madison's wisdom that Madison would consult him individually. [13]

Madison kept his friend Jefferson informed on what was happening in Washington and Europe that year. He wrote on June 27th "that the French Government had made several favorable regulations, among them, one for restoring the cargoes sequestered under the municipal operation of the Berlin Decree; all of which had been arrested by a belief founded on language used in the British Parliament that the U. S. was about to make war on France." Jefferson would see in the newspaper all that was known on the recent battle in Germany. "The Senate passed, unanimously the Bill of non-intercourse with France, with a paragraph admitting French ships of war, in common with British into our waters. The House of Representatives rejected yesterday by a large majority, a motion to discriminate in favor of British ships." [14]

John Quincy Adams did not receive special instructions for his mission to Russia. Secretary of State Robert Smith gave him copies of those for previous missions. They were to create good will and look after American interests in Russia. Favorite treatment of neutral rights were to be protected as they came up. Adams should wait for the Czar's initiative before discussing neutral rights, for which he would be instructed upon on the occasion. Communications would be exacted and ample.

When they met they talked freely. Alexander I and Adams spoke in fluent French. The Czar said that "with regard to the political relations of Europe and those unhappy disturbances which agitate its different states, the system of the United States is wise and just. They may relay upon me not to do anything to withdraw them from it. The Continent of Europe is now in a manner pacified. The only obstacle to a general pacification is England's obstinate adherence to a system of Maritime pretensions which is neither liberal nor just. The only object of the war now is to bring England to reasonable terms on this subject." He spoke of commercial rights for all nations. Adams replied that America did not intervene in European matters. So the meeting went well from the American viewpoint. Americans could count upon the friendship and sympathy of Alexander I. [15]

In Russia, Alexander I had proved to be a divided man. His grandmother had exposed him to a liberal dose of the Enlightenment, but although Alexander had established some reforms in his early year of rule, he did not change much, either to concern what it would do to Russia political, economic, and social life or to a reluctance to give up great power. Alexander never carried through on what he had learned of the change which was limited to Great British as a evolutionary series of events of the United States, both revolutionary and evolutionary. No one lived the Enlightenment like the Americans. Russia remained feudal with only minor developments. Alexander turned out to be the typical Russian absolute ruler. [16]

However, his early liberal upbringing did lead him to be friendly to the United States as is seen in his talk with Adams. But there was also international politics involved. Alexander wanted to weaken Great Britain and America was one of the ways to do this. Also, he wanted justice in the matter, however much that was missing in his own country.

The splendor of Russian courts was not present in the calm of America. In the quiet college town of Cambridge, Massachusetts, Oliver Wendall Holmes Sr. was born to Ariel Holmes and his wife Sally Wendall Holmes' cousin was a representative in Washington from Massachusetts. It was not only the embargo that was Quincy's problem but all those voters in the west who would upset the power that New England had and create economic competition. Those territories in his view should remain such; he wanted no more votes in Congress from the West.

Two years later when it was proposed to make a state of Louisiana, Quincy was to jump to his feet and then thunder that it would be better to dissolve the Union than admit the westerners, since it would be everyone's right, some men's duty, to prepare for separation. This would be amiable or violent. Amiable if possible, violently if not. The road to the Hartford Convention was embarked on over this issue. [17]

It was in this West, Lincoln's western country that democracy which Quincy thought troublesome flourished. The West in Abraham was born was a rugged place of freedom and individual loving men who preferred to enjoy life to a work ethic dominated life. They moved from more settled places to the frontier to avoid taxes and all kinds of restrictions. Living on the cleared acres provided them with a subsistence level of existence.

Some would talk about their rights and against creditors. Others would talk against money hungry Northern businessmen. They did not think of the national government as a rule. It was too far away. For them, there was too much government on the state level, which they tolerated because they were used to it; but on the edge of the frontier even that government was far away. Preferring freedom, they settled for poverty and lived as they wished. The frontiersmen used a gun to hunt, and a rude cabin for shelter and apparatus for the making of corn whiskey. They enjoyed such sports as shooting, boat races, handball, racing, cockfighting, and horse shows. [18]

The American prosperity of these prewar times extended to Kentucky. Its people were mostly energetic and acquisitive, seeking to make good use of their opportunities. This was the other side of the state. The people continued to clear land for farming. Artisans, lawyers, doctors, and merchants expanded their professions and stores and the towns and cities grew; the flood of immigrants coming into the still young state. Over ninety percent still lived on farms or in village settlements, where agriculture was their chief concern.

Besides the large number of hogs being driven to the markets in the east, the Kentuckians had infant industries such as a distillery, tobacco factories, a steam engine factory, a plant to manufacture candles and bars of soap, a steam flour mill, and a sugar refinery. Most of its people were involved in land speculation with an upper spiral of real estate taxes. There was one bank, the Bank of Kentucky, which had a number of branches. [19]

Democratic Kentucky did not remain a common-man state for long. There were educated men with the early settlers and by the time of Lincoln's birth, Kentucky was well under way to be aristocratic base upon the model of Virginia. There were many wealthy merchants and even some rich manufacturers. Near Lexington one could find fifty plus estates after the manner of country gentlemen in England and Virginia. Important leaders from other states partook of the hospitality of these mansions.

Religious leaders denounced Kentuckians as infidels, that is unorthodox or sometimes anti-clerical and even atheistic. To the orthodox everyone who did not believe as they did were infidels. Presbyterian divines took exception to opposition to their attempts to stop the mails on Sunday and introduce religion into politics, and to criticize the war policy of 1812. Their enemies were such as anti-clerical democrats and liberal Unitarians. They could easily call Christian opponents atheists. [20]

Kentucky had educational facilities for a minority. Transylvania Seminary was founded before statehood. Soon afterwards various academies were established, including

The Difficult War: The Era of the War of 1812

one in Elizabethtown, to the west of Lexington, founded in the spring of 1799. When Thomas and Nancy moved to the town, the people were building a new schoolhouse. They built a new brick school building in 1814. A key ingredient of these secondary schools was discipline against all kinds of disorderly conduct such as card playing and gambling, unseemly language and conduct, talkings and whispering, and the use of pop-guns, bows and arrows, pan guns, and throwing stones. The academy required the payment of a substantial tuition of $15 for English, arithmetic, and the use of globes and $30 for the teaching of higher mathematics, navigation, and surveying. There were also primary schools in the country. this was the other side of Kentucky: amid poverty, there was progress.

There was still another side of Kentucky: slavery. One of the themes of the age in which Lincoln lived was runaway slaves and their fate. These situations were eventual to contribute to the fraternal war in which Abraham was to play a prominent role. In nearby Lexington, the closest sizable town to Lincoln's birthplace, the country jailers had a runaway slave named George, a tall (two inches short of six feet) African American in his mid-twenties and deaf. Authorities had captured him. George wore "a few rags under an old blanket."

The jailer was having some trouble in getting someone to claim the slave. He threatened to take the usual course s the law directed if his owner did not come forth. A white man named Robert Peoples told authorities that the runaway slave had been sold by his agent in Nathez. Shortly afterwards the jailer placed in the jail another African American, six foot tall and heavy set in his mid-thirties. This man, named Washington, claimed he was a free man, but jailer Nathaniel Prentiss did not believe this, taking him into custody and advertising for his owner to come to reclaim him. [21]

To the west of Kentucky, guided by a Spaniard named Emmanuel Blanco, three Missourians went on a mercantile expedition for Santa Fe. A journalist wrote that "the enterprise must be toilsome and perilous, the distance being computed at five to six hundred miles, altogether through wilderness heretofore unexplored." If they had expected welcome for their goods, they were sadly disappointed. This welcome was exactly what they did not expect. At the red water of the Red River, a Spanish detachment seized them and took them to Santa Fe. The governor held an examination and put them in prison. They lay there for two years. Folks back home thought them dead. An editor wrote that "the assassins of Mexico have ere this butchered these respectable citizens of Louisiana. Yet a little while and a day of terrible retribution will arrive."

Months later, it was known that they were in prison. The editor wrote in March of 1811 that there were three hundred well equipped men who were preparing to set off to secure of them the three men "and to bring fairer prospects of success, join the revolutionary party". In 1812, the government set the three men free and they returned home. But the Roger McKnight party was also seized and they spent nine years in prison.[22]

Both the British and the Americans competed for Indian support but the march of American frontiersmen into their lands created an anti-Americanism among the Indians. This William Hull could not eradicate. Still he entertained them saying that it was better to feed them than to fight the Indians. The Swanee led the Indians toward a united front and among them the Prophet, from their tribe, preached a return to native virtues. British invited the Prophet and his brothers Tecumseh to Amherstburg in Canada. They restored Matthew Elliott to the Indian Department because he had a Shawnee family and was influential with the tribe. Shawnee messengers went south and reported back that the Southern Indians were divided into pro and anti-American parties. Elliott thought one regiment could join the Indians and they would be sufficient to throw the Americans back east beyond the Ohio. This boded ill for the future. [23]

[1]Lynch, William O., *Fifty Years of Party Warfare 1789-1837*, Bobbs-Merrill, 1931 (1967 reprint), pp. 201-202.

[2]Smith, James Morton (ed.), *The Republic of Letters: The Correspondence between Thomas Jefferson and James Madison, 1776-1826*, 3 vols., New York: W.W. Norton, 1995, III, 1574ff. Quote on p. 1574.

[3]*Ibid.*, 1574-1575. Quote on p. 1575.

[4]*Ibid.*, 1575. See 1611-1613.

[5]White, *Nation*, pp. 59-60.

[6]*Kentucky Gazette*, August 8, 1809, p. 2.

[7]*Ibid.*, Various issues in 1809.

[8]*Ibid.*, May 23, 1809, p. 3.

[9] Ibid., June 6, 1809, p. 3.

[10] Ibid., July 25, 1809, p. 2.

[11] Ibid., August 1, 1809, p. 2.

[12] Adams, Madison, pp. 119-124. .

[13] Lynch, Fifty Years, p. 213. Quotes on p. 213.

[14] Smith (ed.), Republic of Letters, p. 1593. Quote on p. 1593.

[15] Bemis, Samuel Flagg, John Quincy Adams and the Formation of American Foreign Policy, New York: Alfred A. Knopf, 1969, pp. 159-162.

[16] Riasanovsky, Nicholas V., A History of Russia, 2d ed., London: Oxford University Press, 1969, pp. 233-341 and 353.

[17] Bowen, Yankee, pp. 26-27.

[18] Hoskems, George Lee and Johnson, Herbert A. (eds.) History of the Supreme Court of the United States, vol. II: Foundations of Power: John Marshall, 1801-15, New York: Macmillan, 1981, pp. 41-43.

[19] Smith, Elbert B., Francis Preston Blair, New York: Free Press, 1980, pp. 11 and 12.

[20] Sonne, Niels Henry, Liberal Kentucky: 1780-1828, Lexington Ky: University of Lexington Press, 1968, pp. 78-83.

[21] Kentucky Gazette and General Advertiser, January 3, 1809, p. 1.

[22] Duffus, R.L., The Santa Fe Trail, London: Longman, Green, 1930, pp. 56-60.

[23] Wright, J. Leitch Jr., Britain and the American Frontier, 1783-1815, Athens, Ga.: University of Georgia Press, 1975, pp. 147-148.

CHAPTER V

PEOPLE

When Abraham Lincoln was born, a bright and moving Henry Clay was speaker of the Assembly of Kentucky and was spending his early years not far from Lincoln's first log cabin home. For a brief term Clay had already been an United States senator and was soon to be an American congressman once again in Washington across the mountains. Henry Clay was born in Virginia, not far from Richmond. His father, the Reverend John Clay, died poor when the boy was four. Within ten years of that inauspicious day, he received some schooling under a drunken remittance man. At age fourteen, Henry was put to work in a Richmond store under his step-father. One year later, he found a position of clerk in the office of the high court of Chancery of Virginia. There he came to the notice of the great and venerable Chancellor George Wythe, who dated back to colonial times.

Wythe had been a member of the Continental Congress and a signer of the Declaration of Independence. He helped make the Constitution. Next, he was a high judge and a chancellor of the state of Virginia. For all of his renown as a jurist, he was noted as a teacher. He taught Thomas Jefferson, John Marshall, and James Monroe as well as Henry Clay. Wythe was perhaps the first jurist to lay down in 1782, the great principle that a court could nullify statues not in keeping with a constitution. As an early abolitionist, he freed his slaves and made provisions for the ex-slaves in his will. He was poisoned by a great nephew who hoped to come into his estates .

The august Wythe drew upon Clay's services as a secretary for four years before arranging his transfer to the attorney-general's office as a regular student of law for one year. Clay was admitted to the practice of law in 1797, the next year, but migrated to Kentucky seeking a brighter future. This he was to find in the west where he could shine as a lawyer and politician. The young man made his way and soon had a successful practice. He preferred the defense and enjoying freeing and helping his men clients. Even before he was hardly settled, he met, courted, and married Lucretia, daughter of Colonel Thomas Hart. In 1803, he entered the legislature as a member. While in Congress Clay voted against the recharter of the first Bank of the United States. [1]

William Cary Nicholas was an important addition to Madison's arsenal in the House. Jefferson had asked him to enter Congress to become his floor leader shortly after the Randolph schism of 1806. When the federal embargo failed, he became convinced that the only choice for Americans was war or submission. He wrote Jefferson that "we have tried negotiation until it is disgraceful to think of renewing it. Commercial restrictions have been so managed as to operate only to our only injury. War then or submission only remain. In deciding between them I cannot hesitate a moment."

Madison would not abandon the policy and so Nicholas resigned in the autumn of 1809 rather than going into opposition. When he was sure of the his course after the *Chesapeake* affair, George Washington Campbell of Tennessee elected to advocate military preparedness. Then when the embargo was repealed Richie led his Richmond *Enquirer* into the then small war camp. William Duane of the Philadelphia *Aurora* advocated military preparations. If this failed he would wage a "defensive war."

Nathaniel Macon sought the other alternative. He joined with John Randolph in trying to reduce the size of the national military force. Going to the extreme of abolishing the navy and army altogether, Macon seemed to favor submission. He felt the non-intercourse bill of April of 1810 was too provocative although it bore his name. Only later did he see war as the only alternative when the British seized the ships with American agricultural products aboard. Although he joined the War Hawks, Macon inconsistently voted against all bills increasing the size of the navy and to finance the upcoming war by raising taxes. He was no realist, or a student of real international politics. [2]

Carter Tarrant was a fearless worker in Christianity. He helped make the Baptist Church in Kentucky strong and successful. His group ended sectarianism in his church. Going forth into the remote areas of the state, he organized new churches. The friendships he made among Baptists and non-Baptists aided his work in God's causes. Soon he rode high upon the spiritual awakening. Tarrant had long been a slaveholder, but when he was converted to religion in 1784, he was troubled about this institution.

Soon he had become an avowed abolitionist. At first, he was slow in denouncing slavery although he made his views known quietly. After 1800, he became militant on the issue and with John Sutton and David Barrow spoke out. Shortly, he resigned from Mt. Tabor church because the congregation would not repudiate slavery. His new church contained a vocal proslavery minority and conflict erupted. He became most uncompromising when he realized that the religious revival of his days was not a prelude to ending slavery. Soon he was speaking out against the advocated gradual freedom for the African Americans. For him it was too slow.

Abolitionism was causing rifts around 1803. By 1805, pro-slavery groups began to gain the upper hand. The Church excommunicated Tarrant on the charge he was encouraging slaves to rebel. Men began to threaten him and the other abolitionists. He and his friends formed their own church and continued to speak out against slavery. Next they founded an abolition society on September 27, 1808. Tarrant remained with it about five years and it lasted for almost twenty. The rest of his life was downhill; his retail store lost money because he gave credit freely and he soon lost his capital. By 1814, he was very poor, but he preached still. He was an unpaid chaplain in the upcoming war and was with Jackson at New Orleans. On February 17, 1816, Tarrant died and met his good reward. He had lived a good life and fought against an evil at great cost to himself. [3]

The descendant of a long line of lowland Scots, Sam Houston was born near Lexington, Virginia, on March 2, 1793. The location was Timber Ridge, a small community in hill country of beautiful rolling hills, to the west of the Blue Ridge Mountains. His father was a plantation owner, a military man, and an avid reader with a good stock of books. The boy was poorly educated in formal terms, but found a life-long interest in the classics of Rome and Greece. With a powerful mind and superb memory, he was able to recite more and more of the lives of Pope's translation of *The Iliad*.

The rhetoric of the classics influenced his style, literary and oratorical. The memory Houston developed helped him in studying law and speaking extemporaneously for hours. He and his relatives, who were generally doers and leaders in their communities. High living and neglect of his properties put Houston's father into deep debt. In order to begin again, the elder Houston decided to go west. He died on the way to a last inspection of the militia. The family went to the frontier near Knoxville.

Sam went to live with the Cherokee, interested only in the classics and adventure. He marched to the beat of a different drummer. Working behind a counter or ploughing was of no interest to him. At age sixteen in the year in which Lincoln was born, he began his first period of escaping into Indian life to avoid working and civilization. At this time, the Cherokee were largely peaceful and not too far from civil life. Houston and the Cherokee liked each other and his Indian mentor called him "The Raven." [4]

The Indians on the frontier were generally at the mercy of the settlers. White hunters invaded the native territory in search of game depleting that available to the Indian for subsistence. This was done in violation of treaties with the Indians. Parts of the northwest frontier had plenty of game in the nineties, but were to be found in insufficient numbers by the time of Lincoln's birth. Indian tribes in the border areas were forced to withdraw westward into the wilderness or cede their lands for supplies of annuities. Those who remained close to the settlement were addicts to whiskey and would, when drunk, kill anyone they saw including their own kind. White juries would convict the murderers to hang, while they would acquit any white men who killed an Indian. In white cases witnesses would usually never appear when a guilty white life was at stake. One of Abe's uncles thought it was a virtue to murder an Indian on sight. [5]

The first great man of letters in the American republic was Washington Irving. Not only was he loved at home, but he was the first United States author to be respected in Europe. Born in New York City on April 3, 1783, he was named after the great general. His father was a well-to-do importer in the city's merchant community. After a few years in public schools, he returned home to read freely and maintain a liking for human affairs. In 1804, Irving made a tour of France and Italy, returning home to study law. In 1807, he was one of the counsels for Aaron Burr.

His first work was the serial *Salmagundi*, which later came out in book form. It was a humorous book which gave a good picture of social life in the New York of the times. One of his most famous works came out in 1809 under the title of the *History of New York*, which was credited to the fictional Diedrich Knickenbocker. His name was established in the year of Lincoln's birth, but he worked in the family merchant firm for another nine years until it collapsed in 1818. [6]

Another New Yorker, Nicholas Roosevelt was rather the adventurous sort. He had been financed by Robert Livingston in an attempt at building a steamboat and took out a patent on side-wheelers. These things rested until Livingston and his associates backed Robert Fulton in his steamboat invention. It was a success. Livingston involved Roosevelt because of his patent and his abilities. The New York great uncle of Teddy was sent to western waters to investigate the possibility of using steam navigation on those rivers.

It was in 1809 that Nicholas went down the Mississippi and learned of the difficulties in encounters with Indians after whiskey, snakes, bars in the river and both submerged islands and river ledges. He noted the currents and depths and made judgments about opportunities for trade and transport. Although rivermen told the changes in the river would make steam transport impossible, Nicholas formed the opinion that steamboats would be feasible transports on the western rivers.

Having gone down the river in a flatboat, he embarked at New Orleans on a ship for New York where he arrived in 1810. He reported favorably and the investors, Fulton and Roosevelt, formed the Ohio Steamboat Navigation Company for western transportation. Roosevelt went to Pittsburgh, where he supervised the building of a steamboat. The company's managers got a monopoly for the company.

In 1811, in the spring months, Roosevelt set forth with his ship down the Ohio and Mississippi for New Orleans. There were eleven crewmen and the Roosevelts with two servant. A son was born on board to Mrs. Roosevelt. No passengers would embark upon such a chance filled voyage and with seeming good reason. They had their perils. Once there was a fire aboard. Also they were cashed by Indians. Coal ran out and they had to stop for wood which they chopped themselves. Worst yet they were caught in the famous New Madrid earthquake. The ship and its complement of men and women made it to New Orleans on January 12, 1812. This was the start of a long lived transportation system in the waters of the Ohio, Mississippi, and Missouri and other rivers throughout the nineteenth century. The lack of passengers on the first trip was to be compensated for by the millions who would travel. on the Mississippi steamboats over the decades ahead. Soon they were saying what a marvelous invention this was and then later to take the steamboat for granted. [7]

Shortly before Lincoln's birth, David Low Dodge was on the point of death in New York City. The Connecticut merchant had regrets that he had not publicly denounced the war as scripturally unlawful. His illness over, Dodge wrote and printed in 1809, a pamphlet for peace entitled *The Mediators, Kingdom Not of This World*, an anonymous work on non-resistance based upon the Sermon on the Mount. Someone differed with him and wrote an answer to Dodge's arguments. Dodge set out another pamphlet on the subject. Friends talked with him and discussed the idea of forming a peace society. They did not do so fearing the people would think it a political organization given the prospect of war with England. [8]

The prospects of trouble between the United States and Great Britain was direful to Alexander I of Russia. The Russians and their czar were interested in their trade with the United States. The Russian merchants prospered in the Baltic avenues to commerce and Americans took an important role in this business. When John Quincy Adams went to St. Petersburg one of his major aims was to help this Russo-American trade connection. Alexander I of Russia was alarmed when diplomatic relations with America began to fade in 1811. They wanted a strong alliance with Britain to counter Napoleon and did not wish Britain and America to go to war. They did their best to prevent it, but this was to be to no avail. [9]

Convinced that violations of American rights justified war with both Great Britain and France, Henry Clay, Virginia born Kentucky lawyer and planter, rose to speak in the Senate. He told his fellow senators that he preferred "the troubled ocean of war...to the tranquil, putrescent pool of ignominious peace." He said British influence in stirring up Indian activity against the settlers was the reason for war. Besides, the Americans could conquer Canada; the Kentucky militia alone, he bragged, could take Montreal and Upper Canada (that land to the west of Montreal). [10]

A newcomer in the U. S. Senate, Clay from Lexington, Kentucky, said that war was needed. With all the enthusiasm of a young man and the brashness of a westerners, Clay stated that the conquest of Canada was within the power of senators. This was an important goal in a war. The expansion would bring new blood in American life and present new vistas. The Canadians in the United States would provide new heroes in the dream of achievement. He would have the Senate stand up for American rights. The Senate was not interested, passing the resolution which Clay felt would surrender the national rights. The time was not now and the Senate was not the place for action. It was to remain months later and the House of Representatives for Clay to achieve what he hoped for at this time. [11]

The acts for trade restrictions led the maverick representative John Randolph to denounce the idea which was so unpopular but which remained on the books. He told the House that everyone had reviled them, but Congress had not repealed the acts of almost five months of their session. Asking if the non-intercourse act was a scarecrow to frighten the European powers or a toy to amuse them, he proposed its repeal. It had done a great amount of harm to the economy and a limit to the freedom to trade. Randolph wanted a vote upon the issue directly. Furthermore he thought bad feeling against England should not be used to excuse acts of a government against its own people. [12]

It was not just the English who were cracking down upon American commerce. The French secretly drew up the Rambouillet decree which was published in Paris on May 14, 1810, and made retroactive to May 20th of the preceding year. This decree authorized French officials to seize and confiscate all American ships and their cargoes in the ports of France, French colonies, and French occupied countries. Frenchmen blamed their need to do so on the American non-intercourse act. Everything was sold for the benefit of the French government. When the American act was repealed, the French continued to seize and steal. Americans were outraged. Instead of backing off, Napoleon secretly ordered the sale of the seized ships and their cargoes.

Instead of continuing to restrict trade, the American Government opened up unrestricted trade with the world. Should the European powers cease to violate neutral trade, they would be freed of American acts against trade. At first neither power acted. Madison wrote in a negative vein early on. "Great Britain"`, he wrote to William Pinkney in London, "may conceive that she had not a complete interest in perpetuating the actual state of things, which gives her the full enjoyment of our trade, and enables her to cut off with every other part of the world; at the same time that it increases the chance of such resentment in France and the inequality as may lead to hostilities with the United States."

In order to harm Anglo-American trade relations, France issued the Codore letter which said that if the British would revoke their orders-in-council and the United States apply an act forbidding trade with Britain, then France would act favorably toward trade with America. In other words, France wanted everything to go her way. Such acceptance would win France the economic aspects of the war and in effect ally the United States to France. Madison did not see the catch. He hoped to maneuver both powers by accepting the Codore letter at face value. He had no success except to press the British with an embargo against Great Britain. [13]

None of this helped in the least at getting the powers to conciliate their actions with the Americans. Neither were interested in the welfare of the Americans. They were at war and everything which they thought worked for this end was possible and desirable. Their attitude was to let the United States suffer if they would not join their side. With a disinterest in foreign affairs, the Americans just wanted freedom of trade and protection for the actions of either side against their shipping.

Son of a militia colonel in the Revolutionary War, John Rodgers also had a military bent, but he chose the seas over the land. Born on the family farm near the village of

Havre de Grace on the road between Baltimore and Philadelphia in 1773, he had a happy and robust early life. The countryside and the opportunities for a young boy was delightful. One could look inward at the hills or outward over the bay. There was fishing and fowling, and swimming and games and he early proved a leader. Educated at the village school, he read books about sailors and their seafaring life.

When he showed himself determined to go to sea and had run away from home to do so, his father who had overtaken him bound him for five years of apprenticeship to prominent shipmaster Captain Benjamin Folger. John promised his father he would never drink rum or other alcoholic beverages and kept this promise in an era when all men drank and in which rum was the accepted drink at sea.

In the months and years under the Folger tutelage, Rodgers proved a born sailor. He gained a mastery of seamanship and navigation, an acceptance of responsibility and duty, and had the steady habits and stern appreciation for the necessities of the time that resulted in command of his own ship before he reached the age of twenty. The *Jane* was twice the size of the average vessels of the closing years of the eighteenth century. Baltimore merchants Samuel and John Smith owned the ship. His men soon learned to fear and respect Rodgers.

When trouble broke out with France, President John Adams raised a navy. There was a great need for officers and Rodgers was one of those commissioned. He served abroad the *Constellation* under the strict discipline of Commodore Thomas Truxtun with his thirty-two years of naval experience. His ship searched for French ships and did convoy duty. In early February of 1799, Rodgers saw his first naval action. He was executive officer and wrote up the report. He told of the chase battle, and surrender of the French frigate *Insurgente*. Soon Secretary Benjamin Stoddert promoted Rodgers to a captaincy and shortly the captain commanded the *Maryland*. Peace replaced war and Rodgers returned to the merchant marine. He purchased a schooner and traded with Santo Domingo, witnessing the war between the French and the black general Toussaint L'Ouverture. He proved one of the heroes when Cape Francois was burnt. He was a leader of a largely successful affair of rescue and succor for men, women, and children in the Quasi War with France.

Then, suddenly, war broke out with Tripoli in North Africa. Rodgers returned to the Navy and took command of the *John Adams*. He reached Malta and went with the flotilla of Commodore R. V. Morris toward North Africa. Storms forced them back to Malta. Sailing to visit Tunis and Algiers, Morris soon was involved in a diplomatic difficulty with the beys of the two cities. Later Rodgers and his crew seized the Tripolitan cruiser *Merhouda*. Once disposed of, he returned off Tripoli and was put in charge of the blockade.

The Americans had an encounter with ships sent forth by the pasha. They were successful, but Rodgers was ordered to lift the blockade. Shortly, he helped arrange a treaty with the emperor of Morocco. After a term back in the United States, Rodgers returned to the shores of Tripoli, which once again was being blockaded. In mid-1805, a treaty of peace was signed with the pasha. Rodgers also had good success with Hamuda of Tunis. During the summer of 1806, Rodgers reached home. He got married and continued his services to his country.

In the last days of May of 1810, Rodgers led his three ships to Annapolis, and went to Washington DC to confer with the secretary of the navy. The non-resistance of Jeffersonians had given way to the stronger view of American right. Paul Hamilton, the official in question, reorganized the fleet. Then he issued new orders. Hamilton assigned

The Difficult War: The Era of the War of 1812 41

Rodgers to protect the northern coastlines and Commodore Stephen Decatur Jr. to guard the southern coast. There were also small flotillas to operate out of Charleston and New Orleans. The mission was to protect merchantmen within a league of the coast and to seize private armed vessels in ports. [14]

Almost as poor as the Lincolns, the Vanderbilts produced a son who by hard work and sharp business practices became the richest American in his and Lincoln's lifetime. This child was named Cornelius Vanderbilt and saw the light of day on May 27, 1794, in a small farmhouse on Staten Island on the shores of New York Bay. Of Dutch and English ancestry, the boy grew up to work on the farm and spend hours on the waterfront, intensively interested in sailing ships. He took to the waters off New York with his father to carry crops and fish with an occasional passenger five miles away to Manhattan. With a lack of interest in school, he learned only rudimentary reading, writing, and arithmetic, but was soon a messenger of sailing.

At age sixteen he entered a bargain with his mother to work on the family tract in return for money to buy a boat, a loan of $100. He got his boat and soon was a ferry boat operator in the waters he knew best. His competitors laughed and called him commodore, but he made money, paid off his loan and gave her his year's profit of a large $1,000. In the years ahead, Vanderbilt profited, saved, and expanded. He and his new wife were frugal and he was a miser, but with her hard work they saved more and more and raised thirteen kids while working at their inn. She was a one woman cyclone. Later they moved to Manhattan and Vanderbilt increased his wealth into the millions in a growing America. He was to build a shipping empire and was known for shipping what Astor was known for furs. He followed Astor into the financial upper class. Their descendants formed the elite. [15]

Americans like Vanderbilt had a good opinion of themselves but many overseas and in Mexico did not think well of Americans. America was viewed with suspicion and hostility in a monarchical and stratified world where wealth and position ruled and where ambition was frowned upon by those of a royal and noble birth. America was a land, in their view of the world, of common ambition and a thirst for wealth. The nobles liked to spend money and lived in great splendor, but they hated those who made it possible. Wealth was not to be gained by the seeking for it, it was to spent for the comfort of men and women of class. Money making was disgusting to the kings and nobles of the world. Not only did they look down on those who made it, but they considered them to be below dignity. Nobility and a long ancestral background was what counted in their world, a generally closed society which let in a few who could prove of value to them and whose descendants were to make up nobles in their families.

They also feared the United States and its people. They had already upset their world but were dangerous looking to the future. One example of feeling was what General Bernardo Bonavia y Zapata wrote on May 17, 1810. He expressed himself clearly: "We can never depend upon the government of the United States with their present singular constitution, and should always dread the ambitious, restless, and enterprising character of the people, and their misconceived idea of liberty...Self interest and the lure being the only object of the Anglo-American who cares not whence it comes. Hence, even in time of peace, we must be watchful and keep our arms in our hand against people amongst whom the scum of all nations is to be found."

Soon he was to have to be careful of his own countrymen. Problems were great under the surface. The people were restless in his own land. In September, priest Miguel Hidalgo y Costilla led a mob of Indians on the quest for independence and liberty, for a better life. They hated the oppression under which they endured. The educated Hidalgo started the road to freedom in Mexico and proved that the people of Mexico like those of the United States were moved by the ideas of liberty which Bonavia thought so misconceived. Hidalgo was affected by the ideas of the Spanish born who ruled, and felt the pain of social injustices expressed toward the lower classes such as the poor Indians, who lived in peonage in Mexico. This was a political revolution, but more than that was a social revolution. It was bloody but did not end with Hidalgo's defeat and execution. [16]

In another land and a different clime, events were occurring which changed history radically and affected the history of the United States in the time of Abraham Lincoln. The revolutionary thought, which had molded the United States, had been influencing the peoples of America under the rule of the Spanish king. A liberalism expressed by English, French, and American philosophers in books were spreading in Mexico and Hispanic colonies to the south. Men like Mariano Moreno in Argentina and Miguel Hidalgo y Castillo in Mexico were reading the writers of the Enlightenment in private and were to play major roles in revolutions in their countries. New ideas affected the clergy and it was priests that had libraries of the forbidden books which Moreno could read. Hidalgo himself was a priest. Moreno used the press to promote the ideas of the Enlightenment, while Hidalgo resorted to force. [17]

Hidalgo sympathized with the peasants in his parish and worked to improve their lives economically and spiritually. The viceroy of Mexico, governing the colony for his king, learned about Hidalgo teaching the Indians to plant olives, mulberries, and grapevines and to use improved methods to manufacture pottery of leather, which was against the law. The Spanish had strict rules on economical concerns devised to crush competition in the Americas against products grown and produced in Spain. Conspirators in Queretaro joined him. When authorities issued arrest orders for Hidalgo, the wife of an officer warned the revolutionaries. On September 16, 1810, Hidalgo led his parishioners to overthrow the government. Marching southward toward Mexico City, the rebels engaged in a bloody conquest, but were defeated. Hidalgo was executed, but others such as Jose Maria Morelos fought a guerrilla campaign.

Ten years passed and the anti-liberal Agustin de Iturbide achieved Mexican independence with his army in a sudden blow with the blessings of the clergy in Mexico. Under the plan espoused by Iturbide and his backers, a Spanish prince was to reign over Mexico, but instead Iturbide made himself emperor, only to fall through a revolt started by Antonio Lopez de Santa Anna. This ambitious general was to fight Houston and then Scott in his later career and affect the history of the United States. The Mexicans established a shaky republic. [18]

In New York on June 2, 1810, and in Philadelphia on June 3, 1810, some Americans read in their newspapers about the overthrow of the government at Caracas and the establishment of a popular junta in its place. In August they heard rumors of an insurrection in the Spanish province of West Florida and on the 18th of that month read in the *Philadelphia Aurora* of an uprising in Buenos Aires and the institution of a junta there also.

The uprising in Florida directly affected the United States because the government laid claim to Florida. Upon learning of the declaration of independence in Baton Rouge, the government sent troops into West Florida. This was what the government was waiting for. Governor Claiborne of Louisiana and Holmes of Mississippi Territory had encouraged the revolt and gained the tacit consent of President Madison for it. American citizens had joined the revolt. Spanish officials at Pensacola and Mobile were right in believing that it was a thinly disguised intrigue to gain the territory for the United States.

Federalists Josiah Quincy and Timothy Pickering protested, but Congress went along. Claiborne on the other hand wanted the capture of Mobile and suggested the annexation of Cuba. One Georgia newspaper called for the acquisition of all Florida. All over the South and West there were Americans who wanted strong measures against Spain. J. Minor wrote Secretary of State Monroe pleading him to "lay aside all fastidious delicacy and strike the blow called for by national safety."

This news arrived while the Americans were intent upon the news of events in Europe. Their attention was drawn to the problems that these events caused for Americans. What happened in Hispanic America was subordinate but a part of the general trend, because the people of the region were intent on counteracting Napoleon in Spain and the western hemisphere. One Federalist newspaper called upon the Madison Administration to recognize Spain's battling patriot junta and accept its representative Onis. This was necessary to foil Napoleon, who wanted to revolutionize the Spanish colonies in America. The editor evidently believed that Napoleon must be stopped. A few months passed and the editor took the stand that the Venezuelan revolution was a product of the resistance to French domination in Spain. There had after all been no declaration of independence. American party ideology influenced what the politicians were saying. When they commented on the events of West Florida, the Federalists were fearful of French influence in the province, while the Republicans talked on their part about the dangers of British attack. When it was realized that no European governments were involved all Federalists deplored them, while some Republicans supported the rebel cause.[19]

When the news of revolutions in Venezuela, Buenos Aires, and West Florida reached the United States, the party press immediately took them as a danger. Federalists thought French influence was behind them and Republicans thought British influence was in back of them. At the time, Federalists feared revolutions in general and the Federalist *New York Spectator*, upon learning of the Caracas uprising immediately called for a recognition of Spain to upset Bonaparte's projects for revolutionizing Spanish America. That Bonaparte sought to gain influence and build an American Empire was known and the obvious was determined upon, all revolution in Hispanic America must be French inspired. When it was realized that no European governments were involved, all Federalists deplored them, while some Republicans supported the rebel cause. [20]

---

[1]Poage, George Rawlings, *Henry Clay and the Whig Party*, University of North Carolina Press, Reprint Gloucester, Mass: Peter Smith, 1965, pp. 2-3.

[2]Risjord, N.K., "1812," *William and Mary Quarterly*, 3rd series, XVIII (1961), 206-207.

[3]Tarrant, Charles, "Carter Tarrant (1763-1816): Baptist and Emanicipationist," *Register of the Kentucky Historical Society*, LXXXVIII No. 2 (Spring 1990), 121-147.

[4]Hopewell, Clifford, *Sam Houston: Man of Destiny*, Austin TX: Eakin Press, 1987, pp. 3, 6-15.

[5]Adams, *Madison*, pp. 343, 346-347.

[6]Putnam, George Haven, "Irving," Trent, William Peterfield ed. et al., *The Cambridge History of American Literature*, New York: Macmillan, 1940, I, 245-248.

[7]Robins, Peggy, "Steamboat A-Coming'," *American History Illustrated*, XIV No. 7 (November 1979), 16-18.

[8]Curti, Merle Eugene, *The American Peace Crusade, 1815-1860*, Durham, N.C.: Duke University Press, pp. 6-7.

[9]Biedzynski, James, "Alexander I," Heidler, David S. and Heidler, Jeanne T. (eds.), *Encyclopedia of the War of 1812*, Santa Barbara, Calif. ABC-CIO, 1997, p. 6.

[10]Harrison, Lowell H., "Clay, Henry," Heidler & Heidler, *Encyclopedia*, p. 110.

[11]Adams, *Madison*, pp. 134-135.

[12]*The Annals of America*, 1968, IV: 1792-1820, 248-250.

[13]White, *Nation*, pp. 63-74, 76-80.

[14]Paullin, Charles Oscar, *Commander John Rodgers, Captain, Commondore, and Senior Officer of the American Navy, 1773-1838*, Annapolis: United States Naval Institute, 1967 (Reprint of 1909 ed.), pp. 16-22, 26, 32-81, 97-169, 201-215.

[15]Vanderbilt, Arthur T., *Fortune's Children*, New York: William Morrow, 1989, pp. 5-10ff.

[16]Lukes, Edward A., *De Witt Colony of Texas*, Austin, TX: Jenkins Publishing, Pemberton Press, 1976, p. 30. Quote on p. 30.

[17]Parkes, Henry Bamford, *A History of Mexico*, 3rd ed. rev and enl., Boston: Houghton Mifflin, 1960, pp. 133-154; Wait, Eugene M., "Mariano Moreno: Promoter of Enlightenment," *Hispanic American Historical Review*, XLV No. 2 (August 1965), pp. 359-383.

[18]Parkes, *History of Mexico*, pp. 145-187.

[19]Griffin, C.C., 1937, pp. 15, 28-29, 33-34, 46-47.

[20]*Ibid.*, pp. 46-48.

CHAPTER VI

WAR HAWKS

The War Hawks knew that they could neither attack the British in their homeland nor gain the high seas, but they could attack Canada. Britain was most vulnerable there.

Peter B. Porter averred that the United States "could deprive her of her extensive provinces lying along our border to the north." Canada was valuable for the States and for England. We should, he had stated deprive Britain of such a land. William King opposed territorial expansion for the United States, but insisted we take Canada in order to "wound our enemy in the most vulnerable part." Israel Pickens would seek revenge by conquering Canada as the only way in their reach for defending of universally recognized rights which had been violated. Joseph Desha of Kentucky and Lowndes of South Carolina alike argued to attack Canada and use privateers on the high seas. [1]

As the difficulties progressed, an editorial writer in the *Virginia Argus* expressed a sad and concerned look at relations between Great Britain and the United States. He was not happy with the resentment caused by George III toward America because the young nation used to be his colonies. Because of so many natural ties between the two, Americans and Englishmen should be "on the best terms of concord." The Republicans had worked for harmony, but would not bow to Great Britain on the question of national independence. For their part, the Federalists, he claimed, would acquiesce in the British attitude of dominance. The editorialist warned that that the British would despise servility. [2]

Meanwhile, in a dispute over land, the Indian Tecumseh had persuaded some of the natives to reject their annuity payments. To preserve frontier peace, always a fragile thing, Harrison invited Tecumseh to come to a council. Americans were recognizing the leadership that this Indian, the son of a Swanee father and Creek mother, was exerting on more than one Indian tribe from Canada to the Gulf. Tecumseh and his brother Laulewaikau or Elkswatawa were born in the territory that became Ohio. The first became a war chief and was born in 1768 near the Mad River. The second was born near 1775 and had turned out to be a loafer and drinker until the was transformed by a vision. He became known as the Prophet and preached that the Great Spirit wanted him to crusade against the ways of the white men and for a return to customs and virtues they had before the Europeans had come to the wilderness.

When he was young, Tecumseh fought in individual frontier skirmishes with the white invader, the settlers and their families. He was there at Fallen Timbers, when Anthony Wayne won his notable victory against the Indians in 1794. The years passed and his brother had his vision; Tecumseh became a loyal follower and worked to create an Indian Confederation to prevent land cessions for the future. In 1898, the two leaders founded a camp along the Tippecanoe River near where it emptied into the Wabash, with the permission of Potawatomi and Kickapoo representatives. Forty Shawnee and 100 other Indians made it into a village. They believed that no tribe had the right to cede lands to the whites without the consent of all Indians. It was at this point that he and Harrison crossed paths.

William Henry Harrison was one of the signers of the 1795 treaty extending American ownership into the forests and meadows north of the Ohio River. Tecumseh had refused to sign this Treaty of Greenville. His white adversary, Harrison, was born in Berkeley, in western Virginia, on February 9, 1773. He went to college and took up the study of medicine, although his chief interest was in military history. Only his father's death freed him from the mistake of becoming a physician for which he had neither aptitude nor interest. At his bequest President George Washington commissioned Harrison as an ensign. Ordered to go to Fort Washington (Cincinnati), he arrived there shortly after St. Clair's defeat. He served under Anthony Wayne and fought at the Battle of Fallen Timbers. President John Adams made him secretary of the Northwest Territory. Then to be delegate to Congress of that territory. While in that position, Harrison secured the division of western lands into small tracts.

John Adams appointed him to be the first governor of Indiana Territory which reached as far as Minnesota with a population of almost 5,000 men, women, and children, not counting Indians. This made him and Tecumseh mortal enemies. Harrison then invited the Indian leader to come to Vincennes for a conference with no more than 30 warriors. Tecumseh arrived with 400 well armed braves. The governor averted a conflict with an even temper. Some historians feel that Tecumseh planned a treacherous attack and that only Harrison's conciliatory methods prevented this. They have no solid evidence for this supposition. Nowhere did an explosion result from the intense feeling on both sides.

Tecumseh had arrived at the territorial capital on August 12, 1800. He started off with the statement that he had the authority from the tribes to kill the Indian signers to the Treaty of Fort Wayne, because they were not the official representatives of their tribe. However, he would not do this if the Americans gave the ceded land back. It had been up to the Miami, Harrison replied. Tecumseh was a Swanee and had no right to intervene since the land belonged to the Miami Indians before the Shawnee were there. The governor asked the chief to retire when trouble looked certain and the council broke up. An alarmed Harrison began to drill the soldiers more regularly and brought troops to Vincennes. [3]

The frontier was a rough place and hard on the people who lived there. Some of the roughest of citizens were the Virginia born Kempers. They were the sons of a Baptist minister, who preached fire and damnation. He moved to Cincinnati and three of his seven sons settled in Mississippi, near the Louisiana border. They distrusted the Spaniards and earned their reciprocal dislike. In 1805, the Kempers got ambitious. They wanted to conquer West Florida. Assembling a mounted party, they mounted and rode into West Florida, to spy out the land. Since the Spanish garrison was too strong, they returned to Mississippi. The Spanish governor learned of the incursion and of its military object of reconnaissance.

Spain's West Florida governor gathered a posse of twelve frontiersmen, who had their price, and they invaded the United States to kidnap the brothers. With guns and clubs, they broke into Nathan's house and dragged Reuben Kemper from his bed. They

The Difficult War: The Era of the War of 1812   47

then beat Reuben and Nathan Kemper. They tied them both with ropes and gagged them with sassafras roots. Once outside the attackers put ropes around their necks and forced them to run to the Spanish border. With the same treatment, they brought Samuel Kemper to the rendezvous. Colonel Samuel Alston, the governor's representative, helped in the abduction, and tied them on a boat and started to Baton Rouge. The idea was to take them to Cuba to slavery as mine laborers.

News of the abduction spread like wildfire. Lieutenant Wilson decided to intervene, but the boats were numerous. Then a voice boomed out from one of the vessels: "It is Reuben Kemper the Spanish are taking to the mines." He had chewed up his gag. Wilson moved forward and seized the craft, freeing the Kempers and arresting the kidnappers. The later were closely guarded for trial and the brothers were taken to Washington DC for their testimony. Senator Henry Clay of Kentucky made a fiery speech denouncing the Spaniards.

The Kempers returned home anxious for revenge. Then in the autumn of 1810, they led a strong force and surprised the Spaniards at Baton Rouge. After a brief action in which Governor Grandpre died, the insurgents declared a republic and called for ambassadorial recognition. Baton Rouge's Spaniards headed for Mobile and Pensacola. Madison proclaimed the annexation of West Florida to the west of the Perdido River. The Kempers were outmaneuvered by the president. In this way, West Florida became American. [4]

There had been many American immigrants into Florida, both east and west. They welcomed the American troops, but Madison sent troops only to the Pearl River. This must have disappointed many, but this was the way it was. Great Britain protested the area was occupied and Congress passed a resolution in private to the effect that the United States could not see a foreign power in the territory. Should an European power occupy East Florida the Americans would use force if peaceable means did not work. Congress authorized the seizure of more lands in Florida.

Lincoln's presidential career was entwined around slavery, which is a constant thread in the story of his time. At the time he was an infant, manumission or the granting of freedom to slaves was an individual matter. Masters would free their slaves or certain ones. In 1810, a African American freedman named Henry Birch purchased his two sons from slaveholder William Danridge Claiborne of Virginia to set them free.

The African American petitioned the state legislature as required for the freedom of his sons and the permission for them to live in Virginia. His petition contained an affidavit from Claiborne that they were purchased by Birch and another to attest to the black's good character and industrious nature. The government required certification that his creditors would be protected in the freeing of his property in sons. Several whites testified in a letter that the creditors would not be injured by the manumission of the boys. [5]

The Davis family, unlike the Lincoln's, were the holders of slaves. Samuel had a few in Kentucky and was to become a slaveholder in the Deep South. He moved his family to St. Mary's Parish in Louisiana, but soon went to a farm one mile east of the Woodville on the other side of the Mississippi. The plague of mosquitoes drove him out of Louisiana. It was to be a long time before anyone knew that the pests carried malaria, but Davis knew that they were troublesome and painful.

On high ground amidst a grove of poplars and live oaks and near a spring, he hired carpenters and with the aid of his slaves built a nice plantation home of bricks and cypress. Its mantel was constructed of black Italian marble. Jane laid out a flower garden and planted roses. Soon the plantation would be known as "Rosemont." Samuel never had more than one dozen slaves and had to work in the fields with the slaves, but the religious planter had the influence most small planters did not possess. His neighbors knew him for his integrity and sure judgment. He believed in a just, kind, and merciful God. [6]

John Armstrong, born in Pennsylvania in 1758, had attended--but did not graduate from--Princeton. He kept hearing of the adventures of the American Revolution and wanted to hurry off to war. Since his father had been in the French and Indian War, John Armstrong Sr. had known George Washington and Hugh Mercer, so he was able to get young John a commission as lieutenant in the American army. This suited Armstrong just fine. He fought at Trenton and Princeton before serving under Horatio Gates in New York as an aide. He wrote one of the Newburgh Addresses which was later to harm his political career. He was a congressman and a judge and married well, into the Livingston family. Managing his wife's estate took his time, but he managed to become a U. S. senator and a Jeffersonian Republican.

Serving as U. S. minister in France, he found it hard going. He was unable to achieve anything of substance in France, although he worked at gaining concessions. The French would not bend however. He wanted seized cargoes reimbursed and when in 1810, the French talked about improving relations with the United States, he asked for this again. He was suspicious about the talk and this suspicion was well founded. The French were eager for discussion, but did not wish to do anything which would benefit the Americans. To the French, Armstrong was arbitrary, and Napoleon got angry. The emperor immediately ordered the sale of seized property that had come to France since May 20, `1809. Armstrong left France in October 1810 to retire, only to be called in by the War of 1812. [7]

In the Senate since 1807, William H. Crawford, of a numerous Virginia family moved to South Carolina and Georgia, had a good education and taught and practiced law. He served in the Georgia legislature. Then he was elected by the state legislature to the U. S. Senate, as was then the law. He reached Congress within days of the vote on the Embargo Bill of 1807. Because he did not understand the bill, he voted against it; establishing his conduct of not voting for things he had not yet understood. His was a reflective political career.

He developed his views on the war issue. War was preferable to submission, but he did not believe America could challenge British supremacy on the high seas. Thus he voted against naval construction appropriations. His efforts would be focus on building up the army; land forces could conceivably overmatch the British in Canada.

Resources should, he believed, but used to gain Florida for the United States. He expressed his thoughts on the best way to achieve that goal to Madison and his administration. He recommended Georgia's governor George Mathews as the man for this job. Madison supported the idea in secret; but he soon thought better and disavowed the governor's actions in East Florida as war loomed. This made Crawford angry at Madison. Crawford pushed for annexation even after war was declared. He voted for the war measure in 1812. Later Crawford refused Madison's offer of the secretaryship of the army, pleading he lacked necessary qualifications for the position. He did continue as a Madison adviser, greatly relied on for his views and suggestions. Still later Crawford was sent to France as U. S. minister there. [8]

Meanwhile, Calhoun proved to be successful enough in the state legislature of South Carolina to build a platform of success. He paid off an old debt in a popular move to select De Saussure chancellor of the state with his support for such a selection. Having made a name for himself in the state, Calhoun made a clever speech by which he assumed leadership of the South Carolina Republican War Hawks. It brought him great popularity in the state. In this speech, so applauded by the people, he boldly attacked Jefferson's and Madison's policy and declared war to be inevitable. Next he opposed antiwar George Clinton of New York for the vice-presidency and proposed John Langdon of New Hampshire instead. In 1810, Calhoun had been nominated and elected to Congress as a Jeffersonian Republican.

Despite embargoes, the war in Europe brought prosperity to most Americans, so much so that they were even more satisfied with the Constitution and the Union. Demand from abroad pushed up the price of agricultural products and American ships took over much of the shipping trade between France and her colonies. The Europeans were so busy with their conflict that they did not have the time or inclination to stop American expansion to the west. Indeed, the Napoleonic Wars had gained Louisiana for France and then the United States, whose citizens would have migrated there anyway. The times were generally so good that the Federalists joined the Republicans in thanks for prosperity and for the fact that Jeffersonianism did not radically alter the established domestic policies of the Federalists.

There were two groups that were elected in 1810, who were opposed to the idea of war. First, there was the small Federalist minority. They were not so much alarmed over the violation of their rights that they ignored the prosperity in trade in the bottom line even with the losses at sea subtracted. They believed that the English were in the front line of the battle for civilization against French anarchy. Second there were the northern wing of the Jeffersonian Republicanism whose members were fearful of what would happen to America if she opposed the powerful British. They were so powerful that they were holding back all Europe under Napoleon and once he was defeated they could turn their entire force against the United States which was greatly outnumbered in population. They were also the sea giant of the world. [9]

There were Americans with pride in their country and thought it was the light of the world. America was the hope of civilization and not England to these people. A certain Charles Jared Ingersoll of Northern descent published a booklet with the title *Inchiquin, the Jesuit's Letters, During a Late Residence in the United States of America* in 1810 under a pseudonym, to defend American society, literature, and manners. It was supposed to be a book of letters from a Irish Jesuit in America to a friend in Europe, but it was Ingersoll's work. Grown in America, American republicanism had eradicated peasantry in favor of free farmers, mobbism by a high employment rate, and beggery by opportunity. Except in Southern states, there was only one rank in America according to public opinion at the time. Slavery was not in conflict with republicanism, he believed. Ingersoll followed Burke in the belief that Southern slaveholders were more attached to liberty's spirit than Northerners. Masters were always more freedom-loving than others, non-slaveholders. He defended slavery. In short it took the view that all was right with America and nothing was wrong.

Several years later, poet and clergyman Timothy Dwight defended Ingersoll from an attack from a critic in the London *Quarterly Review*. A Federalist and a New Englander, an avowed Yankee and president of Yale University, Dwight believed that a Southern planter could not be censored if he inherited the slaves from his father, since he did not procure the slaves and could not free them by law. Such fulfilled their duty if they treated the slaves with humanity and tried to turn them into Christians.

Novelist James Kirke Paulding was an even stronger protagonist for the South. He defended the South from Dwight's views on Southern society and culture. Believing no one could characterize Southern slavery without seeing it, he delayed too many remarks until he had the chance to see for himself what slavery was .In 1816, he visited Virginia and return home to write a two volume defense. The writer believed that Southern slaves were well cared for. He was later to attack abolitionists as misguided and fanatical and wrote of the low estate of the English poor. To be poor in England was much worst than to be a slave in America.

Later, in 1819, the book of Robert Walsh on slavery was praised by John Adams, Thomas Jefferson, and James Madison for its systematic and fulsome description of slavery. Walsh defended slavery, while blaming it on British imperialism. The institution was founded in the American colonies under British rule in their North American Empire. Further he thought that the founding fathers should have eradicated slavery, although then, in 1819, the central government could not touch the peculiar institution in the states and would have been unable to do so during the Revolution and founding of the Constitution. Freedom and slavery could co-exist together he averred. He evidently believed that African American slavery tended to make all whites equal, which was hardly the case. It did however draw the rich and poor whites together.

Abolitionists and slaveholders alike suggested the idea of colonization of slaves outside the country as a solution for the problem of slavery. Those like Walsh who were pro-slavery were anti-American. Their idea of colonization was to send the free African American to Africa since both free and enslaved African Americans were a problem in their estimation. It was not slavery which was evil, but the presence of blacks in the United States which was unacceptable to them. Underlying many of their arguments was the idea that slavery was wrong for America, while being at the same time proslavery as it existed in the United States. Behind all of this was the idea that slavery needed defending. [10]

Led by Chief Justice John Marshall from 1801-1835, the Supreme Court broadened the powers of the judicial review of laws of nation and states. His was also a political action of Jeffersonian Republicanism for a Republican judiciary in place of a Federalist one. They impeached District Judge John Pickering, who was ruled insane. Then they charged Samuel Chase of the Supreme Court, who had presided over sedition prosecutions, but failed in the impeachment proceedings.

In economic development, Marshall gave a successful broad interpretation of the contracts cause. This was to be expanded again and again in the years ahead as corporations grew and developed. Corporations saved businesses from the risks of partnerships. Marshall and Chief Justice Judge Spencer Roane of the Virginia Supreme Court of Appeals wrote anonymous newspaper articles in support of their various positions. They also supported government chartered monopolies, although the Court struck down one monopoly in 1824. [11]

Marshall believed in vested rights promoting Locke's principle that connected property and individual liberties. He feared inroads upon this by state legislature and ruled on Federal obligations to renew laws of states as well as those of nation. He would protect property rights and the stability of markets for the promotion of investment needed for the economic growth of the nation. Commerce and manufacturing were important for him and his fellows. Agriculture still reign supreme but Marshall was looking to the future. He championed free interstate commerce without state hindrance. In general he followed the Federalist idea that people and not states were important. [12]

The Difficult War: The Era of the War of 1812   51

In the Supreme Court, the entire seven justices available voted to a man for Marshall's interpretation of national power., in approving the idea of congressional power to charter a bank. Union government was granted power to legislate for the public well-being. Federal government was supreme within its sphere of action. [13]

There were prohibitory state laws against the African slave trade but these did not end the trade completely. Expanding Southern planters still needed more slaves, but they were in a bind. They feared large-scale importation of unruly slaves from Africa and the importation of revolutionary slaves from the Caribbean. They decided to import slaves however. New Englanders carried on their expeditions and Southern slaveholders received Africans from whatever source. Anti-slave enthusiasts continued to work for stronger laws and execution of the laws in effect. There were new laws. They were poorly enforced. [14]

At this time there were the usual lives of the people; they lived day to day. There were births, marriages, and deaths. There manifold examples of this. One was the Taylor-Smith marriage. Educated in the basics and trained in domestic activities, Margaret Smith of a Maryland family of farmers married Zachary Taylor about the time he became a captain in 1810. She made a good wife and was happy at her domestic tasks. She did not want more than the benefit of her army husband. He rose in rank and when peace came, he was to revert back to captain, for which he resigned and took up farming, which pleased Margaret.

When he turned to the army later in the Black Hawk War and still later in other conflicts, she persistently went with him to the field or its vicinity. They had children who, when they met a certain age, were sent back East to family to get an education, while she remained with her husband. She was to do her duty at his side in Florida and help attend the sick and wounded. After Florida, they settled in Baton Rouge.

Their house there had four verandahs full around the house, which was a pleasant place of friends and kin to visit. He was not idle for long with his army duties, he bought and supervised two plantations besides. He next bought a house at Fort Jessup and they lived there for awhile. Their son Richard was to move to Louisiana and become a sugar cane planter before serving in the Civil War. [15]

There were children being educated like the Taylors' and Benjamin Abbot was noteworthy as an educator. He was born on September 17, 1762, at Andover, Massachusetts, the son of John Abbot and his wife. Upon graduating from Harvard in 1788, Benjamin became principal of Phillips Exeter Academy for the next fifty years. He married Hannah Tracy Emery on November 1, 1791, and Mary Perkins in 1798. In his academy, he taught Latin, Greek, and mathematics to such students as Lewis Cass, Daniel Webster, Edward Everett, Jared Sparks, and Francis Bowen. When he retired, Webster, his most renown pupil and a power in the nation, gave a tribute to Abbot. On October 25, 1849, he died in Exeter, Massachusetts, honored in life.

There were Indians in life too, and they had their loves and dreams. There was a gulf between their world and that of the whites. Tecumseh was born and raised to hate the white man. Born in Ohio in 1768, he grew up in this hatred fostered by his widowed mother. When her husband was murdered by hunters, Methoatikes turned to her young son to avenge his death. He grew up to bare a bitter enmity and to be a great hunter and warrior. Soon his guardian and maternal uncle Cornstalk lost his life in 1777 to the white man's weapons. Tecumseh was adopted by Blackfish who excelled in ambush and bushwhacking. Tecumseh became expert in woodcraft, which was to create in him the consummate warrior. On the other side of the brave was compassion for women, children, the sick, and the old. Although he was modest and good natured, he had times when his temper got the best of him. He scorned the musket and favored bow and arrow and tomahawk. He instructed others in their use. He was tall and handsome, and stuck to Indian garb.

He impressed all who saw him, including beautiful Rebecca Galloway, well educated and kind. She was blond and fine. He fell in love with her and was educated by her. In time, he asked her to marry him. She was interested, but it did not work out. Since he would never adopt the white ways nor she the Indian ways, she declined gently. He left forever; they were never to see each other again. Their lives would have eventually been parted by war anyway. The union would never have worked. [16]

---

[1] White, *Nation*, pp. 105-106.

[2] *Kentucky Gazette*, January 1, 1811, p. 2.

[3] Gilpin, Alec R., *The War of 1812 in the Old Northwest*, East Lansing, Mich: Michigan State University Press, 1958, pp. 3-6.

[4] Tucker, Poltroons and Patriots, *pp. 127-129.*

[5] Johnston, James Hugo, Jr., (comp), "Manumission Petitions presented to the Virginia Legislature," *Journal of Negro History*, XIII No. 1 (January 1928), 87-88.

[6] Strode, *Davis*, pp. 8-10.

[7] Heidler, Jeanne T. and Heidler, David S., "Armstrong, John," Heidler & Heidler, *Encyclopedia*, pp. 13-14.

[8] Hiedler, Jeanne T. and Heidler, David S., "Crawford, William H.," Heidler & Heidler, *Encyclopedia*, p. 131.

[9] Capers, *Calhoun*, pp. 23-24, 26, 28.

[10] Tise, Larry E., *Proslavery: A History of the Defense of Slavery in America, 1701-1840*, Athens, Ga.: University of Georgia Press, 1987, pp. 42-43, 45-47, 49-52.

[11] Wiecek, William M., "History of the Court," Hall, *Supreme Court*, pp. 374-377.

[12] Newmyer, R. Kent, "Marshall, John," Hall, *Supreme Court*, pp. 524-526.

[13] Ellis, Richard E., "McCulloch v. Maryland," Hall, *Supreme Court*, pp. 536-538.

[14] Franklin, John Hope, *From Slavery to Freedom: A History of Negro Americans*, 3rd ed., New York: Alfred A. Knopf, 1967, pp. 152-154.

[15] DeGarmo, Mrs. Frank, *Pathfinders of Texas, 1836-1846*, Austin TX: Press of Von Boeckmann-Jones, 1951, pp. 17-19.

[16] Leckie, Robert, *From Sea to Shining Sea: From the War of 1812 to the Mexican War, the Saga of America's Expansion*, New York: Harper-Collins, 1993, pp. 143-147.

CHAPTER VII

THE YEAR 1811

The rechartering of the Bank of the United States came up before the House of Representatives. The issue was hotly debated in Congress and in the nation. Large numbers were opposed to such an chartered organization. The agrarians in the nation had no need of it. Most Republicans were strong against the bank; but Gallatin himself had found it very useful in his personal financial dealings and had good numbers of friends for the bill. Only two of his friends were to vote against it, but his political enemies in the Republican party were numerous and could carry the weight of the nation against it. People in general could not understand the necessity of it and the nation was to pay for this in the upcoming war, out of which was to developed a second Bank of the United States. By then it was believed that a national private bank was good for the country.

Jefferson himself did not oppose the Gallatin position. He wrote that many supported Gallatin for the idea. The secretary of the treasury was not in congress when it was voted years before and Jefferson wrote that he had never heard Gallatin speak of the Bank. "Money in New Orleans and Maine was at his command and by their agency transformed in an instant into money in London, in Paris, in Amsterdam, or Canton." He was therefor cordial to the bank. On January 24, 1811, the House defeated the bill by a one vote majority.[1]

The Senate took up the bill and voted a tie. The tie was broken by Madison's vice-president in the Senate who voted negative. The first national bank was ended by this vote on February 20, 1811. In this vote was the seeds of trouble. The necessity of the bank was demonstrated in succeeding years when the federal government had to deal with a multitude of small state banks for its financial services. They found its dealings to be chaotic. New England banks were serviceable, but banks elsewhere in the country suspended species, that is gold and silver, payments in a short while. Experience in the few years between national banks turned around the views of many opponents and a petition was sent to Congress on the fourth of January, in 1814, asking for a new national bank. After a little more than two years of delay a new bank with $35 million in capital was formed.[2]

When Congress refused to recharter the First Bank of the United States in 1811, Secretary of the Treasury Gallatin saw trouble ahead for government and as soon as he could leave with dignity he resigned. No one of his calibre replaced him. Congressmen had acted on the premise that such a national bank was unconstitutional. They were hostile to Gallatin and it did not bother them that he left the government.

It could not have come at a worst time. Government income fell because of the embargo and the government had trouble borrowing funds. Bonds and treasury notes were issued. Investors were able to buy the $100 bonds at from $80 to $88, a good discount. The government could not raise enough for the war which ensued, and paid a heavy premium for what they did raise.

Congress authorized $61 million in bonds and raised only $45,172,581 from 1812 to 1814. In these years more loans were authorized by Congress and each was troubled. The $25 million dollar loan failed in 1814 since only $10.4 million was secured. In July of 1814, the secretary of the treasury requested six million in loans and received offers for two and a half million. The next discount was $80 in cash for $100 in stock.

In the two and a half years from June, 1812, Congress authorized $35 1/2 million in treasury notes at 5 2/5 per cent interest reimbursable in one year and slightly less than one half were sold. It was reported that only $6 million in treasury notes could be kept in circulation at one time.

Trouble followed. Banking deteriorated and in August of 1813 specie payments were suspended or ended. Now gold and silver would be paid out no longer except in New England. The government now had to accept bank paper from state banks which was risky business. Solid banks would also have to deal in state bank papers. Treasury notes of varying depreciation would have to be accepted.

Worse was yet to come. Specie and New England notes were good in New England but the banks and the governments soon hoarded them and they were in short supply. Many appreciated the value of them and internal payments were harmed and it seemed that they would come to an end. Only the establishment of a national bank would suffice. [3]

The Georgians were fearful that Great Britain would move against them through Florida. They believed that the Spaniards were inciting the Indians against them and "would be even more menacing if Britain reached the Florida coast." Southerners could not be convinced, despite reassurances, "that the British did not pay a regular bounty for American scalps." Georgians would like to have peacefully annexed Florida, but the people there were not interested in joining the Union. They had a good thing going. On Amelia Island, Florida's had a smuggling enclave in goods and lumber. [4]

Revolutionary veteran and former Georgia governor Brigadier General George Matthew's was one of the Madison appointed commissioners to treat with East Florida. Monroe ordered Matthew's to take the Floridas if it could be done peacefully. Should anyone else take them or attempt to take them he was to use force. Naval assistance would be available. Mathews stretched his orders greatly. He and his Georgians infiltrated Rose Bluff overlooking St. Mary's River and had it under his control. They unfurled their flag in early March of 19812 and summoned Ferdandina to surrender. However, they stated that over the next year the settlement could have free port privileges. The presence of an American naval force forced them to surrender. Mathews captured Amelia Island and named Floridian William Craig governor. When news of his victory reached Georgia, Mathews received numerous reinforcements.

The Federalists back at home were in an uproar. They protested strongly and Madison decided quite correctly that Mathews had exceeded his instructions. Previously they had not protested. Mathews, hot under the collar, headed for Washington to defend his actions, but he died enroute. The soldiers were withdrawn and the United States no longer had the future state of Florida. [5]

The Difficult War: The Era of the War of 1812   55

When in the spring of 1811 Harrison received reports of small and uncoordinated Indian raids in the area of the Wabash River, he immediately felt that Tecumseh knew about the attacks on settlers. In his protest letter to the Indian chief, he threatened to attack the tribes unless the Indians stopped their raids. Undaunted Tecumseh called for a council in Vincennes. Harrison said he could come, with only with a few warriors. He feared the settlers would attack the Indians if they came in force. Actually, the whites might attack a small group of Indians without knowing whether they were friendly or a group of raiders, so this was not a realistic distinction. Harrison feared a Trojan Horse or a clash brought on by white settlers. For his part Tecumseh feared a successful attack if he did not have a large escort of fellow Indians.

Harrison did not think of sending an escort of troops, but it was just as well. The chief would worry about his safety in an escort. Tecumseh said the mass were coming of their own accord. Of the three hundred Indians who came, less than thirty were women and children. The general wrote that he allowed them to come to the territorial capital in the little populated area only because President Madison was so intent upon peace on the frontier. There was no real danger for Harrison since he had seven or eight hundred militiamen present. To point up his strength, he showed his troops in a review for Tecumseh's benefit.

On July 30th, the two parties talked, but could not agree. Harrison said that he could not discuses the Fort Wayne Treaty because the president was considering the treaty. Tecumseh would not turn over two Potawatomi who had committed murder in Missouri. They must be forgiven. He had forgiven white murderers in Illinois country. The Indians chief said that he was working for a confederacy. After all, the Indians had not protested the Union. He hoped that the Americans would not expand in his absence. The governor said that the Americans would allow no murders of their own people by Indians. This ended the council. [6]

On February 3, 1811, in a Massachusetts farmhouse in Amherst township was born Horace Greeley, whose paths were to cross with Lincoln in the course of Horace's dynamic life. His father, Zaccheus, was a poor farmer like Lincoln's father. Both Abraham and Horace were to strike forward and reach greater heights of fame from humble beginnings. Born into the world a frail infant with weak eyes and sensitive hearing, Horace grew up sick with solemn owlish air. A smart youngster, he went to school at the age of three and at four bested boys twice his age in spelling bees.

His robust mother, Mary Woodburn Greeley, developed his intelligence with reading at her knee. She told him old Scots and Scots-Irish tales and legends. In time Zaacheus fell into debt more than he could manage and the Panic of 1819 finished him off. The sheriff seized what he had for debts, while Zeccheus hid and fled to Vermont to avoid imprisonment for debt. He soon slipped back and the Greeleys went to Vermont to begin again. There he tried lumbering and small farming. The family had an even greater struggle than the Lincolns were having.

The Greeleys had long been farmers from way back in time, but they were also blacksmiths as a means of additional subsistence. The Woodburns were all farmers. All his kin were not necessarily thrifty by choice. Economy was really a necessity rather than a virtue. Still they did own their farms, small through they were, and bought with credit. They cultivated various crops, including the potato which was used to feed the hogs they raised for a cash crop. Their houses were small and unpainted. From his early childhood Horace worked on the farm. [7]

In the midterm elections of 1810, those for a war with England, called the War Hawks, won the congressional elections by great numbers. The Congress which met on March 4, 1811, consisted of almost more members than not, most of these were in favor of the war they envisioned on the horizon. Chief among them was Clay of Kentucky. He quickly became their spokesman fanning the flames of fevered action and recognized from the start as their leader. There was something about the man's personality that attacked others and since his followers were to have the same nationalistic views as Clay did, he made a natural leader. He had been a short while before in the Senate, so he knew something of parliamentary procedures and of getting around in Washington. This experience, above that of the other members newly elected, gave him a decided edge, but it was his leadership abilities and their dominance in numbers that led the War Hawks to easy victory.

Madison had stood in the way of war, like Jefferson he was a man of peace and was strong in Washington and the nation as a leader and man of high principles. He had been the most influential of framers of the Constitution and none living except Jefferson occupied such a high place in national esteem. This gave him power and it was against his policy that the War Hawks would have to contend. They recognized this in good friendship but in political contrast. After all as president and had of the Jeffersonian Republican party he was their leader too, and his views on political and economic matters were to be greatly respected. Madison had proved himself and now Clay was to do the same.

To the president, the War Hawks were adversaries. His policy and theirs collided. Only one of the two could prevail. Each faction was confident that it would win out in the political battle of the decade. Polite and restrain, his personality was in contrast with that of a Clay, who was all buff and bluster. The exuberance of the new members was a counterpoint to the society of statesmen headed by Madison when Congress opened. Everything seemed to clash except their adherence to the same party.

Madison wrote Jefferson in March that it was as Jefferson had written the reason why Napoleon acted as he did against America. He had some ideas though and he expressed them. Napoleon was influenced by both a lack of money and an ignorance of commerce and how it operated and should operate. Napoleon had "also distrusted the stability and efficiency of our pledge to renew the non-intercourse action against great Britain and had wished to execute his in such a manner that would keep pace only with the execution of ours."

The French emperor acted to counteract Britain to give them no rest. This was folly. "Distrust on one side produces and authorizes it on the other; and must defeat every arrangement between parties at a distance from each other or which is to have a future or a continued execution. Madison wished to turn the two great powers from plunder to "a competition for our commerce and friendship." Neither power was in the least bit interested in such policies. They were in a death grip and that was paramount for them. This was a species of total war. [8]

One historian commented on this. It was interesting that there was a reference to distrust. Madison had exhibited great faith. His reward was humiliation and censure. Napoleon gained little from his sowing distrust. He did not win support from Americans by this, but he was little interested in such objects. He was safe only because Great Britain was in a position to harm America more and due to this the British earned more hatred.

The way was most difficult for the Federalist who looked up to the English. One Federalist even thought that England was the hope for the world. This did not win them votes for themselves. People still remember England as the enemy. Still there were many who tolerated the British. For their part, the British ministry read the Federalists and thought thereby they could get away with much. They relied on the Federalists and would not consider concessions. This was to lead to war. [9]

Meanwhile at sea, there was a violent clash between a British and an American ship of war. Each claimed the other fired first. On May 16, 1811, Commander Arthur Bingham of the *Little Belt* saw a sail and gave chase. Closing in, the British discovered it to be the American frigate the *President*, which had recently supplied two American merchantmen at sea. Bingham did not show his colors and the American Commandore John Rodgers asked without reply what ship it was. The British officer asked the same question. Someone replied with a cannon shot and both ships fired their salvoes. Breaking off the exchange, the officers exchanged information and surveyed the limited danger due to both ships. An American boy was wounded. British Bingham informed Rodgers that between twenty or thirty of his crew were killed or wounded. Fortunately the blows exchanged did not lead to a conflict but bad feeling did result on both sides. [10]

One month later in distant Detroit, Governor William Hull pondered the possibility of a war with Great Britain and the strategic value of his outpost of American society. He expected war and had a firm grasp of the situation in which he would find himself when the conflict began. Hull was born in Derby, Connecticut, on June 14, 1753, graduating with honors from Yale and was a lawyer before joining the Continental Army. Distinguished in battle, he led a detachment which surprised and defeated De Lancey's loyalist force at Morrisania. After the war, he was a judge and state senator and was a 1793 envoy to Upper Canada to ask the lieutenant-governor, Simoe, for help in negotiating a treaty with the Indians.

On June 15, 1811, Hull wrote Secretary of War William Eustis, a New Englander also and a graduate of Harvard, that the land forces, British and American, were equal in numbers. However, the civilian population of Upper Canada had a twenty to one edge on that of Michigan Territory. There was a wilderness between Detroit and the American settlements outside the territory to the east, and even those were thinly inhabited. Detroit could not expect help from them, for they needed all of the men in their states and territories to defend themselves.

His territory, with his population of about five thousand could not depend upon peace with the Indian in case of war, especially because they considered war as an integral part of a warrior's life in which the native men proved their manhood. so outnumbered and isolated, this key to the American west was doomed unless the country took strong steps. The establishment of a superior naval force on Lake Erie would preserve the communication lines between Detroit and the east. This was his essential. Months later, recently returned from France where he was minister from 1804, John Armstrong suggested an army of up to six battalions should be raised from a pool of western men, mounted and capable in Indian warfare, and stationed at Detroit. This would require control of Lake Erie, he wrote. [11]

Appointed territorial governor of Illinois in 1809, Ninian Edwards' chief problem was the Indians in this scarcely populated territory. Relations between native and intruder deteriorated in the next couple of years. Finally, Edwards ordered the building of a series of blockhouses for protection of the frontier in advance of white settlements. Soon several settlers were killed and Edwards called out three militia companies.

He was soon to support Harrison's Indian policy. They had a commonality in interests since they were both frontier governors. Each had his chief aim the protection of whites against the hostile Indians. Each had problems in getting enough support in men and supplies from the Federal government. Each were bold men. Edwards had been a lawyer and militia major and just before his appointment as governor, he was chief justice of the state supreme court of Kentucky. He was well qualified for his job and educated at Dickinson College in Carlisle, Pennsylvania. [12]

With the nation at the verge of war, the final series of negotiations took place in Washington DC between Secretary of State James Monroe and the latest British minister to the United States from July of 1811 and June of 1812. August J. Foster had been charge d'affaires in Sweden and before that had served in the British Washington embassy. The envoy said that the British orders were necessary "as retaliatory measures to counteract Napoleon's attempt to crush British trade." France was the aggressor, he stated. Monroe probably doubted this, but must have believed what Foster stated about French decrees. There was evidence that France did not revoke her decrees. "The *New Orleans Packet* had been seized since the decrees were supposed to have been revoked, and further, that the Emperor in a speech to the delegates of the free cities of Hamburg, Bremen, and Lubeck had declared that the Berlin and Milan decrees should be the public code of France as long as England maintained her orders in council of 1806 and 1807. Indeed, the Secretary knew that American ships had been seized almost daily and continued to be so.

Then when Napoleon ordered all American merchantmen to be released if they had been delayed after November 2, 1810, and admitted American vessels with American made, mined, and cut products. This was not enough for Monroe and he sent Joel Barlow to Paris in July of 1811 for more liberal commerce and payment of American claims for losses from French decrees. By May of 1811, Napoleon received a repeal notification from the French emperor which was sent to the British on May 21, 1811. Meanwhile, Congress debated the question of war. [13]

President Jefferson had appointed William Hull to govern the newly established far flung Michigan Territory. It was no coincidence that the new governor for 1805 had military experience. Because of conflicts with the tribes of the new northern territory, a soldier with Hulls' vast experiences was a requirement for the frontier of the early Republic. Hull had taught school, studied theology, and then took up law, an important background for a governorship. In the Revolutionary War, he had led bayonet charges and was cited twice for bravery.

In 1784, Hull returned to the practice of law. He was twice commissioner to Canada for President George Washington. In 1798, he made a trip to Europe and was made major-general of the Massachusetts militia. His experiences were broadened when he served as a Common Pleas Judge and as state senator in the Massachusetts legislature. Then he became governor and was placed in an environment he little understood. Still his experiences were valuable. as is seen he had experience in education, theology, war, and government before he moved west. In Michigan Territory Hull rebuilt Detroit, and established laws, administration, justice, and a militia in a country in which there were few Americans but many Indian, French, and British. Unfortunately, Hull remained an Easterner and never really understood the frontiersman. This was to cause friction. Except at Detroit, the settlers scattered along the waterways to hunt, trap, and trade.

During the war scare of 1807-09, Hull was alert. In a letter to the secretary of war, he said he would gladly serve and before the secretary could reply, he activated three militia companies. Hull at Detroit and the British at Fort Malden worked their defenses to be ready for war if it came. The Americans hoped to induce the pro-British Indians to be neutral, while the British, who lacked regulars and who did not trust their Canadian militiamen, enlisted the aid of the Indians, given their cruelty and tactics presented a crucial foe as shall be seen. The British also built up their lake fleet, while the Americans did no naval building, a great mistake for which Hull could not be blamed. Hull tried to gain the friendship of the Wyandots, but white intrusions on the tribal lands undercut the Hull policy. [14]

Far from the dirt and log cabins which were Lincoln's world, was polished gentility in the stolid and religious town of Litchfield, Connecticut. It was a town with a history of almost a century by 1811. During the recent Revolutionary War it was a patriots' community, with military stores and a workshop for the Continental army. There one found a law school, the first in the United States. Without buildings it held lectures in its instructor's law offices. The students there over the years attained great renown.

Chief among them was the famous John C. Calhoun, whose fame has survived in the century of the era of American world leadership. Lesser known Levi Woodbury was almost as prominent in their day. Woodbury held a senatorship for better than a decade in two portions, was a Democratic cabinet minister of the navy and the treasury, and a Supreme Court justice for the remainder of his life. He died in 1851. The school graduated a multitude of able men. Local luminary and Judge Tapping Reeve, friend of the Beechers, married the sister of Aaron Burr and founded this Litchfield Law School.

The most famous citizen of Litchfield was Harriet Beecher Stowe. On the day of June 14, 1811, her father Lyman Beecher, the Congregationalist preacher, went to tell Tappping Reeve of the birth of his seventh child and fourth daughter. More were still to come through the joy and pains of her mother, Roxana Beecher. As the Congregational minister, Lyman was one of the chief leaders of Litchfield. Harriet grew up in the culture of the small town elite with the best heredity and environment could provide. We shall meet her again in her life and when she helps write history. Lincoln was to meet her, and she him in the days of the national distress over the issue of slavery. Both had strong views of the subject of the peculiar institution and played important roles in its demise.

The early ancestors of the Beechers came one in the early days of the colonies. They reached back as had the Lincolns' but the forebears of the Beechers siblings were more important. there was an important general and a colonel on the Ward side and a learned blacksmith on the Beecher side, who counciled Congressman Roger Sherman, a signer of the Declaration of Independence. The Beecher household was a busy and exciting one with many children, some relatives, and a few boarders. Lyman's wife loved a certain standard of living, and the large family gathering required the payment of many expenses. Matters were helped along by an inherited life annuity for Roxana.

Two years after Harriet's birth, Roxana delivered another child to be named Henry Ward Beecher, in the midst of a war of which Lyman Beecher, like the natural New Englander, disapproved. To Lyman the War Hawks had launched a conspiracy to wipe out American liberties. This was of course nonsense, but it did destroy the annuity in the financial failure of Uncle Justin Foote's company. Shortly Lyman's sister-in-law Mary Hubbard came to live with them. The lady had a great influence on Harriet's life. Having married an English settler and planter in Jamaica, she saw the full horrors of slavery and imported to the young Harriet her hatred of slavers as a sin and a source of misery, through others in the family. Mary died soon after moving in. This was Mary's contribution to history. Suddenly Roxane was stricken with tuberculosis and died. Lyman was to remarry. [15]

---

[1]Lynch, *Fifty Years*, p. 214.

[2]Madeleine, *Monetary and Banking Theories of Jacksonian Democracy*, Reprint 1970, p. 12-13.

[3]Catterall, Ralph C.H., *The Second Bank of the United States*, Chicago: University of Chicago Press, 1960 (Reprint), pp. 1--7

[4]Tucker, *Poltroons* and Patriots, *I, 131. Quotes on p. 131.*

[5]*Ibid.*, pp. 131-135.

[6]Gilpin, *War*, pp. 6-7.

[7]Hale, William Harlan, *Horace Greeley: Voice of the People*, New York: Harper, 1950, pp. 3-7; Greeley, Horace, *Recollections of a Busy Life*, New York: J.B. Ford, 1868 (Reprint New York: Arno, 1970, pp. 34-50.

[8]Lynch, *Fifty Years*, p. 212. Quote on p. 212

[9]*Ibid.*, pp. 212-213.

[10]Dudley, *War*, pp. 40-50.

[11]Cruikshank, E.A. (ed.), *Documents Relating to the Invasion of Canada and the Surrender of Detroit, 1812*, Ottawa, Can.: Government Printing Bureau, 1912, pp. 1-3.

[12]Holden, Robert J., "Edwards, Ninian," Haidler & Haidler, *Encyclopedia*, p. 163.

[13]Updyke, Frank A., *The Diplomacy of the War of 1812*, Baltimore: John Hopkins Press, 1915, pp. 116-120. Quote on p. 116.

[14]Gilpin, *War*, pp. 23-25.

[15]Wilson, Forrest, *Crusader in Crinoline: The Life of Harriet Beecher Stowe*, Philadelphia: J.B. Lippincott, 1941, pp. 1931.

CHAPTER VIII

DANGERS

On September 7, 1811, newspaperman Hezekiah Niles issued his first copy of a weekly compendium of the news, written in the evening of the day for its weekly publication. It was the forerunner of a newsmagazine although decidedly a newspaper. He expected it to be used by future writers as a source of history, and Americans were not to disappointed him. Niles recorded wars and was himself born a refugee. The newborn's parents were residents of Wilmington, Delaware. Some two months before his birth, British soldiers approached that city and the parents fled to the refuge of fellow Quaker near the forks of the Brandywine and were almost in the line of march of Lord Cornwallis. Hekekiah was born on October 10, 1777, in the Chester County farmhouse of James Jefferis. Soon the Niles family moved back to Wilmington. It was there that Hezekiah received a classic education. In 1790 the boy's father died when struck by a falling signpost. About four years later he went to work as an apprentice to Benjamin Johnson, a publisher and bookseller in Philadelphia. He awoke early and read for an hour or so until the family was stirring about.

His interests in politics were further awakened when he saw President George Washington on his morning walk. He taught in later writings that the president "frequently seemed to give me an encouraging look, if our eyes happened to meet; to which he would sometimes add a kind nod of recognition." Some of Niles' views on political and economic issues came to him when the was young. Niles was a lifelong protectionist. At about age nine or younger he saw some gentlemen paraded in homespun clothes. He father said they were wearing domestic clothes because they wanted to keep America independent. There were other forms of protection, he late wrote, that is, to protect persons, pursuits, and property at home and abroad. Every president and congress had agreed upon that. He would at an early age see a tariff which would protect industry at home and commerce abroad. [1]

In 1794, young Hezekiah published a small number of small articles in support of domestic industry in Colonel Oswald's newspaper in Philadelphia for the independence of the United States. In 1797, back in Wilmington, he joined a debating society where he met an older unlettered blacksmith by the name of David Chandler. The brawny man "possessed one of the strongest and most original minds, concerning the principles and properties of labor, that I had ever met with before, or have encountered since--and his lectures, so happily adapted to my own youthful notions of the subject, laid the *foundation* of all my since expressed opinions, though rejecting many of his theories." He joined a democratic caucus of some 50 or 60 persons in that year as it most junior member, being still a minor. Some of his most steadfast friends over the years came from that group. Although political fashions might change, Nile's ideas had remained the same, he was to report in later years. [2]

Young Niles was an early supporter of Thomas Jefferson. In 1796, he wrote a number of letters for the *Aurora* and other Jeffersonian Republican papers in support of the future president. This attachment grew with Niles' growth and was strengthened with his strength from that early day. Niles had not "regarded him as infallible--supposed that he had not committed errors in opinion and errors in practice, as the head of a great political party; but when distinguished men in his own state opposed him, and would have disgraced him...it was our fortune, as well as every other occasion, to feel it right and proper to support him--so far as we could." These same men would presently laud the memory of Jefferson. [3]

In 1795, the firm of Vincent Bosall and Hezehiah Niles printed the *Delaware Gazette* for Robert Coram and then for others until September 1, 1799. The partners republished the *Political Writings of John Dickinson* which was financially disastrous. Niles was an ardent admirer of Dickinson, but this was only a part of the problem. The firm failed, leaving Niles $25,000 in debt. Instead of disowning his debt, he paid it off over the years. In 1798, he married Anne Ogden, daughter of tavern keeper William Ogden of Philadelphia, a Quaker. [4]

Niles entered Wilmington politics. In the fall of 1801, the people of the city elected him town clerk with a large vote. Next they selected the popular printer assistant burgess. Then they elected him to each position in consecutive years. From 1797 to 1805, Niles was busy in Delaware politics and knew every Jeffersonian Republican politician who was prominent in the state. Looking back in 1834, he saw the parties of the time both patriotic and deprecated the use of the term "federalist" in proscribing opponents of Jacksonianism. Back then, he was a young member of the first caucus in Delaware. [5]

In the last year of Niles' public service, he published a literary magazine of eight pages for $3.00 per year. It was entitled *The Apollo or Delaware Weekly Magazine* and lasted six months. He found contributors of poetry, essays, and short novels. It is assumed that Niles wrote the series of humorous essays which were entitled "Quill Driving by Captain Jeffery Thickneck." Shortly, the editor went to Baltimore to edit and run the newly started Baltimore *Evening Post*. He lasted five and one half years with three pages of advertising and a fourth page of local, national, and foreign news, until he sold it in June of 1811. Two weeks later he came out with the prospectus for the *Weekly Register*. [6]

Among the news stories of the day for Niles and others was what was happening on the western frontier. The Indians of the western frontier were finding a certain unity in 1811 under Tecumseh. This vibrant native dreamed of an Indian confederation to match the union of the whites. He was the Shawnee chief. Because his mother was a Muskogee, he was most welcome among the Creek to whom Major Ridge was an ambassador. Although it was declared that Ridge was there to settle the mutual horse stealing from the north that plagued the two peoples he was there to hear what Tedumseh and the delegation had to say after Tecumseh's stay of several weeks among the Chickasaws and the Choctaws. Ridge and his Cherokees were there now as were others to hear what the great leader of the north had to say.

The first step for the northern visitors was a war dance called the Dance of the Lakes, a wild dance which roused all watching. Tecumseh did not talk for a few days and regular council affairs were taken up by the Indians. Colonel Benjamin Hawkins, the agent, was old and sick, so he then went to his home on the Flint River, but his spies were able to

The Difficult War: The Era of the War of 1812 63

keep him informed of what went on in council. He learned that Tecumseh time came about September 30th and the Indians turned down the Sioux idea of an immediate attack upon the Americans. Despite his hatred of the whites, Tecumseh knew how to bide his time and that first the Indians would have to be united. The Creeks had lost lands and would, like the other Indians, be certainly forced westward and die off, perhaps into extermination. They would have to wait first for unity among themselves.

He told the assembled Indians that they had friends in the British. The white man would have to live their own way and the red man his. Indians would have to return to their own ways, and heed the revelations of his brother the Prophet. To the Cherokees and others it was a failed message that Tecumseh carried south, because they did not wish to give up the ways of the white man that they had acquired. They did not regret the departure of Tecumseh.

However, at this point in time there was the famous New Madrid earthquake. The Cherokees were concerned and many panicked and Major Ridge feared that the world might be coming to the end. This series of earthquakes strengthened the conservative Indians and they remembered that Tecumseh had predicted them. Agitators among the Indians made claims they had caused the earthquakes or that Tecumseh had caused them.

One half-blood prophet called Charley came forth and spoke words against the paleface ways. He won the allegiance of those who wished to return to the old ways and when Major Ridge defeated them, they rushed the Indian chief. However Ridge's friends rescued him and a blooded Ridge continued his defiance. When a hail-storm to kill all but the faithful did not materialize as Charley said it would, the prophet was rejected. The peace party prevailed among the Cherokees while the Creeks favored war. [7]

There were fears among people of Kentucky and elsewhere over dangers from Indians and from slaves. In Lincoln's territory, postriders came from Frankfort to Lexington, Kentucky, with news from Governor Harrison to Governor Scott. The rumor mill started when it was learned of the messages' arrival. People speculated that the Indians were marching on Vincennes. Lexington's gazette editor had heard no call for assistance, but if volunteers were needed, he was sure that Scott would be prompt in answering that need. Citizens would respond and a number would not wait for a call but rush to Harrison's aid. [8]

A more distant danger came from Jamaica, but it hit close to home also. Southerners could be fearful of black uprisings. Now their concern was heightened. There were reports that three regiments of African Americans had risen up and killed and sacked. The town of Montego Bay in Jamaica was in flames. They could not be suppressed easily it was reported and Kingston itself was in danger. Later there were rumors that Kingston had been burnt. The British reacted strongly to the information at hand and it was reported that forces were underway for Jamaica. This was interesting to the slaveholders and their neighbors since in the back of everyone's mind was the fear of a slave uprising at home. For now, it was in the forefront of conversation and in the newspapers. [9]

William Henry Harrison was about forty when he rose to prominence during the War of 1812. Born on February 9, 1773, in revolutionary times, at Berkeley, his father's estate in Virginia's tobacco country, Harrison swam, fished, and rode on horseback in his youth. Tutored at home, his life was easy, but it was a bit undecided what he would do in the workaday world. Finally, his father decided he would be a doctor of medicine. Sent to Hampden Sidney, his father withdrew him when a Methodist revival took place there. The Harrisons were traditionally Episcopalians and so they sent him to a sound academy for a few months. In 1790, the young man entered the office of a Richmond physician, but as an abolitionist surge of feeling took place in Richmond, the father sent him to the Medical School of Pennsylvania University at Philadelphia, his first taste of a large city. His father died and Harrison went into the military.

The young Harrison entered the army just after St. Clair's defeat in Indian country and was immediately sent west. He observed the crude situation around him and determined to neither drink nor duel. This stood him in good stead. Harrison proved himself by winter marches with his troops. Often he commanded guard duty. Pleasant duty soon intervened when Harrison escorted the wife of General James Wilkinson and their family back to civilization, back to Philadelphia.

Having gone into the army as an ensign, Harrison was promoted to lieutenant with a captain's brevet. He drilled his troops and led them in sham battles and show skirmishes. Then General Anthony Wayne appointed him his third aide-de-camp. This meant a major's pay. In the broader spectrum, peace talks failed and Wayne called upon Kentucky's General Charles Scott to bring two regiments up to the front. Meanwhile, he marched out until stopped by President George Washington. The head of the government would not "risk defeat during a season when supplies and forage wire difficult to obtain." Wayne ordered his men to build a sizable stockade and settled in for the winter. The next summer Wayne headed for war and Harrison served as dispatch bearer, one of the more important duties of aides. Even more important was the captain's submission of a plan for battle, which Wayne took on as his plan.

They reached a site which had a cyclone created mass of fallen timber which was cover for a thousand Indians and more than one hundred British regulars and Canadian militia. When the enemy fired, the Legion dropped back. Wayne sent Harrison with the order of the day to charge with the bayonet and to personally reform the broken line. The shortest route led Harrison between the lines of both armies but he rode so fast that he escaped injury. Harrison worked at keeping the American lines intact. The American left was threatened so General Wayne brought up reinforcements. Kentucky fire power broke the Indians and they headed for the river. The Americans had cut off their retreat. [10]

The Greenville treaty of peace was signed on August 3, 1795. Harrison served to report infractions of the treaty. At this point, he fell in love with Anna Symmes and she him but her father vetoed the proposed marriage. Judge Symmes ordered Harrison to stay away from his daughter. Harrison met the young lad on occasion and they eloped to marry. Harrison was elected delegate from Ohio to Congress, thus entering politics for the first time. There he worked for the benefit of his constituents, especially in land matters. On January 10, 1801, Harrison became the territorial governor of Indiana.

Harrison looked after the interests of the Indians whenever possible, but without much luck. Unable to prevent them from drinking liquor and loosing their subsistence or to punish the murderers of Indians, Harrison felt indignant and probably hopeless, except for some success in improving the lives of the wretched Indians. On the other hand, the governor oversaw the cession of Indian property at Vincinnes. The Americans saw Indians armed by the British among dissenting Indians and probably were somewhat alarmed.

Indians's first election took place with Harrison wishing a pro-slavery legislature to be elected with its chosen delegate to Congress. The new legislature was six to one in favor of slavery. They advocated this peculiar institution's spread into new territories. This did not change the fact that Indiana laws prevented slaves from being bought and sold in Indiana.

The governor escaped slightly tarred from an encounter with Aaron Burr's plot. But more serious for the governor was Indian intransigence. The Indians were increasingly attracted to Tecumseh and his brother the Prophet; the later was saying that the Great Spirit would destroy all whites in America in a few years. Harrison blamed the British. He had a lot of company. Word reached Harrison of British activity, who passed on the warnings to the legislature. Indeed the Indians needed little encouragement and the British, who wished no war with Americans at that time, had to quiet the natives of the Old Northwest. There was a bite coming up, for the whites desired more land. At a long drawn out conference, Harrison got the Indians to cede about three million acres of land and he was in line for a fourth term as governor. [11]

Harrison was eager to strike a blow against the Indians to prevent an Indian confederation from gaining strength. Westerners were alarmed about the rise of the Indian brothers. Tecumseh wanted the tribes to combine and establish an Indian Congress. He would prevent the piecemeal surrender of Indian lands to the whites by giving title of all the lands to this assembly. In May or June of 1808, the two Indian brothers established a village on Tippecanoe Creek, at a central site. His people did not partake of liquor and farmed for a living. When the Prophet met with Harrison, he talked peace and wanted the two peoples to tend to their own affairs.

There could be no peace, however, as long as the Americans wished to have more Indian lands to the edge of the Wabash. People in Indiana wanted those particular lands, so Harrison wrote Secretary of War William Eustis to ask for authority to purchase the land. Eustis gave him that authorization and Harrison gathered together the tribes of the area and received about three million acres extending past the Wabash. The Indians were forced to withdraw from the given lands toward the lands of their enemies, the Chippawas and Sioux.

When the other Indians learned of this treaty, they looked increasingly favorable upon the idea of confederation. The proud Wyandots or Hurons joined the league and said they would not recognize the cession. Soon Tecumseh was refusing to accept the salt annuity and demanded annullation of the purchase. The British felt that it was to their interest for the confederation to succeed. They loaded the Indians that came to Malden, opposite Detroit, with gifts and weapons. They urged Tecumseh to add more tribes to his Indian league, but not to start a war until they gave a signal. Reports of this reached Washington. [12]

As soon as Tecumseh went on a diplomatic mission to the Creeks, the settlers and Governor Harrison decided to destroy the Indian settlement at Tippecanoe. Madison wanted peace, but he was far away and the governor prepared for war. Harrison had his men build a small wooden fort. Soon Harrison lead a force of over one thousand. On October 28, 1811, he marched his army up the river. Avoiding the woods, Harrison led them up the west bank of the Wabash where the prairie was located.

On November 5th, the army was eleven miles from Tippecanoe and promptly advanced toward the Indian town on the sixth. It was a dark and a rainy night. Two young Winnebagoes approached the sentries. The sentinels fired, wounding both. Alert Americans approached the two Indians who had fell. When they got close, the warriors arose and tomahawked the white soldiers. This decided the question of offense or defense and the chiefs decided to attack the invaders in revenge.

Before sunrise on November 7, 1811, the Indians attacked. At first the Indians had the advantage. The men were about to leave their tents, when a shot was heard and the yells of the Indians pierced the dark. They shot the soldiers who could be seen by their campfires. Lacking strength, the Indians gave the soldiers chance to form a line. Colonel Abraham Owen was killed in the fight, but Harrison reached the area of the heaviest fighting and directed the defense.

It was there that the Indians broke through at the joint between units. The line was broken. Harrison brought forth two companies which rescued the situation. The Indians did not recognize their advantage and were pushed back into the woods by degrees. Harrison moved to the areas of need. Harrison ordered two charges. When he learned that Captain Spier Spencer's company had seen the deaths of Spencer and his lieutenant. Harrison told Ensign John Tipton to hold his position and sent in reinforcements. He then plugged a gap. The old Major Samuel Wells led his infantry on a bayonet attack upon the Indians, who began to flee from the area. The whites had held their position and drove the Indian warriors (who were running out of ammunition and arrows) into the swamp. Soldier losses were heavy, but the soldiers won the battle.

On the 8th, they marched to the deserted town, took needed supplies, and burned the town before retreating back to Vincennes. The Indian women and children had crossed the river while the fighting took place. Twenty-five braves lost their lives in the encounter. Tippecanoe was deemed a great battle in the West. Indeed the army had seized the town which was their objective, but nothing was solved by this success. Warriors were to have their day. They still controlled the forest and prairies. [13]

By the second of December of 1811, Major General Isaac Brock was expecting that the Americans would soon invade Canada and he had a long, long line to defend from Fort Dearborn on the west to Montreal on the east. His plan was to use as many militiamen and Indians as he could possibly raise. He wrote Sir George Prevost that he believed that the strait running "between Niagara and Fort Erie is that which in all probability will be chosen for their main body to penetrate with a view to conquest. All other attacks will be subordinate or merely made to divert our attention." Brock expected to have 3,000 militiamen for his own force and that the Americans would have difficulty with undisciplined soldiers and with bringing up provisions. Brock was a man of action and planted batteries of cannon and beacons and signal stations at various points. [14]

The debate on war as a means and end continued in the Congress. Expansionistic Felix Grundy of Tennessee frankly denied that the carrying trade question was the subject of the contention. At least, it might be observed, it was not a question which he thought interested westerners. Should it be the only question, he would not go to war with Great Britain. He did not think the impressment and confiscation of ships issue was a major concern of the people. However, he did believed that the right to export agricultural and industrial products was paramount as a nation issue.

British depredations on the high seas were not made in accordance with law, but with the British pride and demands of maritime supremacy. The British were jealous of America's commercial greatness, second in the world only to Great Britain. He would not have the United States submit to their regulation, to the arbitrary and capricious rule of British will. The advantage of driving the Britons from North America was important. Grundy thought Florida and Canada should be conquered, ending British intrigues on the frontiers of the United States. He spoke as a true westerner.

Richard M. Johnson, in opposition to the view that Americans had common ties with England that should determine our policy, stressed that the roots of enmity to Great Britain lay in the insidious policy of that nation. If the nations of Great Britain and the United States had mutual obligations of friendship, why did Great Britain rend those ties asunder through injuries of plunder and harm of honor, commerce, and substance.

Johnson believed that Americans had ample reasons for a declaration of war against the British nation. He defended the Republican party and administration against the charge that they were partial to France. Only Great Britain had the means to greatly harm the American people.

On the other hand, representing the minority view, John Randolph defended the pro-peace position on the issue. The Virginian disagreed with Grundy that there was proof that the British government had instigated the Wabash massacre. He thought that the British had not encouraged the Indians and stated he would march upon Canada should his opponents prove their contention. As we have seen the British were encouraging the Indians in the expectation of any war. Also, Randolph did not think, as did War Hawks, that the Canadians would revolt and join the Americans in case of invasion. He was correct. He did not believe that they would be so treacherous as to revolt. The people of the United States would suffer with their blood and taxes from a war, and only a few speculators, merchants, and contractors would benefit. A conquest of Canada would, he stated in Congress, risk the Constitution.

Also, a war would consist of invading Canada and leaving the coast vulnerable to British attacks. The coast was vulnerable as the British were to prove and nothing could be done to protect it enough in case of war. Little had been done so far and there was much that could be accomplished in the near future, but it could never be safe enough for comfort. [15]

The nationalistic John Caldwell Calhoun was born on March 18, 1782, on the South Carolina frontier at Abbeville. His father's house was the first frame house in the country and his father's life was that of a stern Calvinistic Puritan life. John grew up to consider life to be a struggle against evil. Happiness was neither expected or sought. In the process of his early boyhood he heard of the fights and bloody crimes of the recent war and of the regular vigilance and leadership such as "Swamp Fox" Francis Marion and Nathanael Greene. One uncle had died with many wounds at Cowpens and another died on a prison ship off St. Augustine. Young John was brought up on talk of politics. Like Lincoln years later, Calhoun had his first schooling in a frontier log-cabin school, but unlike the future president, John went on to study at an academy.

With his father's death, he returned home to manage and work the several farms himself with his African American slaves. His was a subsistence life. There was little to be marketed from the farm crops. His intellect showed through in these years and his brothers talked him into finishing his education and becoming a lawyer. There he proved to the head and shoulders above his classmates. Calhoun graduated with the class of 1804.

Back in Abbeville, Calhoun began a law practice without the benefit of formal legal training. This was temporary for in the fall of 1805 he entered the established Litchfield (Conn) Law School. His cousin's widow, Floride Bonneau Colhoun (spelt with an "o") took him with her to Newport, Rhode Island, on that trip to Litchfield, and they stopped at Monticello where Calhoun introduce himself to Thomas Jefferson. In those days anyone could meet with a president if he so desired; especially with Jefferson who was always in touch with the common man. They had a long talk in which the young man impressed the president. After one year at the school, he went to Charleston to read law and then to Abbeville to practice the law profession. There the people elected Calhoun to a legislative seat in Columbia and soon to Congress for an easy landslide. On the eighth day of 1811, he married Colhoun's daughter Floride, named after her mother.

Calhoun entered the House of Representatives and immediately became one of the new speaker's lieutenants. Clay found him able and young, but at the time no threat to his ascendancy. Calhoun's report on November 29, 1811, asked for fifty thousand volunteers, warships, and the arming of the American merchant marine. Meanwhile, word had reached the capital of the Indian battle of Tippecanoe and Felix Grundy told Clay that the war had factually began with British weapons in Indian hands. [16]

Professor Herman E. von Holst wrote from Germany in his keystone biography of John C. Calhoun that Calhoun had formed the beginnings a most successful career in politics and statesmanship. He "observed the parliamentary proprieties with the vigor and naturalness of the born gentleman. Often did he proved he could wield with equal force and dexterity the trenchant sword and the massive club, but he always attacked the argument of his adversary and not his person, and he was never guilty of hectoring or bullying tone in which so many of the Southern politicians indulged in keen relish." At the very start of his career in Congress a self-assured Calhoun "entered the lines with the proud conviction of being fully equal of any man, and he always spoke in the weighty tone of authority."

In his first major speech in the House, Calhoun made John Randolph, a Virginian and leader in the House of Representatives, feel the cutting edge of their early adversary relationship. Calhoun had been accepted as a leader from his first meetings with Henry Clay and others as did Clay himself. For all intents and purposes Calhoun was born to lead. Calhoun was for war measures and Randolph was not. The South Carolinian believed it was essential for Americans to fight for their rights against England and he favored war preparations with the majority of the Committee on Foreign Relations. [17]

Calhoun went on to say that "it may be and believe it was said, that the people will not pay taxes because the rights violated are not worth defending; or that the defense will cost more than the gain. Sir, I here enter my solemn protest against this law and 'calculating avarice' entering this hall of legislation. It is only fit for the shops and country-houses; and ought not to disgrace the seat of power by its squalid aspect. Whenever it touches sovereign power, the nation is ruined." Honor must prevail. He was not vexed in this calculating policy, "and will not, therefore, pretend to estimate in dollars and cents the value of national independence. I cannot measure in shillings and pence the misery, the stripes, and the slavery of our imperiled seamen; nor even the value of our shipping, commercial, and agricultural losses under the Orders in Council and the British system of blockade." [18]

Clay's opinion of Calhoun was enhanced. Calhoun's reputation had preceded him and, as one of the new War Hawks, was already dear. Clay recognized his leadership abilities and made him one of his political lieutenants. The South Carolinian had been a legislator at home and made his mark there as a leader; now he was in a bigger stage of history. Calhoun recognized Clay as the man to follow and was delighted to be selected as were several others to be high in the councils of Congress. This was an opportunity that ambition demanded. [19]

At first, Calhoun was a nationalist who believed in a big government strong enough to lead in developing the country politically and economically. He would have the federal government levy tariffs. These would be used to protect and encourage manufacturing. He wanted a strong national bank to provide the credit necessary in this earlier Calhoun cause. Calhoun wished to have a system of highways and waterways to promote commerce in these days before the railroad. Clay and Calhoun joined hands in a government for national development, then called internal improvements. They achieved protective tariffs and a bank, but under the limited government viewpoint of Madison, who like Jefferson, wanted little government, this went against the ideas of the orthodox of the party. Still it was achieved in part and efforts would be made in the future for further action by the government.

Like a true politician, Calhoun preferred to read history and politics, both ancient and modern. Not caring much for fiction, he read and studied Jefferson, Madison, Taylor, and Tucker. More immediately he read Thomas Cooper, who was a college president and antitariff economist. His studies were the Jeffersonian favored John Locke. In addition, he read Demosthenes, Cicero, Polybius, and Machaievelli, Algernon Sidney, and Thomas Hobbes. His economic views where those of Adam Smith. Calhoun's favorites were Aristotle and Edmund Burke. He was no disciple, selecting what he wished from each of these authors. His nullification views were developed from Jefferson and Madison, but he rejected their ideas of human equality and natural rights. His reading of Locke produced his idea that property's worth was developed from the labor people put into it. He borrowed the idea that self-interest was the main motive of the political man. Society and government were with man from the beginning in his view and hence there was no social control to be adopted. [20]

The legal profession's major figure for the first half of the nineteenth century next to John Marshall, Justice Joseph Story and John Marshall worked well together. Story was a hard worker and together the men accomplished a great deal. In addition, Story soon came to become Dane Professor at Harvard Law School when he was not on circuit or in Washington DC. Story had lived in a fishing village into a deeply religious family. Brought up in Congregationalism, he was in time a Unitarian. In either faith, he was deeply faithful, dutiful, and imbued with a gift from God. His father had been a physician in George Washington's army.

In 1798, Story graduated from Harvard. A Jeffersonian Republican, he served in the Massachusetts House from 1805 to 1811, and served two years into the national house, where he voted for the repeal of the embargo. This made Jefferson angry. Returning to law practice, he was soon presented with the main chance of his career. Madison tried to find a justice for the vacancy left by William Cushing, but was not having much success when over Jefferson's objections he turned to Story who agreed. [21]

Meanwhile there were more concerns of a mundane nature. Captain Enos Collins watched on in the Halifax ship docks as a lean and bold ship to be known as the *Black Joke* was put on the auction block. He was forever buying things no one else wanted, at a bargain price. This one was a condemned vessel which had been captured in the slave trade which was still going on in 1811. The month of November saw it's purchased as Collins made the final bid. At first it was a passenger and cargo carrier operating ship between Liverpool township in Nova Scotia and Halifax. This ship was to become a privateer out of Canada in the upcoming war between Britain and the United States. [22]

There were other opportunities for profit. In 1811, Captain Becknell went a trading expedition to exchange goods with the Comanche Indians and ended up with a good profit. Hoping for riches in trade with Santa Fe, he decided to go in 1812 to Santa Fe. Trade with the Indians had been tedious, but he reasoned he could sell out his stock to Spanish merchants. He achieved this objective with great profit on the long road to Taos. Back on the Missouri River Becknell told tales of the great success he had put behind him and there was a popular response. Many listeners wanted to take part in the sale of goods to the New Mexicans. Becknell raised five thousand dollars in merchandise, a large amount for those early days, reaching a peak compared to earlier trade expeditions. Thirty men composed the caravan.

Everything went along all right until they reached "the Coches" on the upper Arkansas. Remembering the long journey of the previous year, Becknell decided to take a shortcut. He reasoned that the mountain route was too long and wanted to take a quicker route, not realizing that there were good reasons for travelers to take the longer journey. Everyone expected there to be plenty of water like the Arkansas valley. Two days later they finished their water and realized that they were in a virtual desert. Thirst soon drove them almost mad and they killed their dogs in order to drink blood. This was not the best drink, but they next killed an old buffalo bull for his stomach contents. Deciding to return to the Arkansas with poor navigational guides, they turned around. The strongest among them followed the bull tracks to water and rescued their compadres with the find of water. All made it back to the Arkansas River and going west on that river, reached Taos.

Later trading was sporadic and largely devoted to the Indians. Auguste P. Chouteau and his partner led a large party of trappers and hunters on the upper Arkansas River to trap beaver and trade with the Indians. Chouteau established a trading post on an island of beauty on the boundary line between New Spain (soon to be Mexico) and the United States. There they were attacked. They won the battle with heavy losses on both sides.

A later trading party reached Santa Fe and were arrested as spies, lost their goods, and were incarcerated at Chihuahua. Most of the traders spent the majority of a decade in prison. Two men escaped reaching St. Louis in 1822. Although they told of this unhappy reception, they spoke about the demand for trade goods and of high possibility for profitable trade. One group left late in the season and were stranded for winter on an island near the site of Cimarron. Losing their animals, they had to hide their goods and the trading expedition failed. Because of the hostility of Santa Fe officials a trade which would have been great, if the Spanish and Mexicans had been for free trade, met with more shoals than smooth water. Men like Collins were more fortunate; even more so were the Astors and Vanderbilts, who played no role in trade with Mexico. [23]

---

[1]Luxon, Norvel Neil, *Nile's Weekly Register: News Magazine of the Nineteenth Century*, Louisiana State University Press, 1947, Westport, Conn.: Greenwood Press, 1970, pp. 17-20 (Quote on p. 19); *Niles Weekly Register*, December 11, 1830, pp. 251-252.

[2]*Niles Weekly Register*, December 11, 1830, p. 252. Quote on p. 252.

[3]*Ibid.*, April 24, 1830, p. 154. Quote on p. 154.

[4]Lincoln, Anna T., *Wilmington, Delaware: Three Centuries Under Four Flags, 1609-1937*, Rutland, Vt: Tuttle, 1937, pp. 355, 358.

[5]*Ibid.*, p. 21; *Niles Weekly Register*, June 14, 1834, pp. 265-266.

[6]Luxon, *Niles' Weekly Register*, pp 21-23.

[7]Wilkins, pp. 52-64.

[8]*Kentucky Gazette*, September 3, 1811, p. 3.

[9]*Ibid.*, September 10, 1811, p. 3.

[10]Cleaves, Freeman, *Old Tippecanoe: William Henry Harrison and His Time*, New York: Charles Scribner's Sons, 1939 (Reprint Port Washington NY: Kennikat Press, 1969, pp. 5-19.

[11]*Ibid.*, pp. 24-39, 45-46, 55-58, 64-68.

[12]Adams, *Madison*, pp. 350-356.

[13]*Ibid.*, pp. 360-370; Cruikshank, *Documents*, p. 7; Leckie, *Sea*, pp. 163-165.

[14]Babcock, *War of 1812*, pp. 31-32.

[15]*The Annals of America*, IV, pp. 291-298.

[16]Coit, Margaret L, *John C. Calhoun: American Portrait*, Boston: Houghton Mifflin, 1950, pp. 1-3, 5-10, 13-14, 18, 32-36, 43, 45-47, 52, 62-65, 67-73.

[17]Von Holst, Hermann E., *John C. Calhoun*, New York: Chelsea House, 1980, (Reprint of the 1899 edition), pp. 15-18. Quote on p. 17.

[18]*Ibid.*, pp. 18-19. Quotes on pp. 18-19.

[19]Coit, *Calhoun*, pp. 54-55, 68-70.

[20]Current, Richard N., *John C.* Calhoun, New York: Washington Square Press, 1966, pp. 6-8, 43-44.

[21]Newmyer, R. Kent, "Story, Joseph," Hall, *Supreme Court*, pp. 841-844.

[22]Snider, C.H.J., *Under the Red Jack: Privateers of the Maritime Provinces of Canada in the War of 1812*, London: Martin Hopkinson, 1928, pp. 9ff.

[23]Inman, Henry, *The Old Santa Fe Trail: The Story of a Great Highway*, Reprint, Minneapolis, Minn: Ross & Haines, 1966, pp. 38-44.

CHAPTER IX

CAUSES OF WAR

Congress was busy in session, but on common and trivial things. They were waiting for reports on bills on December 24, 1811, when Felix Grundy wrote General Andrew Jackson on congressional events. The House was awaiting reports on four subjects. "One was for an increase of the regular military establishment, another for a volunteer corps, and third authorizing the president to call out detachments of militia, and a fourth authoring our merchantmen to arm etc." The increase in soldiers and one on militia were to pass Congress the next February and April.

Grundy wrote that "the first bill will provide for the raising of 15,000 regular troops in addition to the present establishment." This will bring the military up to twenty-five thousand regular troops. There would be a bounty of from 100 to 169 acres, "a bounty in money of $16 besides the usual pay and rations--terms of enlistment five years. I have no doubt, but great exertions will be used in the house to destroy or diminish the land bounty, but I hope it will be without effect. It requires, but little reflection to show, that the Western Country at least will be benefited by it, and I believe the whole United States. The 'volunteer bill will authorize the acceptance by the president of 50,000 men, in companies not less than 60 no more than 80 men in number. They are to nominate their captains and subalterns to the president. The majors, colonels, and generals to be appointed and commissioned by the president, no higher officer than a brigadier general will be attached to the volunteers. In addition to pay heretofore offered to volunteer, some honorable marks of distinction will be conferred on officers and soldiers after their discharge, such as a set of arms used by them in service, with *suitable inscriptions*." Grundy thought war was certain if Great Britain did not recede on his policies and that the war would be fought in Canada and Florida. Failure to enter a war would mean that the Congress would be disgraced.

In Jackson's area of the country, Americans had moved through the Mississippi Territory southward into the region just east of the Mississippi River and west of the Pearl River in East Florida. By 1809, nine-tenths of the inhabitants of that area were Americans, encouraging James Madison to advance the theory that West Florida was a part of the Louisiana Purchase. As a base to the claim, he cited that under France in 1763, the province of Louisiana extended as far east as the Perdido River west of Pensacola. After the Americans heard that the claim was advanced, they turned revolutionary and seized the Spanish fort at Baton Rouge and captured the governor. They requested annexation by the United States, and President Madison issued a proclamation annexing the region to the Perdido River on October 27, 1810. He then seized West Florida. This was the event that encouraged Mathews to move into East Florida as we have seen. The pro-war Southerners were eager for the rest of Florida, which Mathews had failed to take and, if war was declared, they felt sure to take it. The pro-war Northerners were eager for Canada for their part. Meanwhile the frontier was expanding. People were on the move.

In 1811, Thomas Lincoln moved his family to a new farm on Knob Creek, where the farming was much more productive. He rented this farm, located on the road to Bardstown. Whether he moved in search for better land or because of the difficulties he was having with the title to the South Fork farm is unknown, but he was the defendant in a suit in 1813 over that property. Three original owners sought recovery of payment on a note. Richard Mather alleged that the payment was due to him from David Vance, one of the decedents with Lincoln and Isaac Bush.

On Sundays, they would travel back to the Big South Fork to attend services at the Separate Baptist congregation. Like other Baptist churches, this church paid attention to the moral and personal relations of members of the congregation. The first preacher Abraham Lincoln heard was the Reverend William Downs, a man of education and great oratory. This church was called Little Mount Church and Downs was its first minister. On the slavery question, Downs was an emancipationist. This preacher might have influenced Thomas and Abraham's views on the subject. [2]

What Lincoln did remember was the Knob Creek place. The Lincoln farm was made up of three fields in a valley surrounded by high hills and deep gorges. He remembered big rain in the hills which would come down the gorges and flood the valley below. On one Saturday afternoon, the other boys were planting a seven acre field with corn seed. Abraham dropped the pumpkin seed, leaving two seeds every other hill and every other row. During the next Sunday morning it rained in the hills, but not in the valley. The water came racing down the gorges and washed out corn and pumpkin seeds, leaving the work to be done all over again. The land was narrow and rich alluvial soiled along main creek and two streams which led into the creek. [3]

The revolutionary generation was spinning its last. The nation was into the fourth presidency of the early group and there was to be only one more. There was a new generation and the beginning of a new issue; this new group was led by Clay, Calhoun, and Webster and the growing issue was slavery. An old issue republican and revolutionary government was fading and would only last until the end of the coming war. It was the final hostility between the mother and the offspring, between the British nation and the American nation, between monarchy and republicanism.

All three of its rising statesmen were nationalists and still young although grave. They were for a war with a still arch enemy. Victory of Republicans over Federalists insured that Britain would be blamed instead of France, although both were the movers of exclusion of American goods from the markets of the other. Indeed, because Britain was also a power on the seas, their actions hurt the nation of the United States more and sure. The new inheritors were young and inexperienced men, but they proved more capable than the older citizens in government. They were sure of themselves and highly ambitious. The motive force was there however. Daring enough to lead their nation into war, they were also self-reliant. One of their number, Henry Clay was accepted as a leader before he became speaker; he was accepted as a speaker even before he entered office. Believing that war would solve their international problems with the British, they did not hesitate to cut the Gordian knot. [4]

Although the Republicans had very large majorities in both Congressional houses, they disagreed among themselves while the Federalists voted as a block on most issues.

Still the regular Republicans who supported Madison could manage a majority when they were not outmaneuvered. The Clintonian Republicans wanted their president to adopt more Federalist policies while the John Randolph of Roanoke's southern agrarians felt that Jefferson and Madison had gone too far in that direction already. A group of senators called the "Invisibles", or Smith faction, wanted Madison to spend money on military preparedness. And then there were the War Hawks.

Clay immediately set out to manage Congress and give a decisive say to his dozen young patriots in the Congress. On the fifth, one day after Congress organized, Madison made his annual speech. He accused Britain of a commercial war and asked Congress to prepare for war. Nothing could please the War Hawks more. Clay and his supporters arranged for the House's packed committee on foreign relations to resolve to prepare for the conflict that James Monroe, secretary of state, said Madison would favor if the British did not redress American complaints by May the first of 1812. The peaceable Madison had moved toward war. Clay got large majorities for House bills to recruit soldiers and spend money for defense.

Not everyone who voted for defense measures was in favor of a war. There were those Republicans who believed that the British would fear war with the United States so much that with the threat of military conflict, they would make concessions. A critic of these Americans charged that they believed there would be no need of using force or even raising troops. Pro-business Republicans voted yea because they favored a strong defense establishment as a policy to protect their interests. Although the Federalists did not want a war with England, they voted for defense measures for two reasons. They wanted preparedness and wanted to protect themselves from a charge of being bought by British money. [5]

The difficulties with Great Britain were leading to war. Although impressment by British captains and patriotic anger over restrictive trade practices inflamed part of the eastern United States, there were distinct reasons for war fever in the land. Because the British had encouraged Indian deprecations in the west, westerners sought to conquer Canada in revenge. There had already been a desire in northern states for the adding of Canada to the American union when it was French and during the American Revolution, but this had subsided with peace. Now that there was a possibility of war with Great Britain once again, there were renewed interest in taking Canada. There were settlers in the West who remembered their interest in acquiring the British land to the north and they were eager once again for the territory.

The westerners were angry; "desperate and angry owning to the lost of overseas markets for their goods, and burning with patriotic anger at British aggressions, particularly impressment." Agrarian depression and the hurt done to the small but important export of produce and grains also drove the westerners to the cause of war. New England shippers were making a profit despite the European conflict and so they did not want further disruption, while the western interests, being producer orientated with export crops of tobacco and cotton, felt bound from a loss of markets. Western farmers needed the income to pay for land, manufactured items, and small luxuries in home and food. From 1808 to 1812, the large Mississippi Valley farmer suffered from depression because of falls in agricultural prices. Some of their costs were even rising. [6]

Westerners and Southerners blamed the depression upon British commercial restrictions in Congress in 1811 and 1812. Congressmen from west of the Appalachians spoke in Congress more of maritime rights than they did of Indian attacks and conquest to the north. Peter B. Porter of western New York spoke on December 6, 1811, on the interruption of direct trade to friendly ports and said that these violations "ought to be resisted by war." Later in that month, Henry Clay stated that "today we are asserting our right to the direct trade--the right to export our cotton, tobacco, and other domestic produce to market." Southerners such as Robert Wright from Maryland and John C. Calhoun from South Carolina said the same thing in Congress that December. In the north even, Adam Boyd of New Jersey said, "you go to war for the right to export our surplus produce--tobacco, cotton, flour, with many other articles." Congressmen received a number of petitions from their states and their districts, telling of tough times in the fall of the prices of such products as cotton. Income was lower than annual costs of family upkeep and there were no funds to pay on mortgages and buy new land. The people blamed the effects of foreign restrictions. [7]

Madison appointed Joel Barlow minister to France in order to persuade Napoleon to treat American trade with more care. He picked Barlow because of the poet's previous standing in France and his history of achieving success in dealing with men of influence. Barlow was very much a man of the world. With his family Joel set sail for France in August of 1811. Once in Paris, he met with French officials, but they were evasive. At this time, Napoleon had been blessed with the birth of a son and busy in a diplomatic war with Russia. Earlier the czar of Russia had opened his ports to an English merchant convoy and Napoleon countered with the seizure of the Duchy of Oldenburg. The duke took refuge in St. Petersburg with his second cousin and brother-in-law Czar Alexander and Alexander closed his ports to French merchants. Barlow was in Paris when Napoleon gave his orders to increase the armies in the east. Bernadotte signed an alliance with Russia on April 5, 1812, and three days later Alexander sent an ultimatum to Napoleon.

Napoleon invaded Russia and found the population gone and the towns burnt to the ground in scorched earth tactics. He lost troops to illness and desertion. They marched far inland, the Russians retreating. On September 7, 1812, was fought the Battle of Borodino in which armies of men lost their lives. Neither army won a clear cut victory, but the Russians retreated after the battle. They could not continue due to the heaviness of their losses. Moscow fell, but the Russians set fire to the city. Alexander would not surrender.

On October 11th, back in Paris, Barlow was told by foreign minister Bassano that Napoleon would met him in Wilna, Poland, to discuss a treaty. While Barlow traveled to Poland, Napoleon faced by winter, began his march back to western Europe. The storms and the Russians took a heavy toll of French and other auxiliary soldiers. Barlow reached Wilna on November 18th and waited until December 5th when he had to flee back to Paris. Meanwhile, Napoleon reached France on December 16th. Two days later, Barlow left Warsaw and took seriously ill, dying on December 24, 1812, at Zarnowisc, a little village near Cracow. The Russian campaign had been a disaster for both Napoleon and Barlow. [8]

In America a year earlier, it was a calm night as the Mississippi flowed through its usual course southward south of St. Louis, when the people were suddenly awakened down to Arkansas Post. The ground shook vigorously at 2:00 AM. It was a major earthquake that December 16, 1811. During the next three months there were two more shocks of major proportions and some 1,800 aftershocks. The people lived in a nightmare for three months in the New Madrid earthquake of 1811-1812. This earthquake was so large and terrible that it altered the geography of the Mississippi besides destroying buildings. Among the effects was the destruction of rich farmland, changed courses of the river, the creation of new swamps and later, the landslides of sizable islands, and an occasional temporary flow of the mighty Mississippi upstream. [9]

The Difficult War: The Era of the War of 1812

While the Americans had been resting from their independence war, the English had viewed the area beyond the Alleghenies as fertile lands whose people never would be able to engaged in foreign commerce. Lord Sheffield wrote a book at the end of the American Revolution on American commerce. The lord was hardly a friend of neutral rights, being one of the fathers of the blockading system. He was noteworthy for his lordly view of a degraded American character and the derogerator of the natural advantages of the United States. Americans felt that he would work to prevent emigration to America, retard population increases, and obstruct American industrialization. Now the West was being developed and the English would have to accept a growing power in Lincoln's lifetime. Large numbers of people were emigrating to the Trans-Allegheny and steamboats were traveling on western waters. This was just the beginning. Sheffield was shortsighted, but the Americans were forward looking, and there was a flow westward; along the line from Ohio to Georgia. [10]

During this period, the people of Georgia were known for their excesses. There were a number of duels; men of all classes drink heavily and gambled much. Profanity and drunkenness marred life. At every assemblage there was a boxing exhibition of sorts. They bet on horse races, cards, and dice. Many were rude and lawless. On the other hand, people were generous and hospitable, courageous, and truthful. They upheld their marriage vows taken when they were young. Laws were strict and religion was respected.

Georgia had been prosperous, but the European wars caused distress with the end of all foreign commerce. There had been a wild speculation, with great debts on the purchase of enslaved persons and land. Cotton was grown in increased amounts and large plantations were carved on the lands of Georgia. Now the United States Bank and its branches called in their loans and bankruptcy was overwhelming the people of the cotton states and territory. In 1808, the legislature of Georgia passed an act for the relief of debtors. One third of the debt was to be paid when due. The rest was to be paid in subsequent intervals. In 1809, the Planters Bank incorporated, but it failed to open. In the next year, a charter was granted for two other banks; one also called the Planters, and the Bank of Augusta. Hamilton's Bank of the United States continued to operate in Georgia. Lotteries were common in Georgia. Money was raised in lotteries for such things as church building, graveyard enclosures, schools and universities, and the poor of Chatham, and the moving of goods and expenses for improving the navigation of rivers.[11]

American influence in Hispanic America was varied during the revolutionary period there. The United States had had its revolution earlier, but Latin Americans did not always see the northern republic as an older brother. Ties were too close to Europe for that. Light at first, American influence increased somewhat as contacts multiplied. In Buenos Aires British influence was paramount, but the able and brilliant Mariano Moreno had read Jefferson's *Notes on Virginia* and admired Washington. Moreno's colleague Manuel Belgrano looked upon Washington as a model and published the "Farewell Address" in Spanish. The junta president Cornelio Saavedra was conservative and never showed the result of any American influence. When diplomat Joel Poinsett was there, he found the government too moderate and headed for Chile where he had hopes of creating a revolutionary sentiment. [12]

Chileans were highly affected by the example of the United State because of the exertions of Joel Poinsett when he was there and more importantly of Camilio Enriquez, newspaper editor and revolutionary, an enthusiast for all things North American. He translated the speeches of Washington, Jefferson, and Madison and wrote visionary romanticism about the struggles of Chileans and the example of the United States.

Poinsett became friends with Enriquez and political leader Jose Miguel Carrera and had great prestige with Chileans until he was ejected by a government which did not want him around.

Influence was strongest in Venezuela and New Granada where many American books and documents were translated. Constant reference was made to the experience and leadership of the United States. Commercial relations were close. The Venezuelan government was modeled largely upon American federalism although the Venezuelan Declaration of Rights was French inspired. The belief that American support would be forthcoming encouraged the Venezuelans to declare their independence in 1811. Bolivar did not want to adopt American federalism and Miranda looked more to Great Britain, but neither controlled affairs then.

Since the Spanish were in control on Mexico, influence from the United States was light there. Griffin wrote that when "rumors of American help reached the Mexican rebels on one occasion there were laudatory comments in their gazette, but when they were disappointed, articles of a very different nature, containing bitter reproaches against the cold-blooded and ambitious aims of the United States also appeared." [13]

Feelings throughout the United States were stirred up by impression principally above all other causes. One would expect New England and New York to favor war since they were most affect by the seizures at sea. They were angered by the action of Britain and France but what ruled their interest was the trade with the British. They did not want war because that would end imports and exports with Britain and give a greater blow to their pocketbooks than the existing situation. Frontier areas were for war as a matter of principles. They were angered by the seizures and impressment at sea. Their patriotic impulses were of foremost importance to them, unimpeded by economic issues.

The South, being without trading interests, could support war as a means of national honor. Years of great cotton ties with Britain were still ahead. Why did America not go to war with France? The Jeffersonian Republicans were in control and more numerous and favoring France and being anti-English, they could overlook the actions of France and put the entire blame on London. Federalists were largely from New England and they were pro-English and anti-France, which meant that they were against a war with Britain. New England was equally adverse to war with France because that would cut off trade between the United States and France. Economic interest ruled New Englanders, while the South and West could appeal to principle. [14]

The key to the causes of the War of 1812 is to be found in the west of the Lincolns. Grievances against Britain on the high seas were the cry of the Americans to be sure, but it was those complaints of westerners which had the most effect. People in New England were not willing to go to war with England over their shipping rights, but the citizens of the west were determined to war against the British for the protection of their frontiers against the pro-British Indians and had the desire for land in Canada. Since the prairies of the west were believed unsuitable, chiefly because the lack of timber for fences, horses, and fuel, the pioneers looked north to Canada for new land.

The settler wore out their land and was always interested in new land for crops and cattle and Canada's land was inviting. Almost all of the vehement War Hawks were from the northwest where they represented a land hungry people. There was much valuable land in the woodlands of the west, but the settlers considered them essential for their use and preferred a mixture of cleared land and woods. They already had that, and eager for more land, an undeveloped Canada interested them. While others might interest themselves in wrongs at the hands of the British, the westerner was out for conquest. The

Indian could instill fear in isolated settlements, but the hunger for land motivated the westerner. American conquest of Canada was the chief cry. [15]

In his success against the Indians, Harrison had captured almost one hundred fuses and rifles. Most of these weapons were new and had been manufactured in England. This information was soon publicized in American newspapers and added to the war cry. Grimly Felix Grundy spoke in the House of Representatives on the matter. For him the war was already underway. There was an alliance of Redcoats and Redskins. In the view of the War Hawks, the battles were begun at Tippecanoe. [16]

Because of the influence of populations, Americans thought Canada to be an easy target. There were fifteen Americans for each Canadian. Being tied down in Europe, the British presumably could not send a large enough force to protect their colony to the north. In addition, French Canadians could not, in the American view, he counted on to be loyal to Britain. Indeed, the Jeffersonian Republicans thought their troops would be welcomed in Canada. Federalists also believed that Canada could be easily conquered, but they considered such a conquest to be unjust. The Canadians, after all, were not to blame for British violations of maritime rights. [17]

North Carolinians supported war because the British had offended their sense of national honor, instead of the usual expansionist or defending of maritime rights that ruled so many of their fellow citizens. People in that state remembered the Revolutionary War and held long lasting resentments toward their mother country. The politicians expressed themselves in various phases. They rejected the need for new lands.

Instead, an invasion of Canada was deemed necessary to bring the enemy to terms. One congressman spoke of the invasion as an offensive tactic and not an end. Others opposed an invasion altogether. Also, many North Carolinians believed the United States had land enough. An editor in Raleigh did not want to spill the blood of their brethren in Canada. Instead of a land war, they wanted a strong navy or another embargo to resolve the differences between the two countries and force Britons to treat the Americans right on the high seas. Few in the state wanted to acquire Florida either.

Since they were not threatened by the Indians, people in the state did not want war because Britain encouraged or armed the Indians. the Indians on the states frontier were friendly Cherokee, settled farmers and ranchers at this time. People did, however, listen to stories and rumors that the Cherokee were getting arms from the British. This talk was groundless. People in the state were not very concerned about trade restriction because the state was an important exporter. Their biggest product was naval stores, whose price had climbed during the war. North Carolina had few merchants and was yet to produce tobacco and cotton on the large scale. Impressment was not an issue in the state since few people in the state sailors. Only a handful of the state's were sailors were foreign born lessening the possibility of conflict even more. [18]

John Henry was Irish born, having come across in the steerage passage of an ship. Steerage was below decks by which the poor traveled in crowded cabins and spent their time during the light above decks in huddled passages. His early years in the United States were spent a Philadelphia grocer and as a natural course of events was naturalized. Current affairs interested Henry and he wrote letters to editors of American newspapers. Next, he began to edit a newspaper of his own. With the growth of the XYZ Affair, it seemed that war was possible with France and he obtained a commission as captain and commanded an artillery detachment on Governor's Island. He did not stagnate but was sent to assist in the construction of the federal arsenal at Harper's Ferry, Virginia. Then as a prank he dislodged "Jefferson's Rock," mentioned in Jefferson's *Notes on Virginia*. It plunged down the hill and caused a furor in the two states of Virginia and Maryland.

When the danger with a French conflict died down, he resigned his commission, there being an possibility of promotion. John Henry took up farming in Vermont. There he wrote newspaper articles attacking republican forms of government. Sir James Craig read them as a part of his intelligence gathering. When Criag learned that the monarchist writer lived just across the border in the United States, he invited him to visit him in Quebec. Henry was polite and talked frequently and Craig paid Henry to agitate among the Federalists of New England and New York to arrange the separation of this area from the rest of the United States. Upon being informed, Lord Liverpool of the British home ministry sanctioned this procedure.

In January of 1809, Craig's secretary Herman W. Ryland gave him a cipher and Craig a letter of instruction. Henry spent the next three years sounding out sentiment and making contacts. He was not successful at accomplishing anything important but went to London in 1811 to put in a claim for 32,000 pounds sterling for his services, a very hefty sum. The British would not pay that amount of money and sent him to Canada where he found that Sir James Craig had died. Abroad ship, Henry met the bogus count Edouard de Crillon, a man guilty of embezzlement of army accounts. De Crillon hid out on the Isle of Wight and then took passage to America. The army account tamperer became friends with the traitor. Henry took his story and they allied to get money. They called upon Massachusetts' governor Elbridge Gerry who sent them to President Madison. De Crillon had Henry's papers and sold them to Monroe for $125,000, but Gallatin would pay only $50,000.

Madison sent the papers to the Congress and the fat was in the fire. The Federalists were fearful at first, but since no names were mentioned could soon rest. De Brillon had escaped with the money and left Henry a non-existing estate in France. The American public was outraged and war was brought one step closer. War was inevitable, but the Henry affair led to a more secure war spirit in the nation in which Great Britain was the enemy. Americans now felt that Great Britain was intent on dividing the Union. Joseph Desha of Kentucky asked if any American could now doubt that Britain could be ousted from the North American continent? [19]

Andrew Jackson treated the need of a passport on the way to Natchez with anger and contempt. He considered this requirement to be a violation of "the rights of the honest American citizen." The agency where a passport was required was on the Natchez Trace, near present day Jackson, Mississippi. There were three families from Georgia in their three wagons with twenty-two slaves along at this agency. He told the deputy there that the measure was illegal. Since America was on the verge of war, he said, the wish of the government should be to strengthen that particular frontier with the best people and good citizens. The Georgians were forced to obtain a passport from the territorial governor, but Jackson himself would not bend and insisted upon going his own way without a passport. The secretary of the territory, acting as governor, offered Jackson a passport, but the general refused. The general would not yield when threatened for not having a passport, but he was not stopped. [20]

Future American senator and statesman, Thomas Hart Benton was born on March 14, 1782, in Orange County, near Hillsbrough, North Carolina. His parents were Colonel Jesse Benton and his wife Anne Gooch of a prominent family in Hanover County, Virginia. Young Thomas' name came from his maternal uncle Colonel Thomas Hart of Lexingron, Virginia, and Thomas Benton was cousin to Lucretia Hart who married Henry

The Difficult War: The Era of the War of 1812

Clay. He was not a relative of Clay as was so often thought and stated in his lifetime. When he was eight young Thomas' father died and left a sizable family of which Thomas Benton was the eldest child. Anne continued to devote herself to her family and passed on her education by reading and observations to the children. Within two years of learning his alphabet, Thomas was reading adult books of history from his father's library. He read the edition of the famous English state trials among other books.

His mother was a pious and religious woman who imported those qualities to Thomas and the other children. She cherished all the virtues including temperance, modesty, decorum, and would not allow a pack of cards in her house. Yankee emigrant Richard Stanford taught him in a North Carolina grammar school and later became a representative in Congress. With these bases, Thomas went to the University of North Carolina in Chapel Hill, but when his mother moved to Tennessee where his father had bought 40,000 acres before he died, Thomas headed there to take charge of the settlement as the eldest in the family. It was on the edge of the wilderness south of Nashville.

Because of the dangers and the need for workers, the Bentons invited other settlers to form a community called Benton Town. The settlers did not have to pay any rent for seven years. Afterward the rent would be moderate. They found a rich earth, fine wood, and sufficient streams. Prospering on the farm, Thomas continued reading. He considered his books of history and geography to be light reading. He tagged law studies heavy reading and it prepared him for a legal career in subsequent years. With this career started he received support and encouragement from the leaders of the state including General Andrew Jackson. [21]

In Tennessee, Thomas studied law and in bad years he stopped farming and taught school. A friend Nicholas Hardeman helped finance Benton's studies. Benton was admitted to the bar in the summer of 1806. He soon had a good practice. He entered politics in 1808 with a long series of articles against the judicial system, complaining of delays, constant concerns with minor judicial organization. Also the judges often got drunk on the job. A reform program was a part of the campaign. Benton wanted a single supreme court meeting in Knoxville and Nashville, alternatively six judicial circuits, and county courts mainly involved with county administration. This attack made him famous and popular. In 1809, he was elected a state senator. In the senate he achieved his program of reform. Further reform, in favor of slaves in the legal court died on the vine. He was to become a captain, major, and then colonel under Jackson in the war. [22]

---

[1] Jackson, Andrew, *The Papers of Andrew Jackson*, Vol. II 1804-1813, Harold D. Moser and Sharon MacPherson eds, Knoxville: University of Tennessee, 1984, pp. 274-276. Quote pp. 274-275.

[2] Warren, *Lincoln's*, pp. 110-113, 239-244.

[3] Booth, *Country*, p. 197.

[4] Von Holst, *Calhoun*, pp. 12-15.

[5] Hickey, *War of 1812*, pp. 29-33.

[6] Horseman, Reginald, "Western War Aims, 1811-1812," *Indiana Magazine of History*, III No. 1 (March 1957), pp. 4-6. Quote on p. 4.

[7] *Ibid.*, pp. 6-9 (Quotes on p. 6); Pratt, Julius W.A., *History of United States Foreign Policy*, Englewood Cliffs, NJ: Prentice Hall, 1955, p. 125.

[8] *Dictionary of American Biography*, I, 612; Castelot, Andre, *Napoleon*, New York: Harper & Row, 1971, pp. 403-447.

[9] Vitanen, Waynes, "The Winter the Mississippi Ran Backwards: Early Kentuckians Report the New Madrid, Missouri Earthquake of 1811-12," *Register of the Kentucky Historical Society*, LXXI No. 1 (January 1973), pp. 51-52.

[10] *Niles Weekly Register*, September 7, 1811, pp. 9-10.

[11]Smith, George Gillman, *The Story of Georgia and the Georgia People, 1732 to 1860*, 2d ed. 1901, Reprint Baltimore: Genealogical, 1968, pp. 235-238, 247.

[12]Griffin, pp. 57-60; Wait, Eugene M., *"Warriors and Revolutionaries"* MS book.

[13]Griffin, pp. 60-68.

[14]Lewis, Howard T., "A Re-Analysis of the Causes of the War of 1812," Part One, *Americana (American Historical Magazine), VI (1911), pp. 506-516.*

[15]Coleman, Christopher B., "The Ohio Valley in the Preliminaries of the War of 1812," *Mississippi Valley Historical Review*, VII (1920), pp. 39-50; Hacker, Louis Morton, "Western Land Hunger and the War of 1812: A Conjector," Mississippi Historical Review, *X (1924), pp. 365-395.*

[16]Coit, *Calhoun*, p. 73.

[17]Hickey, *War of 1812*, pp. 72-75.

[18]Lemmon, Sarah McCulloh, *Frustrated Patriots: North Carolina and the War of 1812*, Chapel Hill, NC: University of North Carolina Press, 1973, pp. 6-12.

[19]Tucker, *Poltroons and Patriots*, pp. 71-77.

[20]Jackson, *Papers*, II, 277-279.

[21]Benton, Thomas Hart, *Thirty Years View, or, A History of the American Government for Thirty Years, from 1820 to 1850*, New York: D. Appleton, 1856, (1968 reprint, I, i-iii; Smith, Elbert B., *Magnificent Missourian: The Life of Thomas Hart Benton*, 1958, pp. 13-23.

[22]Smith, *Magnificent*, pp. 24-29, 33-37.

CHAPTER X

THE ROAD TO WAR

The new governor of Virginia, elected in January of 1812, was concerned about the approaching conflict and his states' lack of preparation for defense. Governor James Barbour was a man of great legislative experience in the Virginia assembly and had been four times speaker of the House of Delegates. He had little executive experience, but rose to the occasion. At the time the powers of the governorship were very limited. Barbour's chief aim was to widen those powers and protect the state in the approaching war he foresaw. The demands of state overrode his governmental philosophy of limited powers, held since childhood. Like Jefferson earlier, Barbour had to meet reality and modify his views. His father had been an Orange county planter and James was born into the gentry. The elder Barbour met economic difficulty and James had to forego a college education. However, he studied law and rapidly rose to enter the legislature in 1798. A success there, led his fellow legislators to make him governor after the death of the then governor in a Richmond theater fire.

Barbour worked to meet the challenges as best he could. Since he could not assume powers which did not belong to the governorship, he tried to change the law in order to increase the powers of his office through constitutional change. In his years in office, Barbour tried to persuade the legislature to broaden executive powers. He used his office to persuade others to take such action as he deemed prudent to protect Virginia.

One of his chief problems was to deal with the militia system. His experience as captain of the Orange militia had convinced him that America could not rely upon their state militia forces for protection. Still he was in a hurry for the declaration of war against Britain. The United States was not strong enough for a war as event were to soon show in the difficult war. Barbour must have known this. Of course, he was determined to improve the Virginia militia for a time when the English might land on the coast of Virginia. He did have self-confidence, persistence and energy.

Since the attack on the *Chesapeake* in 1807, Barbour had been in favor of war. He did not say anything at the time because of his loyalty to Jefferson and then Madison. Shortly after his election, Barbour has espoused war and talked about the insults heaped upon the United States by perfidious Albion. America had tolerated these for long enough, he said in March. We must vindicate national honor. Barbour told his legislature. He had already asked for emergency powers. The assemblymen responded only by authorizing him to buy lead and gunpowder for the militia. There were to be no special powers.[1]

In Canada, Major General Isaac Brock felt anxiety concerning the lack of readiness of his British and militia forces for a war he saw the Americans preparing for to the south across the border of the lakes. He informed Sir George Prevost, New York born major general in the British army and his wife, of the needs of his command. Prevost had been a governor (civil and military in succession) of St. Lucia and governor of Dominica, two British islands in the West Indies. Three months earlier, London put him in command of all the forces in British Canada. Brock had a long military career behind him and was a native of the British island of Guernsey between Great Britain and France.

Brock found the military forces inadequate to their mission of defending a long frontier. His key was Amherstburg as a center for an offensive action which would be needed to gain co-operation from the Indians on both side of the border in Amherstburg's vicinity. Their example would bring support from the many tribes along the Missouri River. All were already hostile to the Americans. Detroit would be a difficult objective because the Americans had plenty of time to make it formidable. Already the fort was too strong to assault, and they needed mortars if they were to bombard it in a siege. Hull also had enough arms, according to Brock's sources.

Delay benefited the Americans who were raising six companies of Rangers to overawe the Indians and collecting regulars to reinforce Detroit. Indians were important to the King's army and the officers must be free to provide ammunition to them if the Empire was to keep the country from falling into the hands of the Americans. The British had a certain advantage. While they worked to gain warriors for battles, the American agents and officers were limited to convincing the Indians to be neutral. American policy forbade them to recruit or accept Indian volunteers into the American forces.

The Americans had less than one hundred regulars at Detroit; the British had the same numbers in the fort at Amherstburg. However, the British had command of Lake Erie with their two armed ships. This would have to be met by the Americans. American troops, supplies, and communications from Fort Detroit would have to come overland through Indian territory. But what was even worse, they must build roads for passage of men and supplies. It was most necessary to send men to Detroit for its defense. Without them and control of the lake to the east of Detroit, the Northwest would fall to the British. Hull did not hesitate to point this out to Washington. [2]

President Madison appointed Henry Dearborn and Thomas Pinckney major-generals in that order. Neither men had major service in the war, but they did have some military service in the Revolutionary War. Dearborn was the head of the customhouse of Boston, having retired in 1809 from the Jeffersonian cabinet. He and Pinckney were both in their early sixties. In the war for independence Dearborn rose to become deputy quartermaster-general in 1781. After the war, he became colonel of a New Hampshire regiment. Pinckney took part in the guerrilla actions of Marion and Sumter and as aide to General Gates in the South. After diplomatic duties, Pinckney served in Congress from 1797 to 1801. He had been a Federalist. [3]

At the time of the spring of 1812, the Cherokee Major Ridge was a set proponent of civilization and friend of the Americans. He was a natural ally of the Americans. While at the council which the Cherokee called, the chiefs in general were neutral. The Ridge with John Lowrey and John Walker joined the forces to offer their agent, Colonel Meigs, Cherokee tribesmen to fight by the American side against the British. Meigs could not authorize this, but wrote the secretary of war about the offer, suggesting that it was a good idea.

The Cherokees might be able to furnish infantry and cavalry and make a real contribution. They were good horsemen according to Meigs who was in a position to know. The secretary of war had his doubts. General Andrew Jackson thought he could use Cherokee scouts to guide his army to the Creek towns. Should a method be devised to distinguish Cherokee from Creek, he would like to him them in his regiment in the field. The secretary of war was not favorable, fearing the consequence of setting one tribe against the other. [4]

On March 7, 1812, in the rough and rugged state of Tennessee, near the Cumberland River, at his Hermitage plantation outside of Nashville, Andrew Jackson issued a call for volunteers. Beginning with the statement that their government had yielded to the nation's impulse, he claimed that war was near with Great Britain. Because they were free men and not English slaves, French conscripts, or frozen Russian peasants, the men of the frontier must respond to the invitation for 50,000 volunteers. Americans had clamored for war and must act to protect their maritime rights. He did not mention any desire to annex Canada, but did call for an army to invade Canada and carry their flag to the Heights of Abraham. Unsaid was that there was all the more need for western response due to the eastern opposition to the war. Jackson as a Republican and a westerner favored France and Napoleon and was eager to fight against the British. He was clearly angered over British supplying of the Indians.

The future president offered Madison his services and his militia division, but he had no orders until his friend Governor William Blount managed to enlist his talent in spite of disagreement with Jackson and his unpopularity with the war department. Secretary John Armstrong found an opportunity to send Jackson back to Nashville. The general insisted on taking his men. On the way back from Natchez through the wilderness he showed such toughness that one of the soldiers called him tough on hickory, the toughest that he knew. Andrew liked the word and soon he was known as "Old Hickory." The name appealed to others and lasted his lifetime and beyond. [5]

John Adams had a singular opinion for a Federalist leader, supposedly devoted to England. The ex-president was a practical man and a moderate in public endeavor. As president in the closing years of the eighteenth century, he had avoided war with France when most Americans were clamoring for action. He preferred peace, but by March 11, 1812, Adams was certain that war with Great Britain was certain and unlike most New Englanders, he wanted to win this one if it was to be war. Because of this world view, Adams secretly supported the Republican , the incumbent, for the governorship of Massachusetts. Federalist candidate Caleb Strong, who won the election months later, opposed a war against Britain and would not cooperate for victory. Gerry hated neither nation.

Adams did not always agree with Jefferson, or even Washington, but he national government was as he said, their only rock of safety against the storm. Madison was coming around to more and more of Adams' views. Overall, Adams wished more generosity and liberalism in existing government. It would not do to release these views and Benjamin Waterhouse knew when to keep his mouth shut and follow the wishes of Adams to secrecy. Indeed, at the time, there would have been an uproar should the ex-president from Massachusetts let his views be known. Adams was right when he said this series of opinions would hurt Gerry in his election bid for governor. Opinions of Madison and Adams were coming closer to verging. [6]

The war movement gathered strength and its call could well have been Calhoun's speech in which he said that he only knew "if one principle to make a nation great, to produce in this country not the form but real spirit of union, and this is to protect every citizen in the lawful pursuit of his business." Speaker Henry Clay and his henchmen managed to pass, by narrow margins bills to increase the size of the army, raise taxes, and authorize loans. However he failed to produce a larger navy by vote in Congress. At the end of March of 1812, the War Hawks made a demand for war, but Madison compromised with a ninety-day embargo. In mid-April Madison's *National Intelligencer* preached war. Madison was barely moved because he knew that his country was still not prepared. Few people were interested in being soldiers for any amount of time. If glory could not be had immediately, they were not interested. [7] [8]

In March, General George Mathews of Georgia marched into northeast Florida with some seventy or eighty men. Once there, he declared that there was the beginnings of a rebellion in Florida. Hoping to gain support from Anglo-Americans there and from Madison in Washington, Mathews organized a provisional government. He moved against Spanish Castillo de San Marcos, but the commander there would not surrender. Unable to take the fort, he withdrew and was followed by Spanish soldiers and Seminole Indians who were ready for battle. He had not gained local support and Congress repudiated the action. Madison followed suit. Mathews stayed on the northern borders for a year and then withdrew. He had failed to take Florida and the Spanish could rest awhile and tend to their private pursuits and government.[9]

On April 1, 1812, James Madison recommended an embargo of Great Britain to Congress. Representative Felix Grundy understood it, he said, to be "a war measure, and it was meant that it should directly tend for war." Calhoun declared "its manifest propriety as a prelude to war." Congressmen were generally favorable and on April 4th, they passed a bill or an embargo of all ships for sixty days. Madison took the next step, by leaving it up to Congress with its sole power to declare war. The Committee on Foreign Affairs was to advise war later in the year. [10]

Driven by interest and ideology, the Federalists of New England strongly opposed the foreign policy of the Republicans. In case of war with Great Britain, an already crippled economy would become worse. The British would devastate the maritime enterprises with their control of the seas. Already the Yankees of the northeast had suffered greatly because of the embargoes and British seizures. The situation would be worst in case of an all-out war. Seamen and laborers would be thrown out of work, merchants would lose, and the farmer would not be able to market his production. They would suffer impressment and orders in council gladly to avoid the destruction of the economy. While impressment was the rallying cry of the country, the Yankees were more realistic. Aware of the problems of his region, he knew what was in store for him in a war.

Politically, they had opposed the Republicans as rabble who endangered the country with their devilish ideologies born in the French Revolution or so they thought. Federalist believed that America would prosper if it was ruled by the propertied and hard working Christian gentry of their party. God would reward those who feared him and were virtuous like they were. They wanted a civilized and cultural republic; a nation of good people. Republicans would lead the nation to mob rule and violence. Should they continue to rule there would be an economic collapse.

To the Federalist, the Southern Democrat was a hypocrite with his egalitarian talk and his slaveholding fact. They accused the Republican of sacrificing national interests to that of party. That they were doing the same did not occur to them. Still they were most apprehensive over the prospects of war. They asked themselves why the war was to be against Great Britain and not France, which had done damage to American shipping also.

The Federalists wanted peace and especially did not wish an invasion of Canada which some were talking about. [11]

There was a measure of hope and a measure of hopefulness by April 14th. It looked possible or indeed favorable that France would establish a new policy for freedom of the seas. The pro-French attitude of the Republicans made them optimistic about France and Henry Clay shared in this as an important member of the ruling party. There was no hope about the achievement of honorable accommodation with Great Britain. Because of this situation, Clay wanted war with the island government. Clay wrote in the leading Washington newspaper that there was no reason for delay and too late to further discuss the origins of the crisis. "It exists; and it is by often and manly war only that we can get through it with honor and advantage to the country. Our ways are great; our cause is just; and if we are decided and firm, success is inevitable."

Clay brushed aside the argument that the United States was not prepared for war. This was a legitimate event, but to the Speaker it was an idle objection and for the timid and not the brave. However, he then wrote that American preparations were adequate. Events were to prove Clay wrong. He did not fear an invasion by England on American soil. This was absurd he said because France was still a threat and English troops had so many men tied down for the defense of Sicily, India, Ireland, and the West Indies. They would not attack from Canada with its meager population of 300,000; indeed, Canada was vulnerable and would not incite the Indian out of fear of retaliation. Although the American coast was exposed, the militia could handle any raids by British marines. fortifications would prevent ships of war from attack. America must act or face contempt from the international community.

Clay was much too optimistic as were most men inclined to war in almost all wars in history. Going into war, everyone expected easy victories and Clay was no exception. France was to disappoint Clay in the months ahead. Still, he wished a war against England alone because they would continue to do harm, while French actions were in the past. Napoleon had limited ships and could not hit the Americans where it hurt. Once Americans silenced Great Britain, we could turn to give the French reprisals for their aggressions. [12]

At this time in Virginia, that state's governor made an inspection tour. Barbour had just galvanized the Tidewater militia and ordered up troops as the state's quota for President Madison. He called for special musters for drilling. In this effort he was supported by his council which the governor dominated. Beginning on April 21, 1812, James Barbour inspected the defenses of the eastern counties. He talked to the local leaders and reviewed their troops. He appealed to patriots to prepare for war. Next, he returned to Richmond and days later informed Secretary of War William Eustis of what he learned. Eustis did not act on the Virginian governor's recommendations. Later, at a big rally he presided and was encouraged by its war resolutions. The gathering took place on May 30th. [13]

In Illinois Territory, there were various Indian troubles. Some settlers were killed and property stolen. The Kickapoo raided and the O'Neal family were massacred. Potawatomi warriors swept down upon farms on the Wabash. Fourteen whites lost their lives there on this raid. Edwards acted to protect the settlers, but many of them fled to the east. The frontier was not a safe place, but such events hindered but did not stop the migration west. The coming war proved to be limiting especially and the West was one of the major battlefields of the war. [14]

A party of Creeks raided into Humphreys County, Tennessee, on May 12, 1812, and killed six whites. Five of the six were children and one was a man living at the Crawly home. The Indians carried Martha Crawly, wife of riverboatman John Crawley, into captivity. General Thomas Johnson in the 2d Division arrived at Humphreys Court House soon after this and learned about the murders. He wasted no time and sent out a small detachment to the scene of the massacre and sent scouts to cross the Duck River. Because of the scarcity of provisions, he discharged his foot soldiers and those without good horses. Then he set out with 270 veterans well mounted through the wilderness, but found nothing. James Barefield shot one Indian, but Johnson found little else. When he returned, he learned from Mrs. Manley, who was wounded and lost three children, that there were only five Indians who killed the whites.

General Andrew Jackson returned to Tennessee from Georgia and wrote his regret "that General Johnson at the head of 500 men was near this place where the horrid scene was acted, and did not either send a detachment in pursuit or follow the trail of these marauders, with his whole force even to their towns." They had thus far escaped punishment which was intolerable to a man of Jackson's fire, the American frontier must be protected. He believed that the Creeks were urged on "by British agents and tools, the sooner they can be attacked, the less will be their resistance, and the fewer will be the nations or tribes that we will have to war with." He would march into the Creek nation and demand the murderers at the point of the bayonet.

The threat would be to burn down their towns. He only needed the orders of Willie Blount, the governor of Tennessee. The militia burned for revenge. The Cherokees were informing the whites that "the Creeks were making every preparation for war" and they would help the pioneers attack the Creek if the settlers were to show a quick spirit of revenge. He believed that he could raise 2,500 volunteers, enough to suppress the Creeks. Later the captive Mrs. Crawley escaped from her Creek captors and the Creek apprehended and execute the natives of their tribe who had committed the massacre.

Governor Willie Blount had no confidence in the friendship of the Cherokees. Indians could not be trusted. He was to be proved wrong. While the whites were fighting the Creeks, the half Cherokee leaders John Lowry and John Walker provided troops and intelligence to the militia troops. Lowry owned a ferry across the Tennessee River and raised nearly 400 Cherokee warriors to fight under General Jackson. Blount knew these two men as clever men, but still Indians in part and would play into each others' hands. Because Lowry and Walker lived among the Indians, they would be subject to death by Indian hands, if they followed the wrong opinion. Also, there was a strong British party within the Cherokee nation. even the Chickasaw had a British party, although small. The Choctaws also had a British party and this was strong among the Creeks. According to Blunt the American party existed in the neighborhood of the Agency house and those Indians there who benefited from the liberality of the United States. The whites on the frontier must take care of themselves against such British power because Congress will have enough to take care of elsewhere.

In reply in a letter dated June 17, 1812, Jackson expressed his concurrences about the trustworthiness of the Indians, but believed that they should enlist one tribe against the other in a division against Indian unity. Should the Cherokee go to war on the American side, Jackson wrote, they will be obliged to a friendship with the whites for their self-preservation out of fear. He suggested the policy of enlisting Lowry, Walker, and Major Ridge in the American service, to provide scouts and on deceptive marches. Meanwhile Jackson had the militia in readiness and could move in three days some 2,500 volunteers

The Difficult War: The Era of the War of 1812   89

against the Creeks and their alliance with the Prophet. Blount had recommended one company of mounted infantry in each regiment and Jackson said he would be able to comply. Jackson suggested to Blount in July to deliver "a speedy stroke against the Creeks." Given the spirit of the settlers, there would be an immediate move. [15]

In Nashville, Tennessee, a militia force under General Johnson prepared to start out on an expedition against the Sandy River tribe of Indians. He had about 800 men all together. The force did not have the best of arms, but they were better armed than any other militia unit the informant had yet seen. There were rumors that Tecumseh was with them and was hoping for them to advance to battle because the Indian chief was confident of victory. Also he was supposed to have 600 warriors from the Shawnee, Wyandot, Creek, and Cherokee Indian nations. Johnson and his men would have to travel a mere 160 miles to find the Indian town. [16]

On May 18, 1812, the Republicans in the Senate and House of Representatives met in caucus to nominate Madison as president for the second time. They were united and no other person was considered. They voted by ballot and when they were counted, everyone was for Madison. However they were not allowed to go into the campaign undivided. There were Republicans who followed DeWitt Clinton of New York and he was to gather their votes in the election along with the united vote of the Federalists. Clinton wooed the Federalists but made no promise that has survived if any. They wanted to defeat Madison and Clinton was his opponent; they did not have a strong candidate among themselves and their coalition with Clinton had a good chance of defeating Madison. Indeed the vote in November was to be very close. They could not have come nearly that close if they ran one of their own. Because they had realized this, Clinton was their man.

The Clintonians were in almost complete control of New York state and city. Leader George Clinton had recently died, leaving the power in the hands of his relative and fellow leader DeWitt. As one of the most populous states at this time, it was a good base. His alliance with the Federalists would get a block of New England and New York plus hopefully other states; perhaps South Carolina too because it was the only Southern state with large numbers of Federalists, or so it could be hoped.

Days later after the nomination of Madison, the politicians of New York met and announced the candidacy of Clinton, George's nephew as president against Madison with whom he had definitely broken. Many of Clinton's political enemies now saw him as a great man. His support increased. All those who wanted Madison out, joined the band wagon. Later Christopher Gore wrote Rufus King that until Clinton was announced as a presidential candidate he had never heard anyone speak in his support. Since the head not heard but a few who did not extol his character; wanting the imbecile as they called Madison retired. For them the president's measures were ruinous.

Until mid-September the Federalists were in a quandary. They did not have a candidate and had not yet officially declared for Clinton. They met for three days in a secret conference. The chief hope of the Federalists was that Clinton would make peace with the British. This was the strongest suit the man had with the Federalists. Even though Rufus King was unfriendly to Clinton, he recognized that the political leaders of his party were in favor of him as president. Still they did not make an outright announcement but left the conference with the understanding that Federalists would vote for Clinton.

They swallowed the Clintonian position that it would not do to speak too loudly about peace, since it would alienate friends from the war party who would vote for

Clinton. He would have to straddle the issue. They realized this as good politicians and when the time came voted for him. Clinton, although in a final opposition to Madison, would not also attack him head-on, a stand for gaining votes from those who did not hate Madison.

The editor of the *Aurora* wrote an editorial in attack on the Federalists and their position. He did not think their quiet allegiance to Clinton was creditable to their reputation. He menaced no words. As a party, the Federalists was now, "by its own admission and unsought confession a mere remnant hanging on the skirts of the party two which it has been opposed--clinging to the very men who have been most conspicuous in opposition to them as a party, and thereby confessing the justice of all the imputations heretofore laid to them."

This was unfair, because the Federalists had joined Clinton because of their interest in peace and inability to field a strong candidate and not because of a denial of all their previous values. They accepted a half-loaf as better than no loaf at all. That was the long and short of it. There was no way they could improve on this. And it almost worked; Madison was to be saved only by his friends the voters of Pennsylvania, who if they voted for Clinton would have swept DeWitt into office. [17]

On May 20, 1812, General Wade Hampton took as his aide Captain Scott to the war front before Canada. They traveled by ship from New Orleans to Washington. Storms at sea prolonged the voyage and it took a full month. Once there, they knew that the war had been declared and that Scott had been promoted to lieutenant colonel. This promotion was at least partly a result of the efforts of Senator William Giles. He now had new duties in the 2d Artillery in Philadelphia to help his colonel recruit enough men to man the unit. When Scott learned of events on the Niagara frontier, he petitioned Secretary of War William Eustis to be allowed to take two companies to Buffalo. [18]

The second child of amiable parents in England, born on February 7, 1812, Charles Dickens, who was to enthrall America, came into the fascinating world shortly after his mother got home from a dance in which she was a participant. His father was the son of a footman turned butler and a housemaid turned housekeeper, whose master saw to it that John was educated and found for him a place as a clerk in the Navy Department. The Dickens had lived beyond their humble means throughout a life of rising income and even greater expectations.

Charles had a happy childhood although he was sickly. While others played games, he read books but the varied people he met later appeared in his novels as characters. Dickens' education was cut short, but he learned from his readings and observations. Finally his father was imprisoned for debt and Charles had to pawn the furniture for the support of his family. Charles got a job in a warehouse where a man named Bob Fagin befriended him. Since much of his early life was interesting and he used the experiences in his novels, he received a better background in writing than if the had gone to college which was beyond his social status. John Dickens was released from debtor's prison when he inherited about L 250 and his brother paid for his release. Shortly Charles lost his job and his father was rehired, on pension, and the young Dickens got a job as a parliamentary reporter for a newspaper, a position at which he excelled. In time, Dickens was to be a literary sensation in the United States, leading all others. [19]

---

[1]Lowery, Charles D., *James Barbour, A Jeffersonian Republican*, University, Ala: University of Alabama Press, 1934, pp. 2-30, 36, 48, 50-63, 66-83.

[2]Cruikshank, *Documents*, pp. 4 n. 2, 9 n. 3, and 16-17, 19-20.

[3]Adams, Madison, *p. 492*.

[4]Wilkins, pp. 60-61.

[5]James, Marquis, *The Life of Andrew Jackson*, Indianapolis: Bobbs-Merrill, 1938, pp. 141-150.

[6]*The Annals of America*, IV, 311-313.

[7]Capers, *Calhoun*, pp. 31-32. Quote on p. 31.

[8]Harrison, "Clay, Henry," p. 111. Quote on p. 111.

[9]Jarvis, Eric, "Florida," Heidler & Heidler, *Encyclopedia*, pp. 187-188.

[10]Von Holst, *Calhoun*, pp. 20-22. Quote on pp. 20-21.

[11]Dudley, *Naval War*, pp. 68-72.

[12]Clay, Henry, *The Papers of Henry Clay*, James F. Hopkins ed., Volume I: *The Rising Statesman, 1797-1814*, Lexington, Ky: University of Kentucky Press, 1959-, 645-648, 674-675. Quote on p 645.

[13]Lowery, *Barbour*, pp. 67-68.

[14]Holden, Robert J., "Illinois Territory," Heidler & Heidler, *Encyclopedia*, p. 251.

[15]Jackson, *Papers*, II, 297-312 and 316, n. 4. Quotes on pp 300, 307.

[16]*Kentucky Gazette*, May 26, 1812, p. 3.

[17]Lynch, *Fifty Years*, pp. 224-229.

[18]Eisenhower, *Agent*, pp. 26-28.

[19]Pearson, Hesketh, *Dickens: His Character, Comedy, and Career*, New York: Harper, 1949, passim; Manowitz, Wolf, *Dickens of London*, New York: Macmillan, 1976, pp. 8-26.

CHAPTER XI

WAR

John Randolph of Roanoke wrote his constituents that the United States was about to join France against England. He was wholly opposed to Bonaparte and stated that Napoleon's war was a war directed "against the liberties and the happiness of mankind; it is a war in which the whole human race are the victims to gratify the pride and lust of power of a single individual. I beseech you, put it to your bosoms how far it becomes you as freemen, as Christians, to give your aid and sanction to this impious and bloody war against your brethren of the human family.

Randolph asked them to answer if they were willing to become allies, the virtual allies of Napoleon. Would his Virginians be willing in order for the North to have Canada and submit to that overgrowing system of taxations which the European laborer gives up his supper to. He tried to influence them by threatened the future as being one given over to military dictatorship. It was this danger that he wished to induce them to work against the war.

Even if the United States won Canada would it benefit them any. Would it make them freer or more secure, richer or happier? Was it a boon for them to joined in an international warfare to be against the liberties of man in the other hemisphere. Would they jeopardize their own ? Would they abandon the lucrative trade with Great Britain, Spain, Portugal and their colonies for a license trade with France? It was against that commerce which gave them markets for their tobacco, grain, flour, and cotton, already denied a market in France. [1]

On the other side of the coin was one historian's view that the "War of 1812 resulted from the unsuccessful efforts of the United States to maintain its interests and its honor in a world divided into two armed camps." In previous times, Washington, Adams, and Jefferson had trouble with the two warring powers bent on mutual destruction and now it was Madison's turn. Madison had acquired Jeffersonian policies and tried to avert conflict with diplomatic negotiation and economic coercion. That policy had been a abject failure and Madison with one last try had finally been forced to abandon the policy. Britons impressed more sailors and boarded more ships. There was no end to this and the War Hawks had finally forced military action to protest and remedy. Madison had to give away. [2]

Feeling was strong on both sides. The Americans and the British were long at odds. Many in Britain felt it was incredible that their ex-colonies were now free and independent. The Americans had been so disunited before, and these Britishers believed that mob rule would soon bring it down. Those who like Charles James Fox looked at the new experiment with hopes were in the minority.. The majority saw in Britain tyranny and corruption. They believed America was an example of how freedom would work elsewhere. Britain should follow the American way. There was much to admire in Great Britain, but only in New England was there firm support for the mother country. The minority in England was for a close alliance between Britain and the United States, but the majority believed that close ties with America would lead to competition and national decline at home. [3]

In America, there was a group of waverers in the Republican party. One historian analyses one in particular. Hugh Nelson was elected in 1811 and followed John Randolph whose innate honesty impressed him. In his maiden speech he used all the usual anti-war arguments. Nelson said a war would centralize the government and strength the executive in comparison to the legislature. It would add new taxes, armies, and navies. There would be no more republican simplicity, and further more would subvert the Constitution.

Principle came above economics. "I care not for the prices of cotton and tobacco as compared with the Constitution." An invasion of Canada would not enforce our rights., Only a great maritime force would do that, but the United States could not raise and support such a navy. However the country should prepare for any eventuality. Unless Great Britain backed down, there would be no alternative to war. "I shall vote for the increase of the regular force to go hand in hand with my friends, even in a war, if necessary and just." [4]

Talk had run out soon after this. Presidential patience was fully at an end, and on June 1, 1812, Madison turned over to Congress the decision on war or peace. He did not directly ask for war, but certainly he must have been sure that Congress would declare war, since he wrote, he was happy in the assurance that the decision would be the in keeping with the councils of a virtuous, a free, and a powerful nation. Congressmen noted Madisonian views of international events in the British violations of the American flag and the laws of nations. Americans seized on the high seas had been literally exiled and subject to harsh discipline on foreign ships. Britain had violated American territorial waters and plundered American ships on the high seas. Madison noted also the British blockade. They ignored neutral rights and tried to subvert the American government and dismember a happy Union. Britain was warring against the United States, Madison told Congress. [5]

The *Hornet* had recently arrived in late May with no concessions from London. There could be no time for delay. The War Hawks then put a declaration of war through the House in days. The Senate was slower. They passed the measure on the 17th, the president signed it on the 18th, and announced it on the 19th. Madison's indictment had arraigned the English nation for impressment, violations of American coastal waters, illegal blockade, subversion, and an evil influence over Northwestern Indians. Official war was in effect on June 19th, but on the first of June, when Madison sent his message, his first army began its march. [6]

The grand plan for the war included invasion routes up the Lake Champlain Valley and at Sackett's Harbor, Niagara, and Detroit. Detroit was a most strategic point, guarding the West from the British and Indians. Madison sent William Hull with a force of four regiments and a troop of Ohio dragoons or sixteen hundred effective men to Detroit. This army began its march on June 1, 1812, and cut its way through the forests, building bridges and constructing causeways. British officials in Canada were surprised at its rapid movement. Thirty days after starting, Hull and his main units reached the

Miami, or Maumee River. On that same day news of the war vote of Congress reached Malden. [7]

A British view drawn forth by the Liberals as opposed the Tories appeared in the *London Statesman* on June 10, 1812. When the Tories stated that the United States had nothing to gain from the impending war with England, the Whigs wrote that it could be equally correct to say that England had nothing to gain, and much to lose. Although America lacked a strong navy, it had a hundred thousand "as good seamen as any in the world, all of whom would be actively employed against our trade on every part at the ocean in their fast-sailing ships-of-war, many of which will be able to cope with our small cruisers; and they will be found to be sweeping the West Indies seas, and even carrying desolation with the chops of the channel." The editor referred the British reader of what happened in the previous war with America. They could do more at sea than the French. [8]

About mid-June of 1812, a group of thirty Kickapoos, Winnebagoes, and Shawnee arrived at Fort Harrison to see Governor William Henry Harrison, who was at Vincennes. These natives sent him a speech emphasizing their friendship towards the United States and pleading for corn which they could take to their families who were on the verge of starvation. They said that twenty Potawatomies were marching through the forests for the Kashaskias road, determined to kill all Americans which they could. Three braves had passed through their village.

Harrison replied that they lacked sincerity. After all, they had allowed the braves to pass when with their seven hundred braves, they could have stopped them. They would not get any American assistance until they captured this small war party and turn them over to the American authorities in the territory. Harrison then informed Colonel Russell so the colonel would intercept this hostile party with a detachment of rangers. He wrote the secretary of war on July 7th that he thought the needed Indians had made up the story of the marauders to gain support for their suffering families in their limited precincts. The warriors in the camp would not leave their families unprotected to attack Vincennes or join Brook's army. [9]

On June 18, 1812, the House of Representatives had voted on the resolution for war. The vote was for the war by 79 to 47 with 14 absentees. In the Senate vote was 19 to 13. This was not overwhelming and it would not have been passed if Madison had not pressured 34 congressmen to vote for the bill. Many of these said that the war was undertaken to conquer Canada and predicted heavy losses and higher taxes. Federalists feared a British naval descent on coastal towns and maritime vessels. John Adams had said that the war would result in dangers with the general more popular than the president and the army more powerful than the Congress. [10]

It was mid-afternoon on a hot day of June 18th when Madison signed his name to the engrossed resolution. America was officially at war. Two days hard riding on horses brought the news to New York, four days later the word had spread to Boston, and six plus days it was known in interior Lexington, Kentucky. Lexington was one of the few places prepared for the event. Recruiters had been working there for weeks. The home of Clay, the young city was expecting it.

A certain Billy Phillips had already left Washington and was to report the news to Nashville, Tennessee, on the night of June 21st even before he knew for sure that war was declared. He found that that capital of the state was also raising troops under the auspices of Andrew Jackson, a most fiery citizen who was to become president. Another, Mr. Cozens, had announced a schedule before the feat of reaching New Orleans in twelve days, an average of 125 miles daily. Ready now he was underway with the signature still wet on the parchment and made his record to the cheers of prowar Kentuckians in New Orleans. Meanwhile, Madison had made the rounds of his departments to rally the bureaucrats at a time when criticism of the war proclamation was high and furious in the nation at large. [11]

Among the leading senators who delayed the passage of the declaration was John Pope of Kentucky. Pope was against the act and voted against it. When the news of the declaration reached Kentucky, the people celebrated. Learning also of the actions of Pope, the people there were arranged against him. To them, he was a traitor. Mobs, in the towns of Nicholasville and Mount Sterling, burned him in effigy. Elsewhere in the state, they denounced the senator. At the time they made great preparations to secure the volunteering of the ten regiments or 5,500 troops that were their quota. [12]

With the arrival of war there were a number of things to decide and do in the department of ships. One decision involved what strategy to agree upon. Navy secretary Paul Hamilton was for a defensive policy given the weakness of the American navy and the shortage of supplies and men. Madison favored the ideas of the more aggressive captains, believing lost ships could always be replaced. How they should be used on the offensive was another question. Commodore John Rodgers wanted to make attacks on selective shipping lanes. One of his ideas was to make a mass descent upon his East India convoys on occasion. He would keep the enemy on the defensive. Given its small size, the American navy should keep moving. Because of its closeness to the West Indies, Charleston was the best port from which to operate.

Commodore Stephen Decatur would have the ships stock up with provisions and make long voyages single or in pairs to attack at will. By this means the United States would not lose the major part of its fleet in any single sea battle or be caught in port so easily. Decatur favored northern and middle ports from which to operate.

Naval stations were short of supplies. Their commanders would ask the secretary of the navy for this and that necessity, and he would often pass them on to the Washington Navy Yard which usually had enough supplies to fill the requests. When this was lacking, the Navy sent orders to navy agents to contract with commercial or industrial firms for the items needed. Much of the powder was old and damaged and had to be replenished. Funds were required for facilities, but were often not supplied. At Charlestown, Captain William Bainbridge wanted a good wharf. The necessary 20,000 dollars were unavailable.

An unprepared Navy needed so much, and there was only so much to spend from an economy minded administration. Fortunately for the United States there were only two dozen or so British vessels of war between Halifax and Bermuda. Furthermore the two services shared munitions, supplying each other when one was low on munitions. Surgeons had improved surgeons' needles. Robert Fulton was experimenting with mines for use against British warships. He had to deal with the idea that using mines was not honorable war to which he answered that war was not "confined within the limits of honor."[13]

The War Hawks were eager for the war to begin and happy with the declaration of war on June 19, 1812, but they had failed to provide adequately for the war over the years of the peacetime conflict with Britain. They felt that the people would rise easily and crush the enemy. When they learned the difficulties of war and saw the war go against them, the hawks realized that long preparations were necessary. But for the time they

The Difficult War: The Era of the War of 1812

were very optimistic and passed bills which would hurriedly increase the military force of the nation to army, equip, and train. [14]

A Baltimore newspaper, *The Federalist-Republican* editorialized against the war. Men in Baltimore read this and went on rampages through the streets in June and July. Congressman Harmanus Bleechker of New York said in the House of Representatives that this war "might expose our happy form of Government--our excellent political institutions-- to a dangerous trial." [15]

Because Baltimore was a major commercial center, the merchants there were greatly hurt by the embargo and were to be damaged by any declaration of war. Alexander Chanson's the *Federal Republican* led the fight against Jefferson and Madison and their policies. The newspaper was critical and continued its statements after war was declared. On Saturday June 20th, Chanson wrote that "we mean to represent, in as strong colors as we are capable, that the war in unnecessary, inexpedient, and entered into from partial, personal, and, as we believe, motive bearing upon their front marks of undisguised foreign influences which cannot be mistaken." Like all Federalists, Hanson leaned toward Britain and accused the Federalists of French influence, which was equally true.

People had a chance over the weekend of mulling over the editorial and conspiring to attack the newspaper office. After work on Monday, a French apothecary led a mob to demolish the offices and then march to the wharves to torch some Federalist ships and property. Hanson moved to Washington, continued to publish the paper for Baltimoreans, and then found a new place in Baltimore. War supporters plotted for another attack, but city officials did nothing to protect Hanson's press. Federalists then provided armed men.

On the evening of June 27th, an anti-Federalist mob marched down the streets and threw stones at the office. They them forced open the door. Jeffersonian Republicans led by General Henry "Lighthorse" Lee fired, killing one and wounding several mob leaders. It was only with gunfire on their own that the city magistrates acted. Brigadier General John Stricker took two militia companies forth. Major William Barney brought up the cavalry. They did not do anything to disperse the mob, but Stricker and Mayor Edward Johnson arranged a truce and guaranteed safe conduct to the jail for Lee and his men; however they could not stop the mob from stoning the militia and the Federalists.

The mob destroyed the office and press. That night mob leaders talked the jailer into letting them in to seize Lee and company. At this Lee and his men fled. On the way out many were seized and savagely beaten. Lee was to suffer the rest of his life from the torture. General James Lingan was murdered. Both Lee and Ligan had honored their country in the Revolutionary War. This was their reward. Baltimore's officials were gravely amiss in this riot. They blamed the Federalists when they should have disbursed the mob. This was a strain on the city's record. An investigation whitewashed the officials and their infamy. [16]

---

[1]Bruce, I, 384. Quotes on p. 384.
[2]Coles, *The War of 1812*. pp. 1-6. Quote on p. 1.
[3]Horsman, Reginald, *The War of 1812*, 1969, pp. 1-2.
[4]Risjord, "1812", p. 208.
[5]*The Annals of America*, IV, 314-318.
[6]Hickey, *War of 1812*, pp. 43-46.
[7]Adams, Madison, *pp. 497, 500-502.;*
[8]Coggeshall, *History*, pp. 41-42. Quote on p. 41.
[9]Cruikshank. *Documents*, pp. 42-43.
[10]Hawlett, Charles F., "Antiwar Sentiment," Heilder and Heilder, *Encyclopedia*, pp. 8-9.

[11]Tucker, *Poltroons and Patriots*, I, 19-21.

[12]Clark, Thomas D., *A History of Kentucky*, 1988. Reprint, Ashland, KY: Jesse Stuart Foundation, 1992, p. 127.

[13]Dudley, *Naval War*, I, 117-123, 128-134, 136, 138-141, 143-147.

[14]Meyer, Leland W., *Johnson of Kentucky*, 1967, p. 55; Elliott, Charles W., *Winfield Scott: The Soldier and the Man, 1937, p. 46.*

[15]Howlett, "Antiwar Sentiment," p. 8.

[16]Howlett, Charles F., "Baltimore Riots," Heidler & Headier, *Encyclopedia*, pp. 32-33.

CHAPTER XII

CANADA

When war broke out, Upper Canada was lightly defended. General Brock had at his command the 41st Regiment from Britain, one detachment of the 10th Royal Veteran Battalion and another of the Royal Newfoundland Fencibles, and a single artillery company. To be true, Upper Canada had a militia, but like that on the American side it was not fully effective. All men of a certain age had to join, but they had no training as a force. Lower Canada had a fine battalion of the line. Both had roughly 7,000 troops of regulars, about twenty-three percent located in the western or upper province.

Brock could not expect much help from Quebec which had its own defenses to look after and which was also to be the victim of American attacks. Although the Americans had more troops they were less effective and the two countries were about equally matched in one scholar's estimation. This expert in Canadian military history (C. P. Stacey) believed that the Americans should have concentrated their offensive in Montreal, cutting the essential line of communications and supplies. The Great Lakes naval superiority of the British gave them the advantage west of Kingston where Lake Ontario flowed to from the St. Lawrence River. Both sides did face a critical situation. [1]

Canada seemed very vulnerable to American attack. The great expanse of the northland had small population and many points of attack. An estimated one third of the population were pro-American. British immigrants filled up only a few places, notably the upper St. Lawrence, the Bay of Quinta, and the Niagara peninsula. They were pro-British. The mass of Frenchmen in Canada were more or less neutral. An army existed combined from British and Canadian regulars, a militia, and Indian allies. The militia was a large army only on paper much like the American militia. Regular troops were the only ones to be fully counted upon in view of British officers.

The government of Canada was headed by Lieutenant General Sir George Prevost, the first among equals. There were three other governors, each from a different province. Upper Canada was governed by Major General Isaac Brock who headed up the first and important defense of the area he governed against an early attack in the area by the Americans. Prevost was of the opinion that no offense should be undertaken by British forces in Canada unless it was to promote a good defense. Brock felt that strategy called for naval control of the Great Lakes, use of the Indians, use of the militia, and solution of problems of supply. The governor of Upper Canada would establish a base at Amherstburg and strike Detroit and Michilimakinac without delay. He would promote strong defenses in the vicinity of Lake Erie since it would be there, he thought, that the Americans would direct their main attack.

Meanwhile, Madison thought the main American attack should be at Montreal. For this attack he needed the New England militia, but governors of those states would have to agree to their militia forces, leaving their states. Madison turned to the idea of secondary attacks from Detroit, Niagara, and Sachett's Harbor,. Montreal would still be the main objective and by the use of an army at Montreal could cut out communications in the interior.

Michigan's governor William Hull expected British attacks at Detroit and Michilimackinac, where his action would be required as commander of the Northwest Army. the army met at Dayton, Ohio, and set off for Detroit, making their own track through the forests, avoiding the Black Swamp by taking a detour. Fort McArthur was built as a way station for the concentration of all the troops.

On June 21, 1812, they set out from the fort and ran into heavy rains that mired wagons into a sea of mud and brought out the black flies and mosquitoes. The rain stopped and the army continued its way through the forest. A few days later, the army reached Maumee. There he found a schooner. He filled the ship with barrage, medical supplies, and a trunk of papers, which were caught by the British on July 2d. Hull reached Detroit on July 5th. [2]

Secretary of the Navy Paul Hamilton had consulted Commodore John Rodgers and Stephen Decatur, Jr., about the strategy the navy should pursue. He received conflicting advice. Rodgers was for a concentration of the fleet to capture British privateers and merchantmen. Decatur was for a single or paired ship hunting missions. Hamilton could not decided between them, but after war was declared, Rodgers immediately acted. He sailed his ships to where Decatur was stationed and used his seniority to impress Decatur into joining the two fleets and taking after the British altogether. He promised a fifty-fifty division of the prize money. They sailed forth and captured only seven ships, a discouraging bag. The action of the *Constitution* singly convinced Hamilton that Decatur was right and there was no more combined fleet during the war. [3]

Rodgers was a Marylander who went to sea at age thirteen as an apprentice to a merchant captain for five years. In 1793, he became a qualified master and in 1778, he joined the navy as a lieutenant on the frigate *Constellation*. He fought in the Caribbean in the Quasi-War and was promoted to captain. After this war, he returned to the merchant marine and then back into the navy. [4]

Stephen Decatur Jr. was a son of a Revolutionary War and Quasi-War naval hero, but did not go to sea until 1798 when he tired of being a clerk in a Philadelphia shipping firm. He was soon promoted to lieutenant with his first voyage. James Barron befriended him. This came in handy when the hot-headed Decatur was a second to an officer who killed a man in a duel, one of three duel encounters. Soon he had an independent command and was a hero of the war with Tripoli. For this he received a youthful promotion to captain. Because of an honest disagreement, Decatur later turned on his friend Barron and was one of the members of a court-martial in which Barron was sentenced to a suspension in the *Chesapeake* matter. [5]

The first naval action of the war took place one hundred miles southwest of Nantucket Shoals on June 3, 1812. Rodgers sailed his five ships out to sea as soon as it was possible to get underway. At six in the afternoon he sighted a pilot-boat whose captain told him that an English vessel was to be found to the northeast. Sailing in that direction the sailors brought the ship to within sight of a strong vessel two hours later. A bow shot stopped her, but she proved and American ship bound for France. Sailing on in

The Difficult War: The Era of the War of 1812

the night the squadron commander learned from a brig that that the Jamaica fleet was northwest of Bermuda. Rodgers determined to intercept.

Soon after dawn, they sighted a ship they were to learn was the British 42-gun frigate *Belvidera* under the command of Captain Richard Byron. The Americans gave chase to the approaching ship, which turned around and fled. They slowly gained upon the British warship with *The President* in the lead. Five hours passed. Rodgers ordered the deck of the lead ship to be cleared for action. At noon, Byron did the same thing. The wind became lighter, giving a slight advantage to the British.

At four-twenty that afternoon, it looked as if the American ship would not overtake the British. Byron ordered his stern guns to sight on the Americans and Rodgers ordered his gunners to fire. They fired three shots. One struck the Britisher's rudder coat and one entered the gunroom, and another hit a gun muzzle, while the Third killed and wounded several sailors. The firing was answered. Firing was general. Suddenly an American gun exploded killing a midshipman and wounding fourteen including Rodgers, who was blown into the air and fell with a fractured bone. This did not prevent the commodore to continuing to direct the fight.

Rodgers maneuvered for position, but lost ground. The enemy's stern guns were now damaging *The President*. Closer actions seemed unlikely. Damage was mutual. Both commanders tried to deliver broadsides. Byron tried to lighten his ship. He had his sailors throw boats, waist anchors, and other equipment overboard. The British began gaining space, leaving the Americans behind. Sailing into the night, Rodgers soon had to abandon the chase. Shortly Rodgers and his men captured two brigs and a privateer and later other ships.

Although he did not have as much success as he wished, Rodgers had a great effect which he recognized at the time. He did not take the convoy he was after and that he had searched so hard for, but he kept the British distracted, forced them to concentrate, and prevented single cruisers from seizing merchantmen off American ports. One British office wrote that the had been so completely occupied in keeping an outlook for Rodgers in the North Atlantic that they had taken few prize. This was a major accomplishment since the protection of American merchantmen was a chief object of Rodgers and his squadron. The American navy recognized this success and commended Rodgers for this success. [6]

On June 27, 1812, Captain Richard Byron sailed his Majesty's frigate *Belvidera* into Halifax harbor, severely damage. Commodore Rodgers' and his American squadron had beaten the ship in battle, but the *Belvidera* had escaped at last. This was the first news to reach Halifax that the United States had declared war. Collins acted quickly. He arranged for five rusty cannon barrels used as gate-posts on Halifax as wharves to be placed onboard the *Black Joke* and sailed it to Liverpool, Nova Scotia, where he raise a crew of forty-five men to sail her as a privateer. However, the British still hoped for peace, having recently repealed their council orders, the news of which had not reached the United States in time and the British were not commissioning any privateers yet. Its first mission was to bring back from Boston, a just captured British master. [7]

On June 24th, Calhoun made a ringing speech in Congress. In support of the recently declared war, he said that it was an alarming idea to rely upon a measure of peace when at war instead of courage and energy. It required military measures and not just a non-importation policy. Reliance on the last would lead to a policy base upon that. He called for striking at the false hope of past days, commercial actions and call upon "the resources of the nation for its protection. England will soon find that seven millions of freemen, with every material of war in abundance, are not to be despised with impunity." Any resort to peace was too late for the welfare of the nation. It was war, and America would have to live with it. "We have had a peace like a war; in the name of heaven let us not have the only thing which is worse, a war like a peace." [8]

On that very day, an express rider reached Niagara with news of the war. On both sides of the Niagara River the news was unwelcome; they were connected by marriage and business and friendship for the last six years. On both sides, the women and children watched their menfolk in arming and training. Neither side had experienced concerns over their safety, no anxiety for years. They had never suffered any of the injuries lamented over in the East. The men of the East were taking the place of mercenaries which these particular frontiersmen had fought at Bennington and Saragota. These men of Upper New York wrote that the "renown which you seek is not our renown. It is the renown of Europe, not of America." There would be nothing but desolation coming from this contemplated warfare. Folly would have found new victims. Although frontiersmen in general supported the war on the American side, these men of the woods and clearings did not. [9]

Peter B. Porter believed that the British had immediate plans for an attack on Fort Niagara. Should they pass the river they might advance far, so he sent a message to Major Mullany as did Major General Hall to come to their aid promptly with his men and their arms an ammunition in the Lanandaigus arsenal. Mullany was glad to bring forth three companies of infantry and one of artillery in order to repel invasion and give frontier settlers hope that they would be protected. [10]

Jacob Barker, who had lost his father in infancy after his Maine birth in 1779, was a New York City merchant (since age 22), and a Jeffersonian. He was against the war because it would disrupt the economy. When war did break out, Barker gave his support to Madison. He practiced costly patriotism. The war did cost him his business. He raised money for the government with his connections. Becoming a friend of Madison and other high officials, he was a prime mover in vacating the White House when the British invaded, saving valuables from looting, especially Gilbert Stuart's portrait of George Washington. He then bought food for the dispersed Americans. [11]

New York, city and state, were much involved in the economies and politics of the declaration. Economic interests were involved and in one case, a ruse was engaged in. At Ogdensburg, New York, there was an import-export trade since the town was on the St. Lawrence River. Word quietly reached there and alert businessmen hurried to get goods across the line in this trade. Shortly the custom agents got word of the declaration of war and these officials stopped all trade. Still awaiting export were warehouses of American potash. This did not deter American businessmen. They loaded up a wagon and sent it into the countryside some six miles. Then they told custom agents of its location, saying it would be necessary for them to make haste and stop the smuggling attempt. They hurried forth and captured the wagon, only to find that the potash left in town was on its way to Canada's farmers on six bateau. The price was high and a great profit was made behind the backs of the custom agents.

Economics were usually underfoot where the New Yorkers were about. Recently they were most incensed about accounts of French transgressions. Indeed a young man named Stevens had just visited newspaper offices with tales of Americans in French prisons for no more activity than to sail into French ports on commercial trips. In prison he and others were pressured to enter the French services to prey upon American trade on the highseas. Also current at the time was a report of a French squadron destroying

The next concern of New Yorkers was financial. How would the war be paid for and when. Like so many presidents, Madison would borrow rasher than immediately pay for the war in his administration. Congress passed an appropriation bill of $17 millions, but postponed taxes until after election that fall. This was the usual method. New Yorkers saw a little humor in the situation. Gallatin wanted to establish a whisky tax. It was unusual for a man who had opposed a whisky tax under Washington and was almost caught up in an active insurrection on the matter, was now recommending a whisky tax. [12]

It was a divided concerned people who went to war in June. John C. Calhoun stated that the United States was in a second war for their independence and liberty. British pressure was too much. The relief that Americans had sought for was illusory and her suffering too great for the Americans to take any longer. Negotiation, economic retaliation, and the threat of war had not worked. It was therefore the only honorable, as it seemed to them, alternative of war itself. That is what they thought.

There was no unity, but a large enough segment of the population wanted to take the step. Great Britain was a great power and America was too weak for a successful outcome, but they pushed forward with high hopes for some and dissension from others. They feared only the Royal Navy and the Indians, but hope was high they could withstand both and could take Canada. France had done harm also, but only the Federalists were solidly for a war with France and then only in attune with older politics. [13]

Almost one half of them vote for war; thirty-nine of the seventy nine, came from the South Atlantic states from Maryland in the north to Georgia in the south. Most of these southern congressmen were old Republicans, conservative agrarians, who had no economic motive except for their sale of agricultural products to any who would buy and their old time bias against England. The three new Jeffersonian Republicans either won their seats without opposition or replaced men who were supporters of military preparations and a stronger foreign policy.

Virginia returned a virtually identical delegation of 17 Republicans and five Federalists. The Shenandoah Valley sent forth Federalists as did western Virginia. the five new Republican members were not elected on the issue of peace or war. John Randolph won a close election. John Wayles Eppes ran against him undeclared, because Randolph had vigorously opposed Madison. However, no one expected Eppes would have been any stronger on the issue of peace or war. Eppes had run against Randolph when he moved. Eppes' formal position had been formed from a district in which winner James Pleasants was a new member and a war Republican.

A close friend of Monroe's who felt Madison was too nationalistic, Hugh Nelson won election with a decided preference for peace at any price. Major John P. Hungerford was a winner who had been a supporter of Monroe also. War Republican John Love was replaced by war Republican Dr. Ayler Hawes. Nearly one half the Virginian congressmen were re-elected without opposition. Where there was a contest the foreign policy issue was not the chief issue. Jeffersonian John Clopton won re-election in support of the non-intercourse law (no trade with Great Britain) and against the Bank of the United States.

There was little change in North Carolina. Eight of the twelve North Carolina congressmen were re-elected. Two of them were Federalists and one a Randolph Quid named Richard Stanford. Two of the four newcomers had served in Congress several years earlier. The unanimous vote for war from South Carolina's coincided with state wide feeling and the three great War Hawk leaders from South Carolina were an addition of talent rather than numbers for the war party. These leaders were John C. Calhoun, William Lowndes, and Langdon Cleves. David Rogerson Williams was another War Hawk leader when he finally made his decision. He was a John Randolph Quid in rebellion against Jefferson in 1806, but could not make up his mind whether to support peace or war as late as May of 1812. Now he was for the war.

Support for the embargo and non-intercourse laws had proved a hollow reed and many were connected to a war-hawk position because the masses felt "that the only alternative to war was submission and national disgrace." They would not return to a colonial status anywhere in the nation. [14]

In Ohio, with its concern over Indian attacks, had a division in its representative over the issue. The sole representative in the House from Ohio, Jeremiah Morrow, voted for war. He had voted for the embargo in 1807. This state's two senators were opposed on the grounds that the nation was unprepared and could not protect Ohio from an Indian attack. They would rather the United States stick to commercial retaliation. Such a course would not hurt inland Ohio. [15]

Of all the states, of all the citizens, the men of Kentucky were the most eager for the battlefield, to conquer Canada and Florida, and to cover themselves with glory. They supported their young hero, Henry Clay. He represented them to a tee. Four hundred Kentuckians were recruited for the regular army. Others they volunteered to fill the quota of six-months militia terms. No one volunteered for the one year term. Most of them were farmers who wished to till their farms in the spring and summer and harvest in the early fall. When the disasters of the national army overtook them, Kentuckians decided it was up to them to conquer Canada. The Lincolns and other Kentuckians were too close to the frontier for combat. They were needed at home to protect the state from Indians. Indeed Indians attacks resulted in the massacre of twenty two settlers within 24 miles of Louisville, not too far from the Lincolns. [16]

When the war began there were less than seven thousand regulars and when Congress voted for a 50,000 man increase, only five thousand volunteered. The Americans were for the war but did not want to fight in the war. There was a lack of popular support from the young men of the nation. This looked bad for the War Hawks. However, the government could rely upon some 50,000 or so militia troops, subject to the loyalty and politics of state government men who did not feel themselves obligated to serve outside their states. They were for defense only. Military officers were generally in the top levels of the militia but old and/or incompetent. Henry Dearborn, the senior major general of the army had grown soft in the custom service and was called "Granny," by his men. This was just one example. [17]

In these days in wartime, ship owners were granted letters of marque which authorized them to capture merchant shipping or warships at sea to take to their ports for sale of the ships and tier cargo. The funds would be divided among the owners of the privateer and officers and crew of the each ship. As soon as it was certain war would be declared, ship owners began arming their merchant ships to attack British commerce on the high seas for these benefits. In some aspect they were official pirates, but there were other aspects. They were official warships except that they were used as a warship against private vessels of the nation at war.

The Difficult War: The Era of the War of 1812   105

Privateering operated under a recognized set of rule. Except for an occasional captain, the privateers operated carefully in that code of conduct developed over the years. These ships were kept in action as the only means by which the United States could harm British shipping to the degree made necessary to achieve success in the war, since the American navy had been kept so small by Jeffersonian policies that it would not act in the opening months of the war in a manner to have effect upon the British war vessels and commerce carriers.

At first, the government benefited financially since it charged custom duties and fees which often totaled forty percent of the value of prize goods. However, when a delegation of Baltimore merchants protested on November 12, 1812, these duties were rescinded. Congress agreed and from that moment all profits were divided between owners and crews. The crews generally served without pay since they would profit more from the prizes they took at sea. One man owned several merchantmen and he would pick the fastest schooner of brig to serve as raiders. Since schooners would sail closest to the wind and needed fewer men, they were best for privateering. More often stock companies were formed to finance privateering and profit thereby. One Baltimore advertisement was for a letter of marque vessels of forty shares at $500 each. Also merchant firms would send several of the vessels it owned to sea as privateers with the partners benefiting.

The privateers would seek out the known trade routes or lie off hostile or neutral ports where they would find the right target ships. Once the ship was seen the privateer would give chase. If they were friendly or neutral, the papers would be checked to see if it carried no enemy goods and then allowed to leave. If they were warships, the privateers would flee the opposite direction since they had no prize goods to gain but only unpaying glory and perhaps defeat. They went to sea for money and not because they enjoyed fighting. A type of privateering were ships under letters of marque, regular ships with paid crews which captured hostile merchant vessels. [18]

---

[1]Zaslow, Morris, ed., *The Defended Border: Upper Canada and the War of 1812*, Toronto: Macmillan Co. of Canada, 1964, pp. 12-13.

[2]Coles, *War of 1812*, pp. 38-58.

[3]Seiken, Jeff, "Decatur, Stephen, Jr.," Heidler & Heidler, *Encyclopedia*, p. 149.

[4]Martin, Tyone G., "Rodgers, John," Heidler & Heidler, *Encyclopedia*, p. 452.

[5]Seiken, "Decatur," pp. 148-149.

[6]Paullin, *Rodgers*, pp. 249-259.

[7]Snider, C.H.J., *Under the Red Jack*, 1928, pp. 12-13.

[8]Lynch, *Fifty Years*, pp. 237-238. Quote on p. 237-238.

[9]Richardson, J., War of 1812, 1902, pp. 11-12. Quote on p. 12.

[10]Brannan, John (ed.), *Official Letters of the Military and Naval Officers of the United States, During the War with Great Britain in the Years 1812, 13, 14, and 15*, Washington DC: Way & Gideon, 1823, New York Reprint, Arno Press, 1971, pp. 29-30.

[11]Heidler, Jeanne T. and Heidler, David S., "Barker, Jacob," Heidler & Heidler, *Encyclopedia*, pp. 36-37.

[12]Tucker, *Poltroons and Patriots*, pp. 24-25.

[13]White, *Nation*, pp. 1-2.

[14]Risjord, "1812", pp. 197-200. Quote on p. 200.

[15]*Ibid.*, p. 201.

[16]Adams, *Madison*, pp. 567-570.

[17]Leckie, *Sea to Sea*, p. 182.

[18]Cranwell, John Philips and William Bowen Crane, *Men of Marque: A History of Private Armed Vessels out of Baltimore During the War of 1812*, New York: W.W. Norton, 1940, pp. 15-22.

CHAPTER XIII

DETROIT

The *Nonesuch*, a privateer from Baltimore, was the first to leave that harbor on a privateer cruise, although several beat her out to sea. She met stormy weather, but soon its captain Henry Levely took his first prize, under Spanish colors. Another ship fell victim of the *Nonsuch* and then others. In mid September they met a British warship on the high seas and were able to successfully avoid capture in several days of hide-and-seek off the coast of Martinique. Levely sailed between two British ships in a terrible and bloody battle. For awhile he tried to lay his vessel alongside one of the other British ships, but could not. Soon the damage to the rigging was such that it was hard to maneuver. The enemy were too strong for him. Levely hauled off and repaired and the also hard pressed Britishers escaped as best they could. Three days later there was another battle to be fought, one with a tropical gale.

In October, the *Nonesuch* escaped an occasion British warship and, on October 15th, its captain purchased a long 12-pounder, thirty muskets, and a box of olives from the captain of a Spanish schooner. It is now known why he did not merely capture that ship and take its cargo, the Spanish being allies of the British. The next day the *Nonsuch's* crew captured the brig *Francis* with its forty-nine head of cattle, which did not resist. Two days passed. Captain Levely stopped a schooner from the United States with a British license to pass the growing blockade to supply food to the English ships at sea and colonies. He seized the ship and confined the captain, mate, and sailors, as "traitors to their country."

On October 19, 1812, they captured the *Anna Maria* for the same suspicions. It was also from Alexandria. Then at dawn the lookout called out that three sail were in sight. The *Nonsuch* sailed forth and fired a shot. One schooner unfurled an American flag so Levely chased the other two. When they got close, the American privateers discovered they were chasing two brigs, one of which a man-of-war conveyed the other. Levely ordered several shots to be fired and broke off the chase. The Englishmen continued on their way. A strange vessel was seen but then lost sight of.

At two AM, on Thursday, October 20th, the stranger appeared in an attack. Levely tried to keep clear but the other was a superior ship. They got into a fight with injury and death and damage. Both sides fought to a stand-off. The seamen did repairs during the night. In the morning Levely wanted to break off, but the battle of its own volition continued for a long time. Finally the demoralized stranger lowered her colors and Levely found out it was the *Joseph and Mary* out of Boston. It turned out it was an American privateer. In those days the flag could not be trusted since many flew false or no flags at all. There was another capture of an Alexandria ship with provisions for the British Navy. The *Nonsuch* came into Charleston where it became an American warship. [1]

The most noted privateer of the War of 1812 was Joshua Barney who had made a name for himself as a sea fighter. He went to sea early and at the age of fifteen commanded his first ship, something of a record. During the Revolution, Barney had commanded private, state, and national armed ships until he was captured. He escaped from Old Mill Prison. In 1795, he went to France and became a captain in the French Navy. Then first consul Napoleon Bonaparte promoted the captain to the rank of commodore. Serving until 1802, he was never engaged against the American flag, but still it gained him new enemies.

Barney sailed forth on the *Rossie* out of Baltimore. Instructed to sail off the coast of Newfoundland, he did so, capturing small ships of fishermen, telling them about the war. They must head immediately for friendly ports, he said. The captain and crew boarded an American brig and found it guilty of a violation of the Nonimportation Act, forbidding trade with the British. They seized it, their first prize. Small British fishing boats were taken and burnt and an occasional prize taken. After a necessary visit to Newport, Rhode Island, Barney sailed out for the West Indies where they got into a fight with a British ship, a post office packet. It fell to the American after a lively battle. [2]

Unlike so many of the privateers, the *Globe* had many accidents and misfortunes. No sooner was the schooner underway than a seaman was killed by an accident and suffered damage to the mainmast minutes later. Only moderately successful in earnings for the prize seeking crew, she was plagued by bad luck and mischance. The men of the *Globe* had to fight hard for the few prizes and none surrendered to her with one shot fired. Of the owners one could sustain himself because he owned shares in four of the first half dozen privateers to sail from Baltimore. He made lots of money from the privateers, but others such as the seaman Taylor meet with accident and pain. Before they reached the open ocean, a topsail halyard fouled and Taylor went up to clear it. Suddenly he lost his grip and fell to the deck, suffering injuries such as a broken right thigh. Just as suddenly he died. This was just the beginning of its bad luck which plagued the privateer.

Heading for Annapolis, Murphy forgot to hoist his flag. The commander of the fort saw what might have been an enemy ship and fired upon him. Captain Murphy quickly ran up his colors. He sent Taylor's body ashore and the crew went to work stepping up a new mainmast. Setting sail for the West Indies he found only American and neutral ships. Most of the American vessels did not know about the war and the captain advised them to head for American ports nearest them to avoid capture.

They chased what turned out to be an English vessel. There was a long duel capped by musket fire and the British surrendered. Off Bermuda they ran off from a British warship and then, with their water supply low captured a little schooner *Anne*, which provided some water and sent her to Baltimore for sale. They fought another ship with substantial loss of life. In a twenty minute battle, the American boarded it. This provided them with a prize and a cargo of sugar, rum, coffee, logwood, and mahogany. At this point they headed for Hampton Roads, Virginia. [3]

Soon after war was declared, shipbuilders were busy, working long hours to prepare and fit out privateers. By July first, two had left Salem, and ten were being readied for sea. Others were set for sailing in early July. The best were to be underway later. Larger schooners were being better fitted and equipped for an expected large warfare on the seven seas. Before the end of the year, twenty-six ships were readied from New York with 194 guns and 2,233 men. From Baltimore there were seventeen ships with 1,538 men. Also there were twenty-five rapid letter-of-marque schooners, each with from six to ten guns and from thirty to fifty sailors plus officers.

Ships set sail from other ports and there were other armed vessels which brought the numbers to, for example, forty-two armed vessels from Baltimore. The United States government commissioned all of these to capture, burn, sink, and destroy any British ships or ships which traded with Great Britain. All of this shipbuilding fueled the economy to help make up for loss trade with the British. Gains from privateering also heaped up profits for the Northeast. There was a large prosperity because of these two activities, joined as they were in economics. [4]

Meanwhile in Mexico, after Hidalgo's defeat many of his followers scattered. Some of these went into exile in the United States close to the borders of Louisiana. From there they were to move into Texas later when opportunity opened up in the next decade with Mexican Independence and colonization of Texas. Loyal Spaniards viewed the exiles with distaste and feared they would some day come back to disrupt harmony of the Spanish Empire.

One Spaniard Manuel de Salcedo in an official capacity wrote that it appeared that "that the Government of the United States intends, as preliminary to its conquest, to cut off vagabonds and revolutionists, and consummate them afterwards with their arms and taking of possessions. In fact all indicates a very considerable upturning if this Province is not attended to, from which it would be difficult to dislodge the Americans if they succeed in occupying it."

Salcedo knew that the province of Texas did not have enough military strength to resist. He tried his best to prepare for that day, but there was not much that he could do. Spain was using its utmost in military power to fight Napoleon in occupied Spain and could not spare the troops needed for Texas. Even if this was not so, there is no likelihood that they would have provided them. This new threat was not being met and Salcedo could not move enough effort in Mexico City to get any sufficient help from the viceroy there.

Miguel Ramos Arizpe, who was a representative of northern Mexico at the Spanish cortes or parliament, could do more by recommending Spanish colonization in the Spanish cortes, but this was insufficient. Should there be a larger population, it was by no means certain that they could have kept Texas free from filibusters who took it for awhile in 1812-814. General Joaquin de Arrendondo swept the province clear of the Green Flag insurrectionists, but Texas lost population as a result of this reconquest. And there was always the problem of the Indians. [5]

There was an American religious reaction to the war divided along sectional lines. Most opposed were the people and religious ministers of New England. During the Essex County Convention, the politicians passed a statement which condemned Madison and company for the violation of the Biblical precept that "they who rule over men, must be just, ruling in fear of God." They wanted also that a French connection "is of itself sufficient to draw down upon our country the judgments of Heaven."

Worchester County citizenry believed that the central government could not be reformed and did not send their resolution to the national capital. Exposed Vermonters wrote a resolution for Congress about the moral dangers of war. Such would corrupt morals. They called loans and taxes evil. Bostonians called hostilities "a wanton and impious rejection of the advantages with which the Almighty had blessed our country." They wished to stay neutral. Much of this was commercial interest speaking, but religion played it part in the beliefs and were drawn upon by secular men.

Philadelphians opposed the war in two petitions. There would be economic hardship said one. The other called the war wicked. There were other citizens who were pacifistic and noted the Christian injunction on peace. In Cumberland County, pacifists wrote of the blessings of peace with which God had blessed the country over the years. God had not yet refrained from punishments of war with "the most awful dispensations-- desolating judgments, and terrific convulsions in the physical and political world, which ever could afflict suffering humanity." Marylanders protested against an aggressive invasion of Canada to defend national honor.

Dissenting congressmen embarked upon a worldly comparison. They gave an address of three pages of trade statistics which proved that it was harmful to preserve commerce with France at a low rate by going to war with a large trading partner Britain. They stated that not only should they be true to self, but should not fail in duty to others. With the idea that the deserters from British ships were Irish, they did not see any need to extend American protection to the Irish. Moral duty called for America to avoid Europe's quarrel. War was not necessary, being unrequired by moral duty or political expediency. [6]

The prospects of a war were dreaded by the 4,762 people of Michigan. The two military posts of 94 men at Detroit and 79 at the Straits of Mackinac were exposed. American successes seemed too weak and British-Indian successes too close for comfort. Kentuckians could pray that they could take Canada but Michiganers were more realistic.

When the War of 1812 broke out, the governor of Michigan was in the east. William Hull, a poor but the only viable choice, headed west through Ohio where he took command of the Ohio militia on May 25, 1812. Ohio governor Return Jonathan Meigs was enthusiastic in a speech in which he stressed the need for discipline, praised Hull, and ended with a ringing charge that American "frontiers must be protected from savage barbarity, our rights maintained, and our wrongs avenged. Go then! fear not! be strong! quit yourselves like men, and may the God of Armies be your shield and buckler."

At first Hull went on the water route, but when he found the waters of the Miami too low, he undertook to build a road through the Black Swamp of northern Ohio. He was joined at Urbana by Lieutenant Colonel James Miller's regiment of Regulars, veterans of the Battle of Tippecanoe. After crushing a militia mutiny with Miller's regulars, he began building the road in spite of heavy rains. He protected his force with scouts, fortifications and occasional blockhouses. Near Fall Timbers he chartered two boats to carry supplies and invalids to Detroit.

On July 2, 1812, he learned of the declaration of war and then on the capture of the two boats by the British off Fort Malden opposite Grosse Island. The enemy captured documents telling of Hull's strength and plans. They were eyeopeners. Hull made it to Detroit and attacked and captured British Sandwich. About half of the Canadian militia deserted. Still Hull had justified worries about his exposed supply lines. They could be cut off from Lake Erie by the British and from the west by Indians.

On July 5, 1812, General Hull and his men had reached Detroit with its fort enclosing about two acres, capable of withstanding a siege but without command of the river. Across the river was the British militia. Detroit had a population of roughly 800 people, without sufficient supplies and 200 miles from support. Hull knew that militarily Detroit was a trap, but following orders he was determined to invade Canada. On July 12th Hull led his army across the river between Lake Erie and Lake Huron without incident. The British retreated twelve miles to Amherstburg, their main position, that night. They were welcomed at Sandwich when they took the Canadian town.

Hull proclaimed the emancipation of Canadians from tyranny. With freedom, he proclaimed, would come peace, security, and prosperity. The Americans would not harm, but would protect their persons, property, and rights. They must pursue their normal lives. Deserters from the British militia and some of the population found protection behind American lines. Hull preferred to besiege Malden as Canadians in large number left British ranks for the United States. On one day sixty arrived. The general wrote to Washington that at that time the British were reduced to less than one hundred men and the Indians were leaving. More were to come later. He noted that it was important for American soldiers to invest Niagara, because without this, "the whole force of the province will be directed against this army.

Hull was prompt with this action, but Dearborn allowed himself to become bogged down in the details of raising an army and preparing for its movement. Madison wished Dearborn to take charge, but allowed him time to suit his own schedule. William Eustis urged Dearborn to march to Albany or Lake Erie with the troops he had and the rest could follow. The rest were insufficient since men were not enlisting in the North in any numbers for the war.

Further into the wilderness and surrounded in the midst of hostile Indians, Lieutenant Porter Hanks had no other alternative except to surrender the American fort at Michilimackinac with promises of the honors of war. British captain Charles Roberts accepted the capitulation. Roberts promised the protection of persons and property. Had they resisted, they would have been massacred by the Indians, whom Roberts would have been unable to control. The British had to make an effort to control the Indians as it was. The Indian threat was used at Michilimakinac to induce the surrender and it was to be used again.

More British troops arrived. A British advance was driven back by Colonel Lewis Cass to within three miles of Fort Malden. When the Indians learned of the fall of Hanks' fort, they adhered to the British with renewed strength. A small Indian force ambushed an American column needed to escort a supply train and it was evident that the supply line with Ohio was cut by the Indians. Hull retreated to Detroit with most of his force. He withdrew completely when the supply line was not reestablished by a small victory by Miller and his men. Hull would have retreated to Ohio, but he was told that disillusioned soldiers in his force would desert in large numbers on any withdrawal.

The British commander Sir Isaac Brock, informed of the condition of U. S. troops by the captured mail bags, then demanded the surrender of Detroit citing the hostility of the Indians to the Americans and the dangers should Detroit be attacked. Thinking that a force of Cass and McArthur were far away and faced with desertions, bombarded by the British, and learning from a bogus document engineered by Brock that swarms of Indians were underway, Hull surrendered Detroit on August 15, 1812.

The American might have won had he been more aggressive earlier, but now he was faced with the fear of Indian massacre of men, women, and children. A late court martial convicted Hull of cowardice and neglect of duty, but no one could have resisted Brock long. Hull was cut off and had to think of the welfare of the defenseless among his people. His people at Detroit survived, but Indians murdered a detachment retreating from Fort Dearborn at the site of Chicago, after they surrendered. Thus the Northwest was exposed with the surrender of its three forts. However, Captain Zachery Taylor successfully defended Fort Harrison in Indiana on the night of September 4-5, and became a hero for the first time. [7]

Orders were issued for the gathering of a volunteer army. They came to Buffalo, Black Rock, Lewiston, and Fort Niagara in northwestern most New York until the Americans had about 1,500 men, regular and militiamen. They were unprepared for warfare, lacking in tents, equipment, and discipline. Nothing was done to receive them. The War Department had made no plans, much less any provisions. The only weapons were those that the solders brought with them. Poor quarters, improper food, and a lack of control led the men into sickness. Those militiamen who had come earlier had returned home. [8]

When the war came to Maine, that the channeling of funds for forts were to Republican and not Federalist sections was made obvious. Two of the three rivers were adequately defended but the Federalist Penobscot in the northwest was ignored. In eastern Maine the only fortification was a small redoubt at Eastport. There was no naval defense east of Portland in the southwestern corner of Maine. Portland had nine inferior gunboats, part of a money saving expenditure from Jefferson's administration time. Even this poor excuse for a defense was withdrawn when the war was barely started.

The people of Maine were like those of Massachusetts. They were lukewarm about the war. Residents in Eastport even unanimously voted to preserve good relations with the people of nearby New Brunswick. When Massachusetts governor Caleb Strong refused to send militia to help Henry Dearborn to protect Massachusetts' southern coastline, Dearborn pulled his federal troops from coastal garrisons in Massachusetts and Maine. Dearborn left only one regiment to protect the long coastline from Cape Cod to Eastport in northern Maine. Militiamen from the Penobscot region sent to the border behaved so badly that the local citizens of the northern wilds sent them back to central Maine. The militia was so bad that one of its division commanders stated that there could be no reliance placed upon the militia and none ought to be. This was the opinion of so many Maine citizens.

Maine merchants, farmers, and working men were worried about subsistence. Trade had been reduced by the embargo and now British privateers raided the coastal trade from ports in Nova Scotia and New Brunswick. Crop failures hurt the farmers. Economic depression made things hard for the working men. [9]

Neither side in this emerging war was prepared. Both sides had few brilliant leaders and many incompetent officers. The British officers were largely the poor sort. The best were fighting in Spain against Napoleon. Many had bought their rank as was customary in the British army, similar to American political appointees to its military. American forces did not contain enough experienced officers. They were largely militiamen and political appointees. British commanders also relied heavily on militia soldiers. Neither side wished to fight the other, but with the War Hawks on the American side and official arrogance on the British side, the two nations were at war. [10]

An early wartime encounter on the high seas after the American declaration of war took place on July 10th. Captain Carroway's privateer *Dash* seized in Hampton Roads the British government schooner there. This British captain had not heard of the declaration of war and had dispatches from Britain to the United States, government to government. Carroway went on, bound for captures of British merchantmen.

Eight days later, the letter-of-Marque schooner *Falcon*, on the way to Bordeaux with its four guns and sixteen men, skeleton arms and crew were off the coast of France. The British cutter *Hero* with five guns and fifty men attacked the *Falcon*. They fought for two hours and a half and the *Falcon*, with losses on both sides, finally got free. It repulsed the Britons three times and attempted to board the British. On the next day, a British

The Difficult War: The Era of the War of 1812

privateer fought her for an hour and a half. A weakened *Falcon* was finally boarded. The wounded were disembarked into Guernsey, that British isle between Great Britain and France. There were more captures on both sides in the month of July. *Gypsey's* crew retook her. A British transport with a rich cargo was taken, it mostly carried uniforms and cloth. There were numerous other captures. [11]

Brigadier General Wilkinson assumed his command of the Mississippi soon after he heard of the proclamation of war. he wrote of eventful moments, pride, spirit, honor, zeal, and patriotism. American had drained the last cup of conciliation and it was time to assert inalienable rights. They should put behind them their political feuds and personal animosities for personal glory and national welfare. Justice should come from above and cooperation from the subordinate. This was a natural view from a military man like Wilkinson. [12]

The war against the British produced fear in the Northeast. Not only did the New Englanders have a fear of unemployment and business failure due to the disruptions of trade, but they had British citizens in their midst, men whom they feared would help the British with naval action and perhaps invasion. Other areas had citizens who were concerned over the presence of British subjects among them.

It only took a month after the declaration of war for the state department to take action. It ordered male enemy aliens of fourteen or older to report to the U. S. marshal in their districts. The marshal would then compile census of the aliens in their area. The various census were not complete, some ten thousand only reported to their marshal. An internment order was issued, but it had little effect beyond preventing enemy aliens from moving along the coasts or to move at all in many instances. Exceptions had been allowed for those who had already declared their intentions of becoming citizens, owned real property or married American women. These exceptions were not already allowed. Limitations were made on instituting suits in federal or state courts.[13]

---

[1]Cranwell and Crane, *Men of Marque*, pp. 49-59.

[2]*Ibid.*, pp. 63-70.

[3]*Ibid.*, pp. 85-89.

[4]Coggeshall, *History*, pp. 1-7.

[5]Lukes, *DeWitt*, pp. 31-34.

[6]Gribben, William, *The Churches Militant: The War of 1812 and American Religion*, New Haven: Yale University Press 1973, pp. 16-18. Quote on pp. 16, 17.

[7]Adams, *Madison*, pp. 501-508 (Quote on p. 504); Cruikshank, *Documents*, pp. 57-69; Scott, Leonard H., "The Surrender of Detroit," *American History Illustrated*, XII NO. 3 (June 1977), pp. 218-36; Hickey, *1812*, pp. 80-85.

[8]Babcock, *War of 1812*, p. 35.

[9]Lohnes, Barry J., "A New Look at the Invasion of Eastern Maine, 1814," *Maine Historical Society Quarterly*, XV (Summer 1975), pp. 5-9.

[10]Berton, Pierre, *The Invasion of Canada*, Boston: Little, Brown, 1980.

[11]Coggleshall, *History*, p. 37-41.

[12]Brannan, *Official Letters*, p. 32.

[13]Coleman, Peter J. and Majeske, Penelope K., "British Immigrants in Rhode Island during the War of 1812," *Rhode Island History*, XXXIV (August 1975), pp. 66-75.

CHAPTER XIV

ISSAC HULL

The opposition to the efforts of redress of wrongs and to the war was the Federalists party in the states and in the nation as a whole. Federalist blamed the Republicans who went to war, they said, to combine themselves in power. The South and West directed the war effort and the Northeast's citizens said they would furnish neither men nor money. Further they denied that the Federals could draft state militiamen. Madison responded by allowing militia soldiers to remain under state officers. The Federals petitioned Congress. To them the war was a mistake. Federalists held a mass meeting in Fanueil Hall in Boston on July 15, 1812, to protest the war.

Massachusetts Federalists took a narrow view of the war. State senators resolved "that in a war, like the present, urged without justifiable cause, and prosecuted in a manner which indicates that conquest and ambition are its real motives, it is not becoming a moral and religious people to express any approbation of military or naval exploits, which are not immediately connected with the defense of our sea-coast and soil." To one Federalist editor the Madison Administration was its enemy and not England. Madison was rapidly proceeding to ruin the country with a unredeemable debt and disgrace.

Federalists were pro-British, despite what the British had done to them in now and past years, and it was nature they would claim as late as 1814 that the Jeffersonian Republicans were gratifying an old hatred against the British and were assisting the French to subdue the English. The war would strengthen the Republicans and silence the opposition and "command their wealth for the purposes of keeping them still." Further they would establish a government like Napoleon's.

The British were naturally angered at the American action. Unwilling to listen to American complaints, they felt they had been stabbed in the back while fighting the Napoleonic menace. Their American policy was vital to the war effort and they were outraged that the Americans could rake up a fuss. The *Edinburgh Review*, a highly influential periodical criticized the British policy as did the Liverpool *Advertiser*. Most liberals might view impressment as essential, but Britain practice of that right to be immoderate and unjust. The exporting British manufacturers continued to be hurt and they exerted a pressure which was eventually to lead to peace. [1]

The redoubtable Isaac Hull was born on March 9, 1773, at Derby on the Housatonic River of Connecticut, navigable to lesser ships, twelve miles from Long Island Sound near New Haven. Ships back from distant lands docked at Derby and the town became a center of supplies for the inland to the north. Workers built the smaller ships in Derby.

The Hulls had settled in Derby early in its existence, but did not go to sea until Isaac's father Joseph became a whale fisherman and then plied the Caribbean on a merchantman. They were an influential family. Joseph had served in the Revolutionary War. Second son Isaac played war while his father spent a year as a prisoner of war of the British. Although he learned to read and write, Isaac did not like school. He grew up a brave lad and he went to sea. His first voyage was to the West Indies. On a later trip he was shipwrecked off the coast of Ireland.

In those days of the early republic, ship masters were faced with the terror of capture by the pirates of North Africa and then also by the French and British who were now at war once again. Neutral ships in the ports of one of the two great powers were subject to seizure by the other. French privateers twice captured Hull and his ships. Later, in the early spring of 1798, President Adams appointed Hull a lieutenant of the Navy. His first assignment was abroad the *Constitution*, in time to be known as "Old Ironsides."

His first great exploit was in the capture of the *Sandwich* in a neutral port. The details of the success can be read in the Bruce Grant biography of Hull. His duty off North Africa was similar to that of John Rodgers. Both men proved brave and able sailors on that mission. Hull took part in the action against Tripoli in 1804. He continued his service and on June 17, 1810, he became captain of the *Constitution*.

On a 1811 voyage, Hull and his ship encountered a British squadron blockading the Harbor of Cherbourg. The situation was intense. Everyone remembered the *Chesapeake* affair. Hull insisted upon landing the American minister to France who was abroad. The British backed down and Hull landed his passengers. Despite British hostility, he also managed to land at Texel to be delivered to the Dutch a shipment of $28,000 in gold. The French fired upon the American *Constitution*, thinking it was British, but soon Hull was able to make his signal. After other events, Hull and his men returned to America on board the ship.

With the declaration of war, Hull and his ship set out for sea. He did not know that there was a British squadron in his path. In fact he was expecting to see Rodgers on the high seas. In his first days of his sail he was busy training his new crew. On the afternoon of July 16th, his lookout reported four sailing ships in sight. Hull directed his sailors to close in to determine the nationality of the vessels. When night fell he gave the night signal. There was no reply so he knew that they were foreign ships. They must be enemy. Upon the second day, he discovered enemy ships at hand moving in. Hull cleared the ship for action. Upon a suggestion from his lieutenant, he decided to warp his ship out of range. The British could see what was happening and they did the same.

Hull targeted a fifth ship away from the four. With a light wind his ship came to the windward and the two ships cleared each other. He sailed that night and at the morning watch. The other ship, the *Guerriere*, warned the other British four that an enemy frigate was near. In the morning light Hull saw several British men of war an they were in hot pursuit of the American.

The *Constitution* let down her boats and used them to tow the ship out of the reach of British guns. The *British* towing boats were helping that swift ship to move along. Hull mustered her hawsers using all her spare rope. They played them down into the cutters. A kedge was turn out and let go. One kedge was run up and a second was carried ahead. In this way the *Constitution* began outdistancing the British warships. However this was set to change when there was a wind the American warship could take advantage of.

In the seesaw of events, it was calm once again. Hull had two thousand gallons of water pumped out and the boats were soon towing the ship. There were great efforts on both sides. They relaxed their labor for awhile. Captain Hull ordered the firing to begin, but when it did little good, he ordered it to cease. Neither the British fleet nor *Constitution* could gain enough advantage. Eleven sail were in sight. The British were intent upon taking the American ship so they were interested in nothing else, not even an American merchantman. The American captain gained an escape when he entered a squall. Soon after three days, the English gave up the chase. Days later, Hull edged his ship into Boston harbor to tell the story of his close escape. Captain James R. Dacres of the *Guerriere* issued a challenge for a British ship to duel with any American ship of equal force. [2]

Meanwhile on mainland America, there was equal conflict. Stung by Hull's proclamation to the Canadians, Brock issued one of his own. Brock wrote that it was an unprovoked declaration of war that Congress had passed. Actually it was hardly unprovoked. He stated that the Americans had been the invaders. To Brock the American proclamation was indeed slander. The Government had not injured the Canadian subject in his person, his liberty, or his property. Canada had wealth and prosperity, settled by exiles who had been forced to leave the old colonies because of their loyalty. They had been rewarded with prosperity of the northern colony, superior to that of their ancestors. Canadians had a safe access to markets across the ocean. Separation would lose them this advantage, he told the people. Threatened as they were by Napoleon, they must arise and fight off the American invader or risk the oppression of the French emperor. Canadians were bound to defend the English monarchy. To aid the Americans would be unforgivable treason. Britain would not consent to any peace terms which would give Canada to the United States. [3]

Because of their guilt as a people and individuals, God was punishing the Americans in the estimation of the antiwar citizens. We must, they said, hear the voice of God on such occasions. The declaration of war was just "the beginning of sorrows." Governors of New England states set up fast days. They were to plead for their alliance with infidel France and seek justice for persecution of the Indians.

On the other side of the coin, Madison set aside a day of fast, not for America's guilt, but for a blessing of God on American arms. The conflict he stated was due to the injustice of a foreign power. He did not use any particular Christian phraseology in order to keep the government free from religious interference. Still, he was attacked by sermons on the issues involved. America was very much divided on the war from its first day and in conflict over political issues from the enjoining of differences between Great Britain and France in Washington's administration. [4]

On July 24, 1812, the schooner *Industry* arrived in New York City, a prize of the privateer *Benjamin Franklin*. It was laden with pickled salmon worth about $2,000 when captured to prevent the ship from giving information to British cruisers of the privateer. When the owners learned that the *Industry* was owned by a poor widow who had a family, they restored the ship and the *Industry* headed along its way.

Nine days later Philadelphia's privateer schooner the *Shadow* discovered a sail on the high seas and chased her for five hours to learn that she was a British warship, which tacked and fired upon the *Shadow*. It lost her by nightfall. On the following day, she chased another ship for five hours or so and engaged her in action. After an exchange of demands and rejections, there was another exchange of fire until it was too dark. On the next morning, the fight continued and the American captain was killed. At this time, the *Shadow* was so damaged that they had to work the pumps. [5]

A bold and able seaman since the age of ten, Thomas Boyle, received command of the *Comet* at age thirty-six to play havoc with the British. He was a strict master and bought forth a disciplined seamanry. Leaving Baltimore, Boyle set sail swiftly and with an accurate fire against the British merchantman *Henry*, with its cargo of sugar and wine, that the captain quickly surrendered. Only three weeks later on August 16, 1812, Boyle and his men chased their second prize which fired. Soon they were at each other's throats with broadsides. The captain ordered his marines to fire their muskets since he could not board the ship *Hopewell*. In the hours fight, the British ship lost use of one gun after another. Finally, the Britisher surrendered. The cargo was made up of sugar, molasses, cotton, coffee, and cocoa. It was sent to Baltimore as a prize. They took an easy third prize bound from Surinam for London. Another prize was taken, the *John*, an English letter of marque, with its load of cotton, sugar, rum, coffee, and fifty calves. All in all it was a rich haul of $400,000, one half of which went for court costs and duty. Boyle was able to buy an interest in the *Comet* with his share of the profits of the voyage.[6]

It was late in the afternoon of July 26, 1812, that the privateer schooner *Highflyer* closed in upon an English schooner *Harriet*. This small ship was carrying ballast with three passengers and a crew of four blacks. Unarmed, Captain Mason could not resist. A careful Captain Gavet placed one of his prizemasters, with instructions to spend the night on the *Harriet*. A nervous Mason volunteered the situation of $8,000 in specie hidden abroad. The ship was brought along sides and searched. The money was found. Although use to their freedom, the blacks were listed as prize goods and sold into slavery. One month later, the *Highflyer* came upon a convoy and tried to entice the frigate in charge. Finally he was able to do so and hurried to reach the ship without their protector. Gavet took out a straggler the barque *Diana*. Gavet chased after the convoy once again and fought the ship the *Jamaica*. They took other ships. He would now return to Baltimore to refit and to sell the ships boarded for sale. There was lots of prize money to go around. [7]

Despite this activity on the ocean, the British were eager to continue their trade with the Americans. They especially wished provisions and wood. Very much engaged in a struggle, a life or death struggle, with Napoleon, they needed grain, flour, and naval stores which they had gotten from the Americans even in troubled times of embargoes. America had been used to shipping supplies for British armies in Portugal and Spain and this supplying continued with British licenses. Consulates instructed the British captains to assist and protect U. S. merchantmen transporting those products so vital to the operations of British armies in important and busy Iberian theater of operations. There they were aiding a people who had risen against Napoleon's older brother Joseph Bonaparte, king of Spain. At first successful and then repulsed, the Spanish people fought on aided by armies under British military leaders Sir John Moore and the Duke of Wellington. [8]

Baltimore was a Republican city in the midst of a Federalist Maryland countryside, This boomtown, founded in 1729, owed much to emigrants who had made Baltimore into the third largest city in the United States. There was a long and bitter conflict between the two political parties in the state legislature. Feeling was high and prolonged. This was heightened by strong ethnic divisions since the English hating Germans, Irish, and Frenchmen, as did the Scots and Scots-Irish, formed separate churches, militia units, and social organizations. Various classes provided a ferment of social differences.

Politics was the concern of all citizens and they clashed frequently and vigorously. Since 1808 there was an increase in Federalist strength in the state and city. One of the chief promoters of the Federalist cause in Baltimore was the editor of the Federalist newspaper, Alexander Contee Hanson. His paper the *Federal Republican* kept him in hot water with Baltimore's Republicans, who did not take kindly to the criticism inflict upon them and Republican national policies by editor Hanson.

The Federalists also had a political organization. This was the Washington Benevolent Society. It was supposed to educate poor children, but actually the society was political. Branches in almost all of the counties aided that party. Federalists used the money granted to the society to print propaganda and fill campaign coffers in the counties of the sate. Alexander Contee Hanson was president of the society and in the pages of his newspaper opposed war with Britain. The Republican editors, William Pechin of the *American* and Baptiste Irvine of *The Whig* supported the war. Name calling was openly scornful on both sides. The Federalists called Madison a dupe of Napoleon and Republicans called Federalists monarchists and aristocrats.

Four days after war was declared a Republican mob destroyed Hanson's newspaper office without any restraint from city officials who were scared of the mob. Hanson and his co-editor, Jacob Wagner, had to flee. During the following two days the mob threatened the property of the Federalists in Baltimore. Some small damage was done. Most of the Federalists in the city were not too unhappy over Hanson's departure since they believed that it was now time for unity and it would be dangerous to their well being to act otherwise. Also they probably feared the violence and wished harmony in their city as well as harmony in the nation.

Hanson returned to Baltimore. A house was secured and an edition printed up in Georgetown as if it were published in Baltimore, there being no press available to use in Baltimore. The house, number 45 on Charles Street near the harbor, was on Saturday evening occupied by Hanson and his men, well armed. The next day the twenty-seventh, they distributed their newspaper in Baltimore with the address of 45 Charles Street. The issue attacked the Baltimore mayor personally and directly. A crowd gathered and was partly dispersed by a city magistrate until the arrival of arms for the Federalists. That brought an even larger crowd. The men in the house were said to be from 50 to 75 well armed men.

Some young boys started yelling curses and throwing rocks at the house. One man tried to stop the rock throwing but a stone from the house caught him on the foot. This angered the crowd. The man's effort at stopping trouble ended, through no fault of his, and affairs were promoted by troublesome men on both sides. More stone throwing followed and soon this evening of the twenty-seventh saw all first story windows broken and inside shutters smashed. The leader of the defenders, General "Light-Horse Harry" Lee, the Virginian, would not allow the men in the house to retaliate further yet.

The danger to the defenders increased by nine in the evening. Hanson came to a second story window and spoke to the crowd. The crowd were told that the defenders were armed and would fire upon the crowd if need be. This angered the crowd and when the defenders fired blanks, the crowd turned into a mob. The front door was rushed.

The mob entered the house and was fired upon by the defenders whom Lee had stationed at the top of the stairs. Three men were wounded and one was killed; the mob retreated. Finally at about ten in the evening, the chief justice of Baltimore's criminal court arrived to try to end the action and fighting in the house and streets. He was a Republican but was not listened to neither the crowd nor the defenders.

Soon an attempt at rousing the militia succeeded in presenting a small unit of the militia under Barney. The defenders would not surrender to the militia and Major William B. Barney was forced to wait outside pending more instructions from militia leader Brigadier General John Stricker. A cannon was taken from a nearby armory by the crowd but no one was able to discover how to work the cannon. It was generally pointed in the wrong direction. The mob almost killed its owner and the few militiamen present.

Baltimore's mayor came with General Stricker and others to the house early on the morning of the 28th after the long night came to a close. They entered the house and pointed out to the defenders their danger from the mob and its cannon. The artillery piece had been loaded, but unknown to the defenders, it would not go off. The Federalists, the defenders, were asked to surrender and be taken to the jail for safe keeping.

At first the combative Hanson preferred to fight and suggested cutting their way out and beyond with swords. It was considered, but rejected by the rest of the defenders. Then they offered to surrender if Sticker would disperse the mob. This though was forgotten when Hanson and Lee were told the militia was the mob. Finally the Federalists gave up to be taken to the jail house by the militia units in service.

Some escaped, others tried and were captured by the mob and beaten. The rest were surrounded by militia units under Barney. They were followed by the threatening mob for the mile journey to jail. Conditions were such that it took two hours for the trip. Stones were thrown and Stricker was wounded along with the Federalists. They must have felt real terror on the slow journey.

During the day an attempt was made to gather enough militiamen to protect the jail. This failed. That night the Republican mob returned and the jail was rushed. The mob took out the Federalists and badly beat and tortured them until they were sure they must be dead. Two men were killed. Finally the authorities gathered the entire militia and protected the post office, where copies of the newspapers were said to be.

News of the savagery reached other towns and the Federalist party gained politically. Hanson became a hero. He was elected from a rural district to Congress, but meanwhile Federalist opposition was silenced in Baltimore. However, in a voters' backlash, Federalists gained control of the Maryland House of Delegates. Federalists in the rest of nation denounced the violence, which Republicans blamed on the Federalists. The publicity and Federalist campaigns made the newspaper widely read, except in Baltimore. Further, the riots fueled Federalist dissent in the nation. [9]

Upon the opening of the War of 1812, Kentucky was the largest and most developed area in the west, the trans-Appalachian west. The center of the state was Lexington in east central Kentucky. It was the largest and richest of towns in the region and at the time, the largest town west of Pittsburgh. There was a college, two newspapers, a public library, several jockey clubs, and schools teaching French, fencing, and dancing. Because of Kentucky's development, it was looked up to as the political and military center of the west. Through this exposure the war indirectly affected the Kentucky Lincoln family, through its beginning young Abe was too young to know the effect the war had upon Kentucky and the west. [10]

---

[1]Updyke, *Diplomacy*, pp. 131, 133-136. Quotes on pp. 133, 134, 136.

[2]Grant, Bruce, *Isaac Hull: Captain of Old Ironsides: The Life and Fighting Times of Isaac Hull and the U.S. Frigate Constitution*, Chicago: Pellegrini & Cudahy, 1947, pp. 7-15, 17, 19-23, 26-28, 46-53, 60-117, 166, 178-191, 205-216; Coggeshall, *History*, pp. 9-20.

[3]Cruikshank, *Documents*, pp. 81-83.

[4]Gribbin, Churches, pp. 19-24.

[5]Coggeshall, *History*, p. 60.

[6]Cranwell and Crane, *Men of Marque*, pp. 125-131.

[7] *Ibid.*, pp. 75-80.

[8] Dudley, *Naval War*, I, 202-203.

[9] Cassell Frank, "The Great Baltimore Riot of 1812," *Maryland Historical Magazine*, LXX (Fall 1975), pp. 241-253; Hickey, *War of 1812*, pp. 56-57, 59, 61-65, 68-71; Richardson, John, *War of 1812*, Toronto: Historical Publishing, 1902, pp. 9-11.

[10] Hammack, *Kentucky*, pp 16-17.

CHAPTER XV

MILITARY ACTION

William Henry Harrison was entrusted with regaining Michigan, but he was hampered unacceptably by being placed under Tennessee planter James Winchester. Finally, President Madison listened to Henry Clay and other Kentuckians and gave Harrison full command of the Northwestern army. He moved forward with his large army but was forced to halt because of heavy rains. A series of frosts and thaws next slowed the advance. Lack of supplies furthered stalled the force.

One W. K. Jordan left the American Fort Wayne on August 1, 1812, with Captain Wells and over one hundred Indians who had pretended to be their friends. They were ordered to go the 200 miles to Fort Dearborn to rescue Captain Hill and his company and bring them back to Fort Wayne. Ten days later they reached the fort without incident and loaded up. They destroyed what they could and started on the homeward journey. Most were not going to reach home. Hill had one hundred soldiers, ten women, and twenty children. They had only gone one mile when some 500 Kickapoo and Winnebago Indians attacked. Jordan's Indiana joined them. The battle last ten minutes. The only American survivors were Jordan and fourteen others. They became captives and Wells was beheaded. Left to live, Jordan wanted to escape and soon did. [1]

The two Canadian fur companies had a great interest in seizing Detroit because it was along one of their routes to the western fur country. Hull noted that it was a channel of supply. These two outfits had a great influence upon the Indians around Lake Superior and to its west and could be expected to bring these native Americans into the fray on the British side. Not remise in his duty, Hull directed that fortifications be made. He and his officers believed the fort at Malden could not be taken without artillery to bombard its strength. Also he directed the construction of floating batteries which he planned to use to drive the British ship, the *Queen Charlotte*, from the mouth of the River Canards.

Hull felt the need of an American victory at Niagara, but although he deplored the inaction there, he did not feel his own lack of bold action contributed to the weakness of his position. There was the time to be bold because time was on the side of the British. The lack of supplies would soon choke his army, while the British could supply their own forces. The key to the Northwest was the lakes and the Indians. Great Britain had the advantage of both at this stage of the war. [2]

William Hull ordered Major Thomas Van Horne to Detroit to command an expedition of some 200 men south to reopen lines and deliver mail. Although Hull had suggested he take back roads, Van Horne went by the main pathway. Nearing Brownstown, he stopped his men for water from a French settler's house. The man warned Van that an Indian ambush was set ahead on the road. Disregarding this vital piece of intelligence, he marched his men forth. Soon they were indeed ambushed by a small band of Indians. Fearing being surrounded, Van Horne ordered a retreat instead of fighting it out. Already fearful, the men panicked and fled. They left the mail behind so eager were they to escape. The British read the mail and were informed that Hull was very nervous. This made them the bolder and they prepared to deal with Hull, which as we have seen they did. [3]

When word of the fall of Detroit reached the more settled frontier area, the people became as much alarmed as those on the edge of the frontier. Panic was general. Fugitives from Detroit covered their cowardice with claims of a hundred fresh scouts being presented to Colonel Matthew Allot for payment at the rate of six dollars each. Indians were gathering all over the Northwest and Canada eager for plunder and to devastate the settlements, towns, and farmlands of Ohio closest to the frontier.

Someone sighted the two British warships on Lake Erie's south shore and the people of Chautaqua County were terrorized with the mere thought of invasion. Settlers remembered the massacres of Cherry Valley and Wyoming and people fled eastward. Militiamen demanded their pay and used every excuse for seeking furloughs. This appeal fell on deaf years so they claimed sickness or actually deserted. [4]

At noon on the first of August, the privateer *Yankee*, at ease off the coast of Nova Scotia, saw a large ship to her lee bow and chased it from four miles away. One hour later, she made preparations for an attack. A firing of cannon followed on the Americans' part. It next gave her a broadside and the other, the *Royal Bounty* replied. The sailors on the *Yankee* fired their muskets. After the Americans cut the British ship's sails and rigging away, the British *Royal Bounty* became unmanageable. After a raking broadside and more musketry the Britisher's Captain Henry Gambles surrendered. Three Americans were wounded and the *Yankee*'s sails and rigging received some damage. The British casualties were two men killed and seven wounded.

Captain Isaac Hull, eager to be once again at sea, hurried his preparations with the *Constitution*, taking only about a week, to refill his water supplies, reprovision his ship, and give his officers and crew some time for relaxation and rest. He left port on August 2d. Cruising to the eastward, he saw and captured the British brig *Adiona* on the way with ship timber. He took her crew off her and had his men set her afire. On the early morning of the 15th, they sighted a convoy of five sail. At dawn the *Constitution* was gaining rapidly and at six the warship cast away her tow and set it afire. Shortly Hull chased a British prize from the convoy and captured it. There were other captures as he tried to take the whole convoy.

On August 3, 1812, the lookout of the American schooner *Atlas* had on that morning, early in the day, sighted two sail to the westward. Captain David Moffet ordered a pursuit. One and a half hours later at ten, he directed a beat to quarters and a clearing for action. The *Atlas* sailed closer and hoisted the American ensign and pendant, and saw the two ships clearly flying English flags. The smaller ship fired a shot and soon he engaged both ships. There was a broadside from the American. Those who were engaged at the cannon or in the sailing of the *Atlas* aimed and fired their guns and muskets.

At noon the small vessel struck her colors, but shortly opened fire once again. Twenty minutes later the large ship lowered her flags in surrender. Captain Moffet took possession of both ships at this point. Both had cargoes of sugar, coffee, cotton, and cocoa from Surinam and were bound for London. Two Americans were killed and five wounded. Because of damages to his ship, Moffet headed for the United States with his prizes, instead of sending them back and proceeding along his way as was usual.

Within one month they came within sight of a large ship to the east. She tacked and gave chase for the Americans, so Moffet dispersed his two prizes with orders to make for safety off a United States port. The frigate, flying an English flag, headed for the prize, the *Planter,* with its American flag, but it turned out that the frigate was an American ship under English flag and the prize subsequently made port. [5]

The frigate *Essex* was heavily armed and a very powerful ship when engaged at close quarters. This was proven in this encounter of August 12, 1812. Captain David Porter sailed it forth from New York City on a voyage to Bermuda. There they saw seven British troopships with an escort of a single warship. This was the HMS *Minerva*, which had the same number of guns as did the *Essex*. Its captain, Richard Hawkins, refused battle and tried to protect his troopships. Porter did manage however to capture one of the ships and continued his trip to take seven more prizes. When she came up against the HMS *Alert*, Porter pretended to be a merchantman by trying to escape. Its captain fell for the feint and came up close. A short fight erupted but the *Alert* was not the equal of the *Essex* and was caught by surprise. The British captain T. L. O. Langharne had to surrender with a hold filling up with water. [6]

The United States navy was beset with problems too, but because of able naval officers and sailors the sea war went better than the land war. Secretary of the Navy Paul Hamilton was a South Carolina rice planter and was not competent and had little knowledge of naval affairs. An alcoholic, he was usually drunk by noon. On the good side, he had been an advocate of preparedness, but was unable to move Gallatin or Congress into providing the necessary money for ships and men.

Those who lead a nation into war had better spend a large amount of money on the military if they hope to win. This was not the case in 1812. Only the privateers provided the margin to win big in the naval side of the conflict. Private enterprise paid off over governmental efforts which were less than necessary to win the war at sea. Beset by a belief in limited government and lower budgets, the Jeffersonian Republicans had failed to provide the necessities of warfare. For their part, the War Hawks expected an easy victory and while they could push the nation into war, they were unwilling to adequately prepare for it. America had but seventeen ships in 1812 to face the greatest navy in the world. Fortunately the British navy was spread in many parts of the world to protect the empire and the island of Britain. Still, the British had superiority in the North Atlantic and was able to deploy more ships in 1813 to augment their modest force in American waters.

Maritime experience had fashioned officers and men into first rate sailors and skilled marksmen. It was the ability of Americans to have better ships and abler cannoneers than British that gave them the edge over the British in the sea battles described here. Most of the officers and many of the men had fought in the naval battles in the naval wars against France and Tripoli. Well trained, the men enjoyed high morale. The navy as opposed to the privateers did not have the choice of men, but so many were available that this did not cripple the American navy. One of the big problems was that recruits could earn bounties in the army or fight as privateers with shorter enlistments, less danger, and the possibility of larger profits. The navy had to take steps to compete with bounties, higher pay, and better terms of enlistment. [7]

On August 19, 1812, Issac Hull was sailing the United States frigate *Constitution* when he saw a sail on the horizon. He began a chase at 2 PM. One and a half hour of chase enabled Hull to decide that the ship was a frigate, awaiting an attack. Hull was ready for an encounter of the most serious kind. It's captain Dacres was most anxious for a battle, as determined as Hull. The *Guerriere*, for it was the British *Guerriere*, gave the American frigate a broadside and pulled away. A second broadside fell short. The British maneuvered for a raking fire. Hull's ship finally got into a good position and he ordered a heavy fire at five minutes before six PM.

Shortly the British ship reeled and trembled with a tremendous shock and there was a crash on deck. The opposing captain lost his mizzen-mast and his main-yard with many of his sail torn to pieces. More damages to sail and hull put the *Guerriere* in danger of sinking should the fire continue. Hull ceased firing and finally closed with the ship whose captain surrendered her. The ship was not worth towing to port so severe were the damages. There were no sails to steady the ship and she lay rolling. The deck was covered with dead men and with wounded men. The American gunners had done their work.

In casualties the Americans got the advantage. One lieutenant of marines and six seamen were killed on the American side and one lieutenant, a master, four seamen, and one American marine was wounded.. This made a total of 14 casualties. The British had seven times this loss. Three British officers, 12 seamen and marines were dead from the fight. Captain J. A. Dacres, four officers, and 57 seamen and marines were wounded. Missing were two lieutenants and 22 seamen and marines who it was believed went overboard with the masts and drowned. [8]

This astounding victory cheered the Americans immensely, in the opening months of a war in which they were greatly outnumbered on the high seas. This preponderance of British naval power could but concern naval officers and all who knew of it. Not all of the frigates and twelve or fifteen sloops-of-war were battle ready and they were completely outnumbered by one thousand and sixty British sail that not even the privateers could counter. Of course some of these were at other posts, but still the balance could be weighted easily in Britain's favor. Only American boldness could begin to make the difference. [9]

It took the victory of August 19, 1812, to transform pessimism about the American Navy into an optimistic outlook and pride in American warships. Most Americans had believed that the British seamen and ships were far superior to those of their nation. The American tars had proved their worth on the high seas. Their newly born faith in the sea arm of the country brought with it renewed interest in the navy which led to increased effort to prevail on the high sea in the Madison Administration. American naval forces had been generally neglected except at times of national crisis. Now, building ships for warfare began the rage and people were glad to pay their taxes for such a triumph to be repeated. Congress reacted by authorizing money to build new warships. Isaac Hull's victory helped Madison to win a second term. Hull's success was a hard blow to British pride, but Britain had other ships which they were to transfer to American waters. The competition was increased. [10]

Governor Sherbrooke, having already issued a privateering license against the French, was persuaded to do so against the Americans on August 29th. The *Black Joke* (officially the *Liverpool Packet*) set sail on a privateering mission on the last day of August. It was supposedly a hunter of French ships, but its captain sought U. S. ships from the first. The ship was sailed to the Georges Bank, fishing grounds off Canada, to await the sailing lanes for American ships. It stopped the *Middlesex* and although it had a British license to trade, the captain of the *Black Joke* seized the ship with its cargo of coal, salt, earthenware, and sundries and sent it to prize court. Next he took captive the *Factor*, bearing Portuguese wine, with its prize crew of an English ship. The prize court held the license of the *Middlesex* to be good and released the ship to the American captain and the *Factor* was sold and the jewelry and specie still aboard were restored to its owner in Philadelphia. [11]

The *Globe* was unsuccessful on its second venture cruising in the Gulf Stream and West Indian waters. In alliance with the *Rossie*, they took one ship and then when parted, they made no other capture. Other ships had better fortune, but the ship *Sarah Ann* after a trip in which she captured, had worst, being captured. The British took six crewmen whom they claimed were British subjects and sent them to Jamaica to be tried for treason. Captain Richard Moon told officials that only one was a British subject. The Americans held hostages of Britons for safety and none of the six were executed. Shortly Moon took over the *Globe*.

This ship continued to suffer from bad luck. It went aground and cleared the Capes on January 30, 1813. Men suffered injuries and sickness and died. Moon had instructions to avoid the Caribbean with its English cruisers and cruised off the coast of Portugal. He had better luck than the previous captains. However, his first prize was probably recaptured because it never arrived in the United States for prize court adjudication. [12]

On August 19, 1812, the day of the famous sea battles, the Mississippi delta and New Orleans were struck by a terrible hurricane, the worst they had had in years. Great damage was done to American warships stationed there. Captain John Shaw had been busy developing a naval force and defense in Louisiana, and the storm interrupted his efforts. He had recently fully manned the Brig *Enterprise* and the hurricane drove it ashore; however, there was no damage to its hull and no loss of life. It would be difficult and require much time to relaunch the ship. The Brig *Viper*, which he was having repaired, was completely unrigged by the wind and the driving of three or four large merchant ships against her. One gunboat was stranded. Two men drown from the crew of the *Ketch Etna*. Wind also damaged the naval hospital and other buildings. Roofs were blown off. New Orleans lost its market house and many people lost their lives when it was completely leveled. The city suffered residential losses. Lieutenant Daniel S. Dexter reported damage to his vessels, although he had made very good preparations when winds increased heralding the hurricane. The Brig *Siren* escaped major damage. [13]

The commissioners at Urbana received a letter from Dayton, Ohio, on August 24, 1812, telling them that the British were in control of the Rapids of Miami. Fort Wayne was the only barrier left and it was in danger, the writer said. General Harrison moved his army quickly to the far frontier. A further advance was made until Harrison joined forces between Lebanon and Dayton on August 31. The cavalry was left behind for rest. It voted Richard M. Johnson as its major before riding during the night to join the general.

Johnson received orders to destroy the Potawatomie villages on the Elkhart. On September 18th, he and his battalion reached Fort Wayne just in time. Meanwhile more mounted riflemen set out from Kentucky and more orders reached Harrison to proceed to Detroit as a step to the conquest of Upper Canada. First a fort was rebuilt and named Fort Winchester. Cold weather began to plague the soldiers who lacked sufficient clothes, shoes, and provisions. Kentucky women folk began to make warm clothing. [14]

From Frankfort, on August 25th, Henry Clay wrote James Monroe that Kentuckians felt very alarming apprehensions for Hull and his army. The general had written on the 11th "that almost all the Indians had become hostile; that owing to the tardy operations of the army and Niagara, and the fall of Michilimackinack, the prospects of his army had entirely changed; that his provisions were scarce, and that unless speedily relieved by a repeated reinforcement, he anticipated the most fatal consequences." Since then the Kentuckians learned that in Hull's army there was no confidence, he was surrounded by enemies, and that batteries would soon destroy his fortress. Governor Charles Scott took steps to come to Hull's aid. Clay and others supported Scott. Before this letter reached Monroe, the Virginian president wrote Clay that the word had reached Washington DC that Hull had surrendered. Monroe surmised that this was the results of panic in the army. Hull had shown a want of energy, and had delayed when he should have advanced. [15]

In his report of August 26, 1812, from Fort George, William Hull stressed the Indian menace his fort at Detroit faced when he surrendered. The victory of the British at Michilimakinac encouraged every Indian tribe in the Midwest to join the British, from the Lake Superior and the Mississippi, from the Ohio and the Wabash, and from all of Upper Canada and in the immediate country. Many of these tribe had assured the Americans of their neutrality. This mass of Indians had cut off the communication lines and supply routes of Detroit. [16]

General Brock was disappointed about the armistice of the seventeenth of August, but nonetheless he headed for Kingston at the northeastern end of Lake Ontario not far from the province of Quebec. Once there the British general inspected fortifications and militia. Then he wrote to Sir George Prevost, asking for his permission to attack Sackett's Harbor in New York on the lake southeast from Kingston. He had reliable information that American ships on Lake Ontario were there for their safety. Because of British superiority on the lake, he could easily capture the American port. He planned also to attack other posts when they sent relief forces for Sackett's Harbor. General Prevost as more cautious and prepared a defensive posture. He even hinted that Brock took too many chances in his attack on Detroit.

No sooner did Prevost reject the offensive ideas of Brock's, then the general learned that Von Rensselaer had given notice for the termination of the momentary peace. By this time Von Rensselaer and his Americans were better ready to fight the British and Canadians. The American preparations and strength convinced Brock that the Americans would soon attack, so he worked to ready his troops. There were four main camps near the Falls. The Americans had erected batteries and now had numerous boats to transport troops from these camps. Von Rensselaer was training his troops with dispatch. Brock immediately worked feverishly to fortify and train, to build artillery batteries and earthworks, and to raise and arm soldiers. He also ordered a communications system of telegraphs by signal flags and beacons by fires in the surrounding countryside. [17]

There was a western movement for William Henry Harrison to lead an invasion force into Upper Canada. Henry Clay promoted the militia general in Washington. Governor Charles Scott made him commander and major general of the Kentucky militia and the new Kentucky governor Isaac Shelby celebrated Harrison's appointment at his inaugural ceremonies. Harrison had feared that his first acts would be defensive instead of aggressive. The new major general wrote that Canada could not be conquered that autumn as the frontiersmen had confidentially expected.

Dressed for effect in a plain hunting shirt, Harrison readied himself and on the next day rode horseback to Cincinnati. Along the way, he learned of Hull's surrender and the massacre of the garrison of Fort Dearborn. Fort Wayne was surrounded being half the size of Anthony Wayne's fort of the nineties. The messenger from the fort with this news, a young settler named William Oliver, volunteered to return with word that relief was on

The Difficult War: The Era of the War of 1812   129

its way. Four friendly Indians were sent with the brave man. The five made it safely while the hostile Indians held council in the woods.

At Cincinnati, Harrison learned of the difficulties of his command. He found out that not surprising he lacked ready munitions and equipment. Nearby Newport had only a single cannon, a four ponder, and only 1200 cartridges. There were no dragoon pistols and little in the way of hospital supplies. Since he was a militia officer he could not draw upon the War Department, but he could and did ask the Cincinnati people for homemade cartridges which were forthcoming in the amount of 12,000 and put on a wagon train for Fort Wayne. More cartridges were made by militiamen. He marched his army toward the fort. Nearly halfway to Fort Wayne, he awaited the supply train and a regiment of Kentucky cavalry from Frankfort. Soon it was time to march again. Since the Americans were in larger numbers, the realistic Indian decided they could not win and they retreated. The siege of Fort Wayne was raised. [18]

In August of 1812 rumors reached the American Indians in New York that the British had seized Grand Island, the ancient home of the Senecas. The Senecas met with American Indian agent Erastus Granger. Red Jacket had his say. The Americans had told them, he said, "that we had nothing to do with the war between you and British, but we find that the war has come to our doors. Our property is taken possession by the British and their Indians friends. It is necessary for us now to take up the business, defend our property and drive the enemy from it."

If they did nothing, then the Americans would claim it by conquest after the war much as the British were doing it now. They soon learned that the rumor was false. However, the settlers in frontier Niagara did not want to join the militia because their family might be subject to Indian attack. Granger was to report on September 23rd, that the young men of the Seneca nation could not be restrained. If the United States would not use their services, they would fight for the British. [19]

Daniel Newman led a detachment of Georgia volunteers against the Florida Indians known as the Lotchaway and Alligator Indians. The unit of about 250 men and officers arrived upon St. Johns about mid-August of 1812. Reporting to Colonel Smith before St. Augustine he was ordered to immediately attack the hostile Indians in East Florida and destroy Indian towns and settlements and provisions. Newman hastened to St. John's and set his men to buy horses from those few inhabitants still in the provinces and prepare for a march with supplies. He reckoned without illnesses which struck him and nearly one half of his force. Finally in later September he prepared again.

Almost set to march, he received an express from the colonel. Smith said that his provision wagons and the escort were attacked by a body of blacks and Indians and he needed him and his transport facilities to remove the baggage, field pieces, and the sick. This Indian attack delayed Newman as the acceded to Smith's request. It took several days before Newman could prepare his detachment again. By this time, his men had only six or seven days to serve in their enlistment. A third of the force volunteered to stay forth three more weeks. Colonel Smith sent 23 volunteer militiamen and nine more volunteered under a Captain Cone. Newman's force now numbered 117 men and officers.

On September 24, 1812, they filed forth. The ground was open for the most part and the nightly encampment was in the form of a triangle with baggage in the center and clothed men laying feet outward, ready for any attack. Four days out they came upon the Indians, ready for battle. Soon the Indians fired and the commander ordered a charge which drove the natives from behind their trees, driving them into a swamp half a mile back. Newman's men captured the Indian baggage and provisions. They fought for two and one half hours. The Indians got the worst of the casualties.

The Indians got more blacks, who had at one time escaped Southern slavery, and Indians who had been hardpressed by white settlers to renew the attack with horrid yells. The whites were steady and then drove them back. They repulsed the Indians and blacks although outnumbered three to one. That night the militiamen prepared a good breastwork of logs and earth. The battles were limited to firing at the long distance by the Indians for several days. Newman and his men were running out of food, but he was not fond of the idea of leaving the rough fort. However some of the men were talking about desertion and the men had then run out of food including the use of horses for their meat, so Newman finally withdrew his forces. The reinforcements and supply train missed its connection with the retreating party.

In the midst of American extremity, the Indians fired upon Newman's force and killed some. The commander ordered a charge which within fifteen minutes routed the Indians. They then marched onward several miles a day in hardship. Finally they came upon a gunboat awaiting them by order of Colonel Smith. They could now eat and they were a most happy detachment. They soon returned to Georgia. [20]

---

[1]*The Washington Post*, July 13, 1902, p. 26.

[2]Cruikshank, *Documents*, pp. 116-117.

[3]Heidler, Jeanne and Heidler, David S., "Brownstown, Battle of," Heidler & Heidler, *Encyclopedia*, p. 68; Richardson, *War of 1812*, pp. 26-27.

[4]Zaslow, M., *Defended Borders*, p. 22.

[5]Coggeshall, *History*, pp. 20-23, 49-50, 79-80.

[6]Tucker, Spencer C., "Essex Versus Alert," Heidler & Heidler, *Encyclopedia*, pp. 173-174.

[7]Hickey, *1812*, pp. 90-93.

[8]Brannan, *Official Letters*, pp. 49-51; Coggeshall, *History*, pp. 25-29.

[9]Coggeshall, *History*, pp. 35-36.

[10]Grant, *History*, pp. 4-5.

[11]Snider, *Under the Red Jack*, pp. 13-18 and ff.

[12]Cranwell & Crane, *Men of Marque*, pp. 89-91.

[13]Dudley, *Naval War*, I, 399-408, 428.

[14]Meyer, L.W., pp. 91-94.

[15]Clay, *Papers*, I, 719-720, 722-723. Quotes on p. 719.

[16]Brannan, *Official Letters*, pp. 44-49.

[17]Zaslow, *Defended*, pp. 22, 24-25.

[18]Cleaves, *Old Tippecanoe*, pp. 112-120.

[19]Babcock, *War of 1812*, pp. 27-28. Quote on p. 27.

[20]Brannan, *Official Letters*, pp., 78-83.

CHAPTER XVI

ZACHERY TAYLOR

Zachery Taylor was born into the American aristocracy on November 24, 1784, at Montebello plantation in Virginia and raised near Louisville. He received only a slight formal education to the degree of Lincoln's. With the crisis of the spring of 1808 over the previous year's *Chesapeake* affair, Congress added eight regiments to the small army. The future president was appointed a first lieutenant in the Kentucky regiment. His first task was to recruit, which was difficult. Next, he joined James Wilkinson's force in New Orleans, which was a rumored British target in 1809. Taylor escaped the horrors of the infected camp near that city because he was put in command at Fort Pickering on the Chickasaw Bluffs, located near the site of Memphis, Tennessee. In 1810, he was ordered back to Louisville where he married Margaret Makall Smith.

Before war broke, out Taylor did meritorious service and in 1812 was put in command of Fort Harrison in western Indiana. Meanwhile, western forts were falling and Fort Harrison was increasingly exposed. When the Indians attacked, Taylor had only sixteen healthy men and he was recovering from bilious fever. He was now twenty-seven. He had been in the army for four years, and was stationed in posts and in recruiting duty most of that time. Already he had a family and land in Kentucky. The fort was not a strong one, but the will of the young captain was strong, although it was difficult to defend when so many soldiers at the post were sick. Surgeon's Mate Lemuel B. Clarke was in charge of thirty-four men on the sick list.

On the afternoon of September 1, 1812, the sentries heard the turkey-call signals of the Indians in the woods. They alerted the garrison. Two civilians said they would investigate. Sentries heard four shot in the woods after they entered the woods. The Indians had killed and scalped the pair. A delegation from four tribes, following the Prophet, came to speak to Taylor and said a representative would come to ask for food for the starving Indians. By this the captain knew the Indians would soon attack. He gave orders for the sentries to be especially alert that night.

At eleven in the dark of night some 450 warriors advanced carefully toward the fort. A guard sighted the band and fired. The Indians replied with rifle shots. A few reached the fort and managed to start fires in a blockhouse. There was whiskey stored there and it caught fire and there was a big blaze. Most of the men thought that this was their end. Nine women and children cried. Two men escaped. Taylor had trouble getting his orders executed in the confusion, but Dr. Charles and a few others got up on the roof to pull off shingles to keep them from catching fire. The Indians killed one of these brave men. The women carried water to the men fighting the blaze. They won and the soldiers bridged the gap with temporary breastworks. Two men had deserted in the middle of the battle; one came back with a broken arm, while the other was hacked to death by the Indians. The Indians drove off the cattle and butchered horses and hogs and began a blockade of Fort Harrison. Taylor managed to get word out to Vincennes. Sixteen days into the month, the ford was relieved with men and their supplies. Taylor had saved the fort against great odds. [1]

At about this time, on the Fifth, large body of Indians attacked Fort Madison. One man with a pass went outside the fort where he was killed, tomahawked and scalped twenty-five paces from a sentinel in a blockhouse. Fire from that guard did not prevent the Indians from this murder. Shortly the Indians moved in upon the fort and a siege began. They retired when it got dark. On the Sixth, they attacked again and killed livestock and fired at the fort to receive fire in return. This continued on the 7th when the Indians set fire to houses and boats. Another house was burnt until the wind fell. The eighth was the last day of the Indian attack.

Governor Harrison learned by September 5, 1812, that the British and Indians had laid siege to Fort Wayne. Once they took that, it was believed that they would go to Fort Harrison and Vincennes. He wrote Governor Shelby that he must relieve those places with mounted men who could carry most of their provisions and supplies with them. Miller's regiment would be marched from the falls, followed by mounted men. Colonel Allen headed 900 Kentucky infantry and would be soon joined by 700 cavalry. Supplying these troops presented some problems to Harrison. [2]

Lincoln's part of the country felt considerable concern when word came of an Indian massacre to the north. On September 3, 1812, a war party of Delaware's descended upon Pigeon Roost, Indiana, and butchered several white families. One man and two children escaped and reached Westport, Kentucky, to spread the alarm. People were terrified. A relief party took out and reached the charred community. Two days later, on the 5th, Indians attacked Vincinnes in Indiana, and Fort Madison, close to St. Louis. Ohio was alarmed and home guards were raised in each community. Near Mansfield, Indians killed four out of eight whites they encountered. Black Bird began the siege of Fort Wayne, fresh from his victory at Chicago. The braves proved the brutality of their race. [3]

Kentucky volunteers gathered at Louisville on the Ohio and at other points on the Ohio River to meet the Indian forces. They received an appeal from Vincennes. Militiamen from Henderson County headed for Vincennes, where Acting Governor John Gibson had tried to relieve Taylor. Two parties were unable to get pass the Indians. Colonel William Rossell arrived with a force of three thousand men, enough to relieve Taylor and Fort Harrison. The Indians destroyed one supply train, but a second got through. [4]

Several units of volunteers marched under Harrison for Fort Wayne which was besieged and in dire straits. Chief John Logan was with them as a scout at first. A Shawnee, he decided that he would not stay. Logan reasoned that since he was an Indian and the war would eventfully end, he would be with the Indians after peace. The Indians would know that he had fought against them and would not be friends with him. Logan left and Harrison marched his army forth northwestwardly. One days march from the fort, the Indians scouted their camp. Alarms went off most of the night.

When the Indians saw that the white force was too strong, they left with the morning. Harrison marched the tired men to Fort Wayne from that camp, to find the fort in a deplorable state. The civilians were all within the walls. Indians had destroyed everything in the vicinity that they could not carry off. Firewood was scarce. They learned that a woodsman party had moved forth with axes and rifles, but when discovered had to retreat with two men killed near the fort. These two were buried.

Because there was not room enough in the small fort, Harrison's men were placed outside the walls around the fort. Indians were seen a couple of times, and did not make them feel secure where they were. General Harrison sent out three columns to pursue the Indians to Indian towns on the Wabash and to Elkhart Prairie. Units sent to the last found that Five Medals Town had just been deserted. Soldiers burnt down the wigwams. The two units found on the Wabash the three Indian towns in the same condition and burnt them also. The Indians had hurried away in both instances. [5]

Word reached Kentucky that Hull was in trouble. Shortly, Kentuckians like Thomas Lincoln learned of Hull's surrender. They did not despair, but indeed were aroused and gained new energies. Soon volunteers headed for the frontier to join forces. Thomas was not one of them. Individuals and companies passed through the towns and along the roads and trails. Company sizes varied from ten to one hundred. Indians were killing settlers and their families living in isolated areas on the frontier. On the headwaters of Silver Creek within two dozen miles of Louisville, natives massacred 22 whites. In his letter to James Monroe, Henry Clay blamed British instigation, American encroachments on Indian lands, the death of native leaders who had maintained a peace program, the young warriors, and the natural propensity of savages to warfare. Clay blamed Hull for either treachery or cowardice at Detroit. It did not matter which for the general should be shot. Clay believed that the large force under Harrison could remedy the situation. [6]

Hull defended himself shortly after his surrender, emphasizing the dangers he had faced from a large number of Indians from a wide region in which there were numerous tribes. They came as far away as beyond Lake Superior and the Mississippi. A large portion of the natives had promised neutrality, but with the war they entered the conflict destroying the American line of communications and supply. Also the British had control of the lakes and rivers through their ships and gunboats. At first the Canadian militiamen had deserted in numbers, but by the time reinforcement arrived from Niagara, they ceased deserting. In his view the situation was critical with British and Indian superiority in numbers and a weak American army worn down his sickness and fatigue.

Lewis Cass counterclaimed that Hull should have ordered an immediate and vigorous attack upon Malden while the British were weak. Time was on the British side as turned out. Cass also wrote that Hull would have been advised to attack rather than surrender later on. Generally he took the view that Hull should have fought under any conditions. Of course Cass was not there, while Hull was there. [7]

Hull's surrender led to other Indian attacks upon settlers. A noted and severe one was upon the Copus family. James Copus had recently moved to Richland County, Ohio, with his family from Pennsylvania. He was a Methodist and frequently preached to the Indians in the vicinity in an effort to reach them and convert them to his Christian faith. Copus tried to protect the Delaware in their land rights, but had to persuade them to move to Ohio. There their human rights were not protected either. Their village was burnt by stragglers in a force sent to escort them. An angered Delaware hit settlers who gathered for safety. Soldiers protected Copus on his farm. Delawares caught soldiers bathing in a creek and killed and scalped five and then killed another later in the woods. The seventh escaped wounded. James Copus was wounded and died. When the Indians left, the survivors were taken by the arriving Captain Martin to the protection of the stockade. [8]

Commodore Isaac Chauncey was very busy mobilizing men and materials of war for the effort on Lakes Erie and Ontario. Proving he was well chosen, he launched into a building program with great success. He sent a stream of workmen, sailors, and marines to the Niagara frontier. General Peter B. Porter, knowledgeable about the geography and ships, was of great help to the war effort of Chauncey's. There was a great deal to be done in a short period of time. Equipment had to come from some distance generally, but there were businessmen in the scarcely settled communities of between Albany and Buffalo. From Rome, New York, James Lynch provided iron ballast and common shot under contract. [9]

Captain Joseph Richardson was sailing for Haiti to procure more ballast when off St. Pierre of Martinique his ship *America* captured the British schooner *Adallah* bound for Barbados with two hundred barrels of flour. Richardson removed the captain and seven crewmen and placed four hands and a prize master abroad, but during the night it sprung a leak. With morning he captured the schooner *Intrepid*. After removing the supplies he wished, he let her go back to port with the earlier captives.

Since it was unsafe to float the *Aballah* despite his carpenter's repairs, Richardson sent the prize to Haiti. He followed to the island on ballast. With an interfering officialdom, he did the best he could by arranging with the English resident to give him $800 for the release of the *Abdallah* to them. He took the ransom money and left. He only ended up with the $800 since the flour had been seized by Haitian officials, but he did manage to escape capture on his venture, although not from the elements, for the *America* was cut ashore on Smith's Island in the Chesapeake and was lost. [10]

Captain Levely directed the privateer *Nonsuch* in an engagement with an English ship and a schooner off Martinique. In the contest, the Americans were outnumbered and outgunned. The opponents exchanged broadsides and merchant shots. During a fight of three hours and twenty minutes, the *Nonesuch* was badly damaged and could not capture the two vessels. The English ships were also greatly damaged and lost more men than the Americans. This encounter took place on September 18th. It was a stand off. [11]

The successful privateer, the *Highflyer* was auctioned off for sale for another venture. Two of the original owners and another man purchased her. They improved her armament both for closing and for close work and then signed on another captain, Jeremiah Grant and another crew. As soon as they got new letters of marque on October 7, 1812, they set sail. Shortly after reaching the open ocean, they captured the brig *Porgy* bounded for Martinique in the West Indies to Newfoundland. *Porgy*'s captain Captain Darrel threw the mail overboard to keep the Americans from capturing the letters he carried, but there were found aboard mostly after-dinner dainties such as 26 boxes of cordials and rum and coffee and sugar to name some of the cargo. Grant placed Thurston Taylor aboard to sail her to the United States and sell her in Baltimore. Forty percent of the $20,000 went to the federal government for duties. Many other ships were taken, but most were small and either burnt or sank.

Then near Barbados, Darrel and his crew took a packet schooner *Burchal* which had a British commissary and his wife. At first they were allowed to stay abroad, but after the Americans captured a small coaster he placed all prisoners on it and sent them back to Demerara under a flag of truce. Once his men were back to the *Highflyer*, the *Borchal* was sent in as a prize ship to bring $2,000 at auction. By this time Grant had already sailed toward Brazil and seen further action. On November 6th, off the coast of Surinam or Dutch Guiana, Grant and his men had captured the *Active* which surrendered after an exchange of cannon fire. Back again in the West Indies they chased a large brig. Unfortunately it turned out to be a man of war. Grant never lived to know what hit him. Sellers took over and under the smoke screen of a broadside wisely took flight in the

Highflyer. Later he had the misfortune of running into an English squadron and the ship, captain, and crew were captured. It was not all success for the Americans on the high seas. [12]

Beginning in 1775 the first runaway slaves appeared in Spanish Florida along with some freed slaves. Several hundred were soon present around Negro Fort on the Apalachiola. They were generally accepted by the Indians of Florida, but were not always on good terms with the natives. At first they were still slaves, but were freed once they delivered about one third of their crops to their masters each year. That is they were subject to provide a third of their crops in a type of sharecropage. They lived in separate or segregated villages. They provided a strong fighting force at the subjection to their Indians against the whites. Their knowledge of both languages, English and Indian, served them well as interpreters and spies.

The presence of slavery provided a great friction, each accusing others of taking slaves. Since the slaves could escape from the American state of Georgia or the Mississippi territory, the institution was threatened. This was just one more reason for the Americans to wish to take Florida. Georgians were most interested in gaining that territory, but the Federal government did not wish to fight Spain, when the war broke out with Great Britain. This was good thinking.

There were however border incidents and actions in Florida. Spanish Governor Kindelan suggested the Indians should attack Georgia. They did so in late July of 1812, with some success. Colonel Daniel Newman led a unit of militia from the state of Georgia into Florida to attack the Indian center. They encountered the Seminole and for two weeks were engaged in a running fight which almost destroyed the Americans from September 27th. Seminole king Payne died. Angered settlers were even more determined to fight the Seminole. A lull followed by more action took place. Colonel John Williams led 250 volunteer cavalry from Tennessee and a detachment into northern Florida in February of 1813. They burnt 386 Indian houses, destroyed up to 2,000 bushel of corn, and drove off several hundred head of horses and cattle. The Seminole were almost staved out and were broken east of the Swannee River. [13]

When Detroit fell, General Brock decided upon an offensive. He would take Fort Wayne some hundreds of miles in the interior of Indiana. It was a depot of stores supplying any advance in the future and must be destroyed. Brock learned that its garrison was closely invested by Indians and had a few hundred troopers with poorly placed cannon. Near the end of September, Major Muir embarked a small detachment, a howitzer and two field pieces on boats and crossed the lake to the Miami village, some fifteen miles beyond the entrance of the Miami. The Indians joined them on their landward march. It required hard labor to transport the guns.

About nine in the dark of evening Muir heard the cry of his scouts. They had killed and scalped several Americans who were around a campfire cooking food. The Indians pretended to be friends and lulled the suspicions of the soldiers, whose officers said they were scouts for an army of 2,500 men marching toward the Miami village. They were escorted toward the British encampment and caught by surprise and killed.

Muir abandoned his expedition against Fort Wayne and decided to assail the Americans on the heights over-looking the ford the Americans would probably cross. After a day's wait, he decided that they knew of the attack and would march down the opposite shore. Muir retired to the old fort of Defiance and discovered that the approaching army was under the command of General James Winchester with orders to construct a fort on the Miami. However, they discovered the attack and stopped to fortify themselves immediately on the spot expecting a large army. The small force of Muir's marched back to Amherstburg with the major's orders and Fort Wayne was safe. Winchester's army put the damper on an already weak attempt to march to Fort Wayne. [14]

When they heard of the partial success of Elliott, at Black Rock, the troops under Steven Van Rensselaer pressed forth to the major-general that they must on the offensive or go home. On the morning of the fourth of October of 1812, he sent forth a spy. The man reported back with intelligence that encouraged the general which Van Rensselaer told his chief officers. This made them eager also. He went through with plans to dislodge the British from Queenston Heights and take the village to prevent the British from obtaining shelter for the troops which were then at Detroit.

The major-general sent forth his orders. Lieutenant Colonel Fenwick's flying artillery and a detachment of regulars were to come forth. General Smyth was to send troops from American Buffalo. Detailed plans were to cross over before daylight on October 11th opposite the heights. Experienced boatman were to be used. However, Lieutenant Sim placed the boat with the oars for the entire expedition on the opposite side and abandoned the expedition. A storm hit at the same time, and the effort frizzled.

Van Rensselaer was determined upon taking the heights and made new plans. Lieutenant Colonel Christie offered his services to the first plan and was now eager for the second. There were to be two columns, Christie was to head one. Things were moving, but the Canadians discovered the preparation and fired with musketry. The American battery fired back. Once over, the Americans stormed the fort. Reinforced by several hundred Indians from Chippawa, the British attacked, but were routed. Success seemed to be at hand, the ardor of the unengaged soldiers would not pass over and a large force from Fort George came up the river. Van Rensselaer sent a fresh supply of cartridges. A terrific battle took place. However the Americans were grieved at the lack of reinforcements and the battle was lost. [15]

The army was waiting to move at Niagara when the newly arrived navy lieutenant Jesse Duncan Elliott saw his opportunity to attack. Elliot was busy fitting out navy vessels on Lake Erie, when on October 8th, he saw anchored off British Fort Erie near Buffalo a couple of enemy ships from Malden where Hull had been defeated. One was the former American ship the *Adams*, captured at Detroit and rename the brig *Detroit*, a 200 ton armed ship. The other was the 90 ton armed merchantman, the *Caledonia*. Both were well manned and armed.

Elliott decided to capture both ships in a surprise attack. He needed those ships to offset the size of the British lake fleet. Fortunately his sailors arrived on the eighth, tired after a 500 mile march across New York, but eager for a fight. However, they needed pistols, cutlasses, and boats. Elliott talked to Winfield Scott and Scott talked to General Alexander Smyth and the men received a number of weapons borrowed from other troops. They also received fifty volunteers, armed with muskets, from Scott's battalion of two companies; men also spoiling for fight even if they had to leave their artillery guns to do it.

No time was wasted and at four o'clock that afternoon, the American were in their boats, hidden in Buffalo Creek. Night fell and the men waited. At midnight they took off and with an hour's rowing reached the two ships. They surprised the British on the *Detroit* and took ships in ten minutes. The men of the *Caldonia* were slightly forewarned by the noise on the *Detroit* and a scuffle followed when the Americans climbed on the ship. The second ship was taken.

American sailors tried to sail the captured ships away but there was no wind and a rapid current in the opposite direction. British troops on shore were awake now and poured shot into the ships. Then the *Caldonia* was brought back to the American side where it was anchored under Yankee guns. The *Detroit* was fought over until it was destroyed. [16]

Meanwhile, the czar of Russia decided it was important to offer mediation between Britain and America for two different reasons. First, he feared the loss of Russo-American trade. Second, he knew that British troops would have to be transferred from the war with Napoleon and sent to Canada. So, in September of 1812, he had Count Romanzoff speak to John Quincy Adams about the idea that Russia mediate the issues of war and peace. The count told the Americans Government that discreet negotiations might resolve the problems easier than direct talks and asked if the American Government would have any objections. Adams did not have any instructions of course on the question but said he knew of none. The Russian Government instructed Russian minister Andre de Daschkoff to offer the czar's mediation and Madison accepted. President Madison sent commissioners to St. Petersburg to talk peace, but while they were on the way, the British rejected any such diplomatic conversations. This had a side effect. Direct talks were opened up between Great British and the United States. [17]

---

[1]Bauer, K. Jack, *Zachary Taylor: Soldier, Planter, Statesman of the Old Southwest*, Baton Rouge: Louisiana State University Press, 1985, pp. 1-14, 16-17; Brannan, *Official Letters*, pp. 61-63.

[2]Brannan, *Official Letters*, pp. 56, 63-64.

[3]Tucker, *Poltroons and Patriots*, pp. 219-220.

[4]Bauer, *Taylor*, p. 17.

[5]Patrick, Jeff L. (ed.), "'We Lay There Doing Nothing': John Jackson's Recollection of the War of 1812," *Indiana Magazine of History*, LXXXVIII No. 2 (June 1962), pp. 116-120.

[6]Clay, *Papers*, pp. 728-729.

[7]*America: Great Crisis In Our History Told by His Makers: A Library of Original Sources*, Chicago: Veterans of Foreign Wars of the United States, 1925, V, 135-153.

[8]Coles, David, "Copus Massacre," Heidler & Heidler, *Encyclopedia*, pp. 128-129.

[9]Dudley, *Naval War*, I, 311-318.

[10]Cranwell and Crane, *Men of Marque*, pp. 154-157.

[11]Coggleshall, *History*, pp. 87-89.

[12]Cranwell and Crane, *Men of Marque*, pp. 80-82.

[13]Mahon, John K., *History of the Second Seminole War, 1835-1842*, Gainesville Fla: University of Florida Press, 1967, pp. 19-21.

[14]Richardson, *War of 1812*, pp. 93-103. See pp. 297-300 also.

[15]Brannan, *Official Letters*, pp. 74-78.

[16]Elliott, C.W., *Winfield Scott*, 1937, pp. 50-52; Brannan, *Official Letters*, pp. 66-67.

[17]White, *Nation*, pp. 137-139, 142-144.

CHAPTER XVII

QUEENSTON

A series of situations moved General Stephen Van Rensselaer, a New York citizen of a wealthy patron family and of personal high standing, to take action. Because forage and provisions were insufficient for the numbers of soldiers in his army and the addition of six regiments of regular infantry, five of New York militia, a battalion of rifles, and several companies of artillery rendered the problem one of crisis, this situation forced the American general to go on the offensive and to seize possible supplies in Canada. Then too he would be joined by Pennsylvanians. Also the approach of autumn rains would make the camp disease ridden if he waited. General Dearborn wanted Van Rensselaer to act. According to Dearborn, Harrison was marching for Detroit with six or seven thousand men, the naval force building at Sachett's Harbor would soon try to gain Lake Ontario, and he, Dearborn, was ready to advance from Lake Champlain toward Montreal. Niagara was the key to all this maneuvering.

In the early days of October, Van Rensselaer gathered his generals and colonels. He had hoped for a two prong attack, but when General Alexander Smyth did not show up at council, Van Rensselaer realized that he could not count on the regular army general. Smyth had contempt for the militia and resented his being placed as regular under militia general Van Resselaer. His spies told him about the force and placement of the British and he felt sure of gaining a foothold at least before winter. Both sides were stretched out along the border. Morale soared when the American soldiers near the Falls learned an American force had seized two British ships on Lake Erie on October 9th as we have seen. [1]

When he learned Hull had surrendered at Detroit, William Henry Harrison took over the command in the Northwest. His aim was to end the Indian raids by striking at their villages. One column marched into Indian country from Fort Wayne and destroyed the Potawwatomi villages on the banks of the Elkhart River. Another force struck the Miami River villages where the Wabash forked. The third army, composed of two thousand mounted Kentucky militiamen and a few regulars under Major General Samuel Hopkins, was delayed by a rain which discouraged the Kentuckians and many returned home. The rest were none too eager and when they met a fire on the prairies, they thought the Indians had started it and expected attacks, although they saw no Indians. The grass was too poor to keep the horses fed and the guides argued among themselves. A council of officers decided to turn back and the third expedition was a failure. The Kentuckians had bragged about conquering Canada and were not unable to sustain a march to try and do just that. Hopkins set out again with an army of 1,200 men and destroyed two Indian villages deserted by the natives. The Indians attacked one patrol and ambushed another, before disappearing in the wilderness. [2]

General Brock hurried to the border, but decided there was no danger of attack now. The Britisher returned to Niagara. There was an American spy in the vicinity and he reported that Brock had left Niagara and headed for Detroit. This encouraged Van Rensselaer to strike while morale was high. The New Yorker laid plans to cross over the Canada with his army at Queenston, where the river was narrow. He would set his artillery to cover the landings. His goal was to occupy the heights and besiege Fort George. While Van Rensselaer wanted to wait, his men were eager for battle. Lieutenant Colonel Chrystie brought 350 regular soldiers at this point. Spies reported boats and troops were being gathered at Four Mile Creek. However, Van Rensselaer regarded this as a feint. [3]

In northwestern New York, Van Rensselaer did his own gathering in of men of arms until on October 12th, he had present for duty 5,206 men, almost exactly half of whom were regulars. In addition, the garrison at Fort Niagara had upwards of one thousand men. General Smyth was at Buffalo with 1,650 men. The Americans had larger numbers than the British by about sixteen hundred men, and three hundred Indians. These last had to protect over thirty miles of frontier. The logical place to cross was the Niagara River between New York Lewiston and the Canadian town of Queenston. The river flowed due north from Lake Eire to Lake Ontario. Although it was only 250 yards wide, it was a turbulent river near Niagara Falls' bottom, five miles south or upstream. There was a Canadian steep cliff, Queenston Heights, which rose 350 feet above Queenston. Solomon Van Rensselaer did not know British numbers, but knew they had two heavy artillery batteries and they probably outnumbered the Americans. The American militia was ill-equipped and many did not have shoes. [4]

General Brock reached Fort George eight days after the surrender of Detroit intent upon rapidly taking Fort Niagara held by Americans. Instead, he found Sir George Prevost and General Dearborn had established an armistice. This gave the Americans time to work upon his defenses. Early on the morning of October 13, 1812, the sentinel above Fort George, gave an alarm that there was firing coming from Queenston. He hurriedly dressed, got on his horse, and raced alone to Queenston. Halfway to Brown's Point, Lieutenant Jarvis who told him that he was guard on half-moon battery, and observed many flashes of firearms on the water below. The officer in command ordered the two companies under arms. Then they learned that the Americans were crossing in force. The British marched forth to oppose their landing. At this point Jarvis was able to tell Brock what was happening while he raced ahead. [5]

Although he lacked military experience, the rich and powerful Federalist General Stephen Van Rensselaer was in command of the Niagara front and determined to attack soon, fearful of a charge of deliberate delay. There were pressure from the press, the public, and his army, all of whom were interested in action. In his proposed plan the American general had the advantage of some surprise, the British general Brock expected a fight but did not know the exact point it would take. The Britishers had 1,500 men and 250 Indian allies under Brant, Jacobs, and Norton. His best two companies were at Queenston.

Consulting with his lieutenant colonel cousin and aide Solomon Van Rensselaer, selected because of his experience in Indian warfare as the man to advise Stephen, the general decided to attack on the thirteenth in a second attempt. The staff work improved this time, but not enough for the necessary success. There were to be insufficient boats once again, insufficient ammunition, not enough artillery, and no substantial artillery support over the river. Artillery guns were not transported across the river with one exception. As events were to show the brigade of regulars under Smyth should have been used, but regular army officer Alexander Smyth refused to go to Fort George. Preparations were insufficient and, in particular, objectives were not given to the troops, resulting in confusion. [6]

From the north bank, the British general Sir Isaac Brock watched the preparations on the south bank. Conducted in the open as they were, Brock felt the gathering of the army was a maneuver to deceive him into thinking the action was to take place near Queenston, when indeed it was to be elsewhere. Brock decided it was to be elsewhere and made preparations based upon this belief.

At midnight, the Americans massed their troops. The weather was cold and the night dark. After a three-hour wait, they began to embark on the boats to cross the river. The regulars with their professional officers, hard-bitten sergeants, and recruits set out first. They were followed by two hundred volunteers and by two hundred infantrymen. Most of the boats made it across, although the way was difficult and dangerous and the crossing was not made orderly. Some men were captured and others were fired upon.

An alert sentry gave the general alarm and the Americans received a heavy fusillade. The first American losses were heavy. Captain John E. Wool rallied the American soldiers and drove an enemy company back. Artillery units opened up on both sides. British guns fired from Queenston, one fired from a centrally located position on a hillside, and long ranged guns fired from a strongpoint on the river to the right, across from the American camp. American guns hit Queenston repeatedly from Fort Gray on the American side of the bluffs and Winfield Scott's cannon fired in support of the American landing. [7]

Nothing went right with the American advance. The troops fought for hours in the darkness. There was a cold wind and the militiamen were confused. Three of the thirteen boats were captured by the British when to boats strayed. Colonel John Fenwick was among those captured. The British force was small but competent. The Americans had long since lost the advantage of surprise. The British fired their muskets at the Americans. There were many American casualties before they landed. [8]

The fight continued as shots were exchanged and men fell. Colonel Solomon Van Rensselaer, badly wounded early in the fight, was consulted by Captain John E. Wool. The colonel ordered the wounded captain to take the heights at whatever cost was necessary. Then Lieutenant John Gansevoort, having been told of a pathway up he cliff by a native of the region, volunteered the information and suggested going up by the steep way of the bluff. It was so ordered. The captain and the lieutenant had the troops up the cliff until they reached the path and then continued by it. They formed at the top and charged the British artillery. [9]

By this time Brock was directing the fire of his guns and he had to flee after spiking the guns. Brock ordered a counter assault then and more American troops came across the river. The British were repelled, only to charge with a bayonet attack, during which the general, Brock, was killed. This was a terrible loss for the British. They lost their best general in America, a strong fighter and a man of distinguished valor.

Winfield Scott was sent across to take field command of the Americans. Scott worked hard to prepare a defense while British General Roger H. Sheaff set about to prepare a victorious advance. Sheaff knew that no more Americans were coming across and that he was being rapidly reinforced by additional companies. What neither Scott nor

Sheaf knew was that the New Yorkers refused to cross because of fear, despite their commander's orders. [10]

Helped by General William Wadsworth of the New York militia, Scott did all he could. When the Mohawks advanced, a British attack made a dent in the American line. The militia across the river had heard the Indians and again refused to come to Scott's aid. The Americans left on the battlefield tried to turn the outer flank but were met with a destructive fire. Thus stopped, they became confused. As the British enveloped, the Americans, Wadsworth and Scott tried to retreat with their force. This was impossible since the troops were terror struck. Some jumped off the cliff in their panic. At any rate the boatmen had abandoned the American force. The Americans surrendered.

A possible American success ended in defeat. New York Republicans blamed Van Rensselaer and he was relieved, leaving Symth to command as ordered from the War Department. It was not Van Rensselaer's fault that the Americans lost; this lay with the troops and the superior fighting skill of the British aided by the Mohawks. In Smyth's case, a failed attack on Fort Erie ordered by him ran into similar difficulties. The Pennsylvania militia refused to advance across the border in his case. Now it was Symth who was reviled. No one seemed to blame the men for the debacles. Indeed, it was the responsibility of the generals, but they had no control over militiamen who were to say that they did not have to fight out of their state, refusing to cross over into Canada. [11]

When the militiamen claimed that they did not have to fight outside their states, they were echoing what some authorities mostly at the state level were saying. They stated that the militia could be used only at home within state boundaries. The Federal government argued that Congress had full "power to provide for organizing, arming and disciplining the militia and for governing such part of them that might be employed in the service of the United States, reserving to the states respectively the appointment of the officers and the authority of training the militia according to the discipline prescribed by Congress." In the midst of war, there was an internal argument which weakened the nation at a time of stress. The judges of Massachusetts ruled that control over the militia rested with the states, but that that state was largely in favor of peace and friendship with Great Britain. [12]

At sea, the Canadian privateer Joseph Barss headed for the American coastal trade, a prime target. Off Cape Cod, he ran into his first catch. Soon, within a fortnight he had captured four American schooners and had sent into Liverpool, Nova Scotia, all of them for prize courts. Bound for Boston, New York, and Baltimore, they had a profitable cargo of such items as rice, cotton, leather, shoes, gin, peppers, hops, fish, oil, sugar, corn, flour, salt, earthenware, vinegar, cheese, cotton-duck, bonnets, and dry goods. New Englanders were furious and fitful. There was more to come however.

Barss made a fourth cruise, netting four more U. S. vessels. The cargoes from this sweep were food-stuffs at a time when short supply flour was selling for as much as $20 a barrel in Halifax and L 12 a barrel in London, expensive merchandise for the time. There were more ships and captures. He took a rich haul of nine fishing schooners. In the last two cruises, the Canadians had lost enough to cut a canal through Cape Cod, or so it was said. His next cruise was met with a gale, which hurt his hunt. Soon afterwards, Barss had captured two more prizes. The men of the *Black Joke* celebrated a Christmas at home, but they were still awaiting their first prize money since the lawyers were still arguing over this.

They could wait or thought they could, but early in January of 1813, a great gale roared in. It was so strong that the wind sucked the water, leaving the harbor damp but

The Difficult War: The Era of the War of 1812 143

waterless. The prizes were now stranded. This could be suffered in minor concern. However, a great tidal wave struck next and the vessels were driven by main strength on to the rocks in order to prevent them from being swept into the sea. Even more dangerous was a legal squabble which lasted over the years, netting Barss L 1,000 and his seamen L 156 apiece. But it took two years for them to secure the fund for half a year's work. [13]

On October 15, 1812, Captain Stephen Decatur sailed his warship the U. S. *United States* six hundred miles west of the Canaries. The sailors abroad saw a ship heave into view. They were to discover this British frigate to be the H.M.S. *Macedonian* with Captain John S. Carden in command. Despite his ship's limitations, Decatur outmaneuvered Carden's ship. The British frigate had the advantage of being the windward but this did not limit its damage.

Decatur used his advantage of more powerful long-rang guns and superior marksmanship to devastate the *Macedonian* with leaden hail. Decatur got off seventy broadsides to Carden's thirty and because of his splintered ship and heavy casualties of a third of the crew, the British captain had to give up. A prize crew sacked the damage ship into Newport Harbor. The two hundred thousand dollars of prize money made the crew of the *United States* happy and affluent.

In the fall of 1812, the United States Navy had the best of the Atlantic conflict. By their superior firepower of their heavy frigates and skilled seamanship and gunnery, the Americans gained seven ships to three losses and won some notable sea battles. One of these was the victory of the *Constitution* over the H.M.S. *Java* in which was traveling the then governor of India Lieutenant General Thomas Hislop. That year the American navy captured fifty merchantmen, while the American privateers made 450 prizes just in six months. The *Yankee*, out of Bristol, Rhode Island, and the *Rossie*, from Baltimore, were the most successful. Joshua Barney's *Rossie* took almost eighteen vessels worth almost one and a half million dollars.

London learned that the privateers were swarming around the coasts of Canada and the islands of the West Indies. For their cause, the British warships captured 150 privateers, but had to escort their merchantmen in convoys and squadrons to protect them from the aggressive Americans. For the Americans all but the capture of privateers was a happy contrast to events on land and the bad news coming out of the land war. [14]

Once again on the high seas Rodgers led his three warships, chasing one ship which nightfall saved, and capturing a packet which had ten tons of gold and silver specie aboard at a total value of about 175,000 dollars. Next he rescued an American schooner, dismasted on the way to France. He captured one of three ships, but again darkness saved the other two of his prey. This ship, just captured, carried a valuable cargo of whale-oil, whalebone, and ebony. The rest of Rodgers' voyage was uneventful. When his provisions and water were almost exhausted, he returned to Boston. There were other successes. Decatur's squadron captured a frigate and several merchant ships. [15]

The *Wasp* left Delaware Bay on the morning of October 13, 1812, for the hunting ground north of the West Indies with their rich hauls. A sudden gale tormented the American ship costing her jib-boom and two crewmen. When the weather clear, she shadowed some British ships and was prevented from prizes when the Royal sloop the *Frolic* got in the way, allowing the merchantmen to escape. This ship was also damaged by the same gale. There was an exchange of broadsides, with rigging and sail damage to the *Wasp* and hull damage to the *Frolic*. They ran afoul and the American gunners shot such charges that there were heavy losses on the Britisher. Excited, the sailors jumped on board the British ship and took her over without a fight. Commandant Jacob Jones however had no time to celebrate, because a heavy gunned *Poictieres* bore down and forced him to surrender. [16]

On October 23, 1812, our friend Levy joined the U. S. Navy to serve his country as sailing master. In his first assignment to harbor duty, he saw the flogging of sailors as punishment. Previous to this he had seen scarred backs and heard of men flogged to death. He hated this type of punishment and was to be the naval officer to do away with this in the American navy. He enjoyed the dinner and balls of New York, but he wanted to see action. Asking for such service, he was placed on the *Argus* to deliver William H. Crawford to his diplomatic post in France. The men of the ship took the British vessel the *Salamanca,* which was too weak to measure up to the Argus, 2nd surrendered. They burnt it after transferring the crew. They then safely delivered the envoy at a French port. [17]

The final privateer to sail down the Chesapeake in 1812 was on the schooner *Rolla.* She was well armed but James Dooley could not find enough seamen to complete a crew of eighty men. He decided to go to New England ports for men, where he found some men at Boston but none at Newport or Bristol. At first he sought a Nova Scotia privateer which had taken New England coasting vessels, but could not find it. Instead he crossed the Atlantic to the coast of Spain, but along the way disaster struck. A severe gale rolled in and Dooley had to heave the cannonades over the side to prevent them doing damage to the ship and men. They rode out the storm, but had so little armament left that he asked the crew if they would continue the cruise with one 12-pounder. They would continue. Shortly they came alongside a British ship despite a broadside into the *Rolla* which the Americans knew was mismatched. The British did not know what advantage they had and struck their flag.

Next Dooley and his men took after another, the *Elisha*, which immediately surrendered. He maneuvered before another and was on the point of boarding her. More surrendered, until all of the convoy had struck their colors. Only a brazen commander could succeed as Dooley did. More than one half of his crew was aboard the prizes and many prisoners were below ships. She came to the aid of a Portuguese brig which was without water and sailed home. Each member of the American crew netted $223.50 a share, a sizable sum for the day, and Dooley got nearly $4,500 in a day when seamen were doing great to be paid thirty dollars a month. On its next venture, the *Rolla* was tricked into surrendering to the British warship the *Loire* by whaling apparatus on the warship until it got too near the eighteen gun ports to a side. It was Dartmoor Prison for most of the privateers. This was hard punishment. [18]

In October of 1812, the small frigate the *Essex*, in the previous thirteen years a proven warship in battles in the West Indies and off the Barbary coast of Africa, set sail under Captain David Porter for a rendezvous in the Atlantic. Porter had been in command of the *Essex* in the opening months of the war, when he captured the first British ship to fall in the war. He did it by pretending to be a merchantman, an old Yankee trick. It got him close to the British ship until he could fire away and win the battle quickly with only one broadside.

Porter was a good captain, providing plenty of good provisions including fresh vegetables, fruit, and casks of lime juice for the health and welfare of the crew. He made sure that his men who had mostly been with him later received their share of earlier prize money. He treated the men well. They were men like him as he realized and should be treated the same way. Prize money was not the only thing motivating the men as he knew. Treated well the men of the crew proved to serve him ably.

The Difficult War: The Era of the War of 1812

Meeting points were set out with Commodore William Bainbridge, but his instructions had a leeway for his own choices in case he failed to find Bainbridge and his frigate *Constitution* and sloop *Hornet*. Porter sailed the ship to meet him. He stopped off at a Portuguese island for provisioning and then made his way until one of the crew sighted a British warship. Porter ordered the British flag to be flown until he was close enough to compel the ship to surrender. The vessel proved to have $55,000 aboard in pay for English troops, and this would prove beneficial to Porter and his crew in prize money.

Rigged like a British merchantman, the *Essex* sailed into the harbor at Fernando de Noronha and Lieutenant Downes put ashore in civilian clothes. Downes met the governor, passed as a Britisher and learned of the previous arrival of Bainbridge. He sent Downes back for a letter the governor had for London. By possession of the letter, Porter noticed the hints of phrases and treated the bottom with lemon juice to bring out the secret message. In it Bainbridge stated he would soon be off Cape Frio in Brazil and Porter was to meet him there.

At Cape Frio, Porter and his men waited for Bainbridge, but the American commodore did not show up, being busy elsewhere. With rum and other supplies running out, Porter set his men and ship toward Portuguese St. Catherine where the men could buy items and water could be put in the ship's casks. Some rum was bought but the small supply of meat was rotten and had to be thrown overboard. Porter learned of the approach of British ships and set out for safer waters.

Long wanting to go into the Pacific, Porter decided that now was the time. He had been allowed action at his discretion in his orders and he took it. The captain fleet he could play havoc with the British whaling industry in the southeastern segment of the Pacific and collect many prizes. Also he knew of no British warships in the area. this would cause cries of anguish in London and contribute toward victory and peace.

The ship and its crew suffered dangers and had been seen in passing through the channels around the Horn. It had looked like the passage would be easy when winds and currents almost wrecked the *Essex*. They went up the coast of Chile, barren in its southern extension, but some hunting helped alleviate short food supplies at a point along the coast. Finally they reached Valparaiso where they got provisions and enjoyed celebrations with the Chileans living there.

It was there that they learned from an American whaler captain that the whalers usually put in at the Galapagos Islands. Porter decided that this would be a good place to take prizes so the *Essex* with its crew set out north for these islands. The prospect was rich indeed since the captains agreed that there could be more than twenty English whalers in the southeastern Pacific near South America.

Off Lima, the men of the *Essex* captured a British whaler, but with the use of flags, it seemed to the people of that town that it was the opposite, a British man of war capturing an American whaler. They sailed on until they reached the Galapagos, where they had an interesting sojourn among the animals of those islands. It seems though that there were no British whalers to take in the islands' waters.

Then suddenly at dawn on April 29, 1813, ship sails were sighted. Porter had the British flag run up. He headed for them in his ship and the crew prepared for any action necessary. They reached the British whaler *Montezuma* and invited the captain aboard. While Porter and the captain ate and drank, the crew set about to board the *Montezuma* and reach the other two ships. The first ship had a bountiful supply of sperm whale oil as did the others. Porter then could reveal that his ship was an American frigate. The other two ships quickly surrendered. The American sailors on board were put in command of three whalers. The ample supplies of the three ships provided needed supplies for the Americans in the *Essex* and were hauled abroad by the crew. More ships were caught. Some of the ships were sent back to civilization with excess prisoners and to take prizes to the United States.

Porter ordered his ships west-southwest to the Marquesas Islands to repair and scrape the ships hull. He also planned to fumigate the ships because of a large rat population on board. They reached the Marquesas and found a welcome from the natives. There was an American and another officer on the island with the natives and they acted as interpreters.

The maidens and young married women of the islands proved a delight for the sailors, eager to accommodate them, but the men involved the sailors in their local wars. Few were killed in the local wars, but the American guns made havoc at the first encounter with an opposing tribe. Another tribe was less fearful even with heavy losses. Porter had to go up to the island mountains, with great difficulty and come by the back routes. The second tribe was defeated with more heavy losses for them.

Once he was ready, Porter commanded his ship out of there and returned for Chile. He was off Valaraiso in February of 1814. There was a stalemate at Valpariso when two British men-of-war arrived. Porter attempted an escape, but the two British ships destroyed the *Essex* in a very bloody battle with heavy losses for the Americans. [19]

[1] Zaslow, *Defended*, pp. 25-27; Eisenhower, *Agent*, p. 34.

[2] Baur, *Taylor*, pp. 17-19.

[3] Zaslow, *Defended*, pp. 27-28ff.

[4] Babcock, *War of 1812*, p. 39; Eisenhower, *Agent*, pp. 34-35.

[5] Richardson, *War of 1812*, pp. 101-105.

[6] Elliott, *Scott*, pp. 54-56, 69-70; Hickey, *1812*, pp. 86-87.

[7] Elliott, *Scott*, pp. 58-60.

[8] Eisenhower, Agent, *p. 37.*

[9] Elliott, *Scott*, p. 60; Eisenhower, *Agent*, xp. 38.

[10] Elliott, *Scott*, pp. 60-63; Richardson, *War of 1812*, p. 111.

[11] Elliott, *Scott*, pp. 63-68; Hickey, *1812*, pp. 87-88; Richardson, *War of 1812*, p. 112.

[12] Babcock, *War of 1812*, pp. 7-9. Quote on p. 8.

[13] Snider, *Under the Union Jack*, pp. 18-24, 27-30.

[14] Hickey, *1812*, pp. 94, 96; Dudley, *Naval War*, I, pp. 548-549, 551-553; Paullin, *Rodgers*, pp. 260-263.

[15] Paullin, *Rodgers*, pp. 260-263.

[16] Bunker, Robert J., "Wasp Versus Frolic," Heidler & Heidler, *Encyclopedia*, p. 546.

[17] Felton, H.W., *Levy*, 1978, p. 42.

[18] Cranwell and Crane, *Men of Marque*, pp. 172-177.

[19] Donovan, Frank, *The Odyssey of the Essex*, 1969, *passim*.

CHAPTER XVIII

AMERICANS AT WAR

There had been successes at sea, and one of the American land victories was at St. Regis which Major G. D. Young achieved. Confidential friends reconnoitered St. Regis to report at least 110 British soldiers there. They would soon have reinforcements however, so Young knew that he had to make an immediate attack. On October 22, 1812, they marched in a circular route and arrived at a little rise half a mile from the village after a night march. Captain Lyon was sent forth to take the road and rear of the house where the British were. Captain Dilden secured boats and prevented the British retreat by seizing the boats. Young led the frontal assault. The attack was successful and the Americans took 40 prisoners. Five British died and there were no American casualties in the short surprise attack. [1]

General Hopkins having marched his mounted riflemen to Fort Harrison, Colonel W. Russell took a part of three ranger companies to join Governor Edwards, who had mounted riflemen. Their combined strength had 360 privates. They marched deeply into Indian country for Peoria on the Illinois River, but did not meet General Hopkins as planned. They reached the celebrated Pimartam's town, some 21 miles above Peoria and at the hand of the lake of that name.

The Indians fled for the swamp for shelter against the soldiers, who caught them by surprise. A few shattered shots ploughed through the soldiers, but this hardly affected the soldiers who pursued them into the swamp and across the river. Upwards of 20 Indians fell dead. Edwards and Russell saw the corn and other belongings committed to the flames. They captured 80 horses. Casualties mounted to four wounded soldiers on the white's side. It took 13 days to make the successful expedition. [2]

Meanwhile, Colonel Benjamin Hawkins was busy among the Creeks as an agent. He was instructed and did his tasks. The chiefs and Hawkins were too alarmed over Tecumseh. They did not realize the effect of their rouster of war spirit among the Indians. Tecumseh had dramatic effect. His promise of British guns and military support made them brave and bold. Hawkins had called the Creeks into council in time for Tecumseh to appear. The painted bodies of the braves sat with the leader and listened to Hawkins make his usual report and recommendations. Finally after eight days the agent finished.

He left in confidence, but that very evening, Tecumseh rose to address the assembled Creeks with vigor. He urged the Creek "to destroy their livestock, abandon their plows and looms, and return to the old ways. The white man would turn their beautiful forest into field, muddy their clear streams, and reduce them to slavery. The king of England would help them to expel their enemies. Those who joined in this holy war would be invulnerable; the unseen powers would lead the white men into quagmire and drive them back to Savannah." [3]

Friendly chiefs tried to keep their people from listening to Tecumseh, but their efforts were of little avail. Tecumseh predicted supernatural forces and it seemed that they came true. Running dates together lead the Creek to believe that this happened. The Indians lost sequence and place. However, he predicted an earthquake and when the earth shook, they were convinced.

They were ready to go to war and indeed there was an incident of war. When opportunity did present itself a band, on the way back from listening to the Indian leader, killed seven white families at the mouth of the Ohio. Creeks killed possibly two or three others. Tennessee reacted and issued a call for ten thousand militiamen to exterminate the Creek. Hawkins told the chief that they must punish the murderers and this they did with death. Eleven were killed. The hostiles retaliated and there was civil war among the Creek. [4]

Almost half or sixty one of the 142 membership in the new House of the Twelfth Congress had been new members and they were drawn to the youthful Henry Clay of Lexington, Kentucky. No one knew which way they would go by and large. Seniority was not an important concept to these men. They were ardent Jeffersonians but had only a vague leader in Jefferson or Madison. They would allow no appeasement. Peace and prosperity would be purchased not by them if it meant debasement, isolation, and humility in foreign affairs.

The previous speaker was Joseph B. Varnum of Massachusetts, but he was set for the Senate; Clay had succeeded him with his strong and masculine handshake. With a melodious voice, he swayed his audiences in a fluent manner, but his speeches lacked the flow of information to make his speech enjoyable and instructed reading. Supposedly substance and not rhetoric made his speeches great. Clay was most popular, but never achieved this main goal in life, to become president. His chief asset was his ability to lead and arrange compromises which saved the Union on several occasions, but this was to come in the future. [5]

Lieutenant Colonel John B. Campbell marched his men three days and one night from Greenville to a surprise attack on an Indian town inhabited by Delaware and Miami Indians early in the morning. Some surrendered while others crossed the river to fire back. Seven warriors were killed, and thirty-seven were taken prisoner, mostly women and children. The Americans set fire to the village and killed the cattle and stock. Campbell then marched forth, and had his men burn three villages. They returned to the first village where they were attacked by a large body of Indians. The whites held out for three quarters of an hour. When the Indians retreated, Captain Trotter led a charge of horsemen. Indian dead amounted to forty, while nine whites were killed. The wounded list was higher. [6]

American troops spent three days in destroying the evacuated Prophet's town and the larger Kickapoo village on the west side of the village. On the 21st a party of Indians fired upon the Americans and killed one soldier. Lieutenant Colonels Miller and Wilcox took upwards of sixty horsemen on the next day, but fell into an ambuscade with 18 killed, wounded, and missing. Seeking to avenge themselves upon the Indians they made prompt preparations but were delayed by a violent storm and snowfall. This was more snow than seasonable. The American soldiers were in summer dress, so the hunt was called off. They were marched to Fort Harrison instead. [7]

On November 8, 1812, Isaac Chauncey sailed his lakeside vessel and sighted the *Royal George*. Upon chasing this British ship into the Bay of Quanti, he lost her in the dark. During the next morning he saw her in Kingston channel and followed her into the harbor, fighting her and the shore batteries for almost two hours. She was so well protected, he could not board her as he would have liked. On the tenth, he sailed into the open lake and chased the *Governor Sincoe* into Kingston harbor. Other American ships joined in the action. Chauncey and his men took a schooner and burnt her. They next captured the schooner *Mary*. At this time Chauncey had control of the lake.[8]

The next campaign underway was directed against Montreal, but because of delays it lacked the needed coordination with Isaac Hull and Van Rensselaer. Had all attacked at the same time under competent generals and willing men, Canada might had fallen to the Americans. It was American weakness and not Canadian strength that decided the issue. However, the basic lesson was that the nation needed a professional army and recruits outside the framework of the militia system, so lauded in early America popular views and such a disappointment in the War of 1812. Although the generals were of low quality, the blame laid on many people from the president to the private.

Dearborn lost because of sadly deficient generals, but the worst cause of defeat was a militia which would not cross into Canada. The one fighting was a skirmish in which darkness prevailed and the Americans fired upon one another. Slow enlistments plagued Dearborn and he concentrated upon recruiting New Englanders and prepared coastal defenses there. It took a direct order to send him to southern New York in November. In sum the Americans did not have their hearts in the war; when even Dearborn preferred an office to the field. [9]

On November 21, 1812, the British batteries at and near Fort George pounded the American Fort Niagara all day. This set some of the buildings aflame, but these were quenched before the British could see this. In reply, Lieutenant Colonel George M'Feeley set his batteries to pound the artillery and fort on the British side. The town of Newark was repeatedly set ablaze and one British battery fell silent for awhile. One woman, a Mrs. Doyle, wife of a captured American artilleryman, attended a six-pounder with red hot shot in great bravery and effort during the day. M'Feeley wrote that she showed a fortitude that was equal to the maid of Orleans.

Toward the end of October, Brigadier General Alexander Smyth ordered his men to build 20 scows to transport horses and artillery. One month later they had completed ten. Smyth brought forth sixty boats from Lake Ontario. He expected that he would have 2,300 men for duty from colonels Smith and M'Clure. Four hundred thirteen men volunteered to cross into Canada from General Tannehill's brigade. With some 300 volunteers from New York, this would get him about 3,000 men to go at once. On the 27th of November, 1812, Smyth sent over two parties under Lieutenant Colonel Boerstler and Captain King. Lieutenant Angus, of the navy, headed the seamen.

Boerstler received orders to capture a guard and destroy a bridge near Fort Erie. King was to take and spike a British battery. Although at first they captured some prisoners, they failed to destroy the bridge. King fulfilled his assigned mission but when Angus took all of the boats they brought, he left King stranded. The latter did manage to get some two boats to send back prisoners and half of his men, but he stayed with half and was captured. Angus had attacked the British at the Red House and routed them, spiked their guns, and fired the barracks. Unfortunately he left too early.

In agreement with his leading officers, Smyth decided to await a more opportune time to attack. Early in the morning of November 30th, the troops crossed over to the

British side. They did not have sufficient flour. Smyth took the question again and his officers decided that it was not wise to act at such a time. An opportunity was lost to achieve a success. The high officers were pessimistic and Smyth let them decide what to do. A stronger general might have taken a success and there was no telling what might have transpired.. A lot of time was wasted. [10]

People in Tennessee learned of the repulse of Americans in Florida and the attacks upon them by the Seminole. These Florida Indians not too long before moved from the north in normal migrations, refused white advances and led by King Payne resisted their presence; attacking them in the plantations and killing several Americans. They captured slaves and cattle. Colonel Daniel Newman and his Georgian militiamen came to the rescue of their fellow Americans and made an assault of Payne' town. The Seminole was surprised but fought back. Indians and blacks came up and attacked the Americans in their rear around their flank. Newman led his men on a retreat. They were saved when the Indians ran low on ammunition.

The Tennessseans were angry at all of this and Colonel John Williams, militia adjutant general marching southeast from Knoxville with 165 men; he had bought arms for his men out of his own pocket. They had muskets, pistols, tomahawks, and butcher knives to make their way into Seminole territory. In Georgia they met Governor David B. Mitchell and Indian agent Hawkins asked them to return home. Mitchell wanted them to go home because he wanted to use his own militia to attack the Seminole and garner all of the glory for himself. He kept secret the approval of his legislature to undertake a raid.. Since the Creek would tell of the planned operation and warn the Seminole it had to be kept quiet. He did not want the Indians to flee to the protection of the woods or Spanish forts.

General Thomas Pinckney, commander of the federal forces in southeastern Georgia, encouraged Williams to march on and join forces with militiamen from Georgia for an attack. They would destroy their fields and houses and kill opposing blacks and take back to slavery the rest. They made their way down, but found Payne's town deserted. Indians fired upon them from cover and there was a skirmish until darkness. Faced with a force four times their numbers, the Seminoles retreated into the swamps. The soldiers destroyed towns, and took cattle and deerskins; killing Indians and blacks. They returned to Georgia but a horde of cattle thieves replaced them. Spanish cattle and Seminole cattle were taken. [11]

The war did not bring popularity to Madison and the Republicans. Most Federalists supported Lieutenant Governor DeWitt Clinton of New York, while some rallied behind Rufus King. Federalists came close to winning the election. The margin of Madison's victory was thin. Only a Republican victory by a margin of 20,000 in Pennsylvania decided the election for Madison. His party remained in the majority in the House of Representatives, but their lead was narrow. The Federalists had held one quarter of the seats before the election of 1812, but now increased their minority to almost two-fifths of the lower house. The War Hawk Congress continued in power for a lame duck session, but made only minor contributions to the war effort. They made the decision to avoid many war taxes and did little substantial on preparing and supporting the war effort. [12]

The failures in the American war effort belonged to the administration of affairs in Washington DC as well as the commanders in the field and their men, Americans lacked the energy, efficiency, and commitment necessary for a successful war. The war was unpopular and lacked the determination necessary for successful warfare. The leaders could not rise to the demands of the situation. Civilians and generals alike were generally incompetent. The people had no great war leader in Madison and no organization genius in Secretary of War William Eustis, where leadership and organization reside respectively. Too many had gained high position because they were good politicians and not because they were adept at administration. They also had inexperienced clerks and were understaffed. Eustis concerned himself with the details, which a good staff should have managed for him. He gave no proper direction to his commanders and at times bypassed the chain of command to deal with junior officers. There was no delegation of duties in the department which would free Eustis to concentrate over policy and direction.

Madison depended upon officers who had been appointed because of their political pull or connections. The senior generals were too old for competent service; even when they had showed ability on the way up, they lacked energy and experience. They had shown their lack of leadership skills in the first years of the war. The president and his secretary of war had failed to appoint new officers of ability because they depended upon Republican congressmen and their states to recommend men. Even with the press of war, they were to name political and familial nominations. The army was to continue political.

Not only were the officers unsuited, but the enlisted men did not have experience. Morale was low. There were many desertions. After four months, Madison had to pardon the deserters in order to fill the ranks. Discipline was strict, but ineffective. Punishment was harsh and manifold. In serious cases commanders resorted to branding, ear cropping, and executions. The government had to rely upon large bounties for recruitment. It could not rely upon the militia of most states, although westerners and Yankees had the best militiamen. Not only was pay low, but it was often in arrears for as much as a year or more. The war department had had no quartermaster from 1802 to 1812, but depended upon civilian agents.

Then in March of 1812, they established quartermaster and commissary departments, but during the war were never successful in keeping abreast of the needs of the army. Often the soldiers had no shoes, clothing, blankets, or other necessary supplies. Civilian contractors did not deliver the daily rations which were required according to government regulations. They provided bad provisions frequently. Many soldiers died because of contaminated and insufficient food. Dysentery was common. The medical system was incompetent. In short, Americans were sadly unprepared for warfare and never fully caught up with the requirements of military action. Their problems showed up early and frequently. Americans did not have their hearts in the war. They believed it would be an early victory and were not set for a protracted war. [13]

On December 3, 1812, Secretary of War William Eustis submitted his letter of resignation to Madison. His had not been a successful administration of the department since he came into the post in March of 1809. However, he did work amid great difficulties. It was a hard position to hold anyway, made doubly so because of the tight budget imposed upon him by party and nation. Historians generally considered that he was unfit for the job. Perhaps he was more interested in politics than military matters.

His critics contended that he dealt too much with trivial matters and was too obsessed with cutting costs. But although he did not delegate authority, his interest in cheaper operation was imposed upon him by the tight governmental ideas of himself and the rest of the Jeffersonians. He needed to sit back and view the overall measures of the department. The need for economy led to his shelving of the idea of horse drawn light artillery, which innovation was especially suited to American conditions. However, when it came to supplying and providing for men for the army, this expense was rightfully excessive. This was only so because Congress and the nation did not want to spend the money necessary to good military actions and procedures.

His effectiveness was limited not only by the lack of money, but by conflicts with his generals and between the generals themselves. In this war as was true later in the Civil War to an even greater degree, military men were in disagreements concerning the war and their individual actions. Eustis tried unsuccessfully to get good actions by his subordinates. His minor failings did hurt the military development, but his good ideas were not listened to by the generals; and finally difficulties in action rest more upon them than with Eustis.

On the positive side, Eustis did help the war effort in many ways. He added to defense measures and increased small arms production in both quality and quantity. He worked for the re-establishment of the quartermaster and commissary departments which were so necessary to the units in post and field. He organized the military in districts. This did not keep away criticism which was intense and warring, despite the loyalty of Madison to Eustis. Senator William Crawford wrote Madison that he must be satisfied with defeat and disgrace if he kept Eustis in office and it was clear that Eustis was a political liability for the Administration. Finally it was the secretary who resigned. Later he served Madison as a diplomat and was a congressman and governor. [14]

In the winter campaign of 1812, the chief problem was the lack of supplies and even more important the difficulties of transportation. Harrison's troops were in great need of woolen clothes and coats and blankets. Since the men expected a quick victory they took only cotton or linen clothing and so were caught in the freezing weather without adequate clothing. Harrison called upon Kentucky ladies to send clothing and knit mittens and socks. Men were put forward to build roads. In the face of mutiny, Harrison was able to announce the arrival of packhorses with supplies and the passage of 200 wagons of biscuits, flour, and bacon from St. Mary's. There was no more talk of desertion.

Harrison's ambitions were held in check by the prospect of icy weather and the presence of great amount of rain which left the country so swampy. Drivers pushed the horses unmercifully. Oxen were used and droves of hogs were driven to bring supplies and food on the hoof. Still there were broken down wagons and contractors shorted the supplies with bloated prices, shoddy materials, and planned delays. Frozen weather came and the rivers froze so that they could not be used to transport supply and provisions.

Regular Lieutenant Colonel John B. Campbell led a command of 600 regulars, mounted riflemen, and dragoons to attack the Indians. They marched forth in December 14th on a three day trip. They traveled quickly. Soon they had destroyed four Indian towns, killed eight warriors, and took 42 prisoners. When their fortified camp was attacked by furious Indians, the soldiers did not yield an inch. The Americans won the battle with fewer losses than the Indians, but they had a painful march back to Greenville, being rescued with necessary promises on the way. [15]

Meanwhile on the waters, another able ship which powered the high seas was the *Dolphin* which was sent off the coasts of Portugal, a less crowded field than the West Indies. English ships were bound for the port of Lisbon with supplies for Wellington's army, and the waters were clearly grounds for the passage of ships to and from the Mediterranean. Along the way, the *Dolphin* came upon the *John Hamilton* which fought back so spiritedly that the American captain William J. Stafford thought it was a heavy armed and well manned opponent of great power. He reconsidered and the next morning regained a position of two hours fighting until it surrendered along with its cargo of mahogany which was used for the *Java* being built at Baltimore.

The men of the *Dolphin* had further adventures. Off the coast of Portugal it was quiet sailing for awhile, but on January 6, 1813, Stafford ran in with the ship *Hebe* and the brig *Three Brothers* and captured them. One prizemaster took the *Hebe* toward American ports, but she was recaptured. The *Three Brothers* reached New York City. With men wounded and dead and aboard the three prizes, the *Dophin* was undermanned and returned to Baltimore, passing into Chesapeake Bay under cover of darkness, escaping capture by the British blockaders lying in wait for American ships. [16]

On the first of December, Captain Miller, in the privateer-schooner *Jack's Favorite* of New York City, was adding water and refreshments to his ship's stores at the island of St. Barthowmew in the West Indies. While he was there, his Majesty's ship the schooner *Subtle* sailed into port. Its captain threatened to take Miller's ship, but in his good time, Miller sailed his ship away unharmed. However, the English captain sailed his warship in pursuit. Both ships were beset on their way by a squall with its fury. When it was over, Miller searched for the *Subtle* and saw a few hats and caps, and hammrock-cloths floating by. [17]

The finest of five clipper schooners, the "Pride of Baltimore," the *Chasseur* was launched on the waves on December 12, 1812. It was then the largest schooner yet built. The renown Thomas Bohle was her skipper in the war years. Later she made a record sail from Canton to the Virginia Capes in ninety-four days. His first voyage was supposed to be to France with freight, but the blockading British prevented this despite the best the master of the *Chasseur* could do. The day after Christmas of 1813, Captain William Wade set sail with her. When bad weather set in, the *Chasseur* made its escape from the Bay.

Shortly, Wade seized the British ship *Galatea* flying Swedish colors with its hardware, glass, white lead, and wine cargo. Soon he was sailing off the Spanish Main and captured the *Miranda* on the way from Cork to Guadaloupe with dry goods, flour, and sundries. He burnt the ship. His next capture was the sloop *Martha* with its government stores. The American schooner the *William* had been trading with the British when captured and Wade took off the gold and other specie before burning the ship. There were other captures. [18]

Another one of the privateers, the schooner *Saratoga*, under the command of Captain Charles W. Wooster sailed off Laguira, twenty-four days from New York. While anchored off the coast, it received word from the American consul to stay out of the reach of the batteries for safety sake. Wooster did so, and shortly. boarded and captured a schooner of dry goods. When the fog rolled away on the eleventh, he saw a brig of the British navy and began a pursuit. The bet was that this brig, the *Rachel*, would win any battle with the *Saratoga*. The people on shore flocked to see the engagement. Soon however the two ships were too far to be easily seen. Then the two ships came in closer and the American ship fired and received a sally. People saw columns of fire and smoke and it was seen, when it cleared, that only the American flag was flying. The British brig had the worst of the battle by far with heavy losses to the Americans. [19]

Meanwhile there were peace talks early in the conflict in St. Petersburg, the then capital of Russia, between John Quincy Adams and British Ambassador Lord Cathcart. Minister Adams had just opened a dispatch from Secretary of State James Monroe that the United States, despite its war with England, would not form any close ties with France. The American envoy told this to Russian diplomat Count Rumiantzov, who asked if he would object to his telling the Britisher what Monroe had written. This was done and subsequently both diplomats, Adams and Cathcart, exchanged the view and wish that their countries could settle their differences amicably.

Adams had already sent to Washington DC the Russian offer to mediate. He expressed his desire for friendship and harmony between the United States and Britain. Sure that it was to the interest of Russia for British-American friendship to be established. The war would be highly injurious to the two nations at war and no one would benefit. Monroe was to approve of Adams' diplomacy in Russia and Madison took up the idea of Russian mediation. Despite this good start, there was no end to the war, and nothing was developing from the Adams-Cathcart talks. Both countries were locked into the war by severe disagreements. [20]

---

[1]Brannan, *Official Letters*, pp. 86-87.

[2]*Ibid.*, pp. 88-89.

[3]Debo, Angie, *The Road to Disappearance*, Norman: University of Oklahoma Press, 1941, pp. 77. Quote on p. 77.

[4]*Ibid.*, pp. 77-78.

[5]Tucker, *Patroon and Patriot*, pp. 31-39.

[6]Brannan, *Official Letters*, pp. 104-105, 111.

[7]*Ibid.*, pp. 95-97.

[8]*Ibid.*, pp 90-91.

[9]Hickey, *1812*, pp. 88-89.

[10]Brannan, *Official Letters*, pp. 93-95, 97-100, 106.

[11]Covington, James W., *The Seminoles of Florida*, Gainesville, Fla.: University of Florida Press, 1993, pp. 28-32.

[12]Perkins, Bradford, *Castlereagh and Adams: England and the United States, 1812-1823*, Berkeley, Calif: University of California Press, 1964, p. 7.

[13]Hickey, *1812*, pp. 75-80, 89.

[14]Coles, David, "Eustis, William," Heidler & Heidler, *Encyclopedia*, pp. 175-177.

[15]Cleaves, *Old Tippecanoe*, pp. 123-130.

[16]Cranwell & Crane, *Men of Marque*, pp. 100-103.

[17]Coggeshall, *History*, p. 67.

[18]Cranwell & Crane, *Men of Marque*, pp. 226-234.

[19]Coggeshall, History, pp. 70-71.

[20]Bemis, Samuel *Flagg*, John Quincy Adams and the Foundations of American Foreign Policy, *New York: Alfred A. Knopf, 1969, pp. 185-186.*

CHAPTER XIX

POLITICS AND WARFARE

In New York, Republican Martin Van Buren won an upset victory over a coalition of Robert Jenkins, the Van Nesses, Livingstons, and Federalists for a seat in the state capitol for a special session on November 2, 1812, to help choose electors for the presidency. In 1808, Van Buren had been caught between two loyalties, that to Clinton and that of the party's congressional caucus. His support for DeWitt's uncle George Clinton's try for the presidency in the place of James Madison had been a mistake, but fortunately the setback was temporary and Martin was to support Clinton again.

After calling the 1812 session to order and in accordance with routine, the lieutenant governor allowed an one day adjournment of the state senate, and Van Buren and others separated by party and had their secret caucuses. Despite the inexpediency of Clinton's nomination. Van Buren felt he must support him because the caucus action that that spring had bound New York Republicans. Before his Jeffersonian Republican colleagues, Van Buren took the lead and expressed both doubts that Clinton could win the presidency and that he would support whoever won, but that he wanted them to vote for Clinton. There were to be no bargains with the Federalists he said. Everyone agreed on this. Some of the legislators did not like the idea of supporting Clinton, but the Clintonians had a majority. However, Van Buren proposed a proportionate vote between Madisonians and Clintonians, but the Clinton selection was rammed through the two houses of the New York legislators. [1]

The Federalists were all opposed to the war. No Federalist voted for the war and all vehemently opposed the war effort in any way that they could. It was a Jeffersonian Republican war. A partisan issue, they felt the war was the wrong war fought against the wrong enemy a the wrong time. The war was fought in the wrong places, mainly against Canada. It was an offensive war and not a defensive war. The only thing they voted for was the raising of money for coastal fortifications and the navy. They voted against all money bills for the army and other aspects of the war effort. They did everything they could to oppose the war, efforts which were to go to some extreme. Never in our history did so many so strongly oppose an existing war.

For them it was a Republican war meant for the benefit of that party. Only Republicans would gain by it. The Republicans used it to silence the opposition. They used the Baltimore riots as an example for this. Operations on the high seas against the British might have been understandable for this seaward people, but the conquest of Canada was not only a mistake but even if successful would hurt the United States. The Federalists did not want Canada in the Union. During the war they did not even want the

West as a part of the country. At one time they suggested making the original thirteen states a new nation and leaving the rest out. They looked backward and not forward.

The Republicans were pro-French. If the war was logical, they should fight the French also. After all Napoleon was a monster, the aggressor. For the Federalists the British were admirable and were in the right war against Napoleon. They had learned to live with the impressments and ship seizures, but they had never accepted the economic measures designed to hurt England and quash American commerce. The Republicans were too agrarian and were against the commercial interests. [2]

A middle aged sailor talked to John C. Calhoun in early December of 1812 about the war and politics at Mrs. Bushby's boarding house. Charles Stewart said that the Southerners "are decidedly the aristocratic portion of this Union; you are so in holding persons in perpetuity in slavery; you are so in every domestic quality; so in every habit in your lives, living, and actions; so in habits, customs, intercourse, and manners; you neither work with your hands, heads, nor any machinery, but live and have your own living, not in accordance with the will of your Creator, but by the sweat of slavery, and yet you assume all the attributes, professions, and advantages of democracy."

To this Calhoun replied that "I see you speak through the head of a young statesman, and from the heart of a patriot, but you lose sight of the politician and the sectional policy of the people. I admit our conclusion in respect to us southerners. That we are essentially aristocratic I cannot deny, but we can and do yield much to democracy. This is our sectional policy; we are from necessity thrown upon and solemnly weeded to that party, however it may occasionally clash with our feeling for the conservation of our interests. It is through our affiliation with that party in the middle and western states that we hold power; but when we cease to control the nation through a disjoined democracy, or any material obstacle in that party which shall thrown us out of that rule and control, we shall then resort to the dissolution of the Union. The compromises in the Constitution, under the circumstances, were sufficient for our fathers; but under the altered condition of our country from that period, leave to the South no resource but dissolution; for no amendments to the Constitution could be reached through a convention of the people under their three-fourths rule." [3]

At this time, the Kentuckians and the regulars on the Northwest frontier were in dire straits. They used all the timber within reach for firewood before ordered to move on. General James Winchester, advancing as the Federal Government wished, left a small garrison with all of the sick at Fort Winchester. Step by step they headed down the Maumee to a camp which they named "Fort Starvation" and awaited the arrival of supplies. Those without shoes bound their feet using strips of cloth. Hunters made moccasins with the skins of animals they had shot. Large numbers of the soldiers suffered from influenza and typhus. Not a whole lot could be done to protect them from the icy cold of the ground. They had to eat hickory roots and fresh pork. Many died of the ailments. There were supplies on flatboats frozen in the river and General Winchester sent packhorses to collect these necessities and bring them to camp.

In order to stem talk of proceeding to the flatboats in mass, Winchester issued all the beef and pork he had on hand to the men. Before nightfall of the next day some 300 hogs reached the camp. On the 22d, the all-meat diet was improved with the arrival and issue of flour. On Christmas Eve of 1812, the packhorse train began entering the camp which led the men to a little Christmas celebration. Soon they had some shoes and clothing and could be ready to march forth. More than one hundred men had been buried at the camp and the remaining sick remained behind with guards for their safety. [4]

The Difficult War: The Era of the War of 1812 157

Madison needed a new secretary of war to staunch the blood of failure in the war. He did not have many choices, but decided upon John Armstrong, then in charge of the defenses of New York City. Because Armstrong had developed a reputation for being difficult, he had few friends and many enemies. Monroe and Gallatin for one were opposed to Madison's choice. Madison reluctantly then made Armstrong his secretary of war.

The new army executive found the department inefficient and understaffed. It was a difficult situation for anyone. The supply system was a failure. Armstrong set to work with a vengeance. He supervised the composition of military rules and regulations as a starter. He increased the number of generals and organized them more efficiently into districts. Since fortifications were costly and the government had to economize, Armstrong concentrated on raising more troops for troubled areas. Not enough manpower was volunteering and he suggested a draft. When this was later sent to Congress, Monroe worked behind the scenes to defeat it. As Secretary Monroe had issued another draft idea, but he had done his harm and it was defeated.

When Armstrong made the mistake of going to subordinates of generals with orders, he hurt the war effort. This had caused confusion and created his special interests such as the effort against Kingston, Canada, overwhelming influence in manpower needs and supply dislocations. He played little attention to other operations and they went begging to some degree. [5]

At sunrise on Christmas Day in 1812, the American Nathaniel Shaler noted that there were ships ahead. Aggressive as his fellow Americans at sea, Shaler ordered his crew to set after the three ships. They did not make very fast progress because the wind was so slight that day. Up closer they could see that the ships included a brig and what looked like a transport. The day wore on and at three in the afternoon they were struck by a sudden squall which put the Americans under the guns of a large frigate, a quarter of a mile away. Shaler replaced his English ensigns with American ones. Both ships exchanged fire. There was a fire abroad when a shell exploded a salt-box, and the men had to work to put it out. There were alternative problems and at four the British shot began to fall short of his ship the *Governor Tompkins* for awhile. Shaler lightened the ships' duel and soon was able to escape capture.

Shaler had praise for his officers and boatswain and master's mate. Among the crew were two black sailors who were most seriously wounded, but showed bravery afterwards as much as before. A 24 pound shot hit John Johnson in the hip destroying the lower part of his body. He did not complain from his situation on deck, but several times told his shipmates to fire away. They were never to haul the flag down. John Davis had much the same injury and several times asked to be thrown overboard since he was only in the way of his fellow sailors. Shaler concluded that "while America has such sailors, she has little to fear from the tyrants of the ocean." Both men died soon afterwards. [6]

On the morning of December 29, 1812, off the coast of Brazil, the British *Java* met the American *Constitution* in a battle. Coming upon each other, each maneuvered to get the advantage. Commodore William Bainbridge ordered his American gunners to fire high to demast the Britisher with success. This tactic worked after considerable firing and made the *Java* unmanageable. Its captain was dangerously wounded and carried below decks. The second-in-command Lieutenant Henry D. Cads frantically tired to relieve the situation, but the British had suffered greatly in casualties and guns disabled. Chad's fellow officers agreed that they must surrender. So the *Java* fell into American hands in one of the most important sea battles of the year. It took just short of two hours.

Casualties amounted to nine killed and 25 wounded for the Americans and 60 killed and over a hundred wounded for the British. Because the *Java* was so badly damaged, Bainbridge could only burn that ship. [7]

Learning of the passage of the act which authorized President James Madison to organize and accept volunteer troops, Jackson issued a division order for volunteers. Their government he declared had "at last yielded to the impulse of the nation." Their impatience was no longer restrained and the hour of national vengeance was a hand. "The eternal enemies of American prosperity are again to be taught to reset your rights, after having been compelled to feel, once more, the power of your arms." War would soon break out between the United States and Great Britain. He asked for volunteers. There would be no drafts or compulsory lives yet. America could expect 50,000 volunteers for the present. Jackson issued his division orders to General James Winchester to march with his volunteers. They would meet at Philips horse mill, but would have eight days provision for themselves and their horses. Then baring any further orders, he was to proceed on to the Fishing Ford on Duck River, twenty miles or so downriver from Shelbyville. Other volunteers were to join Jackson and Philips horse mill to protect the frontier. [8]

When the Creek war party struck the frontier and killed a man and five children and took a captive, Jackson was ready for a march into Creek territory. Meanwhile war broke out with the British and war was upon them, but there were delays for the last half of the year 1812. Jackson was ready to march to Canada to find revenge against General William Hull's defeat or to Florida to crush British influence upon the Indians of each area. Both were necessary for peace upon American frontiers. [9]

About this time Captain Zebulon Pike was just back from Mexico with news of a merchants' El Dorado in Santa Fe, capital of the Spanish province of New Mexico southwest of St. Louis. The story of his celebrated exploring party spread throughout the western country. Abraham had not yet been born, but his father doubtless heard of the discoveries of Pike. This young man Zebulon Montgomery Pike had had experience in the army since age fifteen during George Washington's second administration.

In 1805, the first lieutenant explored the Missouri under orders. General Wilkinson commissioned Pike to explore the central part of the Louisiana Purchase. He and his men discovered Pike's Peak in Colorado and saw the Rockies around Leadville. During the winter they thought they were on the banks of the Red River when Spanish authorities arrested them. The Spanish took them to Chihuahua and then were taken to San Antonio and Natchitoches and released on July 1, 1807. He was promoted to captain for his services and by the time of the War of 1812 was a brigadier general.

The westerners were enthusiastic. About one dozen citizens banded together in 1812 and formed an expedition to go over Pike's route to Santa Fe to trade. They reached Santa Fe expecting to be treated well and to sell their goods for high prices. Optimists, they did not consider what had happened to Pike in New Mexico. They might have, but to the Spanish government they were intruders, illegal trades and the expected welcome from free Mexicans did not materialize. They did not realize that Hidalgo had been defeated and that the Spanish viewed foreigners, and especially Americans with distrust. Spanish authorities seized them as spies and confiscated goods and chattels. They were to remain in prison for nine years, when Agustin de Iturbide seized power and liberal sentiments freed them. It was a long imprisonment. [10]

Back on the high seas there was more action. Once underway, through the British blockading squadron off the Chesapeake, Captain Thomas Boyle arrived off Pernambuco on January 8, 1813, and immediately boarded a small Portuguese coasting vessel. Its master told Boyle that several English vessels were loading at Pernambuco and would sail in a few days. Boyle thanked the man. Four days later, they came out, but with an escort from a Portuguese man-of-war whom Boyle told he would fight him, if he interfered with his attack upon the English ship.

Boyle made ready for action and opened broadsides on two English brigs. A general battle ensued, with the Portuguese in on the fight. After two and one half hours of fighting, one English ship was much disabled and surrendered. The American captain ordered a boat out to board the vessel. Soon the moon set. In the morning, it was discovered that the captured ship was the only one in the convoy which was seaworthy at this point. Boyle abandoned the other two and went his way.

About daybreak on January 19th, the lookout saw a sail off the starboard or right bow. Boyle set additional canvas and got within one mile of the vessels before running up the American flag. The other captain flew his Union Jack and soon the two ships were firing at each other. Americans were wounded and when a ball knocked a carronade free it careened across the deck, crushing a gunner's foot as it flew across the deck. The two ships closed in. The Britisher got the worst of the battle and as Boyle got his boarding party ready, the British ship *Adelphi* struck her colors and surrendered. It had a large cargo of salt and dry goods aboard her. Within ten days, Boyle took a Portuguese brig and put his prisoners upon it. [11]

Experienced in the fortunes of tall ships, British Captain Thomas Freeman managed to gain a large sum of prize money during one cruise in the *Liverpool Packet*, sailing the *Columbia* as prize master shortly before Christmas of 1812 to Nova Scotia, home. Then he and Captain Snow Parker bought the *Retaliation* on January 29, 1813. The ship was small as far as schooners went, but big enough for profitable action. The new owners spent additional sums for guns, twelve-pound carronades, twenty muskets and fifteen boarding pikes, plus thirty cutlasses for its fifty man crew.

Shortly Captain Freeman got his privateer commission and then followed the *Liverpool Packet* for the seas off New England. On March 11, 1813, he and his men captured the American sloop *Hunter* around Cape Cod, with its cargo of corn and slaves. Next day, Freeman captured the schooner *Wilburn* off the cape with a supposed British license. The prize court knew better. There were more prizes with four and with salt. This was followed by still more prizes, before he sailed forth for Liverpool, Nova Scotia. Unfortunately Freeman was an ill man by this time and he replaced himself with the able, one of the best Nova Scotia privateersmen, Benjamin Ellenwood. [12]

American James Lawrence sailed the *Hornet* on February 4, 1813, and captured the English brig *Resolution* with its cargo of coffee, jerked beef, flour, and butter bound to Moranham from Rio de Janeiro. He did not have the manpower to put a crew aboard and sent her to a United States prize port, so he took the 25,000 in gold and silver and burnt the ship. Next he cruised off Moranham and off Surinam in February. On the 24th, he saw a brig to leeward and chased it to safe heaven. Another man-of-war was seen and they passed to give broadside volleys. The American had the advantage of common fire and in less than fifteen minutes, the HMS brig *Peacock* surrendered. It was by then sinking. She sank before all of the prisoners and three American sailors could get aboard. The British had the disadvantage of losses. With little water left and more dry mouths, Lawrence set out for the United States. [13]

On February 6, 1813, Boyle sailed off the Island of St. Johns, where he discovered two brigs. He ordered his fellow American sailors to chase them and soon called all to quarters. That morning, he discovered that the newest brig was armed. At six the brig raised English colors, fired a gun, and then surrendered. Boyle had his men board her. The ship was the *Alexis* and had a full cargo of sugar, rum, cotton, and coffee. Boyle put a prize master and six men on board the *Alexis* and sailed after the other. At eight, he found warship upon the wind and learned it was a part of a convoy. The second ship surrendered and received a prize master and seven men aboard. Boyle gave orders to prevent the prize from being seized by the man-of-war brig and diverted the latter.

Next, the American captured the brig *Dominica* with its cargo of rum, sugar, cotton, and coffee. This prize also made gap to escape. Able to outrun the warship, Boyle finished his diversions and outsold her straight, soon being four miles away. There was still another schooner to be captured which surrendered quickly and was boarded. This was the *Jane*, loaded with valuable rum, sugar, and coffee. After this Boyle sailed the *Comet* back to the states, evading the blockaders, one of the most skillful of privateers among many able Americans at sea. [14]

After a successful half year, the *Black Joke* or *Liverpool Packet* was out for the season once again. On March 5, 1813, the sailors seized an American schooner with a license and pass from British Admiral Herbert Sawyer. Joseph Barss did not wish to see it. He would send the ship to prize court and not to Boston with the news that the Liverpool privateer was off their shore. In nine days he made seven prizes all together. News reached Boston of the lightning captures of the ship.

Joseph Barss was a darling sailor. At this time he sailed inside of Halfway Rock, in Casco Bay, off Portland, Maine. In a flash Barss captured the American schooner *Lydia* a short distance from two U.S. brigs of war. Losing no time he sailed 250 miles and made another capture off Point Judith in the Vineyard Sound. This took twenty-four hours or a rate of ten miles an hour, a speedy move for the times.

Shortly after this, he raced back to Liverpool, Nova Scotia, for more hands and made his seventh cruise. He saw nothing in Cape Cod, but trying Maine, he deceived an American convoy on a foggy day. Capturing the sloop, he used it as a decoy to take another ship. With these two captives he made its way home. There were more ships to take in April and May. Among the ship hunting, Brass anchored off Tarpaulin Cove in the thick of the Vineyard Sound passage and had a picnic on shore the next day, a Saturday.

Finally there was an end to the Barss succession of thirty-three prizes. The American *Thomas* took him to task and captured him in a chase and brief fight. Barss had thrown overboard all but one of his guns in order to lighten his weight and escape the *Thomas*. Henceforth the task was uneven. In the greatest of anger the Americans swarmed aboard and did some loss, and the British were made captive. They were marched down unpaved narrow and tortuous streets to prison, guarded by the bayonets of militiamen, of Portsmouth, New Hampshire. Joseph never privateered again when he finally got out. [15]

The American privateer *Globe* was traveling in rough seas not too far distanced from the Straits of Gibraltar. Suddenly at three-thirty on the afternoon of March 10, 1813, the lookout yelled that he saw a sail to the west. Because of a strong wind, he had to be careful not to raise too much additional canvas, but it was sufficiently close enough to set out in pursuit. They gained upon the sail and one hour later, could see it clearly. When Captain Moon raised the British ensign, the stranger put forth the Spanish flag. It was fast and one half hour later, Moon and his men aboard the *Globe* gained but little more. In order to establish a measure of friendship, Moon replaced his British flag with that of the

The Difficult War: The Era of the War of 1812 161

United States. The other ship's captain responded by lowering the Spanish flag. Another one and a half hour later, Moon had gained further.

Firing at each other when they were close enough, that two ships were shortly only about forty yards away. It began to get dark and smoky but they fought for the next three hours. Most of the round shot and grape shot was high and damaged each others rigging. Soon the *Globe* was too damaged to suffer anymore destruction and Moon ordered his men to pull away for repairs. Subsequently, Moon learned that the ship he was trying to take was an Algerian corvette when it sought Lisbon port for repairs.

Once Moon was able to make repairs, he set out and on March 16th captured the schooner *Elizabeth* with its cargo of fruit, and on March 21st, took the schooner *Endeavor* with its cargo of wine. Other ships were taken and burnt. Now it was the *Globe*'s fate to be chased. After capturing the ship *Venus* with its salt and provisions, he headed for home. On the way he took the brig *Kingston Packet* with its cargo of rum, sugar, molasses, and coffee. Since the Chesapeake was blockaded, he sailed his ship to Ocracoke, North Carolina. [16]

The clouds were drifting lazily in the sky and moderate breezes swept the deck of the privateer *General Armstrong* when the Americans of the ship discovered a sail. Captain Guy R. Champlin sailed his vessel closer and found that she was at anchor off the coast of Surinam. At eight that morning she fired three cannon and hoisted the English flag for ships at sea. The Americans fired their center gun and raised the American flag. Britain's ship tacked and stood nearby. Firing briskly at each other, they had in mind the idea of boarding the other. Champlin discovered the British ship was a frigate.

His cannoneers brought down some of the sails including the flag. At first, the Americans thought she had struck her colors, but continued fire from the Britisher spoke different and the Americans fired again and again. A musket ball wounded the captain and he walked to see the surgeon and had his wound dressed. Others were wounded or killed. There was sizable damage to the ship. Finally, Champlin decided they were getting the worst of it and was able to escape the British ship. [17]

The ship *Sir John Sherbrooke* was the largest and finest British privateer to move out of Nova Scotia with eighteen long nine-pounders, nine on each side, with two chase guns set for firing ahead on each side. The men were well equipped for boarding or firing with muskets. They had room for a ton of gunpowder and sixteen hundred rounds of grape, canister, chain, bar, and round shot. It was equipped with three anchors and four cables. In a day when hemp was costly, she had one half ton of it. Collins and his partners owned the vessel. On board were fifty marines or sea infantrymen and one hundred sailors and gunners. It had foreigners aboard as soldiers and sailors of fortune. Captain Joseph Freeman belonged to a fine family in Nova Scotia, was a militia colonel, and after the War of 1812 was to be a member of Parliament for 25 years. He was experienced in the French wars from 1798 to 1805 and was a merchant as well as a mariner.

Freeman sailed his ship for Block Island, where Long Island Sound traffic met with the traffic down the coast of New Jersey to Georgia. He and his crew captured fifteen prizes which reached British port for judication and selling. It was successful as a privateer. However, in October of 1814, the American privateer *Syren* captured her on a voyage from Halifax with a cargo of oil and dried fish. A prize crew attempted to get past the squadron of blockading ships but when hard pressed ran her ashore. They then set a torch to her to keep the ship out of British hands. Twenty days later the *Syren* met the same fate. [18]

Coal was in short supply during the war but efforts were made to transport it under danger. Coal was first found in the Wyoming region of Pennsylvania as early as 1762 when Connecticut pioneers reported the discovery at the mouth of a small creek. The first problem was how to ignite the "black stones." Seven years passed until blacksmith Obadiah Gore managed to burn it in his forge. Blacksmiths adopted it throughout the Wyoming Valley. At that point it was limited to use for blacksmiths with the aid of a strong forced draft. In 1776 under the impetus of war, Pennsylvania's government ordered several tons loaded on flatboats which were towed down the Susquehanna to Harris Ferry, soon to be Harrisburg. From there it was hauled to Carlisle for the arsenal, where they manufactured firearms. Other shipments followed. When anthracite was discovered in the Lehigh in 1791, unsuccessful attempts were made to introduce the hard coal into seaboard cities.

The year 1808 saw a breakthrough. Judge Jesse Fell of Wilkes Barre demonstrated "that anthracite coal could be burned in grates for domestic purposes. Within a few years after his experiment was reported, grates had come into general use in the coal region and shortly thereafter stoves were introduced." Four years later in 1812, people accused Colonel George Shoemaker of Potttersville "of being a swindler when he offered Schuylkill coal for sale in Philadelphia." An industrial firm proved that coal could be burnt and Shoemaker was vindicated. [19]

During the war, coastal regions were unable to obtain Virginian coal and the usual supplies of coals from Liverpool. In addition these areas of population concentration were running out of wood for fuel, so coal became a precious commodity. The price per ton for coal went up to twenty-one dollars. To take advantage of the market, several groups mined and transported coal despite the dangers and high cost of transportation. There was a profit to be made and they willingly took the risk. [20]

---

[1]Niven, Van Buren, *pp. 25-34.*

[2]Hickley, Donald R., "Federalist Party," Heidler & Heidler, *Encyclopedia*, pp. 18-19.

[3]Moore, Frank (ed.), *The Rebellion Record: A Diary of American Events*, New York: Putnam, 1861, Rep. New York: Arno Press, 1977, pp. 186-187. Quotes on pp. 186-187.

[4]Cleaves, *Old Tippecanoe*, pp. 134-135.

[5]Heidler, Jeane, and Heidler, David S., "Armstrong, John," Heidler & Heidler, *Encyclopedia*, pp. 14-15.

[6]Coggeshall, *History*, pp. 140-143.

[7]Dudley, *Naval War*, pp. 639-649; Brannan, *Official Letters*, pp. 118-119.

[8]Jackson, *Papers*, II, 290-294. Quotes on pp. 290, 294.

[9]*Ibid.*, pp. 297-312, 352.

[10]Gregg, Josiah, *Commerce of the Prairies,* Norman, Okla: University of Oklahoma Press, 1954, pp. 10-12.

[11]Cranwell & Crane, *Men of Marque*, pp. 131-136; Coggleshall, *History*, pp. 132-136.

[12]Snider, *Under the Red Jack*, p. 151.

[13]Brannan, *Official Letters*, pp. 142-143.

[14]Coggleshall, *History*, pp. 136-139.

[15]Snider, *Under the Red Jack*, pp. 30-44.

[16]Cranwell & Crane, *Men of Marque*, pp. 92-94.

[17]Coggeshall, *History*, pp. 105-107.

[18]Snider, *Under the Red Jack*, pp. 143-148.

[19]Cornell, Richard J., *The Anthracite Coal Strike of 1902*, Washington DC: Catholic University of America Press, 1957, pp. 2-4. Quotes on pp. 3-4.

[20]*Ibid.*, p. 4.

CHAPTER XX

SAILORS AND SOLDIERS

The British navy wished to make the Americans pay for their depredations or destruction and raided in and about Chesapeake Bay in the spring of 1813. Admiral Sir George Cockburn was guided by escaped slaves through the countryside to show those upstart Americans what it meant to challenge the British Empire on her high seas domain. In late April he burnt Frenchtown, Maryland, and the ships docked there. Soon they burned three other towns, which the weak American militia could not protect. With no resistance the British admiral ordered his men to destroy a cannon foundry and moved freely about. However, in June, General Robert B. Taylor prevented Sir John Borlase Warren from taking Norfolk, Virginia. Prepared obstacles and heavy artillery fire forced Warren to take his troops back on board his ship and sail off. Hampton fell and the French recruits, former prisoners of war, raped, murdered, and pillaged. Warren sent them to Halifax where these worthless ones terrorized loyal British subjects.

At sea the Americans lost three out of four naval duels. Because the British ships of war now traveled in squadrons and British merchant ships in convoys, American chances of victory were limited. Also many U. S. ships were unable to sail from blockaded ports. In the encounter between the British *Shannon* and the *Chesapeake*, the Americans lost because of the superior gunnery of the British under Captain Philip Broke. Mortally wounded, Captain James Lawrence uttered his immortal line, "Don't give up the ship," but his men had no other choice. Both captains were made heroes of their respective countries. [1]

James Lawrence was a sailor of the new school of Navy officers who had been promoted with the fighting against Tripoli, as bold and nationalistic in their outlook as were frontier War Hawks. Burlington, New Jersey, saw the birth of James on the first day of October of 1781. He grew up watching the ships on the Delaware River. With his father in the legal profession, his family destined him for a law career, and he studied law for awhile. However, at age eighteen he set out upon a ship, into the surface of the deep. Five years of sailing led to a first lieutenancy aboard the *Enterprise* in the Mediterranean. Lawrence served as second in command when Decatur recaptured and burnt the *Philadelphia*. His activity during the bombardment of Tripoli won him mention in the dispatches home.

He won a captaincy and sailed in the War of 1812 in the *Hornet*. This ship was off Georgetown, British Guiana, on February 24, 1813. When the odds were too heavy he had recently passed up a battle with the British *Montagu* off San Salvador, Brazil, but now the odds were just about even when he saw the *Peacock*. They passed well within pistol-shot range and fired broadsides. Lawrence swung his brig around and poured a fire on the *Peacock*. Within fifteen minutes, the American gunners were so able that the British captain was killed, the British casualties were about fifty percent, and she was shipping six feet of water in her hold. She ran up her distress colors as she struck her flag.

Lawrence ordered his lieutenant to board the *Peacock*, remove the wounded, and keep the vessel afloat. Others jettisoned their guns in the British vessel, plug up the holes, and worked the pumps. Then at sunset she went down with nine of her own crew and three Americans of the relief party aboard. The *Hornet* was crowded and her sailors shared their clothing with the British sailors. Lawrence rationed his water and made haste for New York City. The officers of the sunk ship wrote a thank you to the Americans when they arrived in the American port. Lawrence's victory was received with celebration in most American cities and Lawrence was met with the news that he was promoted nine days before he anchored at Holmes Hole, Martha's Vineyard, on March 19, 1813, on his long journey homeward. [2]

There was no wind on Chesapeake Bay in late March, 1813, so Stafford of the *Dolphin* had to use the sweeps and row upbay. Then a breeze blew up with flood tide. The good captain saw three schooners from Mobjack Bay whom he believed to be British. Stafford escaped from two of the three but he shortly learned that the third was the Baltimore letter of marque schooner *Patapsco* which had run the blockade in the storm. Thomas West brought his *Racer* to join the growing number of privateers languishing in the Bay due to the presence of the blockaders. At four PM on the 2d of April they saw an English fleet of seven vessels below the mouth of the Rappahannock River. The American captains decided to seek safer anchorage up the river.

When he saw the American ships, Admiral Sir John Borlase Warren ordered his fleet to pursue the American ships. No sooner than this was underway there was a calm and the British admiral sent out oared boats armed and manned after them. At dawn on April 3, 1813, the four American schooners were lined up in the river. Soon the morning mist lifted. The flotilla of small craft was seen steadily forward and the Americans fired upon them. Next they held a council of war at which the Americans said they intended to defend their ships to the last.

In the ensuing battle of April 3rd, the flotilla pressed on against the American *Arab*. Both sides fired at each other. Two cutters headed directly for the ship. They reached it and cut the *Arab*'s cable. As the ship drifted towards the shore, the Englishmen piled over the side. Crewmen escaped their ship, leaving it captured. This disheartened the crew of the *Dolphin* and Stafford had to urge his men to continue fighting rather than desert. The *Dolphin*, the *Lynx*, and the *Racer* thundered forth and British marines fired their muskets to rake the decks. Then the British boarded the *Lynx* and the *Racer*. The first boarders of the *Racer* were beaten back into the river, but others clambered over the sides and took that ship.

The British turned the guns of the *Racer* on the *Dolphin*. Some of the crew fled into a boat and were fired upon on orders of the captain, angered at the desertion. No one was shot aboard the boat as it made for shore. When one of the defenders saw a blue-clad arm over the rail, he cut it with a cutlass and the possessor lost his second arm and fell back armless. This was the second time Lieutenant William Brand had lost an arm in similar endeavors. The *Dolphin* was shortly taken. [3]

This British success did not reach England in time to soften British criticism of British operations on the seas. The Americans had been successful in the waters of the Atlantic too many times to suit the populace of the islands. Britain's Government reached swiftly to the protests of the king's subjects. Britain's naval leaders beefed up the numbers and quality of their ships in American waters. They warned the newly placed Borlase Warren that he must dispose of the enemy's naval forces. He must either capture the American fleet or blockade them on the American coast.

With his increase in ships, Warren was enabled to extend his previous blockade of George and South Carolina to the Chesapeake and Delaware bays and there to the coast up to New York. He left the New England coast clear to reward their opposition to the war and to allow New England merchants to ship provisions to Canada and the British West Indies. Businessmen in New England and New York upstate had traded with the British during the early war years. Foreign trade fell in the blockaded ports, government revenue dropped off, and the Americans had to rely upon their poor roads to replace their coastal trade routes by water. On one stretch it required 38 hours to travel 50 miles. American roads were notoriously bad. There were shortages and prices soared radically because of the scarcity, and the cost of shipping by land, and the speculations by traders. [4]

Meanwhile, once again Clay spoke out in the House on the war as a vigorous War Hawk. He was for no half-way measures and wanted the strongest effort made in the war. Peace would be nice, but peace could be gained only by efficient war. The Clay plan "would be to call out the ample resources of the country, give them a judicious direction, prosecute the war with the utmost vigor, strike wherever we can reach the enemy, at sea or on land, and negotiate the terms of the peace at Quebec or Halifax." Britain was proud and met challenges against it without undue delay. if America did not listen to the timid, she would prevail. If there was failure than Americans would meet it as men of free trade and sailors' rights. For Clay there was no turning back. It would be fight of die. His cause was just, but it required resources and these were often called upon sufficiently for early victory. The British were haughty and strong and Clay tried to rally the people for the nation. [5]

On the eighth of January, Colonel Thomas Hart Benton of the 2d Regiment of Tennessee Volunteer received order to send the 1st Regiment on boats and to march his 2d Regiment to undertake the defenses of New Orleans and the Lower Mississippi. Jackson found deficient arms and insufficient food supplies along the way. After a month underway, Jackson received orders from Secretary of War John Armstrong to dismiss his men from service, while at Natchez, because of the changing needs of the war. Once more the best general of the war was not used. Jackson was largely ignored in Washington. The future president must have been very frustrated at all this. He longed to be in battle, being a very combative man throughout all his long career. [6]

After the Hull debacle, Madison needed a new commander in the West. His administration preferred the regular army general James Winchester, but Richard M. Johnson and other westerners pressured the Government in favor of Harrison. When Kentucky leaders arranged to make William Henry Harrison a major general of their state militia with command of the local troops, it seemed obvious that the had the advantage. Madison bowed to continued requests of Johnson for Harrison and placed Harrison in charge of the theater of operations.

The general built his army in the fall of 1812, but since provisions were dear in the west because of lack of abundance it require so much of available funds, there were charges, denied in Washington DC that his agents paid $50 to $60 a barrel for flour. With federal money pouring into the western states and territories, the people benefited so much that they forgot Hull's setbacks. In order to secure safety, Harrison sent out raiding parties to destroy Indian villages and provisions and sent Winchester to the rapids of the

Maumee. The raiders had a great deal of success, but Winchester was not lucky in his operations. Once at the rapids, he marched without orders to the Raisin River to protect Americans at Frenchtown, later named Monroe, in Michigan. [7]

Five settlers from Frenchtown, located on the River Raisin, reported to Winchester that some Britishers were arresting suspicious Americans. They were planning to seize 300 barrels of flour and all of the beef, corn, and wheat in the towns. The settlers begged their fellow Americans to come to their rescue. Kentuckians were eager to display their heroism for such a cause. Winchester responded by sending two regiments of 680 all told led by colonels William Lewis and John Allen to come to the aid of the people of Frenchtown. They acted in haste and contrary to Harrison's instructions to Winchester. [8]

Madison sent Brigadier General James Winchester with untrained regular and volunteers to establish a base camp at the Maumee River Rapids. Winchester did not follow Harrison's orders, but marched to Frenchtown at the request of threatened citizens and dispersed a small British unit there on January 18, 1813. His Kentuckians under William Lewis did this successful conquest of the town. He had found the British soldiers and Indians and their three pound cannon. Losses were light in the half hour fight. British Major Ebenezer Reynolds withdrew.

The French villagers met the Americans with a supply of apples, cider, butter, sugar-loaf, and whiskey, items which the soldiers had done without for so many months. They encamped behind a split log fence on the other side of the river. It was approached by a road which was open to attack from the north. They put off building fortifications for another day.

With Frenchtown in his control, Winchester, probably highly elated, decided to march to the town with his now 300 man, Seventeenth regiment, reduced though it was in numbers. Soon Winchester had nearly nine hundred men there and called upon Harrison for more. The axes were insufficient to build fortifications true enough, but he did not make an effort to precede to build them. He also needed fixed ammunition. Meanwhile, Winchester placed his men in exposed positions without the great degree of caution required in the country of the native Americans. He also wrote letters to gain additional soldiers for his expedition. When Harrison learned of the success at the River Raisin, he former governor and now general was sure that they must maintain Winchester's position.

Harrison was interested in knowing what Winchester knew of the Indian strength in southern Michigan close to his goal Detroit, not far to the north. He did not know that Winchester had sent forth no scouts. Instead the general of Frenchtown heard reports from fleeing Frenchmen of danger and relied upon a British sympathizer who assured Winchester that there was no danger.

British Colonel Proctor led a force from Malden, eighteen miles away, to attack Winchester. He brought artillery with him over the ice. He outnumbered Winchester and was the more accomplished military leader. Winchester had not posted a single picket and was surprised, despite warnings from a Frenchman, friendly to the Americans that the British were coming, not realizing that the British were near. He had relied upon the wrong conflicting reports. Proctor met disorganized Americans, who hurriedly dressed to fight. Winchester had position and the British suffered from the fire of American sharpshooters.

This was all a shock to Winchester, and he delayed doing anything for fifteen or so minutes while fighting raged around him. He was not as good a general as proven by this in a similar circumstance facing Harrison at Tippecanoe, who had posted guards and directed his fight from the first attack. In Winchester's situation, the regulars were routed. There was a lack of protection along the banks where Winchester wanted them to form. Shortly the British turned the American right and turned them in the flank. The general was captured and surrendered his troops in order to avoid their being massacred. Both sides had heavy casualties except for the Kentuckians who continued the fight for awhile until their officers surrendered them to the disgust and anguish of the fighting men. Some Americans escaped.

The wounded were put into the small fort, where in a night attack the Indians killed them. Protor had been remised in not posting a guard for the wounded. Winchester had been unready and his failure forced Harrison to cancel his winter campaign. This Battle of Raisin River took place on January 22, 1813. It was to be the rallying cry for the Americans in Ohio where it took place. Such were the state of supply that the Americans still wore summer uniforms, here in the midst of winter, lacking great coats and cloaks, with few exceptions. [9]

At this time, Major W. W. Cotgreave was moving his American troops up from the south. They heard the sounds of battle and a fleeing Frenchman said he supposed the Americans were in retreat. Cotgreave ordered his men to hasten but when he heard more of what was happening he turned his troops around and sought safety in wise movement. The danger of Indian massacre was ever present and exerted a Raisin River, despite British disclaimers that they were softening native warlike habits. They knew that the Indians must be indulged, because they were so necessary to the British cause in America. [10]

There was alarm in St. Louis, War Hawk Samuel D. Solomon wrote William Rodgers Clark that an interpreter for the Sac and Fox tribes by the name of Blondeau had told him that the British had moved a force to Chicago. There they were collecting Indians to descend upon St. Louis in this spring. Canadian fur trader in the Red River north at Green Bay was also assembling two other Canadian tribes for a march on St. Louis. One hundred Indian warriors from ten lodges of Sacs had also joined the enemies of America. Some Sioux had accepted British wampum and were eager for an attack on St. Louis which had had a severe winter with a frozen Mississippi and Missouri.

The winter was not the hardest obstacle the Americans had faced. There was a lack of sufficient munitions of war. Simon and Hyman Gratz in partnership with Charles Wilkins, had an answer. They came to the rescue of the Americans by providing saltpeter for manufacturing gunpowder. They had the land on which twelve years earlier whites had discovered Mammoth Cave, which was the largest source of that mineral in the United States. The Americans had been cut off from the supply of the mineral because of the embargo. Hyman Gratz reported that explorers had found in the same cave an Indian bowl or cup and a skeleton of a human body. Other Jews including two other Gratz siblings joined the army to fight the British for their country. [11]

Now, General Andrew Jackson, with two thousand men, encamped at Fort Strother and he sent out spies into the woods of southern America. The scouts searched hard and discovered the Creek Indians on the bend of the Tallapoosa River descriptively named Horse Shoe Bend, ready for a single decisive battle. Creeks numbered one thousand men and Jackson's Americans had a two to one edge. For a man of Jackson's caliber, the battle was thus certain with all due care despite the Creek advantage in being on the defensive, thus requiring fewer men than any attacker. Jackson learned that the bend with its open end to the north marked off some hundred acres and the isthmus with, in Sam

Houston's words, a breastwork of three tiers of heavy pine trees, which stretched between rivers. They had two rolls of well arranged port holes.

Giving orders to march, Jackson headed forth and reached the site on March 27, 1813. Immediately he ordered General Coffee to cross the river at a ford two miles below the battleground with some mounted rangers and almost all the friendly Indians to cut off any Creek retreat to the east, south, and west. This was done by ten o'clock. Next Jackson advanced the men of his main force and raked the works with two small pieces of artillery. This had no effect of importance because of the heavy construction of the barrier and lightness of the artillery.

At one o'clock in the afternoon Jackson's men heard a musket fire and rifles go off in the south and watched smoke rise from the vicinity. This made them certain that the Coffee detachment were fighting the Creeks from across the river. They were eager for a fight, but Jackson held them back, wanting to move the Creek families to safety before the fighting. He sent a messenger asking the Indians to allow the movement of women and children out of way. The Creeks sent them forth and the army attacked the Indian barricades, happily storming the Creek braves. Meanwhile the Coffee force with the Cherokee chief, his men, Captain Russell and his scouts, had seized canoes from across the river and used them to cross, fire the wigwam, and fight their enemy. They carried the fortification and Sam Houston was wounded to fight again, and wounded once more.

The action now became general. The Indian prophet had told them that they should win the battle. They would see a cloud in the sky and know then that they would have the victory. Jackson ordered the carnage stopped and sent a messenger to the Indians, but the Creeks noticed their cloud in the sky and decided that success would soon be theirs. So they fired upon the envoy and the battle was renewed. There was no quarter given or taken. The Indians were killed right and left, but they did not give up. Indians gathered on the fortification and issued a strong fire upon the whites.

Jackson could not use his artillery, but did order a storming of the position. No captain would embark on such a murderous duty, fearing heavy American losses and maybe defeat. Houston tried to lead his men but they would not advance and so a much wounded Houston fell and was carried off the field, to recover slowly and in pain. Jackson's men fired on the covered ravine and with that most of the Creeks were to lose their lives and never recover to safeguard their land. [12]

By the time the spring thaw freed the northern border with Canada from the icy grip of winter, the United States was stronger and better prepared than they had been that time in the previous year. The leadership of John Armstrong in the War Department and of William Jones in the Navy Department, despite their shortcomings was better than their predecessors. Both were more knowledgeable about military officers in their areas of command. Armstrong proved an intriguer and a political enemy of Gallatin and Monroe, while Jones won admiration for his talents. Madison had chosen better generals and opened the way for William Henry Harrison, Andrew Jackson, Winfield Scott, and Zebulon Pike. The number of soldiers, brought in by higher pay and bounties, doubled in number to about 30,000 men. Most were lacking in the experience of battle, but some were campaign seasoned.

Control of the Great Lakes was the key to the 1813 campaign on land. America, it was decided, would no longer attempt to take Quebec or Montreal because of their heavy fortifications. Armstrong decided to have his armies attack Kingston or York, lakeside naval bases, and Fort George and Fort Erie. Should the Americans have victories at these four points, they would advance against British strongholds elsewhere. He reasoned that command of the lakes would mean control of the U. S.-Canadian border.

In March of 1813, the Americans had one vessel on Lake Ontario to the British six. The American six-gun army ship on Lake Eire had been captured when William Hull surrendered in 1812. Madison and Armstrong worked to build a naval force on these two lakes. The British knew what was happening and tried to counter the Americans with their own program. Commanders on both sides were cautious by nature and decided to take the bases of the other. Neither would risk a naval encounter such as the captain of the *Atlanta* had in the previous year.

The experienced naval captain Isaac Chauncy who was in control of the American force at Sacker's Harbor, loaded ships with 1,700 troops commanded by the famous wide range explorer General Zebulon Pike. Sailing across Lake Ontario, Chauncey landed the soldiers west of York on April 27, 1813. Pike's soldiers marched quickly against the town and overwhelmed the 700 British and Indian defenders. General Sir Roger Sheaffe retreated with his force into the interior. The Americans killed or wounded 150 of the enemy and captured 290, leaving Sheaffe some 260 men in the woods. Pike's men sustained 320 casualties, including those lost in the explosion of the town's magazine. Zebulon himself was hit by a stone in the explosion and died. It was a sad lost for America in a brave man with such promise.

Angry over the tremendous impact of the explosion and heavy losses due to it, the American soldiers found a scalp on the wall of the government building and followed the explosion in an outburst. They began looting the town and the king's subjects came into town from the country to help them sack deserted houses. Finding a printing press they destroyed it. Then the soldiers burnt down York's government buildings. The British destroyed one of their ships and the Americans seized another, bringing the United States up to naval parity on Lake Ontario. [13]

In March of 1813, Sam Houston had joined the war effort as private in the Thirty-ninth Infantry and was soon an ensign and then a third lieutenant by years end. His regimental colonel was Thomas Hart Benton. In the next year, the regiment marched into Fort Strother, where Houston had met Jackson under whom he was cool in battle at Horseshoe Bend.

Houston was the fifth son of Samuel Houston, who was a brigade inspector before being made a major in the Virginia militia. His mother was Elizabeth Paxton Houston. The young boy had some formal education, before the widow Houston moved the family to East Tennessee near Maryville in the hills. Since he did not like farming, Houston went to work at a general store in Maryville, but he did not like the work. He visited the Cherokee Indians for the first time and stayed a year. In Maryville, he beat a drum which disturbed the court and he was fined for this demeanor. Instead of paying, Houston fled to the Indians again. The adopted him and named him the Raven.

He lived among the Indians for three years except for some visits home and a scouting party against Tecumseh in 1811. He got into debt and started a school to pay off his debt. With an aroused patriotism he quit teaching and left to join the army. The young soldiers had had an interest in military tactics which was to serve him as a start in his army career. He was to stay in the army at the end of the war and was adjutant with Jackson at Nashville. As a sub-agent to the Cherokees he then spent time with them once again. Because Calhoun dressed him down for appearing in Indian clothes in Washington on a trip with the Cherokees seeking redress. Houston developed a life-long hatred of Calhoun. In 1818, he left the army and the Indians to study law in six months. [14]

[1]Hickey, *1812*, pp. 153-156.
[2]Tucker, *Poltroons and Patriots*, pp. 259-261.
[3]Cranwell & Crane, *Men of Marque*, pp. 104-109.
[4]Hickey, *1812*, pp. 151-153.
[5]Lynch, *Fifty Years*, p. 238. Quote on p. 238.
[6]Jackson, *Papers*, II, 355-361.
[7]Hickey, *1812, pp. 85-86.*
[8]Cleaves, *Old Tippecanoe*, p. 137.
[9]Skagg, David Curtis, "Frenchtown, Battle of," Heidler & Heidler, *Encyclopedia*, p. 195; Clark, *History*, p. 128; Richardson, *War of 1812*, pp. 132-136, 140-142; Cleaves, *Old Tippecanoe*, pp. 137-145.
[10]Cleaves, *Old Tippecanoe*, pp. 146-150.
[11]Sharfman, I. Harold, *Jews on the Frontier: An Account of Jewish Pioneers and Settlers in Early America*, Malibu Cal: Joseph Simon/Pangloss Press, 1987, pp. 121-122.
[12]Houston, Samuel, *Life of General Sam Houston: A Short Autobiography*, Reprint, Austin, Tx: Pemberton Press, 1964, p. 2.
[13]Hickey, *1812*, pp. 106-107, 126-130.
[14]Friend, Llerena, *Sam Houston: The Great Designer*, Austin Tx: University of Texas Press, 1954, pp. 5-9.

CHAPTER XXI

DEARBORN

Although Lincoln was too young to know it, the country was no more ready for war financially than militarily. Gallatin, at the head of the treasury, moved slowly but finally he recommended that Congress passed tax bills to pay for the war. Congress refused, nor would the two houses of national legislature renew the Bank of the United States, no matter how much it was necessary for the war effort. Albert Gallatin confided in the successful politician lawyer Alexander James Dallas, who helped him raise sixteen million dollar loan on April 6, 1813. However, more money had to be raised. Later Madison offered Dallas the secretaryship of the Treasury when Gallatin left for the peace negotiations in Europe. The Jamaican born Dallas declined the honor because the position did not pay enough for the luxuries to which he had become accustomed. Madison succeeded in getting George W. Campbell for the post. [1]

Meanwhile, the Indians made their usual depredations in the Old Northwest with the early Spring of 1813. Harrison had other problems also. With the melting of ice on Lake Erie the British would be able to sail their gunboats against the American Great Lakes shore and up the rivers. He could expect the militia to go home, after which he would have only 500 men to guard Fort Meigs. Already he began doing less work on Meigs' fortifications and straying soldiers were caught by Indians.

Harrison was still intent upon an aggressive stance on operations in the area, still hoping to take the Fort Detroit that Hull had lost. The idea was not merely an illusionary one for the general collected packhorses that the Kentuckians could use to keep supplied for a quick advance. On April 1, 1813, Harrison headed for the Rapids. Whenever he could, the general picked up fresh detachments and had others come for the advanced points with him. He reached Fort Meigs. Cannoneers saluted his arrival with their guns and frightened off an Indian scouting party nearby.

At this time, the British authorities promoted Proctor to the rank of major general and Proctor made plans for action. The two Indian leaders searched out their tribes and recruited, strengthen by British promises of rich plunder and power over Harrison, whom the Indians could hope and torture and burn. They said that Fort Meigs could not hold out. Only a single day's cannonading was between them and the whole Northwest which could be theirs once again.

General Harrison immediately and successfully encouraged his men to work on the fortifications and daily expected an attack. He wanted them to attack Fort Meigs. Soon Proctor brought forth a large force of two thousand British regulars, Canadian militiamen, and Indians. Once they arrived before Fort Meigs, Proctor's men built two batteries to menace the fort. The American general took counter-measures with his 1,200 effectives. At first the siege was one of sharpshooters. A more sustained undertaking was not fruitful, but since Harrison had limited shot, he did not reply in equal vigor, husbanding his supplies. It was a matter of whom could outwait whom. Then what Harrison had long awaited for came into being, General Green Clay was arriving with 1,200 men. There was a fight between Colonel William Dudley who charged the British force, but when his men pursued the retreating British, they were caught in an Indian ambush. The Indians massacred many of the Americans with the tomahawk and the Kentuckians under Dudley had to surrender.

With the addition of the militiamen in the fort, the pressure was on for a raising of the siege. There were only so many provisions at hand. Colonel John Miller volunteered to lead a select group of men to capture the British cannon. Picking out 300 men, Miller advanced his forces from the fort under heavy fire. As ordered, the Americans did not fire until the command was given within fifty yards of the British. They fired and charged, taking and spiking the guns at the loss of 30 dead and 90 wounded. This created a bad situation for Proctor since the Indians and Canadians began deserting him. Proctor faced defeat and withdrew. Despite this victory, the War Department ordered Harrison to go on the defensive. Once again official will was weak. [2]

An example of New England feeling is found in the letter of George Herbert of Maine to his old college friend Daniel Webster. Herbert cursed the Government and wrote that he would march against Madison if he could get anybody to go with him. In his march, he would reached Georgia and trample the planters down. The planters, in his view, were the aggressors in the war. People of Boston and their leaders had failed to take action necessary to remedy the situation. Meanwhile, the New England states were ruined and starved. Herbert would have relief. Boston had done nothing, was unready until Otis was ready. Starvation would set in before reason was reached. The writer of the letter believed that Boston and Boston folk were timid. [3]

The American Government appointed Albert Gallatin, John Quincy Adams, and James A. Bayard to be envoys to St. Petersburg to work on peace terms with Great Britain under the mediation of the Russian czar. Levitt Harris was to serve as secretary of the mission which hoped to end the war with the British. James Monroe had drawn up varying instructions for the mission for the territorial gains they wished in the Floridas. Americans claimed West Florida by cession from France. They claimed East Florida as an indemnity for spoliations. Monroe informed the envoys that Mobile, the only part of West Florida still possessed by Spain, should have fallen to American troops by the time they had begun their negotiations. The government still planned to take possession of East Florida should any other foreign power attempt to occupy the territory, still under Spanish control.

There were other opportunities to be taken advantage of. Madison thought that the mediation of the emperor of Russia might provide a good time to improve relations with Russia. The envoys were therefore authorized to enter into a commercial treaty with Russia. Hopefully they would reciprocate in a most favored nation treaty. They would also arrange an understanding of neutral rights which would also benefit Russian commerce on the high seas. In addition they should try to enter into another commercial treaty with Great Britain. [4]

Spanish Captain Cayetano Perez led the last of his forces out of Mobile in April of 1813. After they had left, Captain Reuben Chamberlain directed the building of an American fort on Mobile Point on the sand of a four mile peninsula which commanded

The Difficult War: The Era of the War of 1812 173

the narrow entrance to Mobile Bay to protect it from the sea. In June, Colonel John Bowyer arrived under orders to continue the supervision of the work on what was called Fort Bowyer. The fort was a semicircular redoubt rising with bluffs on all sides. There were to be placed their nine cannon without casemates. General Thomas Flournoy inspected the work and expressed his concern that the fort might be vulnerable from the land side. Because of this, he abandoned the fort for Fort Charlotte at Mobile across the bay. In August of 1814, Jackson sent Major William Lawrence to reconstruct the fort.

A British force of marines and Indians were repulsed on September 14, 1814. Before the peace treaty news reached Mobile, another British army arrived. The fighting began, but the enemy swamped Lawrence and his garrison. The bastion fell. Years later the fort was renamed Fort Morgan. The battle for Fort Bowyer has the distinction of being the last engagement of the war. [5]

Dearborn was developing prominent plans. He would take York (Toronto), the capital of Upper Canada, Fort George, and Kingston, capturing Lake Ontario by water and by land. The general and Captain Isaac Chauncey would coordinate their efforts. There was a certain urgency to the campaign. The British were building a brig at York and at Kingston which might when finished swing the American control of the lake waters over to the English under Sir James Lucas Yeo. Dearborn would maintain the command, but the capable and active Brigadier General Zebulon Pike, the explorer, would direct the battle. By way of preparations, he drilled, from the first, his men on snowshoes. The men liked his firmness and sureness, and were eager to follow him in battle.

They embarked on April 22, 1813, and sailed from Sachet's Harbor on the 25th. A letter sped from Pike to his veteran father: "I embark at the head of 1500 select troops on a secret expedition. Should I be the happy mortal destined to turn the scale of war, will you not rejoice, oh my father? May heaven be propitious, and smile on the cause of my country. But if we are destined to fall, may my fall be like Wolfe's to sleep in the arms of victory." At the onset, he ordered his men to refrain from plundering. Anyone caught doing that would be executed. Penalties were harsh in those days. [6]

A speedy wind blew the ships to three miles west of York. Major Forsyth's rifle corps landed on the beach. When Pike saw them receive heavy fire from the woods, he hopped aboard a boat to follow in the second wave, eager to rush the enemy. The British were outnumbered, consisting of two companies only, plus fifty Indians. Pike led the advance against three companies who had had no linking of the battle until they saw troops landing. However, Major General Sir Roger H. Sheaffe did his best to rally and help his troops.

Sheaffe retreated with his regular company, leaving his militia companies to surrender. Two explosions rent the air of York and the second mortally wounded Pike and he died listening to the cheers of his men raise the American flag at York. There were grave casualties on both sides due to the second explosion. Dearborn was no Pike and soon the men were plundering. They left the prisoners out of jail and the men joined in the pursuit of public property in private homes. Dearborn did not reign in his men and soon they were pillaging and torching the legislative halls. [7]

Now aging, General Henry Dearborn was unable to grasp the job and act in a decisive manner. He was sixty-two years old, in ill-health, and a worrier. Distrustful of his subordinates in general, Dearborn was eager to allow Colonel Winfield Scott to make the plans for the attack and supported him fully. The general's thousand worries were happily reduced. Scott's action would suit his military needs. [8]

Dearborn held a council of war on May 10, 1813, to discuss his next step. It was obvious that the Americans should attack Fort George, the British outpost across from Fort Niagara, just across the river. They would have the advantage of numbers with 4,700 men against a British-Canadian force of 1,700. Since Dearborn would assault a fort, he would need this advantage. When asked their opinions by the general, he high-ranking officers came to an agreement that Fort George should be their target. The decision was made, but Dearborn awaited the arrival of his new chief-of-staff Scott to set up the operation.

Scott reached there three days later to find the command in total disarray. Scott took charge. The young chief-of-staff made plans with the navy. He discovered that Oliver Hazard Perry needed the western banks cleared of the British for his Lake Erie campaign and was eager for the Fort George operation. Scott's plan was for an ascent on the shore of Lake Ontario where Perry was, near the Niagara River, north of the Falls. British Brigadier General John Vincent was to be defeated and his fort captured. The goal was the British-Canadian army. Colonel James Burn was to attack at Queenston to cut off any British retreat. Scott himself was to lead the advance. [9]

Much needed to be done. Scott found Dearborn staff-less, plan-less, and ready-less. The troops were untrained (with a few exceptions) and supplies were insufficient. There was no order or plan when Scott took over the preparation at the front in the position of adjutant general. Colonel Scott took out a newly printed textbook on staff work in Napoleon's army written by Thiebault and proceeded from there. Dearborn signed all orders prepared by Scott and order was soon drawn from disorder.

Scott made his plans carefully, taking the necessary time. He did not allow his battle-eager troops to rush him. Plans were made for transportation on the American side of Lake Ontario to take the army pass the mouth of the Niagara River and land them to the west of Fort George on the Canadian side of the lake. A small force commanded by Colonel James Burn was to try to cut off the British retreat by crossing the river behind the chosen battleground. Scott was to insure that the fight be gotten off on the right foot. [10]

On May 27, 1813, after artillery barrages, the men embarked and the American ships set out through a fog that both hid them from the British and made the way difficult. Finally the fog lifted and the British soldiers saw sixteen American ships in a wide arc. The fleet was commanded by Captain Isaac Chauncey. The ship guns silenced the British batteries and the soldiers hit the beaches from the ships and the boats which were strung out behind. The naval planning had been successful and well implemented. [11]

Once there, the battle began with stiff fighting. The British were peppered with fire from the troops and fire from the ships. Men of the British Glengarry Regiment fell back and reformed. They were aided by newly arrived British militiamen and blacks. The blacks were escaped slaves from American soil. Forced back, the British commander retreated in orderly fashion. Having captured a riderless horse, Scott led the troops to destroy the defeated army until recalled by General Morgan Lewis, temporarily in command. Scott thought this was a mistake, but he had to obey. A mistake it was.

Meanwhile, Burn failed in his mission to cut off the retreating British since his force was pinned down by whistling British artillery fire. Vincent escaped with most of his army to fight another day. American losses were light against moderate British killed and wounded and 262 British and Canadians were missing. Scott was successful because of his zeal, energy, audacity, and studies. Scott was at the head of the fighting and had been knocked down twice in the battle. [12]

The victory at Fort George won the abandoned fort for Scott. British general John Vincent had to evacuate exposed forts at Queenston, soon to be occupied by Americans. The end was not decided because the American failure to pursue Vincent allowed him to regroup at Hamilton on the western end of Lake Ontario, the easternmost lake. Thus the American victory at Fort George was incomplete and did not open Canada up to the Americans. It merely shifted forces in favor of the United States. Then Lewis sent two political generals with about 2,600 men to pursue the British. They camped seven miles from the British.

Before dawn, British Colonel John Harvey led 700 men and caught the Americans, superior in numbers, by surprise. Harvey had learned the countersign from a paroled prisoner and using it captured or killed by bayonet the American sentries. All the troops rushed upon the American camp with a great shout. The Americans retreated in confusion and the two generals were captured by the British, a fitting fate. Surprisingly, the British suffered more casualties than the Americans. This canceled out most of Scott's victory because Dearborn withdrew from every fort captured except Fort George, where he left a garrison.

Dearborn tried to recover his position with a raid and its failure left the British to take an offensive, which in its turn led militia general McClure to abandon Fort George. The raid was led by Lieutenant Colonel Charles Boerstler. The 500 man force marched out, but the British were warned by a Canadian lady named Laura Secord who bravely walked 20 miles through unfamiliar woods and plains. Abused by Indians, threatened, and bluffed, Boerstler surrendered in fright. This American defeat led directly to Dearborn's removal from command. So much for the large number of incompetent officers in the American army. Scott would have handled it better. [13]

A brigadier general in the New York militia, Jacob Brown had already proved himself in the war and had been offered a colonelcy in the Regular Army. He was a Quaker. After a farmer's son's work experienced in his youth, Brown surveyed public lands in Ohio, taught school, studied law, and wrote newspaper articles. During the war scare over the XYZ affair, he became military secretary to General Alexander Hamilton, under whom he gave lessons in army leadership. After this, he farmed, served as county judge, and was a militia colonel. He entered the war when his militia unit was called out in the defense of Ogdensburg. [14]

Now he was faced with another military action. Prevost sailed his British garrison of Kingston across to take Sacket's Harbor, on the eastern shore of Lake Ontario. It had few defenders now that the Americans were in action at York. For Prevost the action was a diversion to help Fort George. Prevost's delay of one day, due to the lost of a pilot and adverse winds, enabled a surprised Brown to roundup more militiamen.

Then at dawn, on May 29, 1813, Sir George Prevost landed his Kingston garrison troops. They were under heavy fire. Most of the Americans panicked, but the able Jacob Brown rallied them with effort. A Sacket's Harbor butcher named Westcott helped him bring his men into action. Prevost mistakenly believed they were reinforcements ready to attack his flanks. He reembarked his men and sailed off. His casualties numbered 259, while the Americans lost 137 in the stiff fight. For this victory, Brown was commissioned a regular officer and rose to become commanding general under Monroe and J. Q. Adams. Sir James Yeo took the initiative and attacked the American rear. [15]

On May 13, 1813, there was a report published in the *Missouri Gazette* of a trans-continental journey from Astoria to St. Louis and points east. The editor entitled the account "American Enterprise." It told of the movement of Robert Stewart. a partner of the Pacific Fur Company with others up the Columbia River eastward. Passing toward the Rocky Mountains, they were soon followed by a band of Crow Indians who began stealing their horses until the group was horseless.

The editor wrote that a reader might see what the situation of these men he takes "into consideration that they were now on foot and had a journey of 2000 miles before them, 1500 of which entirely unknown, as they intended and prosecuted it considerably south of Messrs. Lewis and Clark's route; the impossibility of carrying any quantity of provisions on their backs, in addition to their ammunition and bedding, will occur at first view. The danger to be apprehended from starvation was imminent."

This did not deter the travelers. Once across the mountains, they acquired a horse from some Snake Indians and wintered on the Platte River in Wyoming. The next spring the party proceeded down the river to the Missouri and down to St. Louis. The editor noted that according to "information received from these gentlemen, it appears that a journey across the continent of North America might be performed with a wagon, there being no obstruction in the wheel route that any person would dare to call a mountain, in addition to its being much the most direct and short one to go from this place to the mouth of the Columbia River." It was then considered that the better route was the southern one. [16]

The notable 47-ton sloop *Dart* set forth from St. John, New Brunswick, on May 22, 1813. It was a bit of a problem to gather the crew since some had tanked up on cheap rum, but the ship dropped out into the harbor with the Bay of Bundy tide below the rock that is St. John. Sailing off the New England coast the *Dart* captured a number of vessels which were not worth sending to the prize courts. It got disgusting for crewmen to check so many ships and discover them generally empty. No other privateer ever had such bad luck. Finally the captain sent forth a launch to board and take control of an American schooner without any struggle. The *Superb* contained a cargo of salt and a lady passenger, and the other ship captured carried a cargo of lumber.

Next the crew of the British *Dart* sighted a ship which was trying to close with the land. They chased her for two hours. They fired and the vessel surrendered. The boarding party found that the ship was the *Cuba* of New York, with a cargo of flour to deliver to Portland. They took her to the prize court and although they were parted for a good time during the foggy night. the success measured a moderate one with $500 for each man. [17]

On Tuesday, June 1, 1813, Captain James Lawrence had his men aboard ship and get underway on the cruise. They soon saw a ship, which looked like a warship. About 5:45 PM, the ships drew along sides. Each ship fired broadsides which did extensive damage and on the American side, saw Lawrence wounded. After some firing the British boarded the quarter deck. George Budd ordered his men to haul on board the fore-tack to shoot the ship clear and to clear the quarter deck, but soon found the enemy had full control of the American ship. Every officer on the American side was either killed or wounded. This was the battle of the American *Chesapeake* and the British *Shannon*, with heavy casualties. The Americans could not win them all. [18]

The Madison Administration was still economy minded, even in the midst of a dangerous war. Secretary of the Treasury Albert Gallatin reduced expenditure for the northwestern front with the full support of Secretary of War John Armstrong, who wanted economy and a concentration of resources in the East. With no confidence in Harrison, Armstrong restricted the general's freedom of action and forced him to go on the defense. The future president had Eleazer Wood build Fort Meigs on the Maumee Rapids in Ohio. This fort was very strong, fortunately because it was soon attacked by a

The Difficult War: The Era of the War of 1812

superior force of Britons and Indians with artillery. This offensive was led by General Henry Procter. [19]

[1]Walters, Raymond Jr., *Alexander James Dallas, Lawyer-Politician-Financier, 1759-1817*, Philadelphia: University of Pennsylvania Press, 1943, Reprint New York: DaCapo Press, 1969, pp. 177, 180-182, 187.

[2]Cleaves, *Old Tippecanoe*, pp. 159-172; Heidler, Jeanne, and Heidler, David S., "Clay, Green," Heidler & Heidler, *Encyclopedia*, pp. 109-110.

[3]Van Tyne, C. H. (ed.), *The Letters of Daniel Webster from Documents Owned Principally By the New Hampshire Historical Society, 1902, Reprint New York: Haskell House, 1969, pp. 27-28.*

[4]Bayard, James Asheton, *Papers of James A. Bayard*, Elizabeth Donnan,, (ed.), 1915, New York: Da Capo Press, 1971, pp. 211, 214-216.

[5]Smith, Gene A., "Bowyer, Fort," Heidler & Heidler, *Encyclopedia*, pp. 59-60.

[6]Tucker, *Poltroons and Patriots*, pp. 242-244. Quote on p. 243-244.

[7]*Ibid.*, pp. 244-256.

[8]Elliott, *Scott*, p. 91.

[9]Eisenhower, *Agent*, pp. 55-56.

[10]Elliott, *Scott*, pp. 91-94.

[11]*Ibid.*, pp. 94-96; Hickey, *1812*, p. 140; Eisenhower, *Agent*, p. 57.

[12]Elliott, *Scott*, pp. 96-100; Hickey, *1812*, p. 140; Eisenhower, *Agent*, pp. 57-59, Heidler, Jeanne & Heidler, David S., "Burn, James," Heidler & Heidler, *Encyclopedia*, p. 71.

[13]Hickey, *1812*, pp. 140-141.

[14]Tucker, *Poltroons and Patriots*, pp. 256-257.

[15]*Ibid.*, p. 257-258; Drake, "Chauncey, Isaac," p. 90; Drake, Frederick C., "Sacket's Harbor, Battle of," Heidler & Heidler, *Encyclopedia*, pp. 455-461.

[16]Hulbert, Archer Butler (ed.), *Southwest on The Turquoise Trail: The First Diaries on the Road to Santa Fe*, 1933, pp. 8-11.

[17]Snider, *Under the Red Jack*, pp. 55-71. Quote on p. 68.

[18]Brannan, *Official Letters*, pp. 167-168.

[19]Hickey, *1812*, p. 135.

CHAPTER XXII

UNDER ORDERS

Under orders, Lieutenant Sidney Smith patrolled the northern part of Lake Champlain, between New York State and Vermont, with two ships of eleven guns, and ran into trouble. British gunboats ventured out from Isle Aux Noix on June 2, 1813, to capture two American sloops. Smith neared a small fortified British occupied island on the lake's northern end. The Americans got into shallow waters and could not maneuver. British artillerymen, gunboats and musketry disabled the two ships in a three and a half hour fire. Smith surrendered. Opposing British Major George Taylor thought them gallant, but foolhardy for their risks into Canadian territory. Losses were very light on both sides.

The advantage to the enemy was that this opened the way to southward plunge into the United States now that such opposition was captured as presented by the two sloops. In retrospect the Americans should have remained on the defensive, but hindsight is always superior to foresight. Such is life. When the British repaired the two ships and sailed forth they won control of the lake. There could be no successful campaign against eastern or lower Canada with this link lost on the part of the Americans. Unfortunately, Madison placed General James Wilkinson in command of the northeastern theater. This man was unprincipled and had become an enemy to the country in earlier days when he received a pension from Spain for his efforts to join Kentucky to the Spanish Empire. [1]

Dearborn had attempted to exploit the victory before Fort George by sending men forth. He learned that Proctor was headed for Burlington Heights in Upper Canada to assist British Brigadier General John Vincent to regain Fort George. When that information reached him, Dearborn sent out newly promoted Brigadier General William Winder to defeat Vincent before Proctor could arrive. Winder marched his men over difficult terrain across creeks and drew up in front of Burlington Heights. Because he believed he did not have enough men to take the heights, Winder expressed his concern to Dearborn, who sent reinforcements posthaste. These were headed by Brigadier General John Chandler, who as Winder's superior due to time in rank, took command and planned for battle near Stoney Creek.

Vincent ordered a night attack and one hour before dawn, his troops delivered a partial surprise. The fighting raged on with moderate losses on both sides. Both Winder and Chandler were captured. The one hour of battle later, the British withdrew. Reeling, the Americans retreated. They left without tents and tent equipment and without burying their dead. The night attack had hurt the Americans and crushed their morale. They had

180 Eugene M. Wait

to content themselves with Fort George, which was soon lost. Meanwhile, Protor was busy elsewhere and Vincent was left to savor his victory. [2]

There were those British Canadian privateers who made a rich haul and those privateers who had little success. Among the latter was the *Matilda*, a schooner out of Nova Scotia's Annapolis Royal. This fifty-ton ship had only a new hawser and a barrel of flour to show for a month at sea, gained from the American shallop called the *Nymph*, out of Marblehead, seized on June 11th. Captain John Burkett Jr. was thinking of calling it quits when his look-outs sighted two sails on the horizon. It was soon ascertained that it was a chase scene. A brig was in pursuit of the other ship, which was racing for Sequin light on the Maine coast, where the Kennebeck River flowed into the ocean.

Burkett decided he must take his own chances should both be American. He would cut off the lead ship and take her before the brig reached it if the chased should prove American and the chaser be prove British. The *Matilda* clawed to windward. Bad luck seemed to plague Burkett at noon when the wind weakened and shifted. The lead ship was flying the American flag they were now able to observe. They were also able to see the brig was seven miles off. There would be a trading fire with no result. At two o'clock it looked like the lead ship would escape both ships. With the wind falling off, the sailors of the *Matilda* turned to the long oars.

At five o'clock, the gunners of the *Matilda* began firing broadsides with success and the ship was hit in turn. The wind died down and the rowers were too few to move her. In their place, the men of the Canadian *Matilda* fired their muskets. Shortly they launched a boarding boat and returned with six wounded prisoners. American militiamen left the fort near the lighthouse and boarded the distressed American ship. They manned the guns, but the *Matilda* was overshot. The Nova Scotians replied. With great difficulty, the American *Loyal Sam* was boarded by the Canadian privateers. Unknown to either the chaser had reached the American and each side discovered that both were boarding, one from each side. The Americans were caught in between. The boarders overpowered the Americans and divided the prize between them. The *Matilda* sailed home, capturing two American ships on the way.

The *Matilda* had two more cruises, in which she took six coasters, but they tended to be small vessels. She was forced to raid fishermen. However, everything was judged condemned that she sent in to prize courts. One June 15th an American schooner sailed down Long Island Sound with hopes of evading the blockade of the British fleet. Before the *Ramilles* could check on her, the crew had dropped anchor and rowed ashore, a common occurrence. He seized the barrels of flour on its deck and the hold full of powder which had been destined to blow up he flagship of the blockaders. [3]

William Henry Allen next commanded the *Argus* which took William H. Crawford, the new U.S. minister to France, eluding British blockaders off New York and off the Biscay coast in Europe. He landed Crawford in L'Orient in Brittany. Having delivered the envoy set out to take or destroy British shipping in the English Channel and the Irish Sea. In the following month, his ships preyed upon the single ships at sea. He seized 19 ships with cargoes of two million dollars all told, and burnt them. When shippers heard of the raids, they pressed the Admiralty to detail severe man-of-war to take after the *Argus*.

As he sailed off the Welsh coast, Allen seized a merchantman with a cargo of wine, part of which his men consumed and were unable to fight the next morning. Courageous to the point of recklessness, Allen did not flee an approaching British ship. The British brig *Pelran* closed in. Fighting in which Allen was wounded erupted. The British gunners grabbed the edge. The ships came together and the British attempted to board. At this

The Difficult War: The Era of the War of 1812

point, 2d Lieutenant William Howard Allen surrendered the ship. Captain Allen died in a British hospital shortly later. His own drunken sailors had meant his downfall. [4]

British Admiral Sir John Warren returned to Chesapeake Bay with troops under Colonel Sir John Beckwith. Their goal was to capture the *Constellation*, then blockaded at Norfolk, protected by nineteen small gunboats. The key was Craney Island, guarding the mouth of the Elizabeth River and Norfolk. Brigadier General Robert B. Taylor worked to bolster his defenses against the British by installing cannon. Unable to get his ships close enough to bombard Craney Island, Warren landed his troops on the mainland at dawn of June 22, 1813.

Taylor opened up his artillery and the Britons moved inland away from the island. At this time, the British were deploying barges against Craney. Well directed American artillery sunk three large enemy boats. This success was to save the island from British conquest. British losses were heavy in the fighting. Then on the next day, the British took Newport News under cover of rockets. They marched on Hampton and swamped the town's defenses with numbers. They raided up the river, while Captain John Cassin added troops at Craney. The British were not to return, but plundered to the north. They returned to their ships at Lynnhaven Bay and departed. [5]

Earlier, in the spring, the Congress had an able new member in thirty-one year old Daniel Webster from New Hampshire. Like so many congressmen he was a lawyer by profession and duty bound to his constituents. In the contest for a seat in the House, Webster had declared that the War of 1812 was premature and expedient. The people back home, with their eyes on their devastated economy, were very hopeful for their representatives, but could not know how great a career had been launched. In a June tenth speech, Webster verbally attacked the entire Madison war program. He made serious charges. Calboun rose to successfully defend Madison. The heat of debate did not bother Webster, but the hot sun of Washington led him to return home for the rest of the secession. This Webster-Calhoun debate was to continue in the next season [6]

The British were interested in taking New Orleans early on in the war. An English newspaperman noted on June 17th that there were arguments in British colonial journals, sought somewhat successfully to prove that the British should take possession of the province of New Orleans as a necessity. In this way, British would divide the States and cut off the outlet of Western provisions and industry. With this those states would be renown and respected. By this method they would make the people of the West their friends, they thought. In taking New Orleans they would supply the West Indies islands at half price and create allies in Europe, pleasing planters, and guaranteeing Hispanic America from the treason of the colonists. An American leader noted that the taking of New Orleans would only bring forth the Americans in mass to drive the British out. [7]

In the evening of the 23rd of June, 1813, the American command ordered Colonel Boerstler with his 570 men, infantry, artillery, cavalry, and riflemen to march through Queenston to attack and disperse Canadian forces at Beaver Dams procuring provisions and reportedly harassing pro-American Canadians. The British were half as numerous as Boaster's force. His army was ambushed two miles short of the British force at Beaver Dams by 260 Indians. Although he successfully fought the native off, he called upon Dearborn for reinforcements and drove the British into the woods. He had met British Lieutenant James Fitzgibbon with a demand for him to surrender. The American did so fearing the arrival of more British soldiers. Back at headquarters there was already an interest in replacing Dearborn and this was done promptly in early July. [8]

There were divisions in the American army of the north. Armstrong, secretary of the War Department, and James Wilkinson differed greatly on the strategy to undertake. Wade Hampton differed with Wilkinson and would not even speak to him, his erstwhile commander, much less take orders from him. Armstrong avoided a collision by having Wilkinson relay his orders to Hampton through the War Department. This caused dangerous delays at a time when communications were not swift. To achieve this and keep from under Madison's supervision, Armstrong put up his headquarters close to the battlefield of Sacket's Harbor. This alleviated the danger a great deal.

Wilkinson established a large army at Sacket's Harbor. Not having learned from 1812, the American delegation delayed an advance upon Montreal until late in the season. It seemed like the flotilla going downstream was a good idea, but a gale scattered the American vessels. Next the advanced force which was to give the signal for an assault strayed and then was scattered needlessly. It lost only one man in the encounter. Expecting a greater attack, Hampton cowardly retreated.

Lacking determination, Wilkinson failed to press forward when the growing got rough. General Jacob Brown moved forth in the advance on the north and exposed right bank of the St. Lawrence and Colonel Alexander Macomb led the flank. There was no one to protect the rear. Indeed there was something to complain about. British gunboats and some thousand men from Kingston followed the American force. In mid-November, General John Parke Boyd of the American army deployed some one thousand men on Chrysler's Farm in the snow and drizzle. They fought for five hours until faced with defeat. Then suddenly 600 fresh troops led by the American Colonel Timothy Upham arrived and fought a delaying action until night. Then Wilkinson gave up the movement on Montreal. Instead, he went into winter quarters. Soon the boats were frozen in place and the general ordered them burnt. [9]

Colonel William Russell was gathering troops at Fort Vallonia in June. When he had 573 men on hand, mostly rangers and volunteers, he led them out of the fort on July 1st in five columns through central Indiana. They saw no Indians, but were able to burn empty villages. In September, the Indians assaulted Fort Madison where the Des Moines River emptied into the Mississippi. They forced the soldiers there to retreat. [10]

The non-amicable Lieutenant Johnson had the misfortune of commanding the *Old Teazer* which was captured at sea by the British. Soon after being paroled, he entered on board the *Young Teazer* as a lieutenant. Later, at sea, the deranged Johnson was activated by the close pursuit of the American ship by the British and her imminent capture. Unable to bear a new captivity, he carried a burning brand of fire into the ship's magazine. The captain was consulting with his officers about what to do about the pursuing British ship when there was an explosion. Only seven seamen survived and one of those died soon after. The British picked them up to tell their tale. [11]

A stratagem was resolved upon to take the British tender sloop the *Eagle*. Commodore Lewis, in command of a flotilla of gun boat, borrowed a fishing smack and placed on deck a calf, a sheep, and a goose. He hid away over thirty men with their muskets, leaving three men on deck, dressed in fisherman's apparel. They sailed forth and were chased by the *Eagle*. Once caught, the *Yankee* was ordered to go to a certain point. Suddenly the watchword was given and the British were caught by surprise when the men rushed out on the fishing boats decks and began firing. The Englishmen fled below deck. When the firing stopped, none of them came on deck and struck the Union Jack. Americans boarded the *Eagle* and took her into New York Harbor. [12]

The Difficult War: The Era of the War of 1812

After seeing the envoy Crawford in a French port, Captain Allen sailed the *Argus* toward the Irish sea, which was, according to instructions was to be a hunting ground for the American vessel. Once in the English Channel the Americans captured a schooner and its cargo of mahogany and other timbers, coffee, cocoa, wax, chichona, and indigo. In a second capture, they took a large brig with its 3800 pounds sterling and a few pipes of wine. Allen allowed this ship to sail on because it contained two women passengers. He sent with her prisoners from the previous ship. Seven days out of L'Orient they sank the brig *Richard* from Gibraltar. In their turn they barely escaped from an armed brig, a cutter, and a schooner. There were other captures and near escapes.

The hunting ground was heavy and the Americans were at risk. A frigate loomed ahead. Allen sailed rapidly away. The chase was on. Allen maneuvered his way into a fog bank. When evening dropped, he found himself in the middle of a British squadron. Allen extinguished his lights. All was in danger. He filed past hostile ships, coming very close. The ship escaped to make many more captures. They sank the least valuable and sent their sailors home.

Shortly they took the *Betsy* with valuable goods. Levy was to be the prize master. After being underway. Squalls hit and in a high sea they were in the English Channel. It was raining when they saw a large ship coming right at them. Uriah Levy turned the wheel. It was the British *Leonida* out looking for the *Argus*. Without arms, Levy had to surrender her. Days later he was in Dartmoor where he learned that the crew of the *Argus* was imprisoned. The *Argus* had been engaged by *Pelican* and was soon overcome. Sixteen months in Dartmoor prison were passed until he was released in a prisoner exchange.[13]

There had been rumors and hit and run attacks upon the North Carolina coast, but only one major ascent and that was at Ocracoke. On the night of July 12, 1813, British admiral Sir George Cockburn sailed up to the inlet. The British did not have any information on the American defenses and the weather was not the best they could hope for in their effort to take the vessels that they had heard were there and to close down the use of the sound and its wide rivers for commerce. The plan was to attack American shipping and occupy the coast there with a regiment on board. They could hope for surprise, but this was not to be. They were seen and word reached Thomas S. Singleton in time for him to send the custom house money to New Bern and safety.

There was a long distance from the bar to the harbor and there was a heavy swell so it took several hours for the British to land. Two American ships fired upon the vessels but since they had only a few sailors aboard, the British boarded them. Soon the town of Portsmouth on Beacon Island surrendered. Cockburn ordered his officers to pay the Americans for supplies seized. The Americans were to claim that the soldiers tore up and destroyed furniture, beds, law books, and carried off clothing and wounded one man who tried to escape. They captured a privateer and released Singleton, held for two days, before returning to Norfolk. Meanwhile the militia had been ordered to assemble, but the British were gone. [14]

The Creeks of Alabama nursed grievances against the Americans for settling upon their lands. Americans thought they had been gentle and generous, but the younger Creeks or Red Sticks did not feel their way and were eager to join Tecumseh when he called for the compete destruction of the American people. Some Red Sticks visited him in 1812-1813 and took part in the River Raisin victory over the Americans and returned to Alabama with their hatred. On the march they murdered some whites and precipitated a civil war among their fellow Creeks. [15]

Picking up arms given by the Spanish and trading for European goods at Pensacola, they headed back to their home. On July 27, 1813, one hundred and eighty Mississippi militiamen attacked them in the battle of Burnt Corn and seized most of the supplies before the Indians counterattacked and forced them to retreat. In response they were to attack Fort Mims, whose officer Major Daniel Beasley was unprepared and did not listen to a warning from their slaves. In the fight most of the whites, men, women, and children were killed by the bloodthirsty Creeks, who had heavy looses on their side. Fear swept through the area followed by a reaction of vengeance on the part of the Americans under Andrew Jackson in November. [16]

George Washington Campbell advised Andrew Jackson that the government in Washington had decided to lead an expedition against the Creeks. Part of that force would be from western Tennessee under General Jackson's command. In his stead, Jackson wrote Governor Willie Blount that his two thousand volunteers would be ready to march at a moment's warning. General Jackson believed that the British were influencing the Creeks and lower Choctaws toward war. He did not believe he could divide the hostile tribes against segments of their tribe. They could however create divisions between tribes to secure their territory and their property. Judging from the events of the North, true economy was employ enough force to achieve success and crush all opposition at that point with one blow. [17]

Three thousand, five hundred, should be sufficient to crush the hostile Indians and their allies. It would not be necessary under present objectives to burn and destroy their towns, but it would be necessary to crush their hostilities by erecting forts in the very heart of the Creek nation and undertake a military campaign. Should the British land in the south, more force would be necessary to drive the British-Indian force into the ocean. Should the Spanish give the enemy force asylum in Pensacola, they should be able to take possession of that place. [18]

The hostile Creek burned several towns of Creeks in favor of peace and friendship. They destroyed all the elements of civilization, slaughtering animals introduced by the Americans such as horses, hogs, cattle, sheep, and goats, and prepared to root out the Americans. In lower Alabama a band of Americans surprised a Creek pack train with its arms and ammunition. They lost the advantage of surprise when they scrambled for the mules and their plunder. The Creeks counterattacked and beat the Americans loaded down with plunder. One thousand Creeks then had their own surprise when they rushed the open gate of Fort Mims. [19]

About August 23, 1813, General Ferdinand L. Claiborne in the Southern states learned that some 1200 Indians were soon to enter the territory to attack the upper forts on the Tombigbee. Their object was the fort commanded by Colonel Carson in the fork of that river and Alabama River and the fort commanded by Major Beastley on the Tensaw. The first was in danger of those natives from the Black Warrior and the Alabama Indians . Claiborne sent word to the two officers to warn them of the danger. Claiborne took 80 men to Bearsley's. Two detachments reached them there. Claiborne then marched to the cantonment at Mount Vernon, hearing on the way that the fort on the Tensaw had been attacked. [20]

The Indians had been unhappy with the results of the siege of Fort Meigs in the North and the Indians chieftain formed a plan which he felt would reduce the fort. Tecumseh learned through his scouts that Harrison had left the fort and was encamped on the road to Sandusky, Ohio. This plan would have his Indian force land downriver and march through the woods to stage a sham encounter which would draw Harrison and his army

The Difficult War: The Era of the War of 1812

into an ambush. He would rush the fort while its gates were open and take it. When it was put into motion it failed to entice the garrison out of the fort. Having failed to accomplish his plan, Tecumseh had urged Major General Protor to do something.

Proctor decided to reduce Fort Stephenson on the banks of the Sandusky River. Early on August 1, 1813, the British general landed his forces downriver from the fort and marched westward. He came under the guns of the fort whose shots passed overhead. Shortly he had his gunboats fire upon the Americans along with a five and a half inch howitzer all day and night. The British erected their battery to the northward and on the second of that month, their artillerymen had done the firing.

They made no breach in the wooden walls and Protor decided to attempt to take the fort by assault with three columns of about 120 men each. At five o'clock in the afternoon, at quick time, they reached within fifty yards until they were hit by a destructive fire, which did not stop them. When under the wooden walls they discovered that they had no good axes. Making with what they had, the British were mowed down. The only two officers of the second division were killed in acts of bravery. After almost two hours of fighting, the Americans defenses were unharmed and American men were undaunted.

The British followed orders and laid down on the edge of a ravine. At nine o'clock, Protor had them retire and soon they were on their way back to Amherstburg. With no experience in such warfare, the Indians had watched from safety and called the British the bravest of nations for their march to the walls of the fort. The young Major George Croghan, aged 21, had been in command of the Americans and was shortly promoted to lieutenant colonel for his success. He had one killed and seven slightly wounded compared with heavy British looses. [21]

---

[1]Hickey, *1812*, pp. 143-144; Drake, Frederick C., "Isle Aux Noix," Heidler & Heidler, *Encyclopedia*, p. 257.
[2]Barbuto, Richard V., "Stoney Creek, Battle of," Heidler & Heidler, *Encyclopedia*, p. 492.
[3]Snider, *Under the Red Jack*, pp. 169-182.
[4]McArver, "Allen, William Henry," Heidler & Heidler, *Encyclopedia*, pp. 7-8.
[5]Tucker, Spencer C., "Craney Island, Battle of," Heidler & Heidler, *Encyclopedia*, p. 130.
[6]Coit, *Calhoun*, pp. 84-86.
[7]Coggleshall, *History*, pp. 144-145.
[8]Brannan, *Official Letters*, pp. 173-174; Tucker, *Poltroons and Patriots*, p. 413.
[9]Tucker, *Poltroons and Patriots*, pp. 414-416.
[10]Bauer, *Taylor*, p. 20.
[11]Coggleshall, *History*, p. 125.
[12]*Ibid.*, pp. 122-123.
[13]Felton, *Levy*, pp. 46-52, 57.
[14]Lemmon, S.M., *Patriots*, 1973, pp. 128-136.
[15]Hickey *1812*, pp. 146-147.
[16]*Ibid.*, pp. 147-148; Faber, Peter R., "Burnt Corn, Battle of," Heidler & Heidler, *Encyclopedia*, p. 72.
[17]Jackson, *Papers*, II, 416-417.
[18]*Ibid.*, p. 417.
[19]Wilkins, pp. 62.
[20]Brannan, Official Letters, pp. 202-203.
[21]Richardson, *War of 1812, pp. 177-181, 184-185.*

CHAPTER XXIII

BATTLE OF LAKE ERIE

Proctor had led 5,000 British regulars, militiamen, and Indians into Ohio and had attacked Fort Stephenson with them. Croghan had not followed Harrison's orders to retreat and Harrison had rescinded his orders. Proctor's defeat at Fort Stephenson had sent him reeling. Abandoned by his Indian allies, Proctor returned to Canada with his white soldiers. Shortly, Perry won control of Lake Erie and the British had to abandon their northwestern offensive, despite the protests of Tecumseh. [1]

At this time, far to the southwest in Mexico, a young lieutenant named Antonio Lopez de Santa Anna was marching northward into the Spanish province of Texas with the army of General Joaquin de Arredondo. The young son of a prosperous merchant Antonio loved to gamble and wear fine uniforms. Now he was to learn the tactics and strategy of war. They were headed for San Antonio where a group of Mexican liberals and their friends, 450 American filibusters had overthrown the loyal government of Texas. Soon the Mexicans of the province joined in large enough numbers to form a large army for the area.

They marched from San Antonio to intercept Arredondo, but instead were caught in a crude ambush. The Spanish army killed a thousand rebels, murdered those who surrendered, and followed the rest, fleeing for American Louisiana. Arredondo took San Antonio and killed or imprisoned those suspected of rebellion or sympathy of the rebels. Noting the cruelty, Santa Anna was to repeat the policy or murdering prisoners when he next was to be involved in the province. Still later, he was to appear against Americans in the Mexican War. [2]

The American president in that Mexican War was Polk, who was born on November 2, 1795, about noon, near Pineville, North Carolina, to Samuel Polk and his wife Jane Knox Polk. The mother of James Knox Polk was a real religious woman, but Samuel would not agree to the confession of faith required of both parents for the baptism of James, and they took him home unbaptised. James was not to be baptized until he was on his death bed.

Little Jimmy moved with his parents to a farm north of the Duck River not far from Nashville. He was small for his age and very sickly. He could not excel in hunting and boyhood sports and had to stay behind at the campfire when on surveying trips with his father and others. Suffering from stomach pains, his main trouble was diagnosed as gallstones. In a day when gallstone operations were still in a pioneer stage, he had to travel to Danville, Kentucky, for the operation by Dr. Ephraim McDowell in the fall of 1812.

Mental processes and physical determination marked the young man, although he received little education and exercise. Employed for a few week's stint at storekeeping, Jim managed to get his father's approval for more education. In July of 1813, Jim Polk became a student at a small academy in a Presbyterian Zion Church located several miles from town. There he received a classical education. His conduct was good and he learned rapidly. After awhile he moved to a better and larger academy further from home. There he enjoyed a more varied curriculum and Jim worked hard and showed promise.

When he finished his course of studies there he graduated to college in Chapel Hill. Having only a short two years at his studies, he nevertheless passed the entrance tests with high grades. There he succeeded in gaining a thorough education from what was available. He perfected the skills in his later years at college that would make him a sure speaker in the backwoods and formidable in congressional halls. So exhausting was his senior year that Jim had to remain in North Carolina for several months to rest before embarking on the long and hard journey back to Tennessee.

Polk had decided on a law career and picked the prominent Nashville attorney Felix Grundy to study law under. Grundy had been a War Hawk in Congress six years earlier and was now a famous criminal attorney. From Grundy, Jim was to receive an election to the post of clerk of the senate in the Tennessee legislature, taking what another student under Grundy had turned down as not beneficial to his law career as he envisioned it. Polk was very interested in a political career where his companion was not.

Receiving six dollars a day, fifty percent more that the members, Polk was kept busy channeling bills and keeping an accurate record of senate proceedings. He did so well that he was reelected for another two years. Meanwhile, he passed the law examination and was admitted to the bar, establishing his offices in Columbia in his home county with a rented lot and $220 from his father for an one room office on it. His father also helped him buy law books. On his first day in court James got his father off easy on an affrey charge. He took partners for awhile before practicing on his own for the rest of the time. [3]

To the south in Indian territory while Polk was being educated, the Cherokee learned of the Fort Mims massacre at a time when William McIntosh was visiting. He was a friendly Creek, headman of Coweta, and sought aid against the Creek Red Stick insurgents. One of the wives of McIntosh was a Cherokee and so he had the privilege to sit as a chief in the council. He was popular with the Cherokee chiefs who feared for his life because the Creek insurgents had vowed to kill him on sight. The Pathkiller arranged for an escort to see McIntosh safely home. Major Ridge was the head of the escort and reached Coweta to find a Creek council deliberating about what they could do about the insurgents. They had asked the United States for help.

Ridge returned to maintain that the Cherokee could no longer remain neutral. When the Creeks warred with the whites they involved the whole of the Indians in a war. There would be no distinction between Indian tribes. Creek rejection of the chiefs in favor of the prophet, the work of civilization would fall and all of the southern tribes would be destroyed. So Major Ridge said. The chiefs listened to Major Ridge, but voted for nonintervention. Major Ridge asked for volunteers to act against the insurgents and drew so many of the younger men that the council reconsidered and voted for war against the Creek Red Sticks rebels.

The secretary of war had already acted. Colonel Meigs, the Cherokee agent, was ordered to confer with Tennessee's and Georgia's governors about Cherokee co-operation in the war of the frontier. First, however, the Cherokees needed arms. They preferred rifles but would be happy with muskets if the rifles could not be made available. Meigs proposed that armed Cherokees would join the Tennessee volunteers before taking any action. This was to be done to help Jackson. [4]

Meanwhile in the North, months earlier when Chauncey was looking for someone of experience to take charge of operations on Lake Erie, he heard that a twenty-seven year old commodore named Oliver H. Perry was seeking more exciting service than guarding Newport. Chauncey told Perry he was the very person to take vital service at the lake. This was to be a great decision. Perry was eager and the commander of the lakes put him in charge of Erie and devoted himself to Ontario. It was a wise choice for young Perry was a hard worker and most aggressive.

Oliver Hazard Perry wrote Commodore Chauncey from Eire on July 19th that a British fleet of six ships were then off the bar of Perry's harbor. Not knowing the object of the squadron, he thought they might be instituting a blockade, about to attack, or carrying provisions and reinforcements to Malden. Perry would repel them if they launched an assault, but he could not take the offensive himself because he did not have enough men. He awaited men for an attack and every day hoped they would come each day. On the 23rd seventy men arrived with a reply from Chauncey. Immediately, Perry wrote for more men.

During the spring and summer he completed the ships under construction and took them to Presque Isle. His biggest problem was finding seamen. Finally, General Harrison provided one hundred of his best Kentucky sharpshooters and all those in the army who had had experience seamen. His opponent on Lake Erie, Captain Robert H. Barclay, who had served with Lord Nelson at Trafalgar, also had a manpower problem and had to use soldiers. Barclay was also short of provisions since officials at Amherstburg had to feed an estimated 14,000 braves, squaws, and children.

The American fleet was blockading the ports on Lake Erie and the British commander Robert Heriot Barclay knew he would soon have to fight it. However, he could hope to get more seamen. He wrote Commodore Sir James Yeo that he needed more manpower. This was to be promptly coming so Barclay set out to try and defeat the American force on the lake. Barclay felt he must break the blockade in order to get lakeborne supplies of provisions and stores. At the time of the battle he lacked even a day's flour in store and his men were on half allowance of many things. Barclay set sail on September 9, 1813, to find the American fleet. His expectation was that he would run into it on the morning. The events bore this out.

Since he had to act quickly, Barclay sailed his ship forward to meet Perry's fleet. The Americans had the wind at their back so Perry could choose his distance when the two squadrons saw each other on September 10, 1813. The two fleets closed in so that all the ships were viewed in each squadron. Throughout the day the winds were light and the ships were in an irregular line. At ten o'clock they called all hands to quarter. British gunners fired a long range and Perry maneuvered his ship close to the enemy. The fire was intense and damage was extensive. Perry's crew sustained 80 percent casualties so many of the wounded had to fight.

Clearly defeated, he would not surrender. He took command of the *Niagara*, which Elliott had held back to fire at long range and sailed close in. The battle turned as the royal ships now became victims of the firefight. Soon four British ship surrendered. Two others tried to escape, but were captured. Barclay was badly wounded. Perry won the Battle of Lake Erie because he would not surrender and made use of his superior resources. He was courageous and cool under fire. Once again seamen had a victory. This one changed the balance of power in the northwest. With control of Lake Erie, Perry ferried General Harrison' army across the lake to cut-off the retreating British army. This was to lead to the success on the Thames River shortly. [5]

Other naval action, this time on the high seas, had recently taken place. In mid-morning on August 5, 1813, the look-out on board the *Decatur*, a privateer from Charleston, sighted two sail. At eleven o'clock, they made out the two sail to be a ship and a schooner. Captain Dominique Diron maneuvered his privateer around the game. Soon the schooner fired at the *Decatur* without making a hit. When ready, Diron ordered his men to their quarters and made way to board the schooner. His plan was to make a broadside, that is to discharge every gun available on that side, and before the smoke was cleared, join ships and send his men aboard to seize the British vessel. However, the opportunity was not ripe in the conflict which saw maneuver and firing of cannon on both sides.

Finally, after a few attempts at boarding, the time came. While some of the American crew fired their muskets, the rest rushed and boarded the *Dominica*. The men on both sides fought with swords, pistols, and small arms. There was slaughter of both fighting forces in hand to hand combat and the British captains and his leading officers were either killed or wounded. In the battle, there were, from both ships, sixty killed or wounded. Since there was great damage on both ships, they limped their way, prize and captor, to Charleston while the two blockaded English men-of-war brigs. They had lost, the British officers of the captured ship said, due to the superior skill of Diron, the maneuvering, and the American crews' success in musketry. [6]

William Burrows had been disappointed. Although he had served with distinction, he had not been promoted. Finally he resigned. The Navy would not accept his resignation and instead let him go on furlough. During this year, he went on a merchantman for India and China. After seeing the world, he started back home. The British captured the ship he was on, but he was paroled. Returning home he got command of the sloop *Enterprise*. Sailing from Portsmouth, New Hampshire, on September 5, he met the British warship, the *Boxer*. The two ships' gunners exchanged fire for an hour. When the Britisher lost its main-topmast. Its dying captain surrendered the ship to Burrows, who was also dying from the sea battle. News of this successful encounter thrilled the Americans and helped boast morale. [7]

On land, Jackson was on his sickbed, when he learned of the news of the massacre at Fort Mims, in early September. He was galvanized into action. He smashed his fist down and declaimed that "by the eternal these people must be saved!" He looked into the faces of the men around him, and said, "the health of your general is restored. He will command in person." Colonel Coffee immediately went out to organize Jackson's cavalry and soon Governor Blount authorized the army to go south and quell the Indians and their supporters the British. He had been long eager for battle in the war, and never had his chance until now. If he had the war would have been much different, because Jackson was a good general, better than any other in the war, which was soon to be proven.

Under Jackson's orders, Coffee went south to the Tennessee River to lead the way. Jackson soon was underway directing and inspiring, training and supplying his battle happy men. When he received a false report of the cavalry being in trouble, the general forced marched his main body thirty-two miles in nine hours as fast as they could walk without much in the way of rest. It was an arduous trip. He learned that Coffee was in no danger and he joined Coffee. They built Fort Deposit for a supply base and then plugged into Alabama to attack the Indians. [8]

Jackson interests had been turned from a feud with Benton brothers to the idea of defeating the Indian insurgents and conquering Spanish Florida. He marched his troops slower into the wilderness. With reports from his many spies and emissaries, Old Hickory made his plans for an offensive. The civilian contractors of supplies failed him, but he marched on for Mobile. His men built an advance base named Fort Strother.

Then under orders from Jackson, Coffee defeated and wiped out the Creeks at Tallushtchee on November 3rd. Davy Crockett took part in the battle. The Americans lost only five killed and forty one wounded. The Jackson advance and Coffee's victory won over some Indians and kept others neutral. Hostile Indians had laid siege to Talladega with its friendly natives. Jackson led his men to the rescue of the fort. Two Indians from the fort rushed out to meet them and warn the Americans, pointing out the hidden enemy. At first the hostile Indians had the advantage but they were surrounded and the Americans killed 300 Indians at the cost of fifteen whites. Because he had to protect Fort Strother, Jackson could not advance any further.

Despite the two victories, Jackson and his army were in a perilous situation. They had run out of food, because of incompetent contractors. Finally the general ordered a return home. However fifteen miles on the march they met supply trains. They ate their fill. Jackson forced the troops to return to the fort with a threat to fire upon anyone who dared defy him and set out for home. Shortly he learned that the other patriotic armies had failed. Old Hickory was near defeat though no fault of his own. With troops eager for a return to Tennessee, with unsure supplies, and with Indians freed from other war theaters in the South, only his determination kept him and his men in the wilderness. [9]

The balance of power had shifted on the Northwest frontier. Perry's victory on the lake had completely altered things. Despite the limitations placed upon him, Harrison had gone on the offensive. The Americans already had some ten thousand men at such forts as Sandusky and Meigs and the boats to transport these men across the lake. A British council of men who recognized the problem they faced were assembled and General Proctor proposed burning the forts of Detroit and Amherstburg and public buildings at the last. He also wished to withdraw his troops and the Indians to the vicinity of Niagara.

Tecumseh would not retire and rose to give an energetic address in which the Indian accused Proctor of cowardice. He feared that the British would desert his people. They made promises, he said, and now proposed to take actions to run away without informing the chiefs of their intentions. The British had said they would not leave British territory and now were withdrawing out of sight of the enemy. The Americans had not won the land battle and should be met on the ground. The Indians would defend their lands still. His tribesmen let out a loud yell at the end of the speech which echoed from the vaulted roof. Proctor suggested a compromise. They would retire halfway to the Moravian village and establish a defense. This was resolved and done. [10]

Harrison gathered up his large army at westernmost Lake Erie. He authorized Congressman Richard M. Johnson to enter the coming battle with his highly trained 1,200 volunteers who were mounted. The small militia force from Pennsylvania refused to cross into Canada, but the Kentucky militia, eager for battle, went across the border. Harrison followed Henry Proctor, who was slow moving. The British failed to destroy the bridges they marched over, discarded baggage and supplies, and lost two gunboats carrying spare ammunition for the British to the Americans. The Americans retook Detroit and took Malden. The Americans had an army of three thousand as they set out from Detroit on October 2, 1813. After a 25 mile march on that day, eight deserters from the British army were taken and told Harrison that Proctor was only one day's march ahead of them. [11]

A woman came up to the invaders and warned them of an Indian ambush ahead. Harrison ordered a cautious advance by columns. The British failed to catch the Americans at a disadvantage for the day, but instead fled. The Americans captured most of the British provisions and stores and extinguished a burning house which contained a thousand muskets. They were unable to save a burning schooner with its soon exploding military stores. Colonel Richard M. Johnson led the advance column on the next day with the goal of catching Proctor, but came to a halt near a shallow rapid. Scouts went ahead to search for Proctor and his men. They found them. The British and Indians force was awaiting their approach.

When British Brigadier General Henry Proctor retreated, Tecumseh believed him to be cowardly. Tecumseh wanted an advance and would not tolerate any defeat. He was not steadfast since he was thinking of abandoning Proctor. If Proctor would not fight, he would go his own way. The British general told him that he was trying to find stronger ground on which to fight and would make a stand at Chatham. However, an engineer scouted Chatham for Proctor and reported that there was no defensible ground there for the British. Proctor then retreated past Chatham for Moraviantown. Tecumseh went to Chatham and was furious when he discovered that Proctor would not make a stand there. Proctor must be a coward!

Many Indians abandoned Proctor, but Tecumseh ordered an Indian stand at the partially destroyed bridge at McGregor' Creek. Harrison saw them there and believing that this was a part of the main British army, he prepared his troops in battle formation. He fired his cannon and this caused Tecumseh and his Indians to withdraw. They had never gotten used to artillery. Proctor soon decided to make a stand at Moraviantown. Tecumseh joined him there.

Proctor had had to turn around and meet his foe at the Battle of the Thames, fifty miles east of Detroit. Arranging his 800 regulars and 500 Indians in two thin lines from the river to the swamp, the British general regarded the superior numbers of the Americans. He had chosen a clearing in the woods. In the battle of October 5, 1813, the Americans had the advantage. Not only did they have an edge in the fighting, but they were in a good position. However, a swamp to the north and the river to the south prevented a flank attack. Harrison directed a frontal charge. Johnson chose to meet the Indians along the edge of the large swamp to the north.

Somewhat after 2:30 o'clock in the afternoon, the trumpet sounded and the Americans attacked. They galloped forward with the cry of "Remember the Raisin." Under fire Johnson's right wing went through the British lines and began a crossfire against the British. Proctor tried to rally his men and took forty dragoons and fled. Within ten minutes the right wing of the American force had won. The left had trouble with Indian sharpshooters, who killed fifteen of the American soldiers. The Indians had continued to fight on the opposite side. They attacked and were driven back. Tecumseh was killed after more than one hour of hard fighting. Johnson claimed the honor of killing him. As soon as the Indians no longer heard his voice, the braves retreated. Johnson was severely wounded.

Meanwhile, Harrison sent Major Eleazer D. Wood to chase Proctor down, but Proctor escaped through a swamp and made it to safety. The British were allowed to bury their dead. This success was widely greeted as a great American victory and Proctor was court-martialed for his panic in retreat. British and Indian control of the Northwest was

The Difficult War: The Era of the War of 1812

decisively broken. Casualties were relatively low in both armies, because of the shortness of the battle in time. American success in the north ended the Indian threat there, although the British traders continued their profitable fur trade and broke an American attempt to establish a fort at Prairie du Chien. Black Hawk led the Sacs against Zachary Taylor's effort to reopen the upper Mississippi [12]

The Americans arranged a multipronged campaign against the Creeks in northern Alabama. Major General Thomas Pinckney, a Revolutionary War veteran, had overall command of the effort and led troops from the Carolinas. Brigadier General John Floyd would drive westward with his Georgia militia and join the friendly Creeks under McIntosh, a major. Brigadier General F. L. Claiborne led volunteers from Louisiana and Mississippi. The main thrust came from General Andrew Jackson and his militia. Cherokee warriors were joined to various units in the Tennessee brigade and division. They were divided into small bands under various chiefs. Meigs issued supplies and clothing. To distinguish them from the Creeks, the Cherokees wore a deer's tail in back.

Creek warriors endangered the village of The Pathfinder and his principal chief asked Jackson for help. The future president ordered Brigadier General James White from eastern Tennessee to hurry to protect the town from a Creek assault. Major Ridge and his some two hundred Cherokees reached there first. Colonel Return J. Meigs was soon there and spoke of their respectable numbers and the care they would see. The quartermaster would see to their needs for provisions and ammunition. The surgeons would provide necessary medical aid. They would be treated equally and must obey every order and regulation. American soldiers did not war on the aged and helpless and upon women and children, and he was glad to see the Cherokees agree. [13]

Under Jackson's order, John Coffee, commander of cavalry, crossed the Tennessee River at the upper end of the shoals, but could not find a scout, so he took with him the half-breed sons of John Melton, an Irishman and free agent on the river. He was married to a Cherokee squaw. They came across a deserted Indian village which a guide said was the Black Warriors town. [14]

---

[1]Hickey, *1812*, p. 136.

[2]Lavender, David, *Climax at Buena Vista: The American Campaigns in Northeastern Mexico, 1846-47*, Philadelphia: J.B. Lippincott, 1966, pp. 12-13, 15.

[3]Sellers, Charles Grier, Jr., *James K. Polk: Jacksonian 1795-1843*, 1957, pp. 23-25, 35, 39-51, 55-62.

[4]Wilkins, pp. 63, 66.

[5]Hickey, *1812*, pp. 131-133, 135; Paullin, Charles Oscar, *The Battle of Lake Erie: A Collection of Documents, chiefly by Commodore Perry: including the Court-Martial of Commodore Barclay and the Court and Inquiry on Captain Elliott*, Cleveland: Rowfant Club, *1918, pp. 29, 53-54, 57, 67-68, 146-147, 153-159, 188-189;* America: Great Crises..., 1925, pp. 169-171.

[6]Coggeshall, *History*, pp. 172-177.

[7]Paquette, William A., "Burrows, William," Heidler & Heidler, *Encyclopedia*, p. 72.

[8]Albright, Harry, *New Orleans: Battle of the Bayous*, New York: Hippocrene Books, 1990, pp. 19-21; James, Marquis, *Jackson*, 1938, pp. 154ff.

[9]James, *Jackson*, pp. 154, 157-166.

[10]Cleaves, *Old Tippecanoe*, pp. 188; Hickey, *1812, p. 137; Richardson,* War of 1812, *pp. 204-207.*

[11]Hickey, *1812*, p. 137; Cleaves, *Old Tippecanoe*, pp. 188-197.

[12]Cleaves, *Old Tippecanoe*, pp. 197-205; Richardson, *War of 1812*, pp. 209-218, 234; Hickey, *1812*, pp. 137, 139, *America*, V, 181-186; Antal, Sandor, "Thames, Battle of the," Heidler & Heidler, *Encyclopedia*, pp. 509-510; Heidler, Jeanne & Heidler, David S., "Chatham, Upper Canada," Heidler & Heidler, *Encyclopedia*, pp. 89-90.

[13]Wilkins, pp. 66-68.

[14]Jackson, *Papers*, II, 438-439.

CHAPTER XXIV

END OF THE YEAR

According to Armstrong's plans, Wilkinson was to march 7,000 men down the St. Lawrence River from the west and Hampton was to advance from the south with 4,500 men. Major General Wade Hampton was in command of forces around Lake Champlain. Although Wilkinson and Hampton hated each other, Armstrong convinced Hampton to cooperate with Wilkinson. It was for the good of the country. Waiting for orders from the War Department for weeks, Hampton marched his troops northward but when they reached the border almost all of his 1,400 New Yorkers refused to march into Canada. He left them behind and pressed forward with 3,000 poorly trained and largely inexperienced regulars. On October 26, 1813, his army saw ahead a barrier. About 1,700 Canadian fencibles and militia and a few Indians manned the log barriers. They were commanded by Lieutenant Colonel Charles de Salaberry.

Canadian defenses were too strong for a frontal assault. Undismayed, Hampton ordered a strong force to move to the opposite side of the river. Once there they could march through the forest until they gained the Canadian's rear. When Hampton heard the sound of the flank attack, he began his frontal attacks. Because of the swamp on both sides of the road, he could not outflank them without crossing the Chateauguay River. This he tried. Bad luck plagued Hampton when his flanking men got lost in the marshy woods. Although small, a force of Canadians found them and fought them to a standstill. When Hampton learned this he launched a frontal assault on the barrier anyway. His men heard a bugle and cries, they thought they were outnumbered. They failed and Hampton withdrew his forces. He did not prevail in this Battle of Chateauguay and lost about fifty men. The barrier was there and could not be carried. A saddened Hampton withdrew. He did not try again. One barrier had stopped his army stone dead. [1]

It had been thought that they could sever the line of communications with Kingston. Armstrong, Wilkinson, and Chauncey conferred on the matter and decided to take Montreal for itself and to cut off Kingston to the west. The force had been divided between Wilkinson and Hampton. On October 17, Wilkinson led his 8,000 poorly trained regulars and non-veteran regulars from Sackett's Harbor for the St. Lawrence. They rowed or sailed in hundreds of open boats. It was windy and sleeting. It was a miserable trip and dangerous. Many men perished in the hostile weather when boats were overturned. Because Chauncey was not able to seal off the British navy, the Americans were followed in well kept gunboats. The contrast was startling. The British had all the advantage.

Plagued by personal illness, bad weather, and harassment from the rear, Wilkinson took large amounts of laudanum which made him giddy. British Lieutenant Colonel Joseph Morrison followed on the banks. The Americans had the hard task of clearing the rapids. At Chrysler's Farm, a sick Wilkinson directed General John P. Boyd to attack on November 11th. British regulars held their line against each piecemeal assault and counterattacked successfully. Casualties were heavy, especially for the Americans. Floyd retreated, and withdrew into a winter camp where the men suffered from the cold and shortage of hospital supplies and other supplies. Later in March of 1814, Wilkinson lost a battle at La Colle Mill, which he could not destroy. Wilkinson withdrew and marched back to the United States, where he lost his command and ended his military career. [2]

Joseph Almeda was a most resourceful privateer captain in the War of 1812. This war gave him a taste for the privateer life. After the war, Almeda joined, like some other privateers, the Argentine Revolution to attack Spanish shipping on the seas. Almeda made four cruises in all. He took two cruises and more than a score of prizes in the West Indies in the *Caroline*. He sailed from Charleston and ran into an English convoy with a frigate and seven merchantmen. After decoying the warship, he captured five of the merchant ships and returned to port. It took him eight days to gain a prize worth $500,000.

On another cruise he hailed a flagless ship, whose captains thought her an English cruiser. Remarking on the lack of fear Americans felt for an English warship, the merchant captain said that he had no doubt should he meet an American privateer he would be hanged, when exhibiting his British license. Almeda made him a prisoner and seized his sloop. The captain was not hung for his treasonable action. On that cruise Almeda took sixteen prizes without a fight, but they were small and brought in a minimum of prize money. [3]

American Richard Moon, his officers, and his crew were sailing off Madeira in the privateer schooner *Globe* when they noted a sail. They got closer and discovered her to be a large brig. After a few shots, Moon decided to haul off before he was sunk. Next they saw two brigs and waited the night for them. They gave chase early on November 2, 1813, when the two vessels sailed away. When it became dark and windy, they lost sight of them. Continuing in the same direction, they saw them the next day and closed in on the 3rd. They set out to board the nearest enemy vessels, but only the two lieutenants and three sailors got aboard and were overpowered when the schooner fell off. The second brig came up and raked the decks of Moon's ship which cut up sails and rigging. They were hardly enjoying managing their heavy ships under such conditions, but they continued the fight. The largest brig struck colors. Returning the fire of the second ship until they were in danger of sinking, they were surprised when the surrendering ship hoisted her colors once again and fired a broadside. Both brigs together were too much for them and Moon directed his men to haul off to repair damages at the closest island. [4]

In a land battle in the South on November 5, 1813, General White forded the Coosa River flowing southwestward, and sought action on the field of battle. Major General John Cocke countermanded Jackson's orders to hold Fort Strother while he moved against the Creek. The fort was downriver and the junction of Canoe Creek. Like Jackson he ran into an ineffective and corrupt supply system from which he derived no rations. Jackson repeatedly urged Cocke to join him at Fort Strother. Instead the individualistic general built Fort Armstong and decided to seize a chance at the glory he so dearly wanted and to use this as a base for political advancement. Cocke decided to march against the Hillabee towns in revenge for their having warriors fighting the whites.

The Difficult War: The Era of the War of 1812

Cocke's action to move against the Indians left Jackson's rear unprotected, but Andrew Jackson was near his destination and he surrounded the Creek on November ninth and after fifteen minutes of battle routed the Creek warriors at Talledega directly south of Fort Strother, east of the river.

Those Creeks who were left, fled into the mountains. Those who lived on the Tallapoosa sued for peace. The Hillabees sent Robert Grierson, a prisoner of theirs to Jackson to ask for terms. The Hillabees had suffered so much from war that they were ready to abandon it, Gierson said. Jackson said he wanted them to deliver the instigators of war to him and all property, including slaves, that they had seized from the whites. Jackson accepted their surrender.

The glory seeking Cocke was not aware of their surrender and he ordered General James White to move against them with Cherokee warriors and Tennessee mounted men. They destroyed everything along their way. Burning two deserted villages, they reached their objective on the eighteenth. The Cherokee killed sixty-one Creek warriors and took 250 prisoners of the Creek tribes. There was little resistance. Although the Cherokee force had no losses, the battle of the Hillabee Towns was costly. It prolonged the war because the Creek assumed that Jackson had sent an army against them after peace talks had been begun and accepted. Cocke's vainglory cost many unneeded lives as the Creek then fought to exhaustion. He should have followed orders and guarded Fort Strother. The Creek now believed that the American would give no quarter.

Cocke marched his men back northward to the Coosa River upriver from Turkey Town . He had it garrisoned mostly by the Cherokees of his command, which proved a wise move. General Cocke next joined Jackson, but since the terms of his troops were almost over, Jackson who had just put down a mutiny of his own soldiers, sent Cocke back to civilization to raise fifteen hundred fresh troops. However Jackson had Cocke arrested, because he had spoken to the men and encouraged a mutiny. Cocke was tried but found innocent because of his support among the people he was tried by. Major Ridge also moved into his village to raise new warriors for the American cause. [5]

Jackson decided to move south to protect the pro-American Creek town of Talladega. In his advance Brigadier General John Coffee destroyed Tallushatchee on the third of November. He had encircled the Indians and defeated them from all sides. The Indians had fought with a ferocity which however was not enough. At Fort Strother, Jackson received the message that hostile Indians were holding Talladega under siege. He immediately set out with 2,000 men and was promptly at the town. Ever aggressive and bold, he led an attack on the hostile Red Sticks. Ordering an encirclement, he was forced into a premature battle and the Creek found holes in his lines. The fight ended in white victory and losses were heavy on the Red Sticks side and moderate on the white side. Jackson could not pursue because of his precarious situation and lack of supplies. He soon had to return to his fort for this same reason. [6]

There was no food in Fort Strother when they arrived. The men were respectful, idolizing Jackson, but they were hungry and wanted to march back to central Tennessee where they could get full meals. Then they would return to Indian fighting. It looked as if Jackson would have a mutiny on his hands. When the soldiers tried to desert, Jackson ordered a November 13th general order that if supplies did not reach them in two days they would march back home. The next two days became four, and Jackson ordered a march home. He could do no more. The men had to eat. They marched cheerfully for twelve miles. Then there came down the path their supply train. The famished men feasted and then formed to march back to the fort, happier than ever, with the rest of their flour and beef cattle. They were eager for a battle.

Then suddenly one unit started in the wrong direction, back toward home. Others followed and Jackson hurriedly rode up and entered the files with a musket cradled by his sling. Threatening to shoot the first man who did not obey his orders, he gave the order to march back to the fort. They marched back, but shortly enlistments began to expire and at one time there were only 130 men at the fort. Governor Blount had had it. He ordered Jackson to leave the fort for Nashville. Jackson would not obey.

He wrote to Blount for him to rise up from his lethargy with energetic exercise of his functions. If the campaign did not rapidly progress he could be ruined. He wanted Blount to call out the full quota and execute the orders of the secretary of war. He should arrest the officer, who omitted his duty. He should not be concerned about the present popularity. He must save Mobile and the frontier from being drenched in blood. Jackson himself would perish before he entered into a retrograde movement. No sooner was the letter sent when 800 new recruits marched into the fort. He then marched the whole army to Creek Territory. [7]

Meanwhile, General John Floyd left Georgia westward with 950 Georgian militiamen and 400 friendly Creek warriors. Since he had limited supplies he could not make a long campaign of it so he planned to make a hit-and-run assault on the village of Austosee. His force arrived there on the morning of November 29, 1813. Dividing his small army into three columns, he placed his artillery in front of one, his right. He extended his flanks to cover another small town. The fight began. Friendly Indians were to cut off any escape. Floyd's artillery and muskets proved too much for the Indians of Autosse. The battle did not last long. Floyd's men killed 200 Indians, burnt 400 dwellings, with eleven lives lost and 54 wounded. He then returned to his base. [8]

Meanwhile, in the North, when General George McClure of New York left Fort George, he also left a burnt Newark. Wilkinson and McClure did nothing to bring honors upon their names later in the winter. Shortly after asking for a courts-martial to clear his name of any failure over the Montreal campaign, Wilkinson undertook another half-hearted effort upon the road to Montreal. Intent upon showing his capacity to boldness and initiative, Wilkinson only showed that the was incapable of successful conclusions. He marched forth upon a stone mill with plenty of walls and loopholes. His action was unsuccessful, but he acted as if he was vindicated and retreated after two hours.

Before starting forth from the fort, McClure had his men give twelve hours notice to the people of the town to leave their homes. Then he burnt Newark to deny shelter to British troops although he knew it would invite retaliation from the British. Learning that the citizens of Newark had been evicted in zero degree weather, British commander General Sir Gordon Drummond was so furious that he launched several attacks against the Americans.

Five hundred and fifty British soldier surprised the American sentries at Fort Niagara and secured the password to enter the fort which was across the river from Fort George. They bayoneted or shot eighty American soldiers and captured 350 men with the loss of fewer than a dozen casualties. The war material and supplies they seized there were to benefit the British and hurt the American to a large degree from that tenth of December. On the eighteenth, General Phincas Riall destroyed three American towns. His Indians massacred the people. Before the end of 1813, the British had routed the Americans near Black Rock. People fled and the Niagara Valley front collapsed in flames. The United

The Difficult War: The Era of the War of 1812 199

States played a big price for McClure's action, but the British were just as guilty as he had been. [9]

At the varying times that Indians were mutilating, American wagons were providing beef to British troops in Canada and American ships were selling wheat to the British in Spain, all for a profit. Short of nitrate, the Americans mined it in Mammoth Cave in Kentucky. Meanwhile, the national debt was soaring by one million dollars a week to cover the cost of the war. In all this, it cost $125 million to pursue the war and most of this came from loans. [10]

In the South, Ferdinand L. Claiborne began a campaigning against Red Stick William Weatherford's town, the Holy Ground. The general marched his men up the Alabama River to establish Fort Claiborne and other forts in an effort to protect his rear. On the morning of December 23, 1813, he neared the Holy Ground, which had been evacuated by women and children ahead of him.

The remaining warriors listened to prophet Josiah Francis, his Indian name being Hillis Hadjo. He told them that he had provided an invisible ring around the town which would kill any white man who crossed it. However, when Claiborne attacked the town, they saw that their prophet was wrong and fled. William Weatherford rallied the warriors left and fought, but was defeated. He escaped only by riding his horse across the Alabama River. Claiborne's men took what food they could carry from the town and then burnt it down. Claiborne then marched his army upriver, and fought another band of Indians. When he trounced them, he was able to burn another town. He then moved back to his fort and the men ended their enlistments as they expired. This campaign had its effect. [11]

Because Lord Castlereagh, British Foreign Minister, did not wish to be unreasonable about peace talks and ending the war, he suggested to Madison that Britain and America hold direct talks. He did not wish to deal with a third party, especially not Russia, where John Quincy Adams was at to negotiate. This was good news to the peace-loving Madison and so he agreed. He then named five commissioners headed by Adams and including Henry Clay and Gallatin. The others were James A. Bayard and Jonathan Russell.

Adams made his way to neutral ground to hold the negotiations. Castlereagh had wished them to come to London. Clay agreed with Adams about meeting at Ghent, Belgium, a rare time when the two men agreed in the war. The British team was of a lower rank than the Americans and also not as well endowed with ability. Only Henry Goulburn held a high position. Castelreagh sent his best talent to the Congress of Vienna. They were not interested in compromise and held the Americans aloft, believing that these inferiors, the American people, should be grateful that the British would talk to them at all. They did not hide this feeling. The talks were to begin in August of 1814. [12]

At this time little Jefferson Davis was a brave little lad in Mississippi. His father and oldest brother had taught him that cowardice was the worst of all the bad qualities. When he was just five years old, he and his sister Mary, two years older, had to walk a mile through woods to the log cabin schoolhouse. Since he was male, he was her protector and carried the lunch basket. The main danger they faced was the chairmender who carried the chairs upside down on his head. Sober he was fine but when drunk could be violent. The children saw what appeared to be the chairs on the man's head and said, "We will not run." Although frightened they did not budge. Then the upturned chairs turned out to be the antlers of a buck coming into the path. The male deer paused, looked, and left. Jeff and Mary continued their way down the path to the school. Davis had faced his first challenge well. He proved as intelligent as he was brave and Mr. Davis had great hopes for him. [13]

John Charles Fremont was only a few months old, when his parents took him away from Savannah, Georgia, for Nashville, Tennessee. They found there that the talk of the town was about Thomas Hart Benton and Andrew Jackson and a duel which the Benton brother had been engaged in with Jackson as his opponent's violation of their friendship. Benton held his friends in tight conduct once they had become his friends. He had many friends and was known for his loyalty to them. Until this incident he had been loyal to Jackson, but now a duel was threatening between the two men. Benton said that Jackson had behaved in a savage, uncivilized manner. This was reported to Andrew and he took offense so much so that in the Jackson manner he said he would horsewhip him the next time he caught sight of Thomas Benton. The people of the town expected a showdown soon.

The Fremonts arrived at the City Hotel, where Benton was and Jackson took up residence at Nashville Inn across the pubic square. Jackson and a few of his companions strode over to the Hotel and there encountered the Bentons. They exchanged words, and tempers led to gunplay. A bullet from Jesse Benton's gun shattered the left shoulder of Andrew and the future president fell to the lobby's floor. There were more shots and bullets had penetrated the room of the Fremonts, narrowly missing the infant. The mother Anne fainted and when the father Charles returned to the hotel he told the participants off and called their action barbaric. They offered their apologies. Meanwhile, Jackson's wound was attended to. He might have died, but Jackson was too tough to kill in the old phrase.

This 1813 episode illustrated the temperament of the time in Nashville and many other places in the western and southern states. Duels were common enough and sometimes men were killed. Had the infant been killed, the history of the nation would have been changed. Baby Fremont would never have been the worker of exploration and Benton and Jackson would never have lived down the death. They would have been blamed for it and even prosecuted. Jackson probably would never had been president. Had he been killed in the duel, he most certainly would not have been elected. [14]

Samuel Hopkins, an American general and representative, was born in the eighteenth century in Albermarle County, Virginia. With the outbreak of the Revolutionary War, Hopkins joined the patriot army and fought under Washington at the battles of Princeton, Trenton, Monmouth, Brandywine, and Germantown. He advanced in rank to command a battalion of light infantry. Casualties were heavy in Hopkins' battalion and he received a severe wound himself. Promoted to colonel, he was in command of the Tenth Virginia Regiment when captured at the surrender of Charleston on May 20, 1780. He protested the moldy biscuit he was feed as a daily ration; Samuel said that he had never failed to treat his prisoners right and expected the same of the British. Threatened with a mutiny from prisoners, the captain of the prison ship treated the captured colonel and his companions with kindness and respect.

In 1797, he migrated to Kentucky and settled on Greene River. He served in the state legislature and when war broke out in 1812, he led a corps of volunteers against a Kickapoo village, but guides failed and they lost their way. This was too much for the soldiers and they returned to the capital of Indiana. He was more successful later when he destroyed several deserted Indian villages. Returning to Kentucky, Hopkins was elected to Congress and served there from 1813 to 1815. After this, he returned to his farm. [15]

The *Liverpool Packet* alias *Black Joke*, had a varied career after Barss ended up in prison as a captive. An American vessel now it was christened *Young Teaser's Ghost*. However, its luck was gone in the hands of an American captain and crew. It was registered once again by a new captain of the *Portsmouth Packet*, who sailed it in the opening days of October of 1813 for the Bay of Fundy with its strong tides. On the fifth, the British brig-of-war *Fantome* saw it and gave chase for all of thirteen hours. Once again it was British and once again Enos Collins bid successfully for the fleet ship and renamed her the *Liverpool Packet*. With prize money from the small schooner *Star*, Caleb Seely invested in it and was made partner and commander. Sir John Coape Sherbrook issued a warrant on November 25th of 1813. Sheely sailed well and his men had a Christmas feast, having captured three prize sloops before Christmas. [16]

Sailing out of Providence, Rhode Island, with an assorted cargo for Charleston, the schooner *David Porter* made her way down river to Newport. Their aim was to blockade Rodgers. Most vessels trying to escape needed to await moonless nights and bad weather for opportunities to get to the sea. Captain George Coggeshall sailed the American ship through a raging snowstorm and made his way south. Several British vessels chased his ship, but being one of the fleetest ships afloat, he made his escape each time.

Finally off Cape Roman on November 26, 1813, a British warship made chase. Coggleshall knew that warships laying wait at Charleston, so he did not let the pursuing ship box him in. They wanted to drive him leeward, but Coggleshall pushed boldly for the channel. It took four hours to reach Charleston. He gained little for the British had fleet ships too. At the bar, the *Decatur* and *Adeline* sailed forth and headed for the brig. Prudence dictated a retreat, and the British ship took this course. The *David Porter* took the opportunity to cross the bar and deliver or sell their goods to merchants at Charleston.

Once there, he took a cargo for a French port, some 331 bales of cotton. Rainy weather blew fresh from the south, but on December 20th he left on the wing of the right breeze as fine weather, successfully bound to Bordeux. One week later, he fell in with a British brig. However, because of a gale, he had to order the brig to follow him to better weather under a threat. The Britisher fled during a very dark and windy night. There was no British ship in sight on the passage, these being off the coast of North America and Europe. Near France, the Americans were hit by a severe gale and then a hurricane. The sea struck the ship mercilessly, breaking and tearing. It was thrown close to its beam-ends. Sea waves tossed her forward and Coggleshall feared the worst. He took remedial measures of anchoring the vessel head to wind. It stopped its tempest tossed nature and landed safely into La Teste, thirty miles away for Bordeaux.[17]

---

[1]Barbuto, Richard V., "Chateaguay, Battle of," Heidler & Heidler, *Encyclopedia*, p. 89; Hickey, *1812*, pp. 144-145.

[2]Hickey, *1812*, pp. 145-146; Barbuto, Richard V., "Chrysler's Farm, Battle of," Heidler & Heidler,, *Encyclopedia*, p. 104.

[3]Cranwell & Crane, *Men of Marque*, pp. 209-225.

[4]Coggeshall, *History*, pp. 160-162.

[5]Wilkins, pp. 69-72; Heidler, Jeanne T. and Heidler, David S., "Cocke, John," Heidler & Heidler, *Encyclopedia*, p. 117-118; Saunders, Robert, Jr., "Hillabee Massacre, Creek Territory," Heidler & Heidler, *Encyclopedia*, pp. 239-240.

[6]Heidler, Jeanne T. and Heidler, David S., "Talladega, Battle of," Heidler & Heidler, *Encyclopedia*, pp. 499-500; Koerper, Philip E., "Tallushatchee, Battle of," *Ibid.*, pp. 500-501.

[7]Albright, *New Orleans*, pp. 23-24.

[8]Keefe, John M., "Autosse, Battle of," Heidler & Heidler, *Encyclopedia*, p. 27.

[9]Hickey, *1812*, pp. 141-143; Tucker, *Poltroons and Patriots*, pp. 417-420.

[10]*Tucker,* Poltoons and *Patriots*, pp. 422-427.

[11]Heidler, Jeanne T. and Heidler, David S., "Claiborne, Ferdinand L.," Heidler & Heidler, *Encyclopedia*, p. 107.

[12]Heidler, Jeanne T. and Heidler, David S., "Adams, John Quincy," Heidler & Heidler, *Encyclopedia*, pp. 2-3.

[13]Storde, *Davis*, pp. 11-12.

[14]Egan, Ferol, *Fremont: Explorer for a Restless Nation*, Garden City NY: Doubleday, 1977, pp. 5-6.

[15]Collins, Lewis, *History of Kentucky*, Maysville, Ky: Lewis Collins, 1847, Reprint Lexington, Kentucky: Henry Clay Press, 1968, pp. 351-152.

[16]Snider, *Under the Red Jack*, pp. 46-49.

[17]Coggesshall, *History*, pp. 177-183.

CHAPTER XXV

THE YEAR IS 1814

On January 4, 1814, one hundred and fifty citizens of New York petitioned Congress to establish a national bank with a capital of thirty million dollars. Unfortunately John W. Eppes and his committee were strict constructionists and thought treasury notes would be sufficient. Eppes stopped the request in his committee.

Calhoun suggested establishment of the bank in the District of Columbia. He made some progress but his sponsorship was too weak. Then as the situation continued to deteriorate, opposition faded away. Congress met in extra session in September and began considering a bank building which was believed different. The speaker Langdon Cheves appointed all pro-bank men to Epps' Committee of Ways and Means while allowing Epps to remain chairman.

On October of 1814, President Madison had named the capable lawyer Alexander J. Dallas as secretary of the treasury. Madison had long wanted Dallas in that position, but the pro-bank advocates were known and there would be too much stir. Now the need of a national bank was too well known for its opposition to prevent its establishment and soon afterwards a satisfactory bank was chartered. [1]

Meanwhile in the South, eight hundred Tennessee recruits arrived at Fort Strother, replacing the militia, who had finished their three month enlistment. Andrew Jackson led them southward to meet the Red Sticks in battle. Because of the lack of discipline, he knew that he must act quickly while his men were eager for the fight. They were three miles away from Horseshoe Bend when they encamped on the night of January 21, 1814. Ready for an attack all night, the Americans were not surprised when the Creeks attacked before dawn. Jackson's men fired at the flashes of the Indian guns. As soon as they could see well with the light of the new day in the east, Jackson called in his reserve of one company and sent his total force forward. The Indians fell back. Brigadier General Coffee reconnoitered the Creek position at Horseshoe Bend. He reported back to Jackson that it was too strong.

The Indians rushed forward in their main attack. Pickets fired and withdrew to the lines, ready to fight. Coffee led fifty-four men to outflank the Indians. Jackson led a charge, beating the hostile Creek to the punch. The Creek warriors withdrew back into the woods and the commander hurried his men to help the hard-pressed Coffee detachment. There was no clear victory for either side, but Jackson's army was in the territory of a numerous enemy and he withdrew. That night his men slept on their rifles, ready for a surprise attack. The whites marched for the fort. On the twenty-fourth, they were crossing another creek when the Indians moved in. Jackson was counting on his rear guard to blunt any such maneuver, but they fled, pushing the center column back. The general swore at them and they decided they would rather face the warriors than Jackson. They rallied and followed Jackson's example. His men fought bravely then and repulsed the savages. Eager for any success the Administration press played up the battles of Emuckpaw and Enotachopco. There was to be more. [2]

With a six weeks rest, General Floyd set out on a new campaign against hostile Indians, It was made up of volunteers from Georgia and the Carolinas, some 1,300 in number including some 400 Allied Creeks. Marching along the Old Federal Road, Floyd established a supply camp. Hearing about an Indian gathering at nearby Hoithlewallee, he advanced towards the village. When he reached Clabee Swamp on January 26th, he had his men camp on high ground in a pine forest. Indians outnumbering Floyd's force, were nearby. Not all of them had hunting muskets; carrying only bows and arrows or war clubs.

Red Eagle or William Weatherford addressed the Indian council. As their great war chief, he proposed that they wait until the American army crossed the Calabee River and then attack. They did not like his idea and stealthily approached the camp. It was an hour and a half before sunrise, when they shot the sentries and poured into the camp. Completely surprised, Floyd rallied his men and fought.

There was hand-to-hand fighting. Floyd used his cannon, but it was hard going since there was a melee of men on both sides. The hostile Creeks tried to take the artillery, killing many white soldiers. Most of the Allied Creeks deserted, but Captain Timpoochee Barnard led his Uchee warriors bravely for the militia army. Then the sun rose and the Americans charged. Militia bayonets routed the Indians and militiamen pursued the fleeing enemy. Casualties were moderate. Floyd withdrew his army back to Fort Mitchel and the enemy Creeks returned to possess the battlefield. The whites had the victory, but it was incomplete. [3]

Among the men who reinforced Jackson in February of 1814, was twenty year old third lieutenant Sam Houston. On March 24, 1813, army recruiters were in Maryland and intrigued Houston who wanted to fight the British. Short of age, he had to get the consent of his mother which he did. She told him never to disgrace the musket she gave him. She would rather all her sons fill in honorable grave than for one to turn back to save his life. Her cottage door was open to brave men and always shut to cowards. His brothers were angry that young Sam did not get a commission, but the ranks were an honorable position. The six-foot two inch man showed leadership ability and became sergeant, ensign, and third lieutenant over the months, all of which were earned. He was to be wounded in the coming battle and fight on. [4]

Marching to the vicinity of his recent battles, Jackson and his two thousand man army had the advantage of numbers for a change. Eight hundred Creek braves waited for his approach at Horseshoe Bend for a do or die encounter. A determined Jackson surrounded the Indians and had Coffee's scout swim into the river and carried off the canoes. He would allow no escape for his foe. The American artillery fired, but Indian sharpshooters kept the crews down. After allowing the Creek women and children to leave, the general sent his infantry in. They reached the log breastworks. Major Lemuel P. Montgomery climbed the works and was shot dead. Ensign Sam Houston followed. After a hard fight on the logs, the Americans carried the fortifications and the Indians retreated fighting in groups to the last man, believing that the Great Spirit would give them victory. Jackson tried to get the Creek to surrender but they fired upon the messenger with the flag of parley. It was a bloody battle. The Americans set fire to an

Indian stronghold with flaming arrows since the native fighters had to keep them at arms length. No Creek warrior who had been present survived. Jackson lost 49 killed and 157 wounded. [5]

Chief Junalusha of the Cherokee was there with his fellow Indians at Horseshoe Bend; a Creek Indian attacked Jackson. The Cherokee plunged his steel tomahawk into the Creek' skull, killing him. He and his Cherokee five hundred brave warriors had fought for Jackson that day. When the Cherokee were removed from their ancestral home about two decades later, he said that had he known that Jackson would later drove them from their homes, he would have killed him that very day on the Horseshoe battlefield. [6]

The situation became grim for the Americans. Allied victories in Europe over Napoleon would soon free British forces to concentrate upon the war against the United States. Still Federalists and some Republicans could rejoice over Napoleon's defeat. To Federalists, he had been the anti-Christ and Jefferson rightly blamed him for the deaths of over ten million people. Also Federalists believed Great Britain would come to peace terms. Republicans doubted this. It would be a fight for national existence now. Freed from their duty in Europe, British veterans were transported to Canada. Despite the dangers, there were fewer incompetent officers in the American army now, making defense easier. [7]

With the defeat of Napoleon, British leaders were able to look to America. With an increased food supply on the continent the British did not need smuggled American food products. The aggressive Admiral Cochrane was chosen to take charge of naval reinforcements sent to America. On his station, he included New England in the blockade. Britain needed food supplies no more so Cochrane could do this. The debate on what targets to hit held Cochrane back at first. Should Rhode Island or Portsmouth be attacked? The question held the interest of Cochrane for awhile.

Should Cochrane take Portsmouth, he could destroy the large ship on construction there and march overland to Prevost at Lake Champlain, slicing off a part of the new country. Should Cochrane take Rhode Island he could use it as a base to strike other New England states. Instead Cochrane was ordered to move against Baltimore or Washington, allowing Prevost to advance into New York, and a third front issued against eastern Maine and remove the obstacle to land communications between Quebec and Halifax. In wintertime when the St. Lawrence River was frozen over, land contact was essential. There were economic reasons too. Smuggling kept the maritime provinces poor, since smugglers did not pay custom duties. [8]

Major General James Wilkinson left his winter quarters for La Colle Mill, where he heard that a large number of British troopers were fortifying. He was superior numerically and expected a great success to open up his new Canadian campaign. He crossed into Canada, scattered the pickets. Moving on the mill with his patriotic soldiers, Wilkinson observed the British works and its well established stone mill, plus a barn and blockhouse. He also noticed the entrenchments and tree barricades on the road, the only one going to the mill. Melting snow had turned the area into mud and swamps. It was to be a tough nut to crack.

Ignoring such defenses, the general was not one to be stopped. He ordered his men and artillery to fire upon the stone mill. The walls were too thick and the shells did little harm. Besides, he watched reinforcements arrive for the British. Emboldened the British attempted a sortie on the stone bridge, but it failed. Not being able to make headway, Wilkinson ordered his men to withdraw, and not attempt a way around the mill. American losses were moderate and British losses were light. [9]

Meanwhile in Kentucky's placid Knob Creek community, Jonathan Joseph died. Four of his neighbors were named by Hardin Court on May 9 1814, to appraise his property for probate. One of these men was Thomas Lincoln, Abe's father. Another was Joseph LaFollette, grandfather of Senator Robert M. LaFollette, There were several LaFollette families close to Knob Creek. Later in the year of 1814, Thomas purchased a heifer for $9.42 1/2 and a currying comb for 63 cents at a sale. Seventeen days after the sale, Lincoln sold his Mill Creek farm to Charles Melton. Using that money, he purchased a farm of 230 acres on Knob Creek. The bottoms were rich. Unfortunately there was a disagreement over the title and the Lincolns lost the property. [10]

When the British raided Oswego they had not discovered the 36 heavy naval guns and 10 large rope cables at Oswego Falls, needed by the Americans to fit their building at the shipyard. Because of their great weight they had to be hauled by the water route. British commander Sir James Yeo learned of the presence of them and moved to stop and seize them. Master Commandant Melancthon Woolsey led the force and ran up against Daniel Appling and his 150 defending riflemen. The British captured lagging American boats. British ships were in pursuit of the rest.

On May 29th, Woolsey landed at Big Sandy Creek and set out scouts for the nearby naval treasure. On the 30th, they carefully searched for the boats. They saw masts ahead and sent 200 marines and sailors ahead to seize the vital guns. Appling knew they were coming and concealed his rifle men and Oneida warriors, who were among the few western Indians to ally themselves with the Americans, in the woods. They all opened fire when the British arrived. Dozen of Britons fell dead or were wounded in the ambush. The rest fled, but were cut off around their flank. The Americans took 161 prisoners with the loss of one man killed and two wounded. The guns were taken to Sackett's shipyard and Yeo called off his blockader. The successful American fight had lasted fifteen minutes. Major Appling was beveted to lieutenant colonel. [11]

At this point news came into American ports, conflicting news, from Paris. One heard first that Paris had fallen to the Allies, and then that the Czar and Prussian king had been taken prisoners and entered Paris as prisoners. There were bets of which was a true report. Was Napoleon still ruling France? Then on the night of June 8, 1814, a warship was off the coast at New York City. With daylight that vessel came up the bay. Glasses were focused upon the white flag. Those with spyglasses were able to see that it was the flag of the Bourbons and the news spread rapidly in the city and then throughout the country. The officers came ashore with their white cockades. This was the *Olive Branch*, an armed brig of Louis XVIII, king of France. There was the spread of wild rejoicing. The Napoleonic wars were over. Could those of America be further behind? The Federalists were especially happy. [12]

On June 21, 1814, Sir Robert Barrie led an expedition which attacked Thomaston and St. George west of Penobscot, Maine. He captured four ships in the river. Three weeks later, a British force raided Eastport and the Passamaquoddy Islands. Moose Island and Fort Sullivan surrendered. Then Sir Thomas Masterman Hardy bombarded Sonington, but did not try to occupy the town. His was followed by a conquest of Castine in September. The American soldiers there escaped capture. There were other conquests of a minor nature and Castine and other towns were occupied for eight months. This territory was soon restored by the peace treaty. [13]

Captain Johnston Blakely sailed his *Wasp* from Portsmouth, New Hampshire, to raid the sea lanes off southern England. His was a new ship, named after that of the battle of October 18, 1812. In weeks she took seven British merchant vessels. Two warships

The Difficult War: The Era of the War of 1812   207

chased her on the morning of June 28, 1814. A third then showed up. The foremost the *Raindeer* reached her and opened fire. The action was severe. Twice the sailors of the British ship tried to board the American. Each time the American tars repulsed them. The exchange of broadsides continued until the *Raindeer* was destroyed. What was left was burnt after everyone was removed. The victory ship then set sail for L'Orient, France. [14]

Winder was in a bind with Armstrong, secretary of war, dictating difficult orders. For two years Armstrong had delayed measures of defense; for two months he had frustrated Winder's attempts to create an army; and now he wanted to decide matters with the crisis at hand. Now he ordered Winder to take a position close to the enemy, but Winder had few troops to use. His other orders were confused. Armstrong's predictions were equally false. The secretary did not see any danger for Washington DC. At first he believed Baltimore was the object of the British invasion force, which had been seen near the coast.

Next he said that whatever the object of the invasion, their course was simple. They must assemble a large of a force as possible on the Patuxente. They must clear the road of its horses and cattle and break down the bridges. He decided to build abbatis or tree branch defenses with the tops facing outward. Strong points must be defended. When the enemy moved forward, they must harass his front and flanks by night and day attacks and in his rear. All of this was well and good, but Winder did not have troops and time enough to do what should have been done months earlier.

Armstrong was of course acting in a certain darkness. He only knew so much about the British force, but the point is that the secretary was not prepared. The size of the fleet should have told him more. Had he acted earlier he might have brought if off. He was under certain constraints. An abler general and secretary could have defeated the British for the enemy had few horsemen and three cannon.

Winder lacked in boldness on that fateful day. His troops were in Baltimore, even after he wisely chose Bladenburg as the battlefield to meet the British. He dared not ask the people of Baltimore too much. Actually they were eager for a fight like a frontier town and it has been suggested that he could have asked for more militiamen. Perhaps Winder believed quite correctly that Baltimore needed defenses from the British if he was unable to defeat them at Bladenburg. To Baltimoreans like eighteen year old John Kennedy it was a party. Once they saved Washington on the battlefield, there would surely be a ball in the presidential palace in their honor.

At this time, Josh Barney was trapped with his flotilla and so he abandoned it and set out with four hundred sailors to help Winder's army defeat the British. It was at Wood Yard, only half the size of Ross' army. When the British advanced, Winder retreated. Monroe hastily wrote that Ross was on his way to Washington. The governmental records should be removed. However, the Americans got a breathing spell when Robert Ross halted. [15]

Practically everyone in the capital of Washington thought that the city was safe from the British, but that was just the locale in which the British were headed with a fleet although it was not yet decided just where to strike. Admiral Cochrane could not make up his mind. President Madison knew that the British would launch more troops in the war against the United States and could expect that number to be large. Authorities in London had information in their hands that told them they must keep troops in France to maintain the monarchy there and that other troops were needed in Flanders and Canada, but they managed a large fleet and large army for Cochrane.

Since Secretary of War Armstrong protested that no one would attack the capital (he felt it unworthy as a town), Madison wanted a separate command for the District of Columbia. He picked Brigadier General William Henry Winder for the position since his uncle was governor of Maryland and would be the one to supply the militia for the protection of the state and the District. It was a political appointment and slighted better generals. On July 2, 1814, the 10th Military District was established to cover northern Virginia with Maryland and the District of Columbia and on July 4th, requisitions went out to governors of all the states to hold 93,500 militia at the ready. This was apple pie in the sky because so many of the states were not interested in contributing. Pennsylvanian authorities said that they would be unable to go to war until the autumn. Wouldn't the conflict wait until then?

Before the war, General Winder was a Baltimore lawyer and politician. When the war broke out, he fought in one battle and had been captured there on the Canadian front. He had only recently been exchanged. His only qualification as it turned out was his relation to the governor. Winder had some time to prepare, but he had not a single item to begin with and had trouble getting action. Since Armstrong did not believe Washington would be attacked, he practically ignored Winder and although Winder was an independent commander he needed the aid of the secretary of war. Winder asked for at least 4,000 militiamen, but got no answer for even that number. His district had only 612 men for the defense of Maryland, the District of Columbia, and northern Virginia. He had a hard task ahead of him.

The problems that Winder had with Armstrong were enormous and was largely responsible for the troubles that lay ahead for the capital that fall. Meanwhile it was July and Winder learned that Armstrong believed the militia fought best if called out on the spur of the moment. Winder countered that what was the chance of collecting a sufficient force if the British would require only four days to enter Washington, Baltimore, or Annapolis. Armstrong did not reply to most of Winder's letters. He took his time and did not even stockpile military stores as directed by the president. Winder asked for the necessary orders, but never received them. To Armstrong, Winder was excess baggage since he would not be needed to defend Washington. Winder had a hard row to hoe.

Winder did have the aid of Major General John P. Van Ness, commander of the District of Columbia militia. Van Ness was a banker and interested in the future of Washington. He had been urging for the improvement of the city's defenses and when he could not get anywhere with Armstrong, went to Madison himself and asked if the government would deliberately abandon Washington. Madison replied in the negative that every inch would be defended. Still nothing much was being done to insure that despite the ceaseless activity of Winder who got involved in the smallest detail of his weak command. Winder got only 250 militiaman when he gingerly asked help of Major General Samuel Smith, the tough and ready commander of the 3rd Division of Maryland militia. Smith later amply defended Baltimore with his masses.

Progress came slow and Winder managed to gain a few more troops when the British invasion fleet was discovered coming up the Chesapeake. Three hundred and thirty regulars were stationed at Piscatway down the Potomac, and 140 cavalry near Georgetown. The militia under Winder's control now were 240 Maryland militia at Bladensburg and, 1,400 more at Baltimore. Winder's steady work had produced some results, but a bit too late to get ready for men who had defeated Napoleon, considered the greatest general of the age, a genius at war.

The Difficult War: The Era of the War of 1812   209

When the word of the British fleet to the south came to Washington, Winder lost all of his careful complaisant courtesy used to avoid stepping on toes, and sent out his orders. They went out to Van Ness for the calling up of the Washington militia and to General Samuel Smith to federalize the whole 3rd Division. Brigadier general John P. Hungerford, some 120 miles away in northern Virginia was called upon for his 2,000 veteran militiamen and appeals were sent to the governors of Maryland and Pennsylvania for help at the same time that a circular order was sent to militia heads in Maryland for 500 men from each major command.

The big problem came in planning how to use these troops. He had called up the troops ands now they needed some locale to assemble at and marching orders. No one knew where the British soldiers who were surely aboard that large fleet would land, and where they would attack. Winder thought that Annapolis would be the target. According to him it was a fine port, easy to defend, and would make a good base for future operations. As it was, Annapolis would be an easy place for the British to take and when the fleet passed it by it was deserted with fear. The British Cochrane encouraged by Cockburn were decided upon Washington.

Armstrong was consistent, Washington would not be the point, it would be Baltimore; here was a city worth taking. In fact, Armstrong would have loved to live in Baltimore over Washington and figured his value judgments would be shared by the British. James Monroe, secretary of state in Madison's cabinet, felt Washington was the most likely target because it was the nation's capital. If Washington was attacked as he was sure it would be, he would do some scouting for intelligence. Monroe was eager for some action and Madison granted his request for the mission.

Word reached Washington on August 19th that the British planed to destroy Barney's flotilla and dine in Washington after that. That afternoon Monroe had his escort and was on the way to the Chesapeake shore. Secretary of the Navy Jones gave orders to Commodore Barney to take the flotilla as high upstream as he could, burn it if the British followed to capture it, and then bring his men back to Washington. This news did not convince Armstrong that it would be Washington that the British would attack. Secretary of the Navy Jones was sure that it would be Washington evidently when he sent out the calls for help from Commodore John Rodgers in Philadelphia and Commodore David Porter in New York. Both were to be beneficial in the defense of Baltimore so Jones' action was not in vain.

On August 20th, word came from Barney that the British had landed at Benedict on the Patuxent River off the Bay which meant that either Baltimore or Washington would be attacked. At this point there was news of a bloody victory over the British at Fort Erie. Spirits went high in time for a special proclamation from the Commander General Winder, full of stirring words. This uplifting was necessary given the problems that the Americans were faced with in Maryland. [16]

---

[1]Catterall, R.C.H., 1960 Reprint, pp. 7-10, 14-21.

[2]James, *Jackson*, pp. 166-168.

[3]Cole, Brigitte E., "Calabee, Battle of," Heidler & Heidler, *Encyclopedia*, pp. 76-77.

[4]Hopewell, *C., Sam Houston*, 1987, pp. 24-26.

[5]James, *Jackson*, pp. 170-171.

[6]Clarke, Mary Whatley, *Chief Bowles and the Texas Cherokees*, Norman: University of Oklahoma Press, 1971, pp. 5-6.

[7]Hickey, *1812*, pp. 182-183.

[8]Lohnes, Barry J. in *Maine Historical Society Quarterly*, (1975), pp. 9-10.

[9]Heidler, Jeanne T. and Heidler, David S., "La Colle Mill," Heidler & Heidler, *Encyclopedia*, p. 285.

[10]Warren, *Lincoln's*, pp. 113-117.

[11]Barbuto, Richard V., "Appling, Daniel," Heidler & Heidler, *Encyclopedia*, p. 11.

[12]Tucker, *Poltroons and Patriots*, pp. 470-473.

[13]Drake, Frederick C., "Castine, Maine," Heidler & Heidler, *Encyclopedia*, p. 85.

[14]Bunker, Robert J., "Wasp Versus Reindeer," Heidler & Heidler, *Encyclopedia*, pp. 546-547.

[15]Swanson, Neil H., *The Perilous Fight*, New York: Farrar and Rhinehart, 1945, pp. 27-33, 43.

[16]Lord, Walter, *The Dawn's Early Light*, New York: W. W. Norton, 1972, *passim*; Swanson, *Perilous, pp. 16, 18.*

CHAPTER XXVI

WASHINGTON

The men in Maryland marched out into the countryside and discovered that there were no tents and camping equipment waiting for them when they stopped for the night. There were 1,070 men and only 200 flints showed up which meant that 870 could not fire their guns. The British were encamped with all their equipment at Benedict, where they were spied upon by James Monroe who could not see too clearly from three miles away without his spyglasses, which he forgot to bring.

The British feet followed Barney's fleet north up the waterway, while the British army marched parallel to Nottingtham where James Monroe fled ahead of them. Monroe went to the Wood Yard to find Winder collecting his army and gave him news of his discovery of the British army marching along the road from Benedict to Washington by the northern rout they would have to travel. The British troops were meeting with no opposition and were in a festive mood. The fleet caught up with Barney just in time to see him destroy his ships. Barney had already left to join Winder.

Winder and Monroe watched from the Oden farmhouse and saw the British make for the road toward the Wood Yard. They did not see the British reverse themselves and take the road to Upper Marlboro. The Americans fell back, and in Washington putting the state papers in linen bags and prepared to move out. Madison however was restless and intent upon joining with his troops for the battle, so he went to Winder' army, where he was met by the general.

On August 23rd at noon, the British were still in Upper Marlboro and this report reached Winder, who began to think of advancing upon the town and surrounding the British. He could now envision a British defeat, perhaps notably that the British lacked a cavalry force and artillery. Madison was reassured now that a counter-blow seemed in prospect and left for Washington. Winder gave out his orders for an attack on Upper Marlboro.

Meanwhile, the British had moved out of Upper Marlboro heading for Bladensburg and Washington on an afternoon march. American Major George Peter and his force came into contact with the British and American artillery fired upon the British for the first time in the British units advance toward Washington. At Melwood, an estate, the British went into bivouac. The Americans knew nothing of the British stop and Winder feared a night attack by the British, so he pulled his troops back to Washington in a rush which left the troops exhaustingly sublime in a field near the Navy Yard. The sight of the troops scared the Washingtonians and panic took the place of cool withdrawal. People were running, seemingly distracted in the streets when darkness fell.

On August 24th before sunrise, the upper bridge was burnt under Winder's orders to prevent the British from using it. Stansbury and his troops were uneasy at the burning of the bridges and a message from Winder telling of his withdrawal to Washington shocked him with the vision of their being alone to stem the British attack and he set his troops off for a march off to Washington, receiving orders to return on the way. Reaching Bladensburg they did not cross the river to the east side, but stayed on the west side.

The *National Intelligencer* was optimistic in its morning edition. Editors for that Journal wrote that they felt assured that the city of Washington would be protected by the numbers and bravery of their troops. The Georgetown *Federal Republican* felt that the British would not advance any closer to the city, but the people knew better. The city was almost totally abandoned by its populace who found refuge in further fields sure that only distance would protect them from the invasion of the British. William A. Bradley, cashier of the Bank of Washington, was one of the last to leave, with the bank's assets in a cart.

Winder was at his wit's end, he had done nothing right these last few days and with good fortune that comes to those in the last hours of their agony, he sent a letter to Secretary Armstrong that ended that he would be glad of counsel from him and the government. If it was more convenient for Armstrong he would come to him to receive advice. Winder was realizing his own inadequacy in his position, but was wise enough to know he needed advice and help, which so often was not forthcoming. Fortunately it was delivered to the president by mistake.

Madison read it and recognized quickly that it was a desperate plea made to a man who had done nothing but frustrate Winder and who would be the last to render aid. The president ready to do everything he could hurried to Winder where he was joined by James Monroe and William Jones. Monroe promptly went out to determine where the British were going, intelligence that was desperately needed if anything was to be done now, especially now that even Winder could see that the British would be headed for none but Washington.

Finally, a source Winder felt was reliable, told him that the British were headed for Bladensburg. He immediately got everyone on the road, that is everyone but the tough Barney and his equally tough flotilla force. Madison corrected the destruction of the bridge that five men could manage. At last he could manage to get on the road for Bladensburg. Meanwhile Madison had given the slow-moving Armstrong the idea that he could manage the battle with Madison there to decide if any conflict of authority arose between him and Winder. Madison said to give Winder advice and assistance, but Armstrong felt that he was to be in command. When he got to the battlefield, he was disappointed and later resigned from the government when snubbed by Madison. General Stansbury at Bladensburg was unaware of the reinforcements that were coming when he lined his troops into position to resist the expected British attack. [1]

Winder was more certain than ever that the battle for the safety of Washington should be fought at Bladensburg, but Tobias Stansbury and his relied upon left or west wing, had already retreated. The Washington-Baltimore road was uncovered. Stansbury informed Winder that the state of the troops was exhausted and could not meet the British with any prospect of success unless they were reinforced. Stansbury tried several positions about Bladenburg, but failed one suitable to him although with their natural lines of resistance.

Winder once again directed Stansbury to oppose any British march upon the area of Bladensburg. Instead of obeying it, Stansbury held a council of war with his chief officers. The latter wanted him to move further on the road to the city for a better defensive ground. Stansbury agreed. Poor Winder was having trouble with his subordinate as he had with his superior. At last Winder had gotten angry and sent his aide with harsh words for Stansbury. The words pulled the subordinate general up short. Stansbury regarded the last order to be positive. He marched forward for Bladensburg but selected a position back of the bridge over the river but not close enough to counter a British march across the bridge over the river, a branch of the Potomac.

Colonel William Dent Beall was to be an unexpected prize with his men from before Annapolis as a solid port. Stansbury's men saw two columns of smoke. One came from the river road and the other from the Annapolis road. Both were presumed to be the enemy, but soon that from the old capital of Maryland arrived first and it was discovered to be American. Beall had arrived against the orders of Stansbury to travel a different route. The colonel sought danger and the danger was fast approaching by the river road. He had arrived earlier than he would have, had he followed orders. There was no sense in being later.

Finally the men saw the men behind the second dust cloud. Britain's column was impressive. Unlike many of the Americans they had look-alike uniforms of organization, looking hard and solid with a relentless march. They looked back at their own fellow soldiers and saw his infantry regiments move out marching to the rear. Monroe had ordered the men to withdraw. General Winder had reached the field. Stansbury found Winder reconnoitering. British troops had stopped.

There were a number of meddlers on the battlefield. Several gentlemen, including cabinet members, wanted at heart to direct the American side of the battle, seeking glory and duty. Monroe was not the only one. However Winder was late to the battlefield and because of this tardiness he could not adequately direct the preparations. He did not have sufficient forces to command even had he been on the site. His right wing arrived at almost the last minute. Behind the Washington militia infantry came Barney's guns with his flotilla sailors and marines. Barney placed his guns astride the road to Washington on the rise overlooking the creek which flowed into the Eastern Branch of the Potomac River. Cannon were also placed overlooking the Bladensburg bridge. It had its supporters.

In back on the rise was a curved line, supporting Barney. Kramer was in advance of that on the east side of the road and was soon to drop back to join Beall. Stansbury was in the center on the west side of the road. The defenses were strung out on the battlefield and the key to the action, the funnel through which Ross must pass was left poor guarded. Ross would have to cross the river on that bridge over the Potomac Branch, but that was not where the troops were. [2]

The British marched forth to the attack. Fighting erupted. The Americans outnumbered and unorganized were forced back on both wings and center. They were soon lost to the battle and unable to hold their ground. Barney and his sailors reached the field of Bladensburg just when the Americans were routed. He and they were steadfast. They set up their guns with coolness and prepared a defensive line. Captain Samuel Miller came up and put his 150 marines at his disposal. Not everyone had fled in despair. Beall's regiment had not fled. This encouraged Barney.

Soon he could see the British army approach towards Barney's center. Although the British had expected more resistance and were elated, they now halted. Barney and his men held their fire, but formed up in close order. Beall's men fired a volley and then fled the field of battle. Beall was angry but could not hold them back. The American army under Winder was not steady. Barney gave orders and fired into the ranks of the British regulars. He brought up more troops. The British suffered greater losses. British General

Robert Ross came up to urge his men to advance. Ross began the move to envelop the Americans. The Americans fired at close range and caused gaps in the ranks of the British soldiers. Next the seamen yelled the classic cry of the seas, "Board'em! Board'em!" Redcoats recoiled and headed for the safety of the woods. Barney and his men showed what determined men could do against odds.

Barney fell wounded. Once again, other British troopers began their march with their fixed bayonets. It was clear that Barney and his sailors could do no more. He issued his orders to withdraw. General Ross and Admiral Cockburn walked up when the firing stopped. Cockburn turned to Ross and said, "I told you it was the flotilla men" The general replied, "They have given us our only real fighting." When a British soldier found Barney, Ross congratulated the naval captain on his fight and immediately paroled him. Ross said he would convey him whenever he wished. Barney picked the tavern in Bladenburg which the British surgeons had converted into the hospital for the wounded. [3]

With the British victory, the way was fully open to the American capital. General Ross sought a parley whereby any official in Washington could surrender the city to the British and they could hold it for an indemnity or ransom. However the streets were empty. Ross and his force moved into the city lighted by a moon and a bit of day's ending in the skies. He and his small force moved down Maryland street under a white flag with a drum roll. Suddenly he was greeted by a volley from a large corner house rented by Albert Gallatin from Robert Sewall. His horse and a British soldier fell dead. Three more were wounded, but the largest, Ross, was unhurt. The British pushed forward, but could find no one in the house. They had fled and only some curious African Americans could be found in the yard's bushes.

The enemy entered Washington and set fire to the public buildings. Fortunately the paintings and records had been whisked out days and hours before. The White House and the capital buildings were blackened hulls. Madison was now a fugitive along country roads on horseback. His wife Dolley Madison was going south by carriage another way. Looking back each could see the high glow of the fires in Washington, where the naval yard with its ship projects, the treasury, the war department, and the arsenal were ruined. What was left of the American army was also on its way down the back roads. In many ways it was the low point of American history. In an age when the capture of capitals meant a finish to national government and reigns, it seemed like the end of the American experiment. The war was not yet over; it merely looked that way that late August night of 1814.

Baltimoreans, some forty miles to the north, watched the fire from afar and talked about the events of the day, no doubt worried about what it might portend for their city. Theirs was a young city which liked excitement and commotion, crowds and mass celebrations, and money and strong drink. However, this was a little too much for them. The people gathered in small groups and their talk showed their apprehensions. The talk was that of a large army which would plunder and burn Baltimore. One thing especially stuck out: this army was made up of the veterans who had defeated the great Napoleon. What was to be their fate? [4]

A nineteen-year-old boy named Johns Hopkins was in Baltimore, in charge of his uncle's store and his uncle's children. He was very concerned over what he should do. It was his duty, he felt, to stay with the store and send the children out of town to safety, but who would he send them to? He was in a quandary. His uncle, Gerard Hopkins, was a wholesale grocer and commission merchant and a Quaker. As a Quaker, he was sent to attend a Quaker meeting in Ohio with his wife. They left their business and children with

Johns who had gone to live and work with his uncle and learn the business from the ground up. Now with panic shaking Baltimore, he was set down in a bad situation, more than he could handle. However, three days before the bombardment, his uncle and aunt returned on horseback and took over the problem. [5]

Major General Robert Ross, Vice-Admiral Sir Alexander Cochrane, and Rear-Admiral George Cockburn were looking for a new target after their success against Washington DC. They decided to go for nearby Baltimore whose warehouses would yield the loot the Americans had massed from privateering in the Atlantic. The then third largest city in population in the United States with its 45,000 people, Baltimore had been a stronghold of pro-war sentiment. It had one of the best harbors on the coast. However, it was strongly defended against such onslaughts that the British envisioned. Just how tough it was remained to be seen. There were 10,000 militiamen (mostly) and regulars in the city and its environs. They were busy building fortifications and digging trenches. Star shaped Fort McHenry, made of brick, was a dominant landmark.

George Armistead, commander of Fort McHenry, was a Virginian and was born on April 10, 1780, to a long lined prominent family of English and German origins at New Market. Their earliest ancestor had come in 1635. Four of his brothers were militia or regular officers too. In January of 1799, Armistead was commissioned a second lieutenant in the infantry and became an engineer and artilleryman before being promoted to captain. Promoted to major, he played a role in Canada and proved himself at the capture of Fort George. He came to the notice of Secretary of War John Armstrong who valued him highly enough to give him command of Fort McHenry at Baltimore in early 1814.

He was in charge of the fort, the battery opposite, and a flotilla of ships. Immediately busy with organizing its defenses, he led his men of roughly one thousand in number in fortification work. He had 57 cannon, including fifteen huge 24-pounders, which had been loaned to America by the French.

When news reached Baltimore of the disaster at Bladensburg and Washington, Major General Samuel Smith, a U. S. senator, knew that Baltimore would be next. The British would not have to go far in assaulting the city. The Americans there were pessimistic and defeatist after Washington, and there were augments over command authority. This feeling was contrasted with the coolness of Armistead at the fort. Smith was placed over Brigadier General William Henry Winder and he instilled confidence and spirit in the Americans. His men worked on the fortifications on the brow of Hempstead Hill.

An overly optimistic Cochrane sailed his ships northward, planning a joint land and sea attack. While he landed his troops, he would, he thought reduce Fort McHenry. Outlooks sighted the fleet and Smith sent Brigadier General John Stricker to take his brigade to North Point, where the British unknown to him were to land for an attack on the land side of Baltimore. Together the British army and navy could take the fort.

The British sailed up to Fort McHenry and on September 13, 1814, they opened their bombardment a little before seven in the morning. Because the enemy had twice the range as Armistead's guns, they could fire on the fort, safe out of range in the river. Armistead tried everything to increase his gun range, but all failed when with some danger and three explosions and he had to ride out the storm. The ships pounded the fort for eight hours. Since the fort's guns did not fire back after the first few efforts, Admiral Alexander Cochrane assumed the fort was out of action. Actually it had survived in good shape, although missing an explosion in his powder magazine because the shot was a dud. Cochrane sent in three of the bombs and the rocket ship in for the kill, but Armstead waited until they were close and fired. The British withdrew from the murderous fire and began the bombardment again. The Americans had to wait once again.[6]

A veteran of the Revolutionary War, Stricker was militia general. He advanced on the night of the 11th of September to North Point with his 3,200 men to establish a defense line. The next morning he deployed his men in three lines from Bear Creek on the right to the swamp on the left. He expected an attack. There was no attack and Stricker sent out scouts. They returned and reported that the British were at Robert Gorsuch's farm to devour his livestock and produce. Striker sent horsemen and riflemen to provoke Ross into a fight; one of his musket firers hit Ross and mortally wounded him. Ross had narrowly escaped death in Washington, but met his untimely fate near Baltimore.

Colonel Arthur Brooke took command, drove the Americans back and sent his troops against the prepared lines established by Stricker. The British attacked the center in a twenty minute fight. When the British moved against the American left flank, the Americans panicked and it was all Stricker could do to keep them reasonably together for a retreat. News of this reached Baltimore and caused great alarm there. Smith's defenses stopped the British from entering the city.

Firing on Fort McHenry lasted during the night. British Colonel Arthur Brooke on land requested Cochrane give his troops naval gunfire cover. Because this meant that his fleet would have to come under range of the American guns, Cochrane could not help him. It was a long night and dawn arrived to see the firing not making any progress. Then exactly twenty-four hours after it had begun, Armistead had saved Baltimore and was made a hero. He had lost only four dead and 24 wounded because of the protection he had built into the fort. He fell victim to delirium and fever from the ordeal, but recovered to learn that his wife had safely given birth to their daughter. He was promoted to live the good life, but died less than four years later. [7]

Lawyer Francis Scott Key had gone, under a flag of truce to gain the release of Dr. Beans, to the British fleet off Baltimore. While he was there, The British were bombarding the defenses near the city on September 13, 1814. He watched with great anxiety, especially when he learned the British admiral planned to burn Baltimore. Fearing they he would plunder the city first and endanger the safety of the women and children, Key watched during the night.

Between two and three o'clock on the dark morning, the British sent 1,200 picked men past Fort McHenry to land and attack the garrison in the rear. They made it past the fort but Fort Covington which was next poured a murderous fire upon the British force which had cheered too early. In the slaughter from the guns of Fort Covington, the lazaretto, and American barges, they fled but were hit again when they passed McHenry in what seemed like a sheet of fire and brimstone. Houses were shaken in Baltimore. Then all was quiet. At dawn, Key saw the American flag still flying and he was inspired to write "The Star-Spangled Banner" during the day. The song was published and became instantly popular. On the advent of day, Cochrane gave up and soon sailed his navy and army away. [8]

When he fought at Chippewa and Lundy's Lane, Winfield Scott was a twenty-eight year old brigadier general. Under the command of Major General Jacob Brown at Niagara, near the famous falls of that name in western New York, Scott fought well and deserved his great fame which began in the war and lasted until the early months of the American Civil War. Scott's career spanned most of Lincoln's life, and he was an important player in the drama of these years.

A little above Blackrock, the American troops discovered a corps of observation led by the Marquis of Tweedale. American troops were eager for the action and what they considered the glory of war. In the almost unbearable heat and the dust which made breathing difficult, the Americans pursued the corps for sixteen miles that fourth of July. The British had a head start but not enough to completely destroy the bridges along the way of both forces. Finally, the Marquis and his men made it to safety behind the Chippewa River where the main British army under Major General Phineas Riall waited. The pursuit took twelve hours. Seeing the situation across the river, Scott withdrew his men behind Street's Creek where Brown and the reserve reached him early on the next morning.

General Brown ordered men in his command to prepare the materials for a bridge across the Chippawa on July 5, 1814, above the British camp, which was at the river's mouth. Next, the Americans began to build the bridge. While this was underway Canadian militiamen and the Indians fired upon American pickets. Brown ordered his own militiamen to dislodge the enemy and they fought with inconclusive combat. Their fourth of July dinner was brought over that fifth and the Americans ate for the first time since a meal thirty hours before.

That afternoon Brown had planned a parade, but Scott found a fight. General Riall had advanced to do battle. Nine field guns fired upon the Americans when they entered on the bridge and the American artillery responded. Scott's men did not stop. They crossed the bridge with some loss and began forming a line to the left and front. Some of the soldiers fell victim to the fire, but they were brave and Riall exclaimed that they were regulars, having thought their gray uniforms signified that they were militia troops. Barely deployed, the Americans learned that the British had outflanked them. Scott had to maneuver as the enemy advanced. Soon it was a hard fight with thick smokes. Now the British were outflanked and received enfiliated fire. Then Riall's pride broke and fled, pursued by Scott's men until they turned around short of the dangers of the batteries of the British.

Faced with the difficulty of locating the decamped Riall at the heights at the head of Lake Ontario, Brown decided upon a fake panic on the morning of 24th to draw out the British general. The American retreated rapidly for show and on the 25th halted for a day's rest. The stratagem worked. A militia colonel reported that Riall's whole force was in Lundy's Lane recently reinforced. One battalion had already reached Riall and others were on the way in rapid marches. Soon the British and the American were fighting one more battle. An attempt to turn Scott's left failed and the British were driven back. Jesup's men swiped around the British left flank cutting off part of the line and capturing Riall himself. The Americans routed the British that night.

After the night assault, the British regrouped. Scott led a small column which pierced the line in the gloom and enveloped the British extreme left. He had to withdraw when fired upon by his own men. Then both sides entered a spectacular artillery duel. A bullet wounded Scott, who did not know that Brown had just been wounded. Brigadier General Eleazar W. Ripley assumed the command. Against arguments from the officers, Ripley ordered his American army to abandon the field. The British claimed a victory when they discovered that the Americans had left the field. Ripley's action had turned an American victory, which the Americans never ceased to be proud about, into a perceived withdrawal. Nothing was thus accomplished by the American victories at Chippewa and Lundy Lane. Had Brown and Scott not been wounded, the Americans could have marched further into Canada. [9]

The situation Americans found themselves in was a major problem. A war department circular was sent forth to several governors that, in the secretary's words, "the late pacification in Europe, offers to the enemy a large depositable force, both naval and military, and with it the means of giving to the war here, a character if new and increased activity and extent." They were to organize an hold into readiness a corps of 93,000 men to repel any force the British sent against their states. General Dearborn made a requisition on the governor of Massachusetts for a body of militia to guard against British attacks. What would America do? [10]

---

[1]Lord, *Dawn's, passim.*

[2]Swanson, *Perilous*, pp. 42-60, 71-72, 75-77, 80-85.

[3]Tucker, *Poltroons and Patriots*, pp. 544, 548ff.

[4]Swanson, *Perilous*, pp. 3-6; Tucker, *Poltroons and Patriots*, pp. 552-554.

[5]Thom, Helen Hopkins, *Johns Hopkins: A Silhouette*, Baltimore: John Hopkins Press, 1929, pp. 13-17.

[6]Frazier, Donald, "Baltimore, Battle of," Heidler & Heidler, *Encyclopedia*, pp. 30-32; Zabecki, David T., "Armstead, George," Heidler & Heidler, *Encyclopedia*, pp.12-13.

[7]*Ibid.*, p. 32 and 12-13; Heidler, Jeanne T. and David S. Heidler, "Stricker, John," Heidler & Heidler, *Encyclopedia*, p. 494.

[8]*America*, V, 223-227.

[9]*Ibid.*, V, 190-205.

[10]Dwight, Theodore, *History of the Hartford Convention with a Review of the Policy of the United Stases Government, Which Led to the War of 1812*, 1833, Reprint, Freeport, NY: Books for Libraries Press, 1970. pp. 280ff. Quote on p. 280.

CHAPTER XXVII

THE AMERICAN SOLDIER AT WORK

A party of American soldiers had gone to build a frontier fort at Prairie de Chien and visited the Sac village on the way. They received a friendly welcome. The Sac repaired their lodge, worked on their village on Rock River and cleared their cornfields. Reinforcements passed through for Prairie de Chien and these too were well treated. Then the Indian chief Black Hawk learned that the British had taken that fort and wished the Sac to join them. So he collected his warriors and pursued the boats. These vessels were commanded by Lieutenant John Campbell and had sailed with a fair wind. Being on land they could hope to see a boat grounded and indeed this was provided them. When the Indians were about half way up the rapids, Black Hawk could see all of the boats, moving fast with a strong wind, but wind and mismanagement brought one boat to the shore, where it ran hard aground. The sail was lowered. None of the others were having any problems and were passing on.

The Indians moved cautiously ahead. Seeing some soldiers ashore, the natives fired upon them. As Black Hawk described the action, "all that could, hurried aboard, but they were unable to push off, being fast aground." Sac warriors, aided by Renard and Kickapoo braves, fired upon the boat when they reached (without exposing themselves) the river bank. The bullets passed through the planks and killed whites who yelled when hit. Black Hawk urged his braves to continue firing. Several Americans fired from the boat but they did not hit the Indians. The chief had his braves fire flaming arrows to set the sail on fire. After two or three attempts, the sail lying in the boat was ablaze. The boat itself was on fire and it seemed that this was the end for the whites.

Rescue was ahead. While the boat was burning, one of the other boats had returned and dropped anchor, letting their boat swing to the endangered boat and rescue those soldiers who could walk. Black Hawk's men shot at them and wounded one white. Another boat came down, but her anchor did not take hold and she drifted ashore. The other boat cut her cable and the men rowed down the river without an attempt to aid the stranded Americans. The Indians attacked this boat. They fired several rounds. Because the Americans did not shoot back, Black Hawk thought they were afraid or either had few men abroad. He ordered a rush upon that boat. When they got close, the Americans fired upon the approaching Indians and killed two, the total Indian loss. The Americans escaped and Black Hawk led his warriors to put out the conflagration to save the cargo of the captured boat, destroying the whiskey and the drugs abroad and distributing several guns, clothing, and some cloth tents. This ended the engagement of July 21, 1814. [1]

During the summer of 1814 in the east, Thomas Macdonough spent the time of his men patrolling the lower end of Lake Champlain to keep watch on the British to the north. Macdonough was born in 1783 near Middletown, Delaware, to a physician-politician who had served in the Revolutionary War. At age eleven, he lost both of his parents, but received help from prominent friends of his father in the state. This included at age seventeen a commission of midshipman in the American navy. He was in the West Indies in the *Ganges* when he contracted yellow fever. He survived to serve in the Mediterranean for three years and returned home to rest as a well educated in naval affairs man. He took part in the naval action and was promoted to acting lieutenant. In 1811, he captained a merchant vessel.

When war was declared he became a first lieutenant. In September, he was assigned to take charge of the small fleet on Lake Champlain. It was there he was to make his mark and help influence history. However, when he arrived it was a backwater. He immediately set about to improve and develop his two leaky gunboats and three sloops. He added guns, but his great problem was in hiring men who would be good naval gunners and sailors. He made progress but in 1813, as we have seen, he lost two vessels and the naval balance swung in favor of the British. He recovered and soon had two new ships, three sloops, and six gunboats in all. Now the commander was ready for the challenge of his life, as we shall shortly see. [2]

Also Captain David Maffet was at this time commanding the *Rattlesnake* and Captain Samuel Nicoll the *Scourge*. Both men were in Scandinavian water, off the North Cape and the coast of Norway. Maffet took many valuable prizes and inflicted damages to British ships. About the middle of March of 1814, he sailed his ship into La Rochelle, France, to refresh his men and refit for more adventures at sea. Nicoll had sailed his vessel for the poorly protected north coast of England and the waters of Norway. George Coggeshall later wrote that after Maffet had made one or two successful voyages, he found it to be a good idea for himself to remain on shore in Norwegian ports to manage the hauls of his men as prizes to prevent them from falling into the hands of dishonest and incompetent persons in the prize courts. From time to time, he sent one of his lieutenants to command the ship under his instructions while he remained ashore. [3]

The *Ultor* made it to sea from Baltimore aided by bad weather. On April 25, 1814, the schooner was off Echo Bank, northwest of the West Indies. There the lookout sighted a sail which was the *Swift* with its cargo of fish and lumber from Halifax bound for Jamaica. It was captured. The brig *Robert* was sighted on the next day and captured with its cargo of fish and oil. The two ships were sent to prize courts of the United States. Some ten days later they took and burnt another merchantman with its tallow and jerked beef. Ten days later the captain of the *Ultor* was chased by an unknown ship. When it turned out to be a British armed merchantman, the fire fight that ensued led to the surrender of the *Astrea* with its fish and oil. Captain James Mathews set his prize crew aboard. Along the way, the British captured it and then a American privateer took the *Astrea*. There were other captures by Mathews and his crew in rapid secession. [4]

Of obscure background, privateer extraordinary Thomas Boyle captured prizes worth more than a half million dollars in the last half of 1812. He went on to cruise the seas and take British prizes in 1813 on his schooner *Comet*. Early in 1814 he was in command of the *Chausseur* which the people of Baltimore called their pride. And in the swift vessel, it was prove so. During most of 1814, he sailed around the British Isles in havoc for the British shippers. He communicated with London his boast that he alone was establishing a blockade of Britain. Not only was British pride tweaked, but his ventures forced insurance rates up, becoming unobtainable for ships in Boyle's yard between England and Ireland. He evaded British warships and caught almost twenty ships during the year. Then he left for the West Indies where he and his men defeated the HMS *Lawrence* because his cannon were stronger and more numerous. [5]

Thomas Boyle was a most audacious captain. His greatest feat was to "blockade" the British Isles single handedly. He had high hopes to sail off the coast of England as the English had the American coast. Of course this could not be done with one ship, but he could make the effort and make the British pay. There would be the problem of getting prizes home to America through British waters, but the effort could be made. The British were concerned enough over the possibilities that they had convoys underway in the Irish Sea for the protection of linen ships from French privateers.

Along the way, he and the crew of his *Chasseur* made the capture of a brig off the Grand Banks. Boyle took off the *Eclipse* the specie and sent the hides and furs to the United States aboard the captured ship. The *Commerce* was gained with its load of codfish. Next, he captured the sugar laden brig *Antelope* and the fish laden schooner *Fox*. When he captured the sloop *Christiana* he loaded it with all of his prisoners and sent them back to England. Now that this was done, he did not have to feed and house the British sailors on his crowded ship. There would be no danger of an uprising either which he had to guard against previously.

Boyle made various captures off the British coast and was chased by English war vessels. He began carrying it out by capturing various ships. On one of them he sent it out. All did not go well. Running into a man-of-war, which fired upon his *Chasseur*, the captain and the crew soon had their ship outdistance it. On the following day, the *Chasseur* was in trouble with four warships bearing down upon it. On September 3, 814, he ran into warships again and they freed one of his prizes. There were others to make contact with, but the American schooner privateer could outsail them all. Boyle did manage to capture others and soon had a captive cargo in the hold which was worth $100,000. With many prisoners and low on manpower, Boyle set sail for New York City.[6]

The *Wasp* was a successful raider in the Atlantic. On September 1, 1814, the captain saw four sails in the distance. He chased them for almost three hours. Captain Johnston Blakely had his vessel cut out one of the ships. By this time it was dark, but Bakeley ordered his gunners to fire. With no delay the ship surrendered. They discovered that she was the brig *Avon*. They boarded her, but a fast approaching brig loosed a broadside into the American' rigging and two more ships appeared. The *Avon* sunk and the *Wasp* left to capture several more ships, until she had thirteen merchantmen to her credit in this tour. [7]

Before the British moved on Washington and Baltimore, Cochrane received orders to mount an attack on the island in Passamaquoddy Bay and in northeastern Maine. On July 11, 1814, he set forth his amphibious force and secured Fort Sullivan and Eastport. The fort surrendered without a shot. Cochrane wanted to use this port as a base for further action. Orders were issued. British commanders were to destroy government stores and merchant shipping. Private property was to be threatened. Preparations were made in British Halifax for additional action. The British were to march on the rest of northeastern Maine. They believed that western Maine was too populous and too well defended. This was a mistaken belief. It worked to American advantages.

Some weeks later sixteen British ships set out for Maine. A brig in the advance sighted the American corvette *Adams*, commanded by Captain Charles Morris. The Americans had just returned from a cruise in European waters. It was an unsuccessful raiding trip. Trouble was ahead. The American ship headed up the Penobscot seeking safety all the more important because it had stuck a ledge on the way in. At Hampden he dismantled the ship, seeking information on its damage. The British sent a small army after them.

Morris and the local militia commander met but were not able to cooperate with each other. Little was done for a successful defense. It was a cold and foggy morning on September 3, 1814, when the British attacked by land and by river. The British barges stayed out of cannon range while the soldiers attacked up a sloping bluff. They changed the unprotected Massachusetts militia with bayonets and routed them. Losses were minimum on both sides. The Americans escaped harm because they fled so fast. American ships were burnt and eastern Maine was British with the additional capture of Machias in a few days. Rumors and fear spread southward. The militia was called out, but the men lacked arms. Once again militia forces had failed, as they had done so often in the War of 1812. [8]

In the lake region, for almost three weeks, the two armies, the British and the American watched each other until on July 25, 1814, they set out to fight. The British on the heights soon saw Scott lead his 1st American brigade against them through the strip of woods. While Winfield Scott fought, Thomas S. Jesup with his new rank of lieutenant colonel led his troops around the ends of the battlefield to attack the British in back. Jesup saw a great opportunity there to cut the British communication link. His men captured British general Rial and other British officers.

Scott's men were hard pressed in their battle with the whole British army until when towards sunset, General Eleazar Ripley brought his second brigade in to rush up the heights. Ripley asked Colonel Miller of the 21st if he could take the battery of artillery at the top of the eminence. Miller replied, "I can try, sir." The colonel and his men stormed the hill and killed the resisting British artillerists. Meanwhile, Ripley and his men drove the British infantry from their positions. In the dark both sides fought on stubbornly until exhausted. The fighting ended near midnight. The victory was the American. [9]

Former slave owner Edward Coles, private secretary to Madison, wrote Thomas Jefferson on July 31st on the subject of slavery in the midst of this war. This interlude of interest for Coles was in addition to his work for the Administration for the war. The war was not the only thing discussed in America in these years. In frank terms, Coles wrote that his "object is to entreat and beseech you to extend your knowledge and influence in devising and getting into operation some plan for the gradual emancipation of slavery." His concern for the slaves was strong. Coles felt that as one of the founding fathers, Jefferson had a better chance to effect than succeeding statesmen. Coles wrote that "in the calm of this retirement you might, most beneficially to society, and with much addition to your own fame, avail yourself of that love and confidence to put into complete practice those hallowed principles contained in that renown Declaration, of which you were the immortal author, and on which we founded our right to resist oppression and establish our freedom and independence." Actually Jefferson was the main and not the only author of the Declaration of Independence.

Jefferson replied that Coles' ideas were also his own. The question was of what "method by which this difficult work is to be effected, if permitted to be done by ourselves, I have seen no proposition so expedient on the whole, as that of emancipation of those born after a given date, and of their education and expatriation at a proper age. this would give time for a gradual extinction of that species of labor and substitution of another, and lessen the severity of the shock which an operation so fundamental cannot

The Difficult War: The Era of the War of 1812

fail to produce." He would not favor emancipation all at once and retaining them in this country.

He wanted to colonize the black in Africa as was the prevailing idea of those who wanted to free the slaves in the years ahead until the Abolitionists took hold of the issue late in the next decade. At this time African Americans were serving in the war, particularly in the navy and privateers where large numbers were enlisted as sailors. The colonization movement which was getting its beginning with Jefferson would colonize them in Africa. Most free African Americans were going to want to stay in the United States, their home. [10]

In August of 1814, a British invasion fleet was seen off Sandy Hook near New York City. The news spread throughout the city. Major DeWitt Clinton quickly acted. He began to organized the defenses of the city. The people thought back to General William Howe's invasion during the Revolutionary War. They did not wish another occupation. Volunteers from New Jersey joined the thousands of New Yorkers to build fortifications. Various groups vied with each other in friendly competition in doing the work.

Tammany Hall and the Freemasons tried to see who could build the best and strongest ramparts along Brooklyn Heights. Columbia College's entire student body worked on defenses located at 123rd Street. A wealthy Clinton gave the battery. The mayor told them that let us die fighting in the last ditch. This would be better than cowardly surrender of their loved and delightful city. It was not until the coming November that it was clear that there would be no attack. Men returned to their college and occupations, leaving the fortifications to be removed by later workmen in other times. [11]

At Fort Erie to the west, Major Ludowick Morgan deduced from observations that the British were preparing an attack. He secretly had his men build fortifications during the night along the south bank of Conjocta Creek. He then had the ties to the bridge removed. On the next morning pickets told Morgan that the British were advancing upon him. The British reached the bridge and British Colonel John G. P. Tucker ordered his men to replace the ties. While they were doing this, Morgan blew his whistle and his men opened fire. The British panicked but sought shelter behind trees to fire back. The firing stopped. Then the British returned to the bridge but were repulsed for the second time.

Tucker tried turning the American flank, but Morgan was ready there too and fired. The British drew back and shortly Tucker decided to give up and return to Canada. This action safeguarded the American Fort Erie and Buffalo and secured New York against a British campaign. Morgan was to be killed ten days after this August 3rd victory in a minor skirmish. [12]

On August 8, 1814, the American and British commissioners opened up their peace talks at Ghent. The determined British presented their demands as non-negotiable. They said they wanted an Indian buffer state formed in American territory north of the Ohio. There was a necessity for adjustments of the border in Britain's favor and demilitarization of the Great Lakes. New England should give up its fishing rights in Canadian waters. The first was outrageous for Adams and his fellows. Adjustments and a peaceful border were not so hard. But Adams would not give up fishing rights for his section nor would Henry Clay allow the British free navigation of the Mississippi for a bargaining counter.

The British commissioners kept up their insistence on their proposals. They would not budge and Adams was annoyed and pessimistic. This was a waste of time. He became more testy when he saw the other American commissioners led by Clay spend a lot of time playing cards, smoking, drinking, and staying up late. The dour Adams did not approve. This was in keeping with Adams' views as exemplified by both John and John Quincy Adams. They were the usual Puritans of New England.

The British Government noticed that no progress was being made by their negotiators and that they had not made compromises. They were as angered as Adams and his commissioners. They sent over word on this and their men at Ghent lost some of their arrogance and things went smoother. Adams noticed this and recognized what had happened. This gave him new spirit in the conversations. He was aided also by Gallatin who kept Adams and Clay from internal fights. However, Adams was to have other troubles with his colleagues.

Clay and the others believed that the British would never agree to peace unless the were given large chunks of Maine. The also felt that Canadian security was all important to England. This is interesting since in the early months of the war, Clay had been hell-bent to conquer Canada. Now he was concerned for British interest in keeping Canada strong and British. Clay had lost some of his fire. Adams was wisely stubborn and the British gave in on this issue. The British also backed down on the Indians state they wanted on the frontier. For his part Madison dropped the issue of impressment. Now that the war in Europe was ending, there was no need for an American victory on impressment. It was a dying issue.

More negotiations were underway in Ghent especially due to British setbacks at Vienna. The Russian czar and Prussian king had formed a diplomatic alliance and this encouraged Castlereagh to make more moves for a peace with the United States. Diplomats at the Vienna Congress were jeopardizing a peace settlement in Europe. Britain suddenly needed American friendship. This led to final agreements and the Treaty of Ghent was signed on December 14, 1814. Gallatin and Clay then reached trade settlements with the British. Peace was established. But we have gotten ahead of the story. More fighting had taken place and was to take place. [13]

Under orders, Sir Peter Parker tried a raid into the interior of Maryland. Intelligence brought word that 200 militiamen were camped near Chestertown. Late the night of August 30, 1814, Parker led a contingent ashore and marched forth. Militia commander Colonel Philip Reed was alerted and stationed a skirmish line in the pathway. He hid most of his men beyond a rise of ground awaiting with his trap. The British were confident when they met the fire of the Americans and the later then retreated without further opposition. The marched down the road, feeling secure in their strength and success, when the rest of the patriot force attacked them. Parker was mortally wounded and bled to death before his men could get him back to the ship.

With the loss of their leader, the British decided to withdraw. What they did not know was that the opponents were running out of ammunition and would have had to retreat. The Battle of Caulk's Field stopped the British, but the only lasting effect was that sad loss of the promising officer Parker. The rifleman who had killed him had won the battle for his people. [14]

One of the three major thrusts of the British military in 1814 was along Lake Champlain with the goal of splitting the Union into two and encouraging the New England states to succeed. They did not wish to make Burognye mistake of a broken communication line, so the British took the time to strength the flotilla and move the troops southward. However, when Governor General Sir George Prevost took his time, London put pressure upon him to act. Therefore, in August of 1814, he crossed the border

The Difficult War: The Era of the War of 1812

with optimistic veterans of the war in Europe. His superiors were sure of their strategy and troops.

An invasion from the north was expected in the summer of 1814 and the Americans had few resources. Brigadier General Alexander Macomb was given 1,500 regulars and 3,000 militia and volunteers. Lieutenant Thomas Macdonough was ordered to build his own fleet on Lake Champlain. Although times seemed dreary, Macdonough was optimistic remembering Benedict Arnold's success at Valcour Bay, which set back the British timetable a full year. Since the circumstances were the same, Macdonough set about with hope.

Carpenters, shipwrights, and craftsmen were gathered from New York, Vermont, and Connecticut. They worked very hard that summer and produced two ships, two schooners, and ten galleys. Things progressed so fast and well with the enthusiastic lieutenant in command that Macdonough was promoted to Master Commandant and called commodore.

When the British moved forward they were confronted by Thomas Macdonough's comparable fleet, constructed by Noah and Adam Brown at Vergennes, Vermont. They were the same contractors who had built Perry's ships. The English excelled in long-range gunnery while the Americans were superior in short-range guns. With the British needing a quick victory, Macdonough decided upon a defensive. Using the terrain of Plattsburg Bay and the prevailing winds to their advantage, the Americans and their commander placed their ships on a solid line at the southern end of the bay. The British would be able to maneuver in the narrows and have to close in on the Americans to the short-range advantage of the latter. He established a floating battery to defend and hold.

They had finished in time, because George Prevost left Canada, where he was governor, anchored and headed south with 14,000 men, partly from battlefields in Spain and Portugal feeling sure of a successful conquest of the northern states. Captain George Downie led his ships.

Macdonough had to think of the vastly outnumbered American army so he chose to fight in Plattsburg Bay to keep the British ships away from the American army. He set up the ships in special ways to meet the attack. In the morning the British fleet came in view. It's size depressed the Americans, but they fired prematurely at their closest rival. The American rooster crowed, seemingly in response. The Americans had high laughter over that. This broke the tension and American went with cheerful hearts to their guns.

Downie gave orders for his ships to turn the two ends, but Macdonough had stationed his *Eagle* so close to shore that the British ships could not get by. The British *Chubb* was soon cripple by a broadside from the American *Eagle* and was captured. In a fight between the schooner *Eagle* and the two flagships Captain Downie was killed. The battle went on.

The ship *Saratoga* had decks filled with the bodies of dead sailors and some would be in trouble, when Macdonough tired to swing the ship as prepared the night before. With unnecessary sailors and soldiers below, the *Saragota* was turned by bearing down on the kedge anchor cable. Soon afterwards more British ships surrendered. The victory was the American's. Only the British galleys escaped. When Prevost heard of the American success, he fled, leaving most of his supplies behind. For this he was slated to a court-martial, but he died before his trial. [15]

---

[1]Black Hawk, *Autobiography*, pp. 77-79. Quote on p. 78.

[2]Seiken, Jeff, "Macdonough, Thomas," Heidler & Heidler, *Encyclopedia*, pp. 311-312.

[3]Coggeshall, *History*, pp. 219-221.

[4]Cranwell & Crane, *Men of Marque*, pp. 198-208.

[5]Heidler, Jeanne T. and Heidler, David S., "Boyle, Thomas," Heidler & Heidler, *Encyclopedia*, p. 61.

[6]Cranwell & Crane, *Men of Marque*, pp. 235-246.

[7]Bunker, Robert J., "Wasp Versus Avon," Heidler & Heidler, *Encyclopedia*, p. 546.

[8]Lohnes in *Maine Historical Quarterly* (1975). pp. 10-15.

[9]*Niles' Weekly Register*, August 29, 1829, p. 10.

[10]Washburne, E. B., *Sketch of Edward Coles, Second Governor of Illinois and of the Slavery Struggle of 1823-4*, Janson, McClure, 1882, Reprint, New York: Negro Universities Press, 1969, pp. 21-24. Quotes on pp. 21-28, 26.

[11]Lankevich, George J. & Furer, Howard B., *A Brief History of New York City*, Port Washington, NY: Associated Faculty Press, 1984, pp. 75-76.

[12]Fredriksen, John C., "Conjocta Creek, Battle of," Heidler & Heidler, *Encyclopedia*, p. 122.

[13]Heidler, Jeanne and Heidler, David S., "Adams, John Quincy," Heidler & Heidler, *Encyclopedia*, pp. 3-4.

[14]Heidler, Jeanne and Heidler, David S, "Caulk's Field, Battle of," Heidler & Heidler, Encyclopedia, pp. 87-88.

[15]Keller, Allan, "The Battle of Lake Champlain," *American History Illustrated*, XII No. 9 (January 1978), pp. 4-9, 47-48; Perkins, B., *Castlereagh and Adams*, 1964, pp. 36-37; Fischer, William E., Jr., "Lake Champlain, Battle of," Heidler & Heidler, *Encyclopedia*, pp. 288-290.

CHAPTER XXVIII

MORE FIGHTING

Alexander Macomb, who had considerable military experience of the placid kind, was in charge of Plattsburg on Lake Champlain. British General Sir George Prevost led a large force of soldiers which included veterans of Wellington's Peninsula Campaign toward Plattsburg in conjunction with the British fleet. Knowing his army was outnumbered two to one, Macomb made haste to get his defenses in order. He tried unsuccessfully to delay the advance by skirmishing the British. This was a discomfort, but had no result. So he sent a force out to meet the British, which could not match the British in force, but did manage a rearguard action back to Plattsburg. By this time, Prevost knew that he was faced with a fighter.

Prevost reached the river and stopped. He was awaiting the rest of his artillery and troops. For five days, the Americans watched the British establish their batteries. On the night of September 9th, Macomb once again displayed his fighting spirit. His raid which spiked one British cannon returned safety to him. He called up the militia. One sizable Vermont unit arrived. All troops were needed.

The British lake and land offensive was shortly on, and on September 11, 1814, Prevost ordered his men against the two bridges to Plattsburg. The Americans held one bridge but the second was crossed by British troops. Then came news that the British fleet had been defeated, so fearful that his supply lines would now be threatened by the militia, Prevost withdrew. For his valor, Macomb was promoted to major general and many years later became commanding general of the army. [1]

When the British had decided to sever New England away from the United States, they were not very original. The route they had to take was the same, that was essential, but the plans were unchanged too except for the absence of a British military force in New York City which had not operated anyway in 1777. That was their mistake. To succeed it had to be a two pronged attack. Also it acted with the idea that the New England states would revolt. Their intelligence was faulty too. The people of New England was not as greatly pro-British as they thought. They did not wish to rejoin Britain; they merely wished the war to be over. They were anti-Virginian. British planners thought they would quickly rejoin the British empire. This was wrong. Those with secessionist sentiments wanted an independent republic for New England. It was their freedom they wished. New Englanders were much of the same mold and different in many respects from the states from New York to Louisiana as the Southerners and militia state were from each other.

The resurrected plan was less potent than it had been in 1777 since there was no base for the southern pincer force in New York City. The plan had been for one invading army to come down from the north from Montreal to Albany and from their southward or eastward as circumstances might dictate. There was behind the strategy, a need for warm water ports,, a better land outlet from Montreal and inland areas. They desired a strip of Maine coastal outlets or better still possession of Boston as a harbor.

There had been words of British concentrations in America. New York newspapers reported what they had learned from London newspapers about the sending and arrival of British forces in Canada. Madison himself withdrew General George Izard from his position in parts of the New York frontier necessary for the prevention of British success elsewhere. Izard protested his orders to move to Sackett's Harbor, saying this would make for a weak defense which would lead in three days to their fall to the British. He was needed where he was. Izard had reason to believe that the British had a superior force which threatened Lake Champlain. He protested on August 11th and 20th.

The American left Champlain on August 29, 1814, and the British immediately moved in. Vermont's people responded vigorously. One Vermont editor wrote that Madison must consider their people as being unworthy of his protection. They just take care of themselves with high spirit and resolve. The British took the vexations of the Americans as proof that the Americans were as ready to let the British move where they wished in the United States. Once again the British were hoping more than they were thinking.

New England benefited greatly from the war financially, although their shipping interest were damaged so overwhelmingly. the national government relied upon supplies of manufacture goods made in this region. Because the banks there were conservative, financial realism prevailed and because money flowed into New England, they prospered despite the loss of trade with Europe. The rest of the specie reserves of the nation found their way into the region. During the war years, gold and silver coins in New England banks increased from $1.5 million to $3.5 million at a time when Massachusetts bank notes were increased from $1.4 million to $2.7 million. Manufactures and banks benefited enormously. The banks of New England could still give specie for any one wishing it in exchange for notes at a time when all banks outside the region suspended specie payments in August of 1814. [2]

With the Creeks soundly defeated, it was time for a peace treaty. Since the boundaries between the Cherokees and the Creeks were unsettled, the Cherokee had an important interest in the treaty which would draw Creek boundaries. The Cherokees had occupied for one half of a century the lands along the northern bank of the Coosa River down to Will's Creek between Turkey Town and Fort Strothers in northern Alabama. They were of course interested in keeping this land. During the spring of 1814, the national council of the Cherokee told Colonel Meigs to please advise the secretary of war of Cherokee interest in the peace treaty. The agent did this and the secretary wrote Andrew Jackson about the matter.

Jackson was on the way to his new command in Mobile, now a major general in the United States army. He traveled southward from the Hermitage and had reached Fort Strother when a Cherokee delegation caught up with him. Colonel Meigs was with the Cherokees. The agent, Meigs, gave Jackson a memorandum which stated that the Cherokee chiefs wished a boundary that would not leave any Cherokees in the Creek nation boundaries. It should pass below Ten Islands to the boundary with the Chickasaws. The general was impatient and requested the two tribes of Cherokee and

The Difficult War: The Era of the War of 1812

Creek to consult among themselves and decide between them where the boundary should be. He told them that the treaty convention would be held on August 10, 1814, and they could thresh out their differences then. Jackson left to complete arrangements for the treaty council and the Cherokees left for the fort, named Fort Jackson a little over three weeks later.

The council began before the tenth. At its opening Jackson spoke in the half completed fort and outlined terms. He withdrew to allow the Indians and agents to decide upon the boundary. An old method of boundary decision was to draw boundaries halfway between the distance each had advanced into the other territory. At first this was agreed, but the Creeks changed their minds. It was hot and tempers flared. Finally the two Indian nations reached a temporary agreement. The Cherokees could occupy the disputed territory until a permanent treaty was later made. The treaty was completed on the next day, the tenth, and the Americans gained twenty-three million acres of Creek land. This mounted to half of the future state of Alabama.

There was now a grave problem. Peace had been made with friendly Creeks. The hostile Creeks were still looking to the British to support them and peace was not yet made. Hostile Creeks had reached Pensacola where they were welcomed by the Spanish and supplied with arms and ammunition by the British. Soon afterwards, Jackson had won his greatest victory and word reached the Indians that peace had been made earlier in England. Creek hopes for continued encouragement from the British were lost forever in the South. [3]

Meanwhile, the rumors were strong in New Orleans that they would be invaded. People in New Orleans, Mobile, and Natchez felt sure they would be attacked and they awaited anxiously for General Andrew Jackson to force the Indians to come to the peace table and surrender. Reluctant tribes knew they were defeated and could not undertake another war. However, they could not understand why they should cede more land to land-hungry whites. The Indians lacked unity and could not be forced to unite for talks easily, so the summer had passed without war of peace. Then Jackson had his treaty with the Cherokee and Creek, the main native opponents of the whites in the South and the chiefs at least were fairly well reconciled to this. It was doubtful that the braves were satisfied with this bad peace for them. But the Cherokee were more peaceful and the Creek were moving in this direction. In Mobile and in New Orleans, small units of regulars drilled. A Pittsburgh contractor sent a fleet of barges with arms enough for five thousand soldiers. He also had ammunition and tents abroad and was allowed to trade along the way to New Orleans, where the equipment was bound. [4]

On both sides of the war, the captured privateers were subject for sale to serve as privateers for the opposite belligerents. James Caven, a merchant of the island of Barbados, purchased the *Henry Guilder* in Halifax on August 16, 1814. This ship had captured them in Halifax on August 16, 1814. This ship had captured the *Young Farmer* with a great cargo of $40,000 worth of indigo, and was taken in turn by H.M.S. *Niemen*. Caven chose the name *Sherbrooke*, the name of two brigs already. His commission was dated August 27, 1814. It was greatly undermanned, but never needed a large crew for it found no prizes in the several months before the war ended. [5]

Captain Samuel Chester Reid had an interesting encounter at Fayal in the Azores. He had sailed the privateer brig *General Armstrong* on a cruise from Sandy Hook on September 9, 1814, outsailing two British pursuit vessels. He captured a few ships before anchoring in the Fayal Roads to fill up with water. While there the British brig *Carnation* hoved into sight. The British captain would not attack in a neutral port, but he would stick to the *General Armstrong* in preparation of attacking the American at sea when he sailed. Reid continued to take on water and provisions. Reid discussed the arrival with U. S. Consul J. B. Dabney.

They looked out to sea and saw the British ships move closer to the American. Dabney thought that they would not violate Portuguese neutrality. They had never done so. Seeing signal flags on the ships, Reid moved closer to the fort. Dabney went ashore. However, when they got underway, the British captain sent four boats of men to board. They were sure of themselves until Reid ordered his men to open fire on the boats. They called out for quarters and rowed back with many men killed and wounded. Reid suffered one man killed and one man wounded. The British waited for them to attempt to escape. People came forth to watch for the expected attack in the moonlight.

The British captain set forth twelve boats, which started a shooting match. When the British marines were close, the cannons were useless, and the men were fought off with swords, pikes, pistols, and muskets. Reid's men repulsed the enemy several times. Many lives were lost. The damage was so great and the odds so large, Reid sent the wounded and dead ashore and he ordered the crew to save such of their possessions as they could. Soon after daylight, the British fired upon the Americans. Intent upon taking or destroying the American, the British began to plan to take action. Finally Reid had the ship scuttled. The *Carnation* attacked and was severely damaged.

As the *General Armstrong* was sinking, the British boarded her and managed to get off some of the supplies before the ship went to the bottom of the harbor. All this caused a delay in the schedule of the British attack there. Casualties were great on the British side, but the Americans had only two killed and seven wounded on their side. [6]

Six days before this incident, Jackson had ordered Captain William Lawrence to garrison Fort Bowyer at Mobile. He arrived to find the fort in sad condition, and he immediately set about to reconstruct the fort and prepared for an expected British advance from Pensacola. He also moved to establish a post to the dunes overlooking the fort, which could prove disastrous if occupied by the enemy. Before he could be finished, the British arrived led by Major Edward Nicholls on September 12th. The British fired with a howitzer without result and Lawrence ordered his guns to fire back, keeping the enemy at a distance. Because of this cannon work, the British were unable to sound the channel for their disembarkation.

On the 15th the British moved forward in the water. Lawrence held a council of war at which it was voted to continue the fight. Later in the afternoon, the British began firing upon the fort seriously damaging the British *Hermes* and to avoid its capture, the enemy soldier set it afire. Suddenly, there was an explosion; its magazine had caught fire.

There was a charge when the American flag was shot away and the British and Indian thought that its disappearance meant surrender. Instead Lawrence's gunners gave them grapeshot. They fled and soon the British withdrew and sailed away. The council of war was right although the British outnumbered them five to one. Months later the British again move against the fort; this time they successfully bombed the fort and Lawrence was to surrender. [7]

In desperate need of soldiers to meet an challenge in New Orleans, Jackson used Governor William C. C. Claiborne's authorization to allow African American militia units and delivered a stirring speech to the African Americans in New Orleans. Only free black landowners and slaves with the permission of their planter could join the Battalion of Free Men of Color formed by Jackson. They included second lieutenants from that race. Jackson felt that this would keep them from joining the approaching British as spies and couriers. They built defenses and took part in the battle. Afterward, however, they were not allowed to join the victory celebration, given promised bonuses or equal pay, or freedom from slavery. They had played their part and were now denied the rewards of that service. [8]

Captain Ordronaux commanded the privateer *Prince de Neufchatel* of New York City and was the most successful during the war. Her several cruises ended in great loss of from $250,000 to $300,000 to the British merchant marine, not counting the specie he took. Some seventeen warships unsuccessfully chased Ordronaux's ship. One of the adventures dealt with took place on October 11th of 1814, off Nantucket in American waters. A frigate breezed up and approached him rapidly until that same wind reached the *Prince de Neufchatel*. Soon the wind stopped, but the current pushed them toward the shore.

In the early dark the British climbed aboard the boats and rowed forth for the attack. The prize ship signaled their approach and the captain ordered all men to quarters. Ordornaux's ship fired its guns but without effect. The British sailors and marines tried to board the American ship, but were repulsed. One of the five barges were sunk. They suffered large losses. Because he had only eight men fit for duty, the captain kept the men they had made prisoner on one of he launches, instead of allowing them to live among the 37 prisoners confined below the ship. Ordronaux sent prisoners to land under a promise not to serve anyone in the war regularly exchanged. The captain proceeded to Boston that day of the 15th. [9]

On November 2, 1814, a group of Americans bought the schooner *Lee* and put Captain George Cogeshall in command. They suggested that he make short cruises from L'Orient where they were, pick up prizes on the way to Charleston, where they would load it up with a cargo of cotton for the trip back to France. He manned his ship with Americans in French ports and filled her for the trip. The particular danger of that day was that the French Government of Louis XVIII might stop the procedure for the benefit of their English friends. He took on enough stores for fifty days. They had limited arms, but they were ready for the trip when public authorities ordered them back into port. Coggleshall followed the order to take off all of his guns except one. This left him with a long 12-pounder, but he did smuggled aboard some twenty or so muskets and left the port on the 8th.

The crew fired upon an English brig. It surrendered. The American chased another ship, but it was too well armed and Coggleshall returned to his prize. The latter was boarded and sailed to the United States with a prize crew of Americans eager to get home. On the 17th, they boarded a Spanish brig upon which he placed the captain of his first prize. His second prize was an English cutter on the way to London with a cargo of wine. After taking off the cargo and valuable sails and cables, rigging, and blocks, he scuttled her on the 19th.

His lack of sufficient cannon prevented him from taking more ships to battle, but his ship was a superior sailor so he had no problem escaping the well-armed ships he encountered. They did, however, capture a ship with a cargo of fruit and a ship from which he removed guns, powder, shot, and some fruit. A squall broke the foremast twice and they missed a change of taking an English packet. Outside of Lisbon they were captured by a British frigate. This ended their adventures for the war. [10]

Madison had great need of the nation's talented to pursue the difficult war. One of those the president sought to draw on was Alexander James Dallas. This patriot Dallas had been born in Jamaica Kingston in the British West Indies on June 21, 1759. His Scots father, Dr. Robert Dallas, was a medical doctor, educated at the University of Edinburgh, the younger son of upper class parents with Scottish ancestry, traced to Baron William of Ripley in 1279. The descendants of this nobleman took their name from his fief on the Lossie River, the line separating the low lands from the high lands in Scotland.

Alexander's mother was Sarah Cormack, whose father was a colonel. Dr. Dallas took his family back to Edinburgh where Alexander received the progressive education in many subjects instead of the classical education which was the orthodox way to learn. In both there was an emphasis on languages, but English was stressed in the new curriculum of the mid-eighteenth century. In 1769, his father died. While he was able to continue his secondary education, there was no family money for the education he desired at the Inner Temple in London. Instead, Dallas worked in his uncle's mercantile house, clerking and keeping accounts for two years.

Next Dallas fell in love and married. He and Arabella Maria Smith went to Jamaica to live. Because of troubles and sickness they listened to an actor-manager named Lewis Hallam Jr. with interest when he talked of the advantages of the United States. On April 10, 1783, they embarked on a ship bound for New York City and moved to Philadelphia at once, The pair fitted in well into society. Financially, Dallas found a job clerking and keeping accounts and studied law. In Philadelphia, he made many friends in important places. Admitted to the bar, Alexander worked hard in the struggle to establish a practice. On the side, he worked as an editor of a semiweekly newspaper and then a magazine, published by William Spotswood. He filled a gap when he wrote and published a book on Pennsylvania law cases.

The day before Christmas of 1790, newly-elected Pennsylvania governor Thomas Mifflin put Dallas to work in the important position of Secretary of the Commonwealth. Mifflin's lack of administrative abilities meant that young Dallas did most of the work in a virtual partnership with the governor. In ensuing years, Mifflin drank heavily and Dallas performed even more of the high duties of Mifflin's office in the state. Dallas worked on internal improvement projects, supervised the militia, handled Indian affairs, published books on law, and when Thomas McKean became governor, advised him.

Wanting a weak central government and believing Federalists had aristocratic principles, Dallas was hostile to the Washington and Adams administrations. He worked against the Federalists from his position and, in 1792, wrote his first letter to Albert Gallatin. He played a role in turbulent Philadelphia politics. Republicans did poorly in the 1792 election, but continue organizing forming a political society. However they received a powerful blow in the Genet affair and the Whiskey Rebellion which discredited the Republican cause. The French Minister's high-handedness in the Genet episode and the rebellion in the western part of the state disgusted and frighten many citizens and the Jeffersonian Republicans lost in popularity.

They gained popular support against the pro-British Federalists when the Washington Administration made a treaty with Great Britain. Dallas seized upon the Jay Treaty issue, writing a long essay against its ratification. In their view, this treaty was not very favorable for American interests, but it prevented a war between Britain and America. In the first decade of the 19th Century, Dallas was involved with state politics and broke with the new president Jefferson by defending the judiciary. Now a conservative, he worked to put the brakes on change. From 1801 to 1814, Dallas was United States Attorney for the eastern half of the state. [11]

Major General George Izard led his troops to Fort Erie, giving Major General Jacob Brown nearly 7,000 well-equipped and trained men, the greatest body of troops the

The Difficult War: The Era of the War of 1812

Americans had had in the war. Izard and Brown disagreed over deployment. An aggressive Brown wanted an immediate advance upon the British; a cautious Izard did not want a frontal attack, but wished to lure Lieutenant General Gordon Drummond into the open and destroy him. Izard had seniority and won the argument.

On October 25, 1814, the Americans began to bombard the British and then demonstrated. Drummond would not budge. Brown was impatient and marched to Sackett's Harbor. When intelligence reached Izard that there were stores of grain at Cook's Mills, he dispatched Brigadier General Daniel Bissell with his brigade to attack the mill. This would turn the British right and force him into action. Bissell got involved in a skirmish. British troops attacked on October 19th and Bissell stood in their way. He deployed for a counter-attack. With artillery and rockets the Americans assaulted the British. They were successful against the front and British left flank. The British retreated in good order. Losses were light on both sides. The Americans then burnt the wheat. [12]

The Federalists continued to be alarmed and moved into a stronger opposition. One of their own, Timothy Pickering wrote at this time that Union was a talisman of the dominant Republicans, which its opponents dared not attack, although there were at the time those who wished to do so. Picketing was one of them; he did not fear to attack. He wanted the ship of state to run aground, because this would produce the shock he thought needed to throw the present pilots, which meant Madison and company, overboard. They needed new navigators, men who could conduct her safely to port. The Federalists still did not have a candidate to achieve this, but hoped through political pressure to pursue that aim.

The North, according to Pickering, should separate until the South agreed to a new constitution in which New England rights would be written into the compact of the states. He wrote nothing about the West, where the differences were even greater. However the then Federalist view was that the West should be lost permanently in the shuffle. Pickering had the usual negative idea of the planter class of whom their chief opponents Jefferson, Madison, and Monroe were members. They would overthrow the Virginia Dynasty and institute a equable governmental society to bring peace and values cherished by the people of New England. This was their aim and program. [13]

---

[1]Heidler, Jeanne and Heidler, David S., "Macomb, Alexander," Heidler & Heidler, *Encyclopedia*, pp. 313-314; Turner, Wesley B., "Prevost, George," Heidler & Heidler, *Encyclopedia*, p. 429.

[2]Rothbard, Murray N., *The Panic of 1819: Reactions and Policies*, New York: Columbia University Press, 1962, pp. 2-4.

[3]Wilkins, pp. 81-84.

[4]Brooks, Charles B., *The Siege of New Orleans*, Seattle: University of Washington Press, 1961, pp. 31-32.

[5]Snider, *Under the Red Jack*, pp. 207-208.

[6]Coggeshall, *History*, pp. 370-375; Langley, Harold D., "Reid, Samuel Chester." Heidler & Heidler, Encyclopedia, *p. 446; Wilkinson, Dave, "Victory at Fayal," American History Illustrated.* November 1978, pp. 11-12, 14-15, 18-19.

[7]Heidler, Jeanne T. and Heidler, David S., "Lawrence, William," Heidler & Heidler, *Encyclopedia*, pp. 296-297.

[8]Hillman, Elizabeth Lutes, "African Americans," Heidler & Heidler, *Encyclopedia*, p. 5.

[9]Coggeshall, *History*, pp. 241-244.

[10]*Ibid.*, pp. 253-262.

[11]Walters, Raymond Jr, *Alexander James Dallas: Lawyer, Politician, Financier, 1759-1817*, Philadelphia: University of Pennsylvania Press, 1943, Reprint New York: DA CPA Press, 1969, pp. 6-75, 119-159.

[12]Fredriksen, John C., "Cook's Mills, Battle of," Heidler & Heidler, *Encyclopedia*, pp. 127-128.

[13]Lynch, *Fifty Years*, p.233.

CHAPTER XXIX

NEW ORLEANS

The British had moved into West Florida to help the Indians against the United States. The Spanish governor at first reluctantly accepted British occupation but soon friction and the failure of the British troops in operations led to disenchantment. It was a violation of Spanish neutrality the governor said. This left it open for the Americans to send Jackson into West Florida. He arrived with his men before Pensacola on November 6, 1814. He had four thousand men with him. He attacked the town and marched around the town to surprise the Spanish and the British fleet at the harbor. After a number of shots were fired, Governor Manrique surrendered. The British blew up Fort Barrancas and left for Prospect Bluff, still intent on keeping the Indians supplied. Jackson moved on without attacking the British further. He had to protect New Orleans from a reported enemy attack and could deal no further with the British in West Florida. [1]

The British sought the aid of Jean Laffite, the Jewish pirate west of New Orleans. With him they might achieve success before New Orleans for Lafitte knew more about the waterways of southern Louisiana than any other man alive. His brother Pierre was also well acquainted with the territory and he also had large numbers of pirates who could fight well and assuredly. Lafitte had long been a pirate-privateer under authority of the nation of Columbia across the waters in northern South America. This gave him some legality in taking Spanish vessels at sea, but to the Americans he was a mere pirate.

The British got into touch with the Colombians, who provided a ship to guide the British into the waterway of Barataria Pass, which had to be traveled by one who knew the channel. On each side of the pass was the twin of an island, both the same size and shape. These were Grand Terre and Grand Isle. The tall trees in the two islands hid ships in the bay to the north. It was an ideal place for the pirates, where they were safe from the American government and people. They dealt in stolen goods.

Two British officers came down their gangplank and talked with Lafitte. The chief of the pirates wined and dined them in his fine mansion. They then gave him a sealed packet. Lafitte opened it and read that Lieutenant Colonel Edward Nicolls officially offered him 30,000 pounds sterling, a commission in the British navy as captain (colonel) enlistment for his Baratarians in the same. All he had to go on was to guide the British troops through the waterways leading to New Orleans to the bay. By this means they could achieve a surprise upon the Americans and take the city. Lafitte was friendly and the officers left certain that he would help in a fortnight as he feigned.

As soon as they were gone, Lafitte summoned his lieutenant Rancher to his side and delivered a message to Jean Blanque, who was highly regarded in New Orleans. Blanque received it and went to Governor William C. C. Claiborne with an Lafitte offer to serve with the patriots to repel the British whom he said were arriving to take the city. Claiborne had only to pardon Lafitte and remove the posters in the city with a reward of $500 for his pirate head. Claiborne was angry and sent forth a naval force to take Lafitte and destroy his lair. Lafitte did not resist but allowed the Americans to take his base and destroy its buildings including the mansion. The Americans took prisoners and goods and returned to the city with the loot and men.

The situation looked dangerous for the pirate chief, but soon the Americans learned from reliable sources that indeed the British were on the way to take New Orleans. Jackson had arrived and took even some Indians into his army to repel any attack. He could not expect much in the way of reinforcements and Claiborne, relenting, requesting Jackson to release the pirates and arm them for the approaching battle. Jackson did so and sent Major Michael Reynolds to Barataria to fortify it to prevent a British approach in his rear. Jackson consulted Pierre Lafitte and made arrangement for their use.

Captain Dominique Lafitte, the elder of the brothers formed three artillery companies to guard the old Spanish fort to the north of the city in case the British came that way. To Dominque's dismay, the British did not come that way, but he served a purpose of protecting that approach and some of his troops ran six miles to New Orleans to take part in the fight. Pierre was to guide a force to assault the British flank through the marsh, thus playing a major role in the battle. [2]

While Jackson was doing his best at raising troops and preparing to defend New Orleans, Madison had his problems. Volunteers were not enough. With this problem of finding enough troops for the war effort before him, Madison had Monroe draw up a plan for a draft. Clay spent hours in discussion, and then in November of 1814 presented their idea to Congress. They would organize militia units in groups of 100 men aged 18 to 25. Out of each group would be selected four men for actual service. When necessary they would be replaced. Substitutes were allowed. Debate was acrimonious. Senator David Daggett of Connecticut argued that the country should not "compel any man to become a soldier for life, during a war, or for any fixed time." Senator Christopher Gore of Massachusetts said that such a draft was a step on the road to conscription. Senator Jeremiah Mason of New Hampshire noted that the constitution would not have been adopted by a single state if this construction had been known at the time. But these gentlemen were opposed to the war.

The majority wanted the bill. The bill passed the Senate. In the House, Daniel Webster delivered a strong speech against the plan. This had great effect. Morris S. Miller followed up and help defeat it in the House. The Hartford Convention delegates said that their states would retain control of their militia. Militias could be used only in case of actual invasion or insurrection. A convention state summed up their sentiments in saying that it was rank depotism to take men from their homes and make them fight in a war which they did not want. It was just this kind of statement that proved the death kell of a dying Federalist party. [3]

Needing men for the wars, New York's assembly passed a law for the raising of two regiments of African American soldier. These soldiers were to receive the same pay as the rest. It provided that slave who enlisted with owner' permission were to receive their freedom at the end of the war. They served ably. In Philadelphia, some 2,500 African American citizens worked on defenses voluntarily when called upon to do so. African Americans were raised for duty on American ships during the war. [4]

Britishers did not understand the Americans and did not care to. Most Britons "refused to recognize the American people as all of them wished to cripple their proud adversary. They believed that the Americans must submit to strong British demands, must pay for their 1812 war declaration, and give up territory. They feared America would become a rival in agriculture, commerce, naval force, and industry. Britons wanted boundary changes and to exclude them from the Great Lakes with a permanent Indian state in the Old Northwest. They should, the British felt, cede to Britain New Orleans and the privilege to navigate the Mississippi. Americans must recognize British right of search. In short the British wished for revenge.

The Earl of Liverpool and his colleagues were less hostile with a desire for peace and asked only reciprocal security of their mutual essential interests, he told a visiting American. Britain's leaders were well aware that they should not ride shod over the enemy. It would cost too much in the first place adding a tremendous debt beyond the L 86 million which was made necessary, in the British view, by the war against Napoleon. In the first place they realized that they could not be sure of military success and there were European rivalries to deal with. Their allies might decide to support the Americans and then where would they be? Government leaders, in short, wanted peace on both sides of the Atlantic. They were willing to compromise in due time.

Britain's negotiators wished to talk about the Indian question. They could not abandon their Indian allies. America's envoys at Ghent knew that they could not accept a treaty which would not leave the Americans to acquire land from the Indians. Land hungry Americans would not accept the idea of a permanent preserve for Indians in the Old Northwest. The American commissioners were dismayed. British opinion would not accept any stark betrayal of the tribes. They were honor bound not to abandon the natives. Meanwhile, in the United States, some northern tribes had made peace and others worked to fight for the Americans and be on the winning side as the best chance to preserve their existence. Finally the British abandoned the barrier-state idea when the Americans would not give way. Soon, the Americans at Ghent informed the British that the Indians were being won over to the United States side.

The corner was turned when bad news reach Britain. The people of the island nation learned that Americans had repulsed and killed General Robert Ross and defeated and maimed the British expedition before Baltimore. Not only did that victory save the city, but it played a role in forcing peace. Also, they learned that the much hoped for victory in the Lake Champlain area had failed. Sir George Prevost had marched southward, reaching only a limited opposition until American General Alexander Macomb blocked the way with a much smaller, a quarter his size, army. Then on a Sunday morning on September 11, 1814, as we have seen, Thomas Macdonough defeated the British squadron on Lake Champlain with an American flotilla. With this defeat, Sir George had to retreat back to Canada since his line of communications was broken. However this did not repeat Johnny Burgoyne's surrender.

These events broke the back of British negotiations. Suddenly, the people had lost their enthusiasm. Meanwhile, in Europe the threat of war finished the job. British negotiators tried to get their way on the peace treaty after this, but it was probably a brave front and it merely delayed the achievement of peace. In the weeks ahead, the British gave up the Indian settlement and the Americans that of impressment. The latter was no longer necessary. British envoys to the work at Ghent soon agreed to accept the situation as it was at the beginning of the war concerning the boundary of Canada, the Mississippi, and the fisheries. Unknowing to the participants there were to be no more wars between Great Britain and the United States. [5]

Andrew Jackson arrived in New Orleans. It was the first day of December of 1814. The people of that commercial city had looked forward to his arrival, but they presented him with some turmoil. Governor William C. C. Claiborne was eager as usual to burden the respected general with his problems. One of the governor's chief complaints was that the Louisiana legislature concentrated on debates, concerned with what small expenditures would be supplied by which government, national, state, or municipal. Legislators felt he was unfair, since they had a committee which brought in many muskets from donors and had provided Jackson with plenty of money for fortifications through Claiborne. In all of this the people looked to Jackson for leadership qualities from the entire Southwest.

His first step was to be briefed. Four political, military men of the vicinity were there as well as two officers of Jackson's staff. They told him that there were many routes to New Orleans. Since this was so, an adequate defense must be flexible. Governor Claiborne told him what he had done in stationing mobile units in the city and on the river. Naval Commander Daniel T. Patterson told of the inadequacy of his force. The engineer reported and Edward Livingston said everyone was eager to defend their city. After the briefing was over, Jackson began his work by reviewing uniformed companies. He educated himself by the inspection of the area. People were impressed by his activity and the invasion fleet got closer. It soared almost in flight across the seas. The lead ship reached the Louisiana coast on December 8th. Jackson did not have much time left.

The Creek War required the general to be more aggressive and at Mobile he had turned a defensive card into an offensive pack by driving the intruder back at Pensacola. Now, New Orleans was even more defensive. The main defense on the river was Fort St. Philip. Because it was a slow turn of the river, the fort could command the river well downstream. Further, to the south and east were bayous making it difficult for the enemy to get near the fort. Jackson ordered his men to demolish the wooden barracks so that they could not be set afire. In addition he ordered new batteries to be constructed and reinforced. Jackson planned a series of fortifications upriver from Fort St. Philip. Because it was the idle season for the plantation slaves, Jackson was able to gain their hands in working on batteries and forts. The general accepted the work of Jean Lafitte's pirates and a battalion of Choctow Indians to fight the British who had gathered off the coast. He accepted also a battalion of freed African Americans, refugees from Dominica.

The British landed to invade America at New Orleans and to advance up the river. The advance troops of the British force moved to within some miles below the city. There were sixteen hundred of them. Jackson sent his two ships out. One stationed itself on the opposite bank where he could lay an infiltrated sweep against the side of the enemy force.

At New Orleans the Americans were busy; below the city the British had landed, sure of victory. Jackson sent out Felciana dragoons to search out the enemy. Their approach of scouting was seen by the British pickets who hid and fired. They killed an horse, but the rider escape. The sureness of the British vanquished when they heard the gunfire and scurried to find their places in battle. Fear followed due to the confusion, but when they learned it was only a squad of five dragoons they returned to earlier feelings. They felt that Americans never attacked. In this they did not know their history. That was not the only thing they did not learn. Returning to the merriment, they did not learn the panic of the few minutes that they had to prepare themselves for action, as they relaxed.

Jackson decided that now was the time to attack. There was no reason to delay. He ordered Patterson to fire the guns of the *Caroline* at 7:30 and the army to attack upon his signal. Deploying his men, he ordered the march to begin toward the British. The American ship approached the bank of the river and a few British soldiers fired away. It was now time, and the vessel fired at will. British men with arms in their hands soon sought cover behind the levies. Before they could organize, they were attacked by American troops. The pickets formed for battle and fell back, pressed for space before the American onslaught. American troops were making progress in the battle, pressing forth and their marksmanship was causing havoc.

At this point a heavy fog appeared upon the field. There was smoke and darkness also. Soldiers became confused, unable to distinguish friend from foe. One squad of Britishers however was able to attack Jackson's guns on a road, but Jackson urged on his men to drive the English out. The artillerymen were now safe. However, to be sure, they hauled the cannon back. On other parts of the battlefield, confusion enabled both adversaries to take captives by chance and boldness. Expecting that the British would be reinforced and satisfied with the evening's work, Jackson ordered his troops to withdraw and make camp. During the early morning he decided to maintain a defense later the same day. The American had a sense of confidence, having prevailed so well against the British Peninsular heroes, but in order that they should not let down their guard and to prepare for a defense, Jackson had them digging in, making fortifications.

The people of New Orleans were feeling good about the previous days' action. They had many heroes to laud from Jackson down to the foot soldier. Pride swelled up in the people. There were practical considerations also. Wounded soldiers, both American and British found their way into temporary hospital. The Ursline nuns opened their convent to the wounded, as did several Creole's their homes and the men were well cared for. New Orleans women provided lint, linen, wine, and provisions for men in the various hospitals. The British troops were shot up and retreated. Jackson withdrew to the city. British losses were high.

Soon within a battle of a few hours, Admiral Sir Alexander Cochrane destroyed the little lake fleet of the Americans. Both sides suffered heavy casualties. In time, news of the British success reached Jackson. The general and the commander, Andrew Jackson and Daniel T. Patterson looked at the maps and realized that they could not hamper British troops nor spy upon their movements. Jackson sent out orders to Captain Newman to defend the pass into Lake Pontchartain to the last man and to Captain John D. Henley to construct a couple of new batteries at Fort St. John on the entrance to the bayou. [6]

Jackson had set up his headquarters in New Orleans with a throng of fearful well wishers. People there did not act as through they were under siege, but Jackson was able to galvanize the town and its citizens. He gave rapid-fire orders to prepare a defense. He strengthened the forts at the mouth of the river and had engineers and workmen establish obstacles with the militia downriver. Jackson had Commodore Patterson keep two vessels on the Mississippi, a wise decision. He reviewed the volunteer battalion and inspected the forts.

British Admiral Cochrane was also busy planning to destroy Lieutenant Jones' five gunboats, guarding the approach to Lake Borgne. He lowered barges and launches with a thousand seamen and marines. They rowed to the lake and the gunships. They threatened Jones but a strong incoming tide enabled Jones to withdraw. The British came on, and a battle began on December 14th. In fierce fighting they boarded their five small ships and captured them, but Jones had succeeded in delaying the British. Jackson was notified, and he immediately acted to put New Orleans under martial law. The British found by reconnaissance an unguarded avenue to within sight of the city. [7]

Meanwhile, a Spanish agent in Louisiana, loyal to his king, wrote to Madrid on December 7, 1814, still hoping that a Spanish army would reconquer Louisiana. He wrote that at the moment the Americans received the province and early when they thought they would foster revolution in Hispanic America, he had dedicate himself to their enmity. "I knew much about those men, and those particularly who were employed by their government revealed their ambitious designs with no attempt at concealment whatever. They sent spies by way of Nachitoches, on the frontiers of the Internal Provinces of New Spain, to see whether by that means they might incite an insurrection, which did not delay in breaking out."

De Clout had already forwarded some of the American plans and of the aid they had given Jose Bernardo Gutierrez de Lara, Dr. John Hamilton Robinson (part of the Zebulon Pike expedition) and others as spies and revolutionaries. Now there was a new plan afoot. He wrote about it as follows: "in the year 1812, when Louisiana was declared an independent state, its government abandoned caution and showed itself hostile toward the possessions of His Catholic Majesty. The rebellious spirit had greatly increased among the partisans of independence. Those in Hispanic America conspirators had openly formed the intent of aiding the rebels. I knew that their plan was to advance to Natchitoches with six thousand men under the pretext that the state was being threatened; another two thousand were to sail from the Isle of Barataria for the Trinity River, whence they were to join the big army in San Antonio de Bexar." French agents were also involved in the plans, plotting against the Americans and Spanish alike. They wanted to elect in Louisiana men of their choice in a desire to win Louisiana back for France, which had usurped it from Spain and sold it to the United States a decade earlier.

The Spanish agent also noted that "as long as Louisiana belonged to the United States, there would always be disturbances in New Spain (Mexico). And worst if Napoleon's agents had been able to get men of their own choice elected, there would be French interference in Hispanic America which they had feared for some years now. He then gave information on Spanish enemies and military information for an invasion by Spanish soldiers. [8]

At New Orleans, Master Commandant Daniel Todd Patterson directed the operation of many vessels. Because he was certain of a British advance upon New Orleans, Patterson declined a Jackson suggestion that he go to Mobile. Instead of going, he placed his vessels in a formation of defense. He must buy time for Jackson to collect and arrange his troops. British delay was necessary. He decided that the British would adopt the Lake Borgne route and not by way of Mobile. His subordinate Lieutenant Thomas Catesby Jones was sent to the lake with five of his six gunboats.

Cochrane arranged his fleet near Cat Island and then set out his troops in smaller draft craft from the transports. British gun brigs escorted them into Lake Borne. Jones sighted the boats and since the water was low because of winds, he had his men throw overboard much weight in supplies. Shortly an American ship beat back British boats. Next on the next day, the British took an American vessel. When the British came to within range, the American ships opened fire, but the targets were so small little damage was done them. The Americans beat back several attacks easy enough. The Americans lost vessels but gained the vital time. Losses were light on both sides. Jones gave way. He had succeeded in his function against odds. [9]

The Difficult War: The Era of the War of 1812   241

On Christmas Eve on the morning the British had moved up to have Jackson's army confront them. The American vessels bombarded the invading encampment. Jackson, ill and determined, worked to establish as strong defense behind the Rodriquez Canal. He placed the troops with care, sending for more men and more entrenching tools.

The Americans were set to digging breastworks soon after the day of the battle. General Andrew Jackson was eager to inspect the works on Christmas day. He went to the line three times that holiday. There was a great mound of earth along a line from the river bank almost to the swamp. A few cotton bales were used in the works. It was believed that the cotton would prevent the passage of bullets even better than earth. When citizens came downriver to help with their shovels, Jackson sent them to build another breastwork two miles closer to the city than the line at Rodriquez' Canal. Planters sent their slaves to work digging.

American ships, two in number, had pounded the British for days and now the enemy was to get its revenge. English artillerymen heated shot in their furnace on the morning of December 27th. When it was light enough, they dropped the red hot cannon balls on the American schooner and set it afire. Other shells reached the powder filled cabin. In danger of sinking, the vessel was ablaze. Captain John D. Henley ordered his men to abandon ship. They rowed away for their lines. The *Caroline*, exploded. The *Louisiana* reached safety however. It was another withdrawal for the Americans in this battle for New Orleans.

Time was not to stand still. The British generals were eager for an advance against the American lines and a conquest of New Orleans. British bugles sounded on the morning of the 28th, awakening the men and calling them to arms. They hurried forth and were soon inspected by their generals. As soon as they were marching their early morning silence turned into banner. The American pickets fired and withdrew with word of the attack. Major General Edward M. Pakenham halted his men to allow more light and bring up the artillery. This gave the Americans time to get ready for battle behind their breastworks and ready their cannon. General Jackson rode up and encouraged his men who were in good cheer.

On December 28th, the British commander Pakenham advanced on the millrace that was called the Rodriquez Canal. British Major General John Keane marched his column near the American defenses. There was a cannon duel. The cannon shot of the *Louisiana* killed men at the head of the British advance. Keane was surprised at its strength. He ordered his men to drop and find cover. In reply Dickson's rocket teams launched their rockets but they damaged little. On Keane's right (east), Major General Samuel Gibbs also ordered his men to take cover. The latter found a large ditch to shelter them. Some fired back, but they were too far away to hurt anyone. Pakenham's artillery was unloosed upon the American line and the ship.

The Louisiana found the range of the British cannon, and ripped into the artillerymen of their howitzer and then the weapon itself. An artillery sergeant was decapitated while the artillerymen found cover. A British assault was repelled to plan for another attempt. Many hours later the British fired their cannon on the Americans of New Years Day 1815. British Lieutenant Rennie made an advance but he was not supported by the British army and withdrew. Then there was silence when the enemy artillery ran out of ammunition.

In answer to Jackson's call for militia reinforcements, Kentucky militia Brigadier General John Adair raised a force to march to New Orleans. He and his men arrived there on January 2, 1815. Because he had left Kentucky so suddenly he did not have arms for half of his 700 man unit. It was up to Jackson to do what he could to gather arms. It might have been because of their poor arms or to the fact that they arrived late or both, but they were put into the reserve. Adair was born in South Carolina, and moved to Kentucky in 1776. He played a role in the Indian wars and the state's politics. However his involvement with Burr, hurt him politically until he served as aide to Isaac Shelby at the Battle of the Thames and came to help Jackson. Eventually his presence at New Orleans was to enable him to run for governor and serve four years in that office. He did not retire but later was a member of the House of Representatives for one term.

By the end of December, both British and Americans knew the weak point in the American fortification lines. The British observed that the breastworks were weak near their left or east end next to the swamp. Pakenham was certain that he could take advantage of this in his next attack by moving around the end at the British right or east. Admiral Cochrane would not move the British army to the right or west bank, saying that their goal should be to eliminate the breastworks and not bypass it. This was a mistake on the admiral's part. He thought that his action was needed to bring up enough guns from the fleet in three days to destroy the works. Pakenham agreed to this plan.

Meanwhile, well aware of the problem, Jackson ordered his men to extend the works into the swamp to prevent a flank attack. Jackson was the better general. It could be done, the Americans learned, by stacking two long rows of logs and filling them with swamp mud. They got a clear view by clearing the underbrush for thirty or forty yards in front. The days were passed by making other rows of fortifications in back of the front lines to fall back on if needed. Jackson placed the 1st Louisiana as a watch on the swamp to give alarm of any flank attack.

Time passed until Pakenham could delay the battle no longer. He directed his army in an attack. When everything was ready on both sides, there was an artillery duel. Both sides suffered much damage. Shot hitting the cotton bales on the earthworks started fires and others blew up two caissons loaded with one hundred rounds; they exploded. Jackson's troops sought shelter and then returned to push the bales off the mound. Smoke continued to issue forth from the bales and Humphrey's artillerymen could not see to aim. Finally soldiers pushed them into the Mississippi and the cannoneers resumed their fire. Jackson ordered the firing to stop. About this time it began to rain.

The British began their main attack on January 8, 1815, while the Americans watched from their earthworks, ready and awaiting their orders. They were ranged in long lines. Opposite Carroll's position there was a concentration at this deepest in the line. Jackson came up to William Carroll of Tennessee and told him that the enemy was close enough to fire at and Carroll gave his men the order to fire and the rifle battle began.

American firepower began to mow down the advancing British and some sergeants ordered their men to find cover. Others followed their example. The British 93rd and 95th marched forward despite the multitude of losses. Colonel William Thornton led his men on the opposite bank of the Mississippi. He and his men were behind schedule and they moved rapidly. The American artillery had the advantage of the duel because the British were in the open. With more losses the 95th broke and the men hit the ground for safety. British soldiers in the columns of the 93rd, behind them saw this and laid down too.

British soldiers hurried forth in the face of fire from the earthworks. Volley after volley slammed into their ranks. Some were carrying ladders to provide the means to climb the earthworks. In one place they made it to the top only to fall from musket fire. In this battle it was the British who were taking the heavy casualties. Few Americans were hit. There were those English who fell into the canal. Others found shelter against the south side of the breastworks or in the ditches. It was a grim slaughter for the British and a number of the redcoats retreated. Most continued to attack, but it must have been clear that they could not achieve victory. Indeed there was a certain amount of confusion and more British soldiers retreated.

However, on the opposite bank, Thornton was the pursuer. When he and his Britishers came upon the 170 Kentuckians at Mayhew, they were up against stern stuff. Unfortunately David B. Morgan in the rear panicked and ordered a retreat. The Kentuckians withdrew and Captain Arnaud, whom Thornton had followed and who wished to make a safe stand, fled. About this time, Jackson and Carroll were watching the slaughter. Mounted on horseback, Carroll remarked: "Magnificent, is it not General?" Jackson replied: "Yes, its' magnificent. But it isn't war." It was however the end for the British commander. A shot downed General Parkenham and he died on the battlefield.

Across the river, once again, Thornton was achieving success. When General Morgan set the Kentuckians and Louisiana troops to meet Thorton, they deserted him after their first volley. Morgan tried to get the fleeing soldiers to return to battle, but they could not be stopped and Morgan was soon alone on the battlefield. The British success on the American right (west) flank was useless, for the main action was on the left (east) bank where the British continued to lose heavily. By now it was a rout. Major General Lambert was now in command. Admiral Cochrane wanted another assault, one he thought would end in victory. Lambert knew better. He looked at the battlefield and knew utter defeat when he saw it. The pride of the European theater was broken. What was still alive in the British army before New Orleans was scattered in disorder. The British advance was contained after a battle on that day of the eighth of January of 1815. The Americans killed 285 men and wounded 1,186, capturing 484, with relatively light losses. Soon the British were to retreat and return to their ships and England. Jackson had his great victory. [10]

The Hartford Convention grew out of the feud of New England governors and the Federal government over control of the militia. Washington wanted to press the militia into the army and control it there, using it where needed and prosecuting the war successfully. The Federalists did not want the war and the governors wanted full control of their militia. They did not wish their militiamen to serve outside their individual states. However they needed a defense and had to finance such because Federal funds were always low. To do this they had to have a militia at home. This added to their intransigence. Costs were high because of British coastal raids. They were faced with the need for money for their own defensive measures.

With this crisis, Governor Caleb Strong of Massachusetts called his legislature into special session in the fall of 1814. They recommended a convention of New England states. Connecticut and Rhode Island joined in and soon a convention was held. There were 26 delegates in all. Most wanted moderation. They met in secret and no record was kept, so little is known about the deliberations. There was a report, drawn mostly up by Harrison Gray Otis which discussed defense problems, the enlistment of minors by the Federal government (reaching eighteen year olds), and Federal proposals to draft the men. They stated a wish to use Federal tax money collected in their states for state purposes.

The rest of the report was about national changes they wished made. They recommended seven constitutional amendments for a two-thirds vote for declaring war, interdict trade with foreign nations and admit new states. There were others. Being from the Northeast, they protested the overrepresentation of white southerners in Congress.

They feared the growing power of the West. Trade restrictions and the war were protested. They also disliked the influence of foreigners who were Republicans, and the Virginia dynasty's dominance of national politics. Federalists goal was the adoption of these amendments would restore New England's influence in the Union to prevent policies which were, to them, destructive of the region's interests. They were for nullification. [11]

The Hartford participants wished to impose harsh restrictions upon the government in the Constitution. In a strict reaction to then recent events and with sectional bias, they resolved to send to the states for approval seven amendments. They resolved to make on arrangement whereby states or sections might repel invasions of their territory under their control but with federal money. First, the New England delegates would apportion representatives and direct taxes in accord with the number of free persons, including prisoners but excluding Indians. The aim of this suggested amendment was to reduce southern power in Congress. Fearful of losing population and power to western states, they would require two thirds of both houses to admit new states to the Union. Concerned over the strength of immigrants the delegates would have them prevented from holding civil office or membership in the Congress. Concerned also over the power of Virginia from which so many two term presidents had come, they would limit presidents to one term in the highest office and prevent men from the same state to follow one another in office.

Three amendments were tied to recent experience in government. They would require a two third vote of both houses to interdict foreign commercial intercourse. New Englanders wanted to protect their mercantile interest. A related measure would keep Congress from embargoing ships or vessels of American citizens from an embargo in their own ports and harbors for more than sixty days. War and hostilities such as privateering would require a two thirds vote of both houses. [12]

---

[1] Jarvis, Eric, "Florida," Heidler & Heidler, *Encyclopedia*, p. 188.

[2] Sharfman, *Jews*, pp. 125-128.

[3] Howlett, "Antiwar Sentiment," Heidler & Heidler, *Encyclopedia*, p. 9.

[4] Franklin, *Slavery*, pp. 169-170.

[5] Perkins, B., *Castlereagh and Adams, 1964, pp.1-70, 74-75, 78-82, 91-93, 97-128.*

[6] Brooks, C.B., *Siege of New Orleans*, 1961, pp. 71-80, 84-88. 93-96, 103, 106; *Niles Weekly Register*, June 7, 1828; Brooks, *Siege*, pp. 134-152, 164, 166-167.

[7] Albright, *New Orleans*, pp. 74-87.

[8] "Declouet's Memorial to Spanish Government, Dec. 7, 1814," *Louisiana Historical Quarterly*, XXII (1939), pp. 805-818. Quote on pp. 805-806.

[9] Tucker, Spencer C., "Lake Borgne, Battle of," Heidler & Heidler, *Encyclopedia*, pp. 287-288.

[10] Albright, *New Orleans*, pp. 103-170; Brooks, *Siege*, pp. 168, 173, 175, 178-179, 183-184, 187-188, 192, 196-197, 202-205,227-238, 241-245; Heidler, Jeanne T. and Heidler, David S., "Adair, John," Heidler & Heidler, *Encyclopedia*, p. 1.

[11] Hickey, Donald R., "Hartford Convention," Heidler & Heidler, *Encyclopedia*, pp. 233-234.

[12] "Resolutions Adopted by the Hartford Convention, Hartford, December 14, 1814," in Schlesinger, Arthur M. Jr., (ed.) *Elections*, 1788-1968, New York: Chelsea House, 4 v., I (1971), 323-324.

CHAPTER XXX

PEACE

American merchant, financier, and founder of Johns Hopkins University and Johns Hopkins Hospital, Johns Hopkins was born in 1795 on a tobacco plantation in Anne Arundel County, Maryland, midway between Baltimore and Annapolis. His parents were Samuel Hopkins and his wife Hannah Janney Hopkins of Loudon County of Virginia, the second son in a family of eleven children, six of them sons. The house, named "Whitehall," was an unpretentious brick house which was set with large barns and slave log cabins on land once granted by an English king in the not so distant past. It was the headquarters and living place of a slaveowning family on 500 acres of tobacco field. His parents were sociable and there were many friends and relatives entertained in the house. Hopkins family members often went on fox hunts with the hounds.

Young Johns learned to ride and went forth with his elder brother Joseph. They were Quakers, converted in 1671 by Quaker preacher George Fox himself on the latter's visit to America. This Johns' great-grandfather, who married Margaret Johns, daughter of a plantation owner, was originally an Anglican. His name was Gerard Hopkins. The parents of Johns were active in Quaker church where Samuel was an elder and overseer who became a member of a committee to select a site for the first Quaker Meeting house in the nation's capital and she often delivered prayers or sermons from her seat.

When Johns was twelve, there was a sudden decision for his father to make. The Quakers in Anne Arundel were faced with a question of what to do about their slaves and there was a movement to require Quaker slave holders to free their slaves because it was wrong to hold fellow men in slavery. This was a matter of conscience for the Quaker. Even though it was legal to hold slaves in the United States, it was still wrong to keep man in bondage. To manumit the slaves would force the plantation owners and sons to do work on the farm and mothers and daughters to work in the house, thus to do labor when they were used to lives of ease and luxury. Sons would have to leave school and work. The investment in slaves would be lost. The slaves would suffer and old slaves would have to be cared for. Husband and wife agonized over a decision and soon the society required freeing slaves or they would be put out of the meeting. After three more days of thought, the Hopkins decided to free the slaves. It was 1807. Joseph was called home to work and after some schooling in a free school nearby, Johns was back to work on the plantation and to study some at home.

At this juncture his uncle Gerard Hopkins came to visit the Hopkins of Anne Arundel and was impressed by Johns' activity on the farm and asked his mother to allow Johns to come live with him and he would bring up the boy as a merchant. The Hopkins agreed and Hannah told her son that he must not stay on the farm. She said, "thee has business ability and thee must go where the money is." So the seventeen year old boy went to Baltimore to work at the uncle's wholesale grocery and commission store and live with the family. He was fond of the relatives and "Aunt Dolly" was like a mother to him, pleasant, cheerful, and dedicated to his well-being and happiness, moderating the uncle's strict rules.

Johns later wrote that the uncle was a minister in the Society of Friends and was very popular. Like his wife he was cheerful and he transacted a large business. He engaged in mirth and told anecdotes. His uncle and aunt went on a trip to Ohio on Indian paths in Indian country and many rivers to ford. It was deemed a great adventure. He left everything in Johns hands, praising his service so far. [1]

While Johns worked for his uncle, he was impressing his young cousin Elizabeth. He was handsome and strong and she was very pretty. She noticed how her father depended upon Johns, his liking for dogs, children, and women, and his love of fun and his masculinity. They fell in love and made plans to marry. When Gerard learned of the engagement, he told the couple to break off their engagement. They were not to marry. This was buttressed by Quaker belief against the marriage of first cousins and the opposition of the church. Johns tried to change his uncle's mind, but without success. Both cousins were hurt and Johns moved out of the house where he had lived for seven years with Uncle Gerard and his family. Elizabeth helped to persuade him that they could not marry and that she would not marry anybody else. He could have her companionship and advice. Neither ever married, but they remained friends until his death.

Johns Hopkins and his uncle disagreed upon several matters and finally they disagreed too often. Since times were hard, Johns wanted to accept country whiskey in payment for purchases. Gerard would not have anything to do with liquor. The younger Hopkins set up his own wholesale business, providing provisions and accepting liquor in payment. His three brothers, Philip, Gerard, and Mahlon became salesmen for the country of Hopkins Brother and sold whiskey under the brand of "Hopkins' Best." Much later he considered this to be a mistake. Meanwhile however, he had a capital of over thirty thousand dollars mostly lent him by Gerard, uncle John Janney, and his mother and brother Joseph. [2]

The writer from Scotland who impressed the world of letters in his novels and whom Cooper strived to excel, Sir Walter Scott, was born on August 15, 1771, near the old College of Edinburgh. As a boy he narrowly escaped a tubercular nurse and was attacked by infantile paralysis which left him lame in his right leg. He was early interested in his grandmother's tale of Border Affrays and looked forward to the events of the American Revolution, awaiting the latest news, expecting daily to hear of Washington's defeat. Learning to read at an early age, he read among the greats of English literature. Like Dickens, who came later, he heard and remembered what he saw, heard, and learned, in his future great novels. Confined in early life and in school, Walter gained popularity with the tales of war and violence. In November of 1783, he entered Edinburgh University where his professor of Greek told him he was a dunce and would always be so. Scott took up law and learned the countryside and collected tales in prose and song. In the coming years he was rejected in love a few times before marrying Charlotte Charpentier.

Scott made his mark at an early age, when he published old song and ballads in volumes. They were written in Scotland's distant past, but Scott improved some with various minor changes. Scott reached fame at age 33 with the great success of *The Ley*. In

The Difficult War: The Era of the War of 1812   247

the work he had to travel about Scotland and made many friends among the people he meet on his searches. In a visit to London in 1807, the upper class of birth and talent lionized Scott at their evening parties. In the years ahead, Scott ran a publishing firm, did some editing, and served as sheriff and held other government jobs, and wrote poetry. Then the world opened up all the more when his novel entitled *Waverley* sold in 1814 through two printings and was ready for a third printing. [3]

When he published a poem, he gained a disappointing audience. Scott was engaged in a second novel, one entitled *Guy Mannering*, which established Scott as the first of Great Britain's best selling novelists in the modern sense of the phrase. This second novel was much an improvement on his first and was a forerunner of that genre of detective works. His next novel was written in a hurry. Constable published *The Antiquary* about four months after Scott put his pen to paper to create in the midst of building at Abbotsford, his home. This work was his most successful yet. It was rapidly followed by others such as *Rob Roy*, one of his greatest, which took place in northernmost England and in southern Scotland. [4]

Scott was popular in the United States as well as Britain. Almost as well read in the States as in the island nation, Scott's novels were the standard for American authors. From 1814, they used plots, forms, and language similar to the Scotsman. These started critics to ask for a purely American made literature and some to utter or write counterattacks on Scott's style and substance. [5]

The *Snap Dragon* began as a privateer out of North Carolina. She captured two British barques, five brigs, and three schooners, many of whom its captain burnt at sea. On one of her prizes, the brig *Ann*, she collected a cargo of dry goods. There was a change of captains. Captain William Richards Graham of Virginia became the new captain. Searching in Halifax waters, he chased a brig, with these name of *Argus*, bound for Bermuda, and sighted another ship the *Osbourne* of Hull. This second ship had been boarded in the night by the *Teaser*. Placing a prize crew aboard her, the prize master set out for American ports until Captain William Howe Mucaster retook her and brought her into Halifax and she set sail as a merchant vessel.

Graham decided to set out for the larger *Osbourne* and gave chase. Two shots caught the *Snap Dragon* between wind and water, and she began to leak. Her captain changed course again for a still larger ship and discovered that it was the *Thistle*, a brig-of-war. It was soon dark and the *Snap Dragon* escaped only to have a run-in with the brig of war *Martin*. This was no match for the Americans, so Graham surrendered. [6]

In early February of 1815, the British ships blockading the Maryland coastline were frozen in. It was Sunday evening of the fifth when a tender from the British ship the *Dauntless* came near James' Island. Night fell. The tender sent in a barge to the shore and took seven sheep from an American farm. When morning came, the tender went back to the ship and the evening of the sixth came again to James' Island. Meanwhile, American militiamen set out for the island where they found twenty men, boys, and African Americans gathered to watch the British. Ice prevented a British barge from visiting the island. The barge returned to the tender. During that night the tender was iced in between the ice along the shore and ice cakes from the sea.

A group of twenty men gathered on the shore and prepared to attack the tender. The crammed ice provided a good breastwork for the advance. At first they waited for a cannon on that Tuesday morning on the seventh of February. Led by Joseph Stewart they began to cross the dangerous ice to the ice mound. Reaching their objective, they fired on the tender. The British ship tried to set sail and fired back. After two hours of firing, the crew of the tender came up upon its deck and waved their handkerchiefs, crying for quarter. The sailors were made prisoners and took ashore. The Americans had won the Battle of the Ice Mound, the last land fight of the war along the Atlantic coastline. [7]

February 11th was a cold day, but no one minded when news of the peace spread through New York City that evening. Shortly after word of an end to the war reached the people of this city of about one hundred thousand inhabitants, the populace lighted their candles in their windows and took to the streets with torches for illumination. Officials lost no time in adorning all public buildings with transparencies and putting on a colorful display from Governor' Island. Many of the rich citizens put these transparencies on their mansions. These were painted on cloth, with lights in their backs. These contained eagles, doves, olive branches, cornucopias, loaded ships, and a rising sun. [8]

Congress ratified the treaty of peace and the president proclaimed it on February 18, 1815. The people celebrated throughout the country. Church bells rung and cannon fired. The people felt relieved; it was all over this long ordeal, this difficult war. People turned from their interest in Europe and became for almost a century isolationist. They rejected the politics of Europe. They had long been opposed to all that Europe represented except for its literature. They read a lot of London published books. At home they entered a substantial period of inward peace and contentment and turned to their domestic concerns. They had been divided long enough and a new nationalistic feeling was becoming dominant.

The Federalists had lost ground. Suspected of disloyalty because of their opposition to the war, they were on the defensive mostly. However they alienated others by their persistent effort to fight the Republicans in several states. They were in decline and soon dissolved as a party. They entered the war as a minority party and closed the war as a negotiable factor. [9]

On February 20, 1815, the *Cyane* and the *Levant* were sailing in the North Atlantic when the watch of the former spied a ship on the horizon. It gave chase to the two British ships and continued to gain upon them. It was the *Constitution*. The battle commenced and the American ship raked the rigging and sails of the *Cyane*. It was reduced to a hulk within one hour and, as needs must prevail, was forced to surrender. The *Levant* escaped during the battle. [10]

The *Hornet* had escaped the British blockade of New York harbor and headed for Tristan da Cunha for a rendezvous with the frigate *President*. On March 13, 1815, the sloop arrived to see another sail. This was HMS *Penguin*. This Britisher was trying to capture an American privateer. There was a twenty-two minute naval combat. Because of superior American gunnery, the *Penquin* tried to ram the *Hornet*. The two ships collided but neither captain ordered a boarding party forth. The *Hornet* lurched away and fired another broadside, but the captain of the British ship surrendered. the Americans lost only one killed, while the British suffered fourteen killed. Others were wounded on both sides. Once again superior American gunnery prevailed. This was the last naval action of the war, neither knowing that the war had already ended. [11]

War had an effect upon American economics. Foreign trade fell drastically during the war. Goods that were formerly produced in Europe and shipped to the United States had to be manufactured in America. Cotton and woolen textiles were needed for soldier uniforms and clothes. They were increasingly manufactured in New England, New York, and Pennsylvania. Only four new cotton mills were built in 1807, while 43 were erected in 1814 and fifteen were established in 1815. Other new factories were established.

Merchants had no investment opportunities for their capital in stalled trading, so they invested their capital in factories of varying goods.

The federal government needed to borrow large sums from the banks of the nation. Since New England opposed the war, their banks would not loan the money for the war. However, they took in a lot of money for war purchases. Conservative policy attracted coins to New England banks as well as what gold and silver was available. Their capital increased. New England benefited from these economic situations, which countered the loss of trading by these states. Still opposition to the war had continued.

Reliance had to be placed upon mushrooming banks in the west and south. These financial institutions had loose and dangerous policies loaning freely and widely upon little capital. Most of the capital existing was in the form of promissory notes issued by officers and stockholders. The stock became collateral for their borrowings from these banks. Bank notes were printed and served as currency. With their limited specie being in demand, the banks outside New England had to suspend the payment of specie by the banks in August of 1814, leading to larger paper notes. All this caused prices to rise. [12]

The rigors of war being over for the Americans, they were eager to turn a profit. Eastern merchants expected revival of commerce. The had their ships overhauled and rigged and advertised for goods to sell to the Europeans. After waiting until all warships learned of the Anglo-American peace and with preparations complete, a great merchant fleet made its way across the ocean for European ports. The Europeans were once again at war and hungry for American goods. Likewise, the English sent a fleet of ships containing goods, once thought available during the war scarce, but now eagerly sought. The goods included silks, hardware, wine, molasses, and coffee. British merchants sold at auction which prompted the people to bid up the goods they had waited for. Money seemed no object for the buyers.

Next came Waterloo with a final victory over Napoleon and a closing for markets on the continent. This hurt the British and their merchants flooded the United States with goods. The British offered liberal credit extensions and importers, merchants, and manufacturers bought heavily and not wisely. They were soon overstocked with a big debt. A tariff in 1816 was supposed to keep British goods out of the United States, but it failed. Happy at home to pay low wages for a labor force loose from military service, they could and did export, forging documents to get the best deal at customs, and flooded the market before the Americans had their shelves arranged. Cotton and woolen mills were hard hit and shipping lay idle. American businessmen were upset and headed for bankruptcy. [13]

The Southerners hoped to get their slaves that the British took back. Adams and other negotiators had arranged this in the treaty of peace. However, British naval officials would not return the blacks. Since they were free to carry off artillery and munitions of war, the British classified the slaves as contraband under the headings of artillery and other public property. The Americans argued that the African Americans were private property and should be returned as stipulated in the articles of the treaty. Further none of the slaves were taken in forts. James Monroe requested that the slaves should be returned and not carried off.

Under the authority of the president, former governor of South Carolina, Pinkney, sent Thomas Spalding to St. George's, Burmuda, to treat for the slaves and their return to the United States, under the protection of Governor Sir James Cockburn. Spalding sailed from Savannah on May 10, 1815, and arrived on the 19th. The American learned that Admiral Griffith wanted to see him so he immediately went to see the admiral. Griffith was sick, but he saw Spalding, who presented his authority. The British admiral expressed his regrets over the circumstances, but said he could do nothing. Most of the slaves were sent to Halifax. However, he would transmit a letter from Spalding. Next, Spalding saw Governor Cockburn who lost his temper. He would accept no envoy from a governor, only authorization from the American secretary of state was acceptable. Cockburn got more angry and told the American he would rather have Bermuda and its population sunk under the seas than surrender one escaped slave seeking protection under the British flag.

In his letter of May 22d to Rear Admiral Edward Griffith, Spalding wrote that as an agent of the American president, it was not his desire or the president's desire to discuss either the justice or policy of taking private property or slaves, but to achieve the liberal and enlightening task of effecting the provisions of the peace treaty. This called for the restoration of property, including slaves, without delay. To do anything else would be illiberal and unfriendly. At the peace treaty, the British had tried to exempt that property which they had carried away from the forts and other places. They had failed, but now their naval officers were claiming that this was the construction to be taken.

Shortly, evidently at the request of James Monroe, John Quincy Adams, as one of the envoys, wrote about the proceedings at the peace table regarding this point. Under Monroe's instructions he addressed Lord Castlereagh about the situation, claiming payment from the British for the slaves they carried away from Cumberland Island and its waters. The British had stated, Adams wrote Monroe, that they had not been aware that they would have to restore the slaves. whom their officers had promised them freedom. The two sides disagreed about the meaning of the treaty article. Adams felt that the British should either return the slaves or pay for them. Three weeks after the last letter, Castlereagh had not replied.

In early October, Adams wrote Lord Bathurst who replied that His Majesty's Government was looking into the matter. On October 24th, Bathurst wrote a letter. The British were most reluctant to return the black Americans to slavery, earlier during the war or now, months after the treaty was signed, and in between. The British refused to adhere to the American construction of the treaty article though the American position was correct if unjust. Bathurst maintained the verbal British position during the treaty negotiations although the language of the treaty supported Adams. Bathurst, of course, did not take the view of the Americans had at the time. Britain took the moral stand. The slaves would be free. More letters were exchanged and the matter remained unresolved. Time passed and by September 28, 1816, there was still no solution in sight. [14]

The ending of the War of 1812 by the Treaty of Ghent left the West with Indian problems. President Madison named three peace commissioners to meet with the Indians and settle their grievances to allow American settlement. The commissioners met 2,000 warriors at the small village of Portage des Sioux in July of 1815, at which the grievances of the tribes were settled one by one until the conference was over in September. The delegates from the Fox and Sac tribes stalked from the conference grounds after refusing the terms offered to them and the Kickapoos and Winnebago were discontented. Honeyed words were not enough and the worthless promises given the Indians proved to them that the white man could not be trusted.

The government did not waste any time in preparing for trouble and extended the maximum protection to the settlers. In 1816 and 1817 fort improvements and construction were undertaken. Rebuilt forts included Ft. Wayne and Ft Harrison in Indiana; garrisoned forts included Fort Shelby in Detroit, and Forts Gratiot and Mackinac

The Difficult War: The Era of the War of 1812 251

along the eastern shore of Michigan; re-establish forts were Forts Dearborn and Clark; and new fortifications were Fort Edward in western Illinois, Fort Armstrong on Rock Island, Fort Crawford at Prairie du Chien, and Fort Howard near the mouth of the Fox River. Between 1819 and 1822, other forts were constructed,, notably Fort Saginaw in Michigan, Fort Brady at Sault Ste. Marie, and Fort Snelling on the upper Mississippi.

During the period of fortification, Major Stephen Long made a military expedition to the upper Mississippi country and reported back that Montreal fur-traders were swarming in the area and had gained the loyalty of the tribes for England. It was deemed impossible to try to expel the traders and instead it was decided that the Indians must be persuaded to trade with citizens of the United States. The federal government took a direct hand in the situation and established government trading stations to promote trade with the Indians of the upper Northwest. The success of the stations resulted in protests from the upholders of private enterprise and the stations were closed in 1822. They succeeded, during this time, in providing safety for the settlers.

Protection was only a part of the Indian policy. Its harsh counterpart was the expelling of the natives from their land. It was an activity which was brutal in its application. The first action in Indian policy taken after the commissioner conference of 1815 took place in 1817 when the Indians in Ohio were called before officials and told that they must vacate lands for gifts and annuities. During the period from 1817 to 1821, other tribes were forced to move out of the Old Northwest.

---

[1]Thom, *Johns Hopkins*, pp. 1-16. Quote on p. 15.

[2]*Ibid.*, pp. 22-28, 30-32.

[3]Pearson, Hesketh, *Sir Walter Scott: His Life and Personality*, New York: Harpers, 1954, pp. 1-50, 52-68, 91, 110.

[4]*Ibid.*, pp. 121-137.

[5]Perkins, *Castlereagh and Adams, p. 174.*

[6]Snider, *Under the Red Jack*, pp. 209-214.

[7]Stewart, Robert G., "The Battle of the Ice Mound, February 7, 1815," *Maryland Historical Magazine*, LXX (1975), 373-375.

[8]Sellers, Charles, *The Market Revolution: Jacksonian America, 1815-1846, New York: Oxford University Press, 1991, pp. 19-20.*

[9]Dangerfield, George, *The Awakening of American Nationalism, 1815-1828*, New York: Harper & Row, 1965, Reprint. Prospect Heights, Ill: Waveland Press, 1994, pp. 1-3.

[10]Mould, Dephenes D.C. Pochin, "What It Was Like to Be Shot Up by 'Old Ironsides,'" *American Heritage*, XXXIV No. 3 (April/May 1983), pp. 66-67.

[11]Bunker, Robert J., "Hornet Versus Penguin," Heidler & Heidler, *Encyclopedia*, pp. 243-244.

[12]Rothbard, *Panic*, pp. 2-4.

[13]Buley, R. Carlyle, *The Old Northwest: Pioneer Period, 1815-1840*, Bloomington, Ind: Indiana University Press, 1950. Reprint, pp. 8-9.

[14]*American State Papers*. Documents, Legislative and Executive of the Congress of the United States *(Foreign Affairs), Washington: Gates and Seaton, 1834, IV, 106-107, 113-126.*

CHAPTER XXXI

PEACETIME

Military support for domestic and Indian objectives was essential in the early post-war period. Control over the Northwest Indians could be achieved only by the military presence in the Old Northwest. Americans with experience upon the frontier wrote Washington DC to ask for military units on the frontier and the establishment of forts. The acting governor of Michigan Territory William Woodbridge wrote the War Department on May 10, 1815.

He wrote that he knew "nothing that will check the murderous temper among the Indians, unless it be an active, exterminating war on our part--at Michilimackinac--at Green Bay and at Chicago. When they see a large force strongly posted in their country, their fears may keep them quiet." The Indians believed the Americans to be their natural enemies. They considered the Americans to be invaders and the British to be allies and protectors. They now heard that the British were coming back in force at Malden and were happy at the news. Their meek submission had turned to haughty boldness. Motives were proximate. Power near at hand counted for the most. "An imposing military force properly located may probably save the sacrifice of many lives." Governor Cass wanted the establishment of forts which would cut off the access of important trails for British traders and thus assure the United States of the allegiance of Indian tribes. [1]

Officials in Washington were never fully settled on the frontier defense position. They did have the problems of finding the men in the limited army to fulfill the requirements of a larger number of forts in the West. Since Secretary of War John C. Calhoun followed a policy of abandoning forts once the settlements were well under way in its vicinity, Fort Dearborn was evacuated. The relative scarcity of troops decided Calhoun to station the bulk at Jefferson Barracks, south of St Louis and to dispatch them as needed to the frontier posts in case of trouble. He did not want his troops scattered out in the wilderness.

Calhoun's successor, James Barbour, agreed with him, but in 1828 there was a change in policy. Secretary of War Peter B. Porter divided the troops among the frontier posts. He wanted such advanced posts as Fort Snelling abandoned because he was advocating a connected line of defense. This decision took place at the time of the Winnebago Indian uprisings of 1827-28, caused by a withdrawal of white troops from Fort Crawford. The Indian interpreted this as a signal of weakness and attacked and murdered a party of pioneers looking for lead mining possibilities. They also fired upon federal troops. General Atkinson led five hundred men up from St. Louis and two hundred men were led from Fort Snelling for the Winnebago hunting grounds. Seeing such a large force advancing against them, Chief Red Bird and several of the murderers gave themselves up.

The surrender of the Winnebagos did not alleviate the frontiersmen of their fears and additional protection was called for by those who would be the objects of any Indian attack. Fort Crawford was reoccupied at once and a year later Fort Dearborn received a large contingent of troops. Immediately after this, Major David E. Twiggs led troops up the Fox River from Fort Howard and built Fort Winnebago which served a protection at the portage ground between the Fox River and the Wisconsin River.

In 1828, a group of prospectors entered the wilderness territory of the Winnebago Indians stirring up those Indians to the point that a war was threatened. Since the army had authority to remove intruders this was what was done. General Henry Atkinson, who was commander at Jefferson Barracks, gave authority to the commanding officer at Fort Crawford, directing him to remove these whites from the Indian lands. That commander threatened the intruders with forcible action and those whites left the territory. The Secretary of War in Washington acted, instructing General Atkinson to interrupt the visits of any trespassers and to insure peace with the Indians until a treaty could be forced upon them allowing some prospectors freedom to hunt for desirable minerals. This would be forced upon them as the whites did so many others to get their way in life.

In 1829, the white government signed a treaty with the Indians, called the Treaty of Prairie du Chien to open up the land east of the Mississippi to mineral hunters. From this point, the military authorities had trouble keeping intruders from crossing the Mississippi westward and disturbing the Indians there. It was voted by Congress that an office of Indian Affairs be established in the Department of War in 1834. At this time also a bill was passed providing for the regulation of the Indian trade. The power of military officers on the border was strengthen by this law. This was the way it was to come to pass after the war. Beginning in 1815, this was the concentration of interest in the nation until the discords and divisions of the Jackson Administration took stage one. [2]

The men who developed the steamboat in eastern rivers had a great awareness of the need of steamboats in western rivers. At the time the Mississippi network of rivers provided a swift current downriver, but the same swift current meant extra difficulties when goods were moved upstream. Manpower was the chief means of propulsion. Sails were useless because of the winding and narrowness of the rivers. Steampower was needed on western rivers.

It was in 1811-1812 that the first steamboat appeared on the Mississippi and Ohio Rivers and from then on there was an increasing use of these boats on these rivers. First in the field, the *New Orleans*, weighting 371 tons, had Nicholas Roosevelt in command and made its premier voyage from Pittsburgh to New Orleans. Afterwards this boat made the trip between New Orleans and Natchez for several round trips until it hit a stump in 1814 and went down. Three more steamboats were built and found useful in the trade of the Mississippi Valley. Other builders entered the field and in 1819 there were thirty-one ships on western rivers chiefly between Louisville and New Orleans. Meanwhile improvements were made by Henry M. Shreve to adopt the steamboats for use in the waters of the western rivers.

In 1819, the first steamboat to ascend the Missouri did so and thereafter there was some river transportation along the banks of that river. Sparse settlement and commerce limited the number of steamboat going up this difficult river. Later, there was increased trade and in 1829 the first packet service was instituted between St. Louis and Fort Leavenworth. The state of Missouri was developed very slowly. [3]

Right after peace was announced, newspaper readers took notice of the return of Napoleon to Paris. Newspaper editor Thomas Ritchie of Richmond welcomed that news. A Republican extraordinary, he thought Napoleon to be a great man. Then when the Frenchman met his Waterloo, Ritchie was disappointed. He looked all the more to America with its western country and its boundless resources. Like his fellow Americans the editor expressed his new nationality. He turned from Europe to a new felt interest in rivers, canals, roads, bridges, schools, colleges, and scientific institutions. All needed building. He turned to the interests of Virginia, local and industrial. [4]

Daniel Webster, who came into his own after the war, was born at Salisbury, New Hampshire, on January 18, 1782. His father was a revolutionary veteran, and as were most in the war on the American side, an devoted admirer of General George Washington. When Daniel was six, his father went to the state convention which ratified the Constitution. He went to Dartmouth University for his college education in August of 1797. Before this event, Daniel was a well read young man, taking a delight in both reading and playing. He was fond of poetry as well as of prose. Rather ironically, in his early school years, he could not make a speech before the school, despite his ability to memorize a speech. When called upon to do so, he remained rooted to his chair, unable to raise himself from it. One year he edited a small weekly literary newspaper full of selections from books of literature and from contemporary publications.

In July, he and his friends formed the Federal Club and Webster wrote up a constitution. Its project was to promote political information among its members and the acquisition of other useful knowledge. The society was to subscribe to various and manifold newspapers and the periodical publications. The president set on a rotating alphabetical order, shall appoint a member to read such before the society. There was also to be selected a treasurer and secretary to handle business.

Political events in Europe impressed Webster with their novelty and unexpected nature. There were turn-around of major proportions in the life of Napoleon which interested Webster. In other lives too, victory was followed by defeat, and defeat by victory. He did not fear the foreign armies in Europe but divisions at home. The American Whigs of 1796 were opposed now to the idea that American liberty depended upon the balance of power in Europe. The French faction to which he was opposed as a New Englander was still alive. There was commotion in the southern states and trouble in the government of Pennsylvania. Washington was now dead and Adams was almost worried down with years and its cares.

In August of 1801, Webster graduated from Dartmouth and began to read law in Salisbury with a neighbor and friend of his family, Thomas W. Thompson. The lawyer graduated from Harvard in 1786 and went on to serve as a state legislator, congressman, and United States senator. Thompson led the revitalization of the Federalist party in the state. A recent Harvard graduate Daniel Abbott was a fellow student in the law offices. Because of a shortage of money in the Webster clan, Daniel left the law office to teach at the Fryreburg Academy in January of 1802 for several months before returning. At Fryreburg, Webster was well treated and made friends.

In 1804, Webster decided to move to Boston to finish his law studies. His brother Ezekiel was teaching in Boston and offered Daniel a temporary position on the Cyrus W. Perkins school of Boston. The month of July found Daniel entering the office of Christopher gore. Like Thompson, Gore had a political career as a Federalist. He too was a United States senator. Gore served also in the state legislature and was governor. He then served as commissioner to England under the Jay Treaty. Webster was admitted to the Suffolk Bar in March of 1805 and opened a law office in Boscawen. [5]

Thomas W. Thompson was in Congress beginning in December of 1805 and a chief question at his time were the Napoleonic wars, in which the United States tried unsuccessfully to avoid involvement. The Federal House passed a bill to prohibit the exploitation of arms and ammunition and resolutions to spend one million dollars for ship and fortifications. Thompson did not think there would pass the Senate. He believed that the government would use negotiation and remonstrance against Great Britain, France, and Spain. In Europe, Napoleon entered Vienna and Prussia joined the coalition and with this news, the majority of the House, still stung by British actions against American shipping on the seas, prohibited business with Great Britain and her colonies. Daniel Webster wrote to Thompson on March 15, 1806, that is another recess of Congress without doing something to protect American commerce would end the popularity of Jefferson's administration.

Next Webster moved to Portsmouth where he launched his political career campaigning for other Federalists. In that city he became known as a dependable and able party man. On May 29, 1808, Daniel married Grace Fletcher, who had been schoolmistress in the little town of Boscawen. Late in 1898, a full slate of Federalist won election in New Hampshire for the 11th Congress. During the next election, that of 1810, Daniel campaigned for Federalists seeking office. Thompson supplied campaign propaganda. In August of 1810, Daniel Webster issued a message to Federalist committees in New Hampshire warning of the danger of more embargo should Democrats outnumber Federalists in Congress by too many, because there were a number of Democrats only who would vote against further embargoes. Daniel Webster was a leading force of dissent in his state, but he was dismayed to find that Federalists in the nation could not unite.

Webster ran for Congress in 1812 and was elected. A month later he heard that the Russians had burnt down Moscow to deprive Napoleon of a winter quarters. The first session of the Thirteen Congress began on May 24, 1813, with Webster in attendance on the peace ticket. He found the war to be the main issue before Congress. Over two years later, he feared that the British landing at New Orleans would prolong the war, he was so much opposed to, sure that New Orleans was lost. News of the Jackson victory reached Washington on Saturday, February 4, 1815. The city was saved. [6]

Webster had just far played a minor role, but Nicholas Biddle had the ear of important leaders such as James Monroe. On May 5, 1815, Monroe wrote Biddle that he was greatly gratified to find that he and Biddle agreed on the dangers still facing America by Napoleon presence shortly before Waterloo. He also agreed with the precautions they must take. It would not do to send the squad to the Mediterranean or to disband the army until the smoke cleared in Europe. There would be a war in Europe and a new struggle which England could not afford. In Spain, Fernando had destroyed those who had restored him. Britain and Prussia needed Russia. America would not be sure of another period of peace in this future. Monroe said America must be firm and prevent this time a war with England. They must either command the respect of France and Britain or earn their contempt. America must not hesitate, but Waterloo soon decided that this would not be needed. [7]

After a brief naval action off Algeria, William Shaler and Commodore concluded a treaty of amity and peace with Omar Bashaw, Bey of Algiers. This agreement took a matter of hours to draw up in negotiation of the Americans with Omar. The Decatur fleet arrived off Algiers on June 28th. Decatur and Shaler learned that the Algerine squadron was overdue in Algiers. It was spending longer than usual on its raiding expeditions. The Americans suspected that the bey would be uneasy and ill protected, so they decided to deliver the president's letter immediately and to press for a treaty before the pirate fleet returned.

They set forth on the 29th on a vessel flying the Swedish flag (which the bey would honor) and a flag of truce. Sweden's council Norderling came forth to meet what he thought were his countrymen. Sheller and Decatur sent their message of peace to the ruler through Omar's captain of the port. Algier's minister of marine pledged that the envoys would be secure and free to return to their ships when they wished. The American would not accept this truce and insisted that the talks take place abroad the U. S. Mediterranean fleet ships.

The following day, envoys arrived from the Moslem ruler to treat with the Americans who then proposed a treaty, which must be closely followed. Envoys from the Moslem refused the part restoring seized goods to the Americans. Madison's men would not restore the captured Algerian ships. It was an unjust war, the Moslems agreed, but they said it was the previous bey who started it and not Omar. Then the Americans agreed to return the ship if Omar would sign the treaty. Omar's envoys returned to shore, reported to Omar, and returned with his agreement to accept the American proposals. The treaty was signed; a signal victory for American diplomacy. Since the pirate fleet had not returned, Algiers was at the mercy of the U. S. fleet, the bey agreed to the terms for peace.

It was a treaty of friendship, firm, inviolable, and universal, on a most favored nation basis. There would be no tribute and would be an exchange of prisoners on both sides. Omar would compensate his prisoners and return state property. Algiers was bound to return cotton belonging to the Americans and pay ten thousand Spanish dollars. From this point in the treaty followed a number of provisions resolving details of passports, of non-interference, of commerce, of humane treatment of prisoners in case of war, and of justice. [8]

---

[1]Prucha, Francis Paul, *Broadax and Bayonet: The Role of the United States Army in the Development of the Northwest, 1815-1860*, The State Historical Society of Wisconsin, 1953, pp. 17-18. Quotes on p. 17.

[2]*Ibid.*, pp. 22-24. 60-71.

[3]Hunter, Louis C., *Steamboats on the Western Rivers: An Economic and Technological History*, Cambridge, Mass: Harvard University Press, 1949, *passim.*

[4]Ambler, Charles Henry, *Thomas Ritchie: A Study in Virginia Politics*, Richmond: Bell Book, 1913, pp. 62-63.

[5]Wiltse, Charles M., *The Papers of Daniel Webster: Correspondence*, Vol. I, 1798-1824, Hanover NH: University Press of New England, 1974, I, xi, 5-10, 15-28, 32, 35 n. 4, 35-37, 52.

[6]*Ibid., I, 74-76, 82-83, 97, 101, 103, 113, 119-120, 128-133, 137-186.*

[7]Biddle, Nicholas, *The Correspondence of Nicholas Biddle dealing with National Affairs, 1807-1844*, ed. Reginald C. McGrane, Boston: Houghton Mifflin, 1919, pp. 7-9.

[8]*American State Papers (Foreign Affairs) IV, 4-7.*

CHAPTER XXXII

THE WESTERN COUNTRY

Madison had received information that American citizens or residents, especially in the state of Louisiana, were conspiring to undertake an expedition against Spanish dominions. These people were collecting arms, military stores, provisions, and vessels, and recruiting what Madison and Monroe called "honest and well-meaning citizens to engage in their unlawful enterprises. So the president and his secretary of state issued a presidential proclamation, "warning and enjoining all faithful citizens, who have been led, without due knowledge or consideration, to participate in the said unlawful enterprises, to withdraw from the same without delay; and commanding all persons involved to cease this activity or answer to the federal government. The president ordered all officials, federal or state, to prevent the carrying out of the prohibited plans. [1]

Because of the drought of 1813, the rivers of the then southwest had been so low that the food supply of the east could not reach Jackson's army. The Cherokee had come to the rescue of the general and now in 1815, they had claims to submit to the government for the corn and cattle they gave to the army. Colonel Meigs had recorded what the Cherokees had provided and everything was documented. Also the Cherokee agent documented the losses to the friendly Indians from the pillage of their lands by the southern wing of the American army because of the unruly nature of so many frontiersmen. A prideful Jackson took umbrage at all this and said this was all a falsehood. Meigs continued to collect his information and in time Jackson would claim that all of the claims were groundless and was corrupt. Jackson delayed settlement of the claims by his opposition. Major Ridge and the other Cherokees expected gratitude from the stubborn general and found his stand hard to understand.

At this point in time the boundary commissioner began their council because of their old age. Commissioners Colonel Benjamin Hawkins, Colonel William Barnett, and General John Sevier were all old and ailing. At the Tuckabatchee council of September of 1815, the ceding of Creek lands were opening up the necessity of a Creek-Cherokee boundary line. The whites had no record of former boundaries and decision had to be made on the basis of Indian traditions. The Creeks refused to come to an agreement and the Cherokees left the council. Sevier was not present and indeed died in the process of the drawing of the line, to be replaced by General Edmund P. Gaines.

On September 24, 1815, the commissioners present began the line with several prominent Creek chiefs alone. They were protected by a force of 800 friendly warriors who were useful to prevent a threatened attack by hostile Indians at the juncture of the Flint and Chattahoochee rivers. The Cherokees were worried that their claims would not be honored. Finally, the decisions had been made and line was drawn to the satisfaction of the whites, which was what was important to the commissioners. [2]

In the month of September of 1815, Julius Demun and Auguste P. Chouteau finished their preparations for an expedition to the head waters of the Arkansas River. The chief object of this trip was to trade with the Arapahos and other Indians there. They left on the tenth, guided by a mountaineer named Philibert, a trader who had been there before and who had returned to St. Louis to get supplies of goods so that he would be able to return once again with a train of horses bearing his furs. Because it was late in the season this group had a hard time, losing their horses to cold and fatigue and having to walk. They arrived at the Rockies on December 8th.

There they learned that the men awaiting Philibert had given up hope of his returning to the mountains. Being short on food and other necessity, the mountain men had gone over to the Spanish. Demun went to Taos in search of Philibert's men. He found and then paid a visit to Santa Fe to explain his presence in New Mexico. Demun described the governor, Alberto Maynez, to be a polite and well-mannered gentleman who possessed information. Demun asked him permission to trap beaver in the area, which had them in abundance as Demun had seen on his trip. Maynez referred the request to the commandant general. Since he could not delay returning, the American said he could not wait for the reply, and left for the Colorado mountain country.

Chouteau and his party were attacked by Pawnees with one American lost and three wounded. Indian losses were heavier. Five natives were dead and many wounded. When they all met on the Kansas River, they sent the furs by a party to St. Louis. Soon the governor of New Mexico ordered them out of Spanish territory, this being the decision of the commandant general. Because they did not leave, the Americans were found by a Spanish party and escorted to Santa Fe. Maynez was angry and used very abusive language. He claimed that everything west of the Mississippi was Spanish and the Americans had no right to be there. Finally he seized their property, let them out of jail and forced them to return to St. Louis. The Americans did so and made a claim of over thirty thousand dollars on their government for their losses. [3]

Seeking new parishioners in the frontier wilderness, Methodist circuit rider William Stevenson left his home at Belleview, Missouri, on a southwest course in early fall of 1815. He was alone on his journey careful of the weather and hostile Indians. Throughout Arkansas he had preached in individual homes, praying with the people and making a number of conversions. The preacher had heard that a few hunters and troops were operating on the Red River at an old buffalo crossing which the Anglo Americans named Pecan Point where Pecan Bayou entered the river southeast of Shawneetown. Idabel and Clarksville were later founded in the vicinity. At Pecan Point Stevenson found a few people on both side of the river and he preached there. Stevenson found a few people on both sides of the river where he preached. Stevenson was a friend of another pioneer, Stephen F. Austin, in Missouri and then in southeastern Arkansas. [4]

As a part of its usual policy, the War Department sent presents worth almost one thousand dollars to nine chiefs who had distinguished themselves in the late expedition. This annuity was paid at the Cherokee leaders called council and it was decided to send a delegation to the capital during which they could negotiate at the top over all their problems including the boundary line. They went to channels to solicit President Madison to allow them to send a few chiefs to him. This was allowed and word of this was received by the Cherokee on December 19, 1815.

The pre-arranged group of six Cherokee chiefs headed by Colonel John Lowrey with Lieutenant John Ross as clerk were ready to go on Christmas Day. The Pathkiller instructed the six to state their satisfaction that the Cherokees felt in their action in the last war. The business at hand was the notably the boundary question with the Creeks. They also were to sell a certain tract of land in South Carolina. In addition, the delegation was to ask for the establishment of an ironworks in the Cherokee Nation and whatever further business the white government might think important.

The Cherokees were well received in Washington DC socially and in terms of their own work, but were disconcerted to find Jackson there. General Jackson surmised their objectives and proceeded to undermine their case with William Crawford and James Madison, hating the Indian as he did. He thought he won and headed home, but Secretary of War Crawford kept an open mind and the Cherokees were to be successful in most of their efforts. They made the most of the Cherokee grievances at the hands of the white soldiers during the war although they were allies and the hardships suffered in the Creek War by the friendly Cherokee were an issue. They asked for relief like the white families got in similar cases.

Madison promised pensions at fair consideration of destroyed Cherokee property. The United States government could not now provide ironworks, but Colonel Meigs, their agent, could provide them with ironware. Arrangements were made for the sale of South Carolina Indians tracts to South Carolina for $5,000. They were promised fair consideration also of the boundary issue. The Indians signed two treaties, the second of which was generous in the outlay of boundaries. Losses were reimbursed. The United States paid money for free navigation of all rivers and the rights to open road.

Jackson worked to get his way on the drawing of lines which favored the Cherokee wishes. He got himself appointed to a commission to purchase the lands back from the Cherokees. He gave presents to Cherokee chiefs. This maneuver, widely used, in federal-Indian relations, succeeded in winning the American way. The Cherokees settled for a relatively small payment of five thousand dollars down, plus six thousand dollars per year for ten years for a cession of 1.3 million acres south of the Tennessee. Jackson had his victory although he had to buy it. This nearly whetted the appetite of the whites for still more land. Bribery was once again used and a removal policy was first heard by which the Cherokees would move beyond the Mississippi. The Americans took two cessions of land, one in Georgia and the other in Tennessee. [5]

Kentucky was plagued by faulty land titles and Thomas Lincoln had his troubles once again with a title, this time to the Knob Creek Farm. It was part of a ten-thousand acre tract owned originally by Thomas Middleton. Besides Lincoln there were nine neighbors sued jointly because they owned part of the tract. Thomas' suit was the test case in the ten. It was this difficulty with land titles which prompted him to leave Kentucky and move to Indiana the following year. On May 13th of 1816, Thomas Lincoln was appointed road supervisor of the section of the Nolin-Bardstown Road which lay between the Bigg Hill and Rolling Fork. He also signed the marriage bond of Caleb Hazel before the year was out. Hazel was one of the primary teachers of Abraham Lincoln. The other was Zachariah Riney. Abraham and his sister Sarah attended these men's schools, called the A. B. C. schools, and received the rudiments of their education. Lincoln was now going on seven and was the usual young child. [6]

The primary education that young Abe received was basic. His total formal schooling in Kentucky and Indiana provided all together less than twelve months, but must have been intensive. The students read their lessons out aloud so the teacher could know whether they were working at their studies or not. A switch was used when they were silent. Because, after a start with Dillworth's Speller and Noah Webster's book, they learned from the Bible; they learned difficult passages early. This accelerated their education. It was more intensive than modern education. The schools had neither reading books or grammars. Besides the Bible, the book was Lindley Murray's *English Reader* since Lincoln was to say to Herndon that it was the best school book ever used. These twelve months started Lincoln to reading from which he learned. His education was just beginning. [7]

Young Abe attended Knob Creek School. The schoolhouse was two miles from the Lincoln cabin on the same road as the cabin. The road was the main Louisville-Nashville highway. Teacher Zachariah Riney was a Catholic aged about forty-five years when he taught Abe and Sarah for a few weeks. He had a farm without a clear title and he was involved in some suits over it. These titles were basically just, but they were not described accurately in the records, hence the disputes which so many farmers were faced with at the time. The other teacher, Caleb Hazel, is difficult to pin down since there was a father and son with the same name. However, the Lincoln children went to his school only for a brief period. [8]

One of the earliest books he read was Weems' *Life of Washington*. This made an impression on him that lasted. He was to remember the battles of the American Revolution and particularly the sudden crossing of the river and the defeat of the Hessians at Trenton. Patriotism and the American promise of freedom among the world's peoples rose to the front of Lincoln's consciousness. This became the first fixation in his political thought. His earliest political belief was that slavery was wrong. He always thought so, influenced by his father and the ministers of the small churches to which he belonged in his childhood. The Weems biography with its myths was a highly enjoyable book on George Washington and was in the Lincoln home. Thomas also had five other books in the Bible, Pilgrim Progress, Aesop's fables, Robinson Crusoe, and an American history book. [9]

Lincoln's fellow Kentuckian Henry Clay could be jealous of the good fortunes of others. If this was the case his life was made harder by the many who achieved the presidency over him. He wanted to be secretary of state under Monroe. John Quincy Adams achieved this. If Clay had, the Kentuckian would have been president after Monroe. A long list of men of varied ability reached those heights to his failure, in Adams, Jackson, Van Buren, Harrisson, Tyler, Polk, Taylor, and Fillmore. Clay was better qualified than most. Still Henry Clay made great efforts and even founded a party, the Whigs, by which he almost achieved that pinnacle of nineteenth century success. It is certain that Clay had great talents and opportunity, but he never reached that success although he contributed mightily to the success of the young nation and is one of the best known of American leaders of his century. [10]

He was born poor, but he preferred power to money. Achieving great power he never lusted after great wealth, contrary to those who followed in the twentieth century. However, Clay did live well and was an accomplished gambler. His father, John Clay, was a poor Baptist minister who died when Henry was four. The able Clay married well and it has been suggested that his success before the bar was the results of his talents and not a cause of his success. There was something about the young Clay that brought him this early in life. He was naturally able and a born leader of men. Now Clay was in the House once again and speaker by a majority of great size. His position on the stage of American politics was assured and he was to be a giant for the next several decades. [11]

Kentucky was still on the frontier. The national government undertook to guard the frontier from the Indians and to expand that frontier. Garrisons were also established to keep both sides from violating treaty rights. At the same time the soldiers were called upon to fight the Indians and force them westward. There were two lines on the frontier. The first was the rugged line of settlement determined by the desirability of plots and the number of settlers in the area. The complexity of the situation was increased by the variety of the feeling exhibited over the Indians, the stress of their rights and their loss of rights being intertwined. The Indians maintained rights only when so allowed by the whites. This was to be a major problem for the government and an immediate one for the military which had a direct concern for the Indian problem.

Extermination of the Indians was an important policy achieved with warfare. Other policies were the removal of the Indians further west, a difficult and troublesome procedure which required time, tact, and oft times force, and diplomatic, humanitarian, and commercial operations with the Indians.

The War of 1812 which lasted until 1815 brought the problems of the Indians to the forefront. Hostile tribes had been active in the war and now they must be pacified. The Treaty of Ghent required that the Indians be restored to their rights and privilege. Northern tribes were restored and pacified by the Treaty of Spring Wells near Detroit on September 8, 1815. The Indians agreed to be subjected to the United States and to confirm previous treaties. General William Henry Harrison was well pleased with his work.

Belligerent tribes of Sac and Fox were most to be pacified so the Americans built Fort Armstrong at the mouth of Rock River in 1816 to control them. Earlier Fort Clark had been erected to control the Potawatomi in Illinois. Tribes to the south along the Missouri and the Mississippi were to be pacified by commissioners William Clark, Ninian Edwards, and Auguste Chouteau. Clark was the famous explorer to the mouth of the Columbia and was now territorial governor of Missouri from 1813 to 1820. Ninian Edwards was governor of the Illinois Territory from 1809 to 1818. Auguste Chouteau was an elderly fur trader who had important contacts with the Osage tribe, one of the tribes invited to met with the commissioners.

The Indians were invited to assembly on July 6, 1815, and Lieutenant George H. Kennerly was sent to the Missouri River Valley to escort chiefs from that river region. Supplies and presents were provided and the tribes began to gather once the commissioners, a secretary, Indian agent, interpreters, troops, and witnesses took up quarters. Some unauthorized individuals and unimportant members of tribes showed up and had to be sent back. Others came late and some tribes were missing. Negotiations and speeches took up several weeks, and by the end of October twelve treaties were signed with as many tribes. Several undertook treaties when they learned of forts to be constructed in their areas. Cessions were made among the Indians in the southern region by General Andrew Jackson.

Peace did not come easy on the Mississippi-Missouri frontier after the War of 1812. The Indians were not easily convinced of the truth of the peace and the British agents in the region barely cooperated. Governor Ninian Edwards of Illinois Territory notified the Indians of peace between the British and the Americans, but they themselves did not feel that it applied to them. Murders continued of the frontier variety and there were skirmishes including the attack upon Cotes san Dessien and the Sink Hole fight. Finally peace parleys at Portage des Sioux were held, but the Indians were still not yet settled on peace. Most of the Indians had not made peace by September of 1815. Troops were sent to the frontier when the trouble was new early in the year and these were used to occupy the disputed land. [12]

John Jacob Astor took advantage of the War of 1812 in order to acquire a number of ships at low prices. Forced to stay in ports, the ships in American waters had dropped in price. By 1815, Astor had nine vessels, a large fleet for those times. His first action was to send the *Beaver* to Canton to trade. The richness of this port induced him to concentrate his trade upon China. The goods of the orient were popular in the United States, although their consumption had fallen in favor due to the war. He then sent a cargo of 5,405 otter skins, 8,495 fox skins, and $39,000 in specie on the *Seneca* for Canton, trying to get the American government to specify that this was an official ship, carrying the news of peace. The ship made it safely coming back with teas, silks, nankeens, chinaware, and cassia.

His talents were carrying his name forth as a merchant and Astor decided he needed a partner. He chose well when he asked Albert Gallatin to become his partner. Albert was not interested noting Astor's lowly upbringing and distrustful of his action as partner. The able Gallatin had been offered the post of minister to France and would not take Astor's offer. Turning to his son William, Albert Gallatin found a partner for his own house in his own house.[13]

The end of the conflict in Europe and general peace provided an unheard of opportunity for some in addition for Astor. The British had piled up their textile manufactures over the years of war and many faced failure when peace was accomplished. One New Yorker went to the auction beforehand and bid high on a certain lot. Soon he reached the highest he could go and his ex-employer went higher and obtained the merchandise. Soon afterwards peace came and the cost of the goods fell. The young merchant still had his money and could now buy widely at a lower price than that he had bid before. He was fortunate that his first bid was not enough.

Robert G. Albion told of that and also another at the opposite end of luck. The unfortunate merchant had an idea how he could get out of a bad situation with his piles of high cost goods. Merchant Stephen B. Munn from Connecticut exchanged his cloth for land warrants paid the soldiers. His fortune was made when he traded his frontier land warrants for New York real estate. Such deals as that made fortunes. Prosperity affected most of the people in the east who knew how to turn something into much. [14]

Charles Francis Adams, son of John Quincy Adams, was in Paris during Napoleon's return in the Hundred Days and was to remember some incident of that time. His father was in Paris on his way to London as American minister. His mother brought him there by carriage from St. Petersburg, where they had lived while John Quincy Adams was Minster to Russia. Charles was born at Boston on August 18, 1807. After his parents moved to London, he spent two years in an English boarding school. When his father returned to the United States, Charles went to Boston Latin School and then to Harvard College. At age eighteen he graduated. He did not chose a profession for three years. He decided to study law. Later he was to practice law in Boston. He was also to serve as a writer of American history for the *North American Review*. [15]

A humble young man, the free-born mulatto from Virginia, John Stewart became a stalwart in the Christian service of the frontier Methodist Church, when most likely drunk as usual, he came to a Methodist camp meeting in the Ohio town of Marietta. It was a Sunday and he listened to a preacher and was converted. One week later he joined the church and felt the call to preach. There were voices and he followed them to the Old Northwest. Passing through woods and walking on roads in alternative progress, he came upon a Moravian mission for Delaware Indians. He talked with the clergymen. They told him of some Indians to the north. Stewart tramped forth and found the Wyandot Reservation. United States subagent William Walker listened to his mulatto visitor. At first Walker thought he was a runaway slave, but learning the story of the Stewart conversion, he was convinced the young man was sincere. Stewart gained the friendship of Walker and his wife. Walker referred him to mulatto Jonathan Pointer who translated Stewart's preaching to the Indians. These native became enthusiastic Christians and listened to the words of Stewart. When there were rumors that the preacher was an imposture, Steward acted to counteract this mischief by gaining a license to preach from the Methodist Church. Romance came in 1820 and Stewart preached until he died in 1823. [16]

In the months after the war ended, the gates were opened to a flood of products entering and leaving the United States. The South benefited especially. The big Southern crop, cotton, sold at twenty cents a pound and brought seventeen and a half million dollars to the planters. Tobacco planters received eight and a quarter million and rice planters sold two million eight hundred thousand dollars worth of rice. A population in the South equal to the North received an estimated two thirds of the income for exports, and of these a minority, the leading planters received most of the profits. [17]

The Warwick Spinning Mill of Warwick, Rhode Island, under the control of Almy & Brown, prospered greatly in the Jefferson-Madison era because the demand for domestic yarns and fabrics was so great. Since the European war was a story of two powers ravaging neutral trade and trying to destroy each other, there was a hostility between the French and the British who had the greater power to ravage the American merchant marine fleet in their struggle for European and world domination. Imports had fallen and American had to rely upon their own production. This had meant great business for the Warwick and other mills. Due to the great profits, stockholders were interested in increasing their investments rather than liquidating them as was the case of so much of the early history of the textile industry in the United States. Now, however they had renewed competition from Britain. They built and preserved in business. [18]

Because there were few stores in the South and West, Yankees traveled in both sections with goods on their backs, then packhorses for the prosperous, and then to a horse and cart, and finally to a four-wheeled shop wagon. They peddled the small manufactures of New England. At first the Yankee peddlers carried a large number of items. Later he could carry such items as brooms, chairs, and churns for the making of butter in his wagons. Soon he began to specialize. Many times he carried painted tinware, which collectors in later centuries were to prize. It was an era where the buyer must beware. These peddlers became known as cheats, who sold defective merchandise on occasion and quite deliberately at times. Of course, the frontiersmen himself would swindle a man of a horse or farm if he could pull the wool over one eyes. Since hard money was scarce in the southern and especially the western states and territories, Yankee peddlers would, in good service, take the produce of a farm and woods to later sell at a place where the products were in command. Many would settle down and open a store, to contribute more to the economies and needs of the people in their lifetimes. [19]

In the latter half of the eighteenth century and the early nineteenth century, African Americans in and out of slavery had a special days of festival called election day in which they were allowed to celebrate life. It is most recorded in the northeast and existed in the South in some numbers. They had music and dancing, a parade and an election in which an African-American was elected governor or king who had some power of disciplining. A parade was enacted which white observers tolerated. The festival was a celebration, a loosening of the strings of harsh lifestyles to which they were subjected by whites or the general courses of life on the hard style which they suffered amid the conditions of the working class of the United States of the times.

The festivals were to last for almost a century, but finally white opposition caused the end of the holiday. They wanted no one but themselves to enjoy life. This was reserved to whites. They were indeed tyrants in action. There had always been people who felt changes were in order. There were all sorts of restrictions on African Americans which did not apply to the whites. Ministers took a leading part in this. In 1811, the common council of Albany forbade the holding of the festivals in Albany. There were changes among African Americans. In Salem, they stopped electing African American governors, but founded an African Society in 1805. Instead of carousing, they listened to a sermon at the end of their march. There was a blacklist to this new train of events. Whites could laugh at the festivals, but when sober African Americans marched through the streets, the whites resented the invasion of their space. Jokes and stories attacked the African Americans. [20]

In terms of intellectual ferment, the school of romanticism replaced the revolutionary school of the eighteenth century. The readers of the early years of Lincoln preferred to look out of rose colored glasses, whether viewing the South as a paradise of agrarianism or the commercial North as a paradise of responsibility. The most visible of the Southern statesmen and agrarian exponents was Jefferson, but the intellectual proponent was the economist John Taylor. He would have things simple, revolving around gentlemen farmers without cities or commerce. This was wishful thinking. He would have everything made on the plantation for all of its needs and desires. This was much the case for the times when needs were limited. Taylor was the critic of Hamiltonian finance and would have things remain the same always. The Jeffersonians would be met with John Marshall, a conservative Chief Justice who delighted in overturning laws to promote Federalism which had died in politics but lived in the economy. Southern stuck to the plantation theory of statesmanship and Marshall found his match in Andrew Jackson.

William Wirt, that Marylander turned Virginian, was known for his hodge-podge book entitled *The British Spy* and later for his biography of Patrick Henry. He was a busy lawyer and spent twelve years as the attorney general of the United States. The classics of Greece and Rome and of the British recent past were the backbone of his intellectualism. Wirt was to run for president in the party of Anti-Masons in 1832. Soon after he ran for that high office, there were other Southerners who made a literary name for themselves, but Wirt had it all to himself from the time of Jefferson to the time of Jackson in the South. [21]

---

[1] *American State Papers*, (Foreign Affairs), IV, 1.

[2] Wilkins, pp. 84-87.

[3] *American State Papers* (Foreign Affairs), IV, 211-211.

[4] Vernon, Walter N., Robert W. Sledge, Robert C. Monk, and Norman W. Spellmann, *The Methodist Excitement in Texas*, Dallas: Texas United Methodist Historical Society, 1984, pp. 20-23, 27-28.

[5] Wilkins, pp. 87-96.

[6] Warren, *Lincoln's*, pp. 119-123; Basler, IV, 61.

[7] Barton, William E., *Abraham Lincoln and His Books, Chicago: Marshall Field*, 1920, Reprint. Felcroft Library Edition, 1976, pp. 8-12.

[8] Warren, *Lincoln's*, pp. 209-217; Beveridge, A.J., 1928, I, 28.

[9] Warren, *Lincoln's*, pp. 272-273, 282, 284-290; Barton, *Books*, pp. 7-8.

[10]Poage, George Rawlings, *Henry Clay and the Whig Party*, University of North Carolina Press, 1936, Reprint. Gloucester. Mass: Peter Smith, 1965, *passim.*

[11]*Ibid.*, pp. 2-4.

[12]Wesley, p. 1 ff.

[13]Porter, Kenneth Wiggins, *John Jacob Astor: Business Man*, Cambridge, Mass: Harvard University Press, 1931, pp. 589-593, 596-599.

[14]Albion, Robert G., 1939, p. 60.

[15]Ford, Worthington Chauncey, "Adams, Charles Francis," *Dictionary of American Bibliography*, I, 40-41.

[16]Sweet, William Warren, *Methodism in American History*, Nashville: Abingdon Press, 1954, pp. 190-191.

[17]Adams, Madison, p. 1246.

[18]Bagnall, William R., *The Textile Industries of the United States*, Cambridge, Mass: Riverside Press, 1893. Reprint, 1971, I, 218.

[19]Furnas, J.C., *The Americans: A Social History of the United States, 1587-1914*, New York: G.P. Putnam's Sons, 1969, pp. 244-247.

[20]White, Shane, "'It was a Proud Day': African Americans Festivals, and Parades in the North, 1741-1834," *Journal of American History*, LXXXI (June 1994), 15-38.

[21]Parrington, Vernon Louis, *Main Currents in American Thought*, New York: Harcourt, Brace & World, 1927, II, 10-35.

CHAPTER XXXIII

BUSY AMERICANS

The re-establishment of Spanish-American diplomatic relations were difficult until Onis was recognized by the American government as Spanish minister. Once this was done in late 1815, Onis renewed the protests of his unofficial days against the American occupation of West Florida, American failure to prevent filibustering expeditions from entering Spanish territory, and the allowing of rebel ships to enter American ports. Monroe ignored such protests and was intent upon a new treaty with Spain based upon realities.

Onis wrote home to Madrid with warnings about American intentions and urged defense preparations and Spanish application of aid from the European powers. He was hindered, however, by lack of proper contacts and agreements with his government. Fernando's government was ill-organized and ineffective. The most talented men in Spain were in jail because they were liberals. Fernando's government ruled by caprice without a settled policy or system. What the king said was law and he was subject to suspicions. When young he had revolted against his father and at this time was a dark king indeed. It was government by cronies and mismanagement was rife everywhere. This failure linked with a weak government and economy forced the Spaniards to take a more moderate stand than they could otherwise. Still they tried their best to make no concessions to American ambition.

Onis was instructed to ask for the return of Louisiana, but a state was already made out of the territory, and American opinion was such that Onis ignored this instruction. Meanwhile the Spanish government, despite Fernando's ties to Czar Alexander I, turned to Great Britain and France for help. The absolutism of Spain had turned the British public opinion against Spain and the French were unwilling to declare the Louisiana sale null and void. Castlereagh did however tell the Spanish that he told Adams that he would look unfavorably upon any American expansion and when this became known in Madrid it lead the Spanish to expect British support against any American expansion.

John Pintard, a substantial citizen of New York City, wrote his married daughter about feelings of Americans there on the subject of the verbal conflict with Spain over the Louisiana Purchase and the independence of Spanish America. According to him, Americans were somewhat agitated with Spanish demands for New Orleans and its countryside as told in the newspaper. Americans had nothing to fear since Fernando was more vulnerable than Americans and a war would confirm the independence of Hispanic America and a possible union between the United States and the rest of the Americas to the south. This can not be far away since it was inevitable because of self interests.

America would never give up New Orleans. They would rise up in arms and challenge the Spanish to come take Louisiana. America must receive Florida. As no European power could control the flood of the Gulf Stream, none could resist the movement into the northwestern world. [1]

Far from international politics, Oliver Wendell Holmes lived in the boy's world of Cambridge. With his younger brother John, he played toy soldier among the ruins of forts of the Revolution, in which history was soon stepped. There was a hurricanes that September. As a boy he was told of superstition which he readily believed. He heard from a hired hand, drinking tea in the kitchen, of the Evil One who roamed at night. A boy only had to write his name in his own blood and Satan would pocket it. Henceforth he would belong to the power of darkness. Hell was close by, he was told. There was a breach in the walls of a Harvard University building in which the Devil lived. A curious Oliver climbed into the hole halfway down, but soon fled in terror.

His grandfather took the boys down to the wharves. There were earring sailors and strong sea smells. John looked at the tall crossed yards of ships, but the religious Oliver looked up to his minister fathers church steeple and was seized by fear. When he was assailed by this terror he would go to his grandfather. His father's talk about right behavior was not comforting or convincing about this bulwark to Satan. Judge Wendell, the grandfather, was calm; he was awaiting his own departure and would go willingly and gladly. Soon he died. Josiah Quincy delivered the eulogy. He said that full of years, Holmes had descended to the grave. He was missed and beloved by all his friends. It was a life well spent, and survivors rejoiced in the prospects of his felicity in a future state, assured by faith in Jesus. [2]

If Boston looked to the sea with Holmes' visited wharves, St. Louis looked to the western lands. When Joseph Philibert collected goods at St. Louis, he encountered Jules Demun and Auguste Pierre Chouteau. He joined them in a fur trading ship. Philibert's men had been awaiting him at the rendezvous, but when he did not show, they went to Taos for food. They were at the mercy of Spanish authorities there. The fur trading party went to the meeting place, Philibert learned from Indians that the men had gone to Taos. Demun went after them where he was treated politely. Spanish soldiers took Demun to hunt for the trappers. They found them and ordered them out of the country. Because of mountain snow, they could not leave and were arrested. The governor confiscated their valuable property and gave them one horse each, and they returned to St. Louis almost starved to death. [3]

Napoleon's brother Joseph Bonaparte, once king of Spain, escaped to the United States after Napoleon fought unsuccessfully at Waterloo. He enjoyed the social whirl in New York and Philadelphia, the dinners and balls in his honor, and the gifts he garnered from those eager to do favors to such an exalted personage. One year later, Michael Bouvier, a cabinetmaker of lowly origins who also escaped from France as a soldier at Waterloo arrived. In 1818, he was to do some work for Joseph at his summer estate Point Breeze. In 1819, Bouvier was able to open up his own shop and then when Point Breeze burned down in 1820, Joseph selected him to superintend its building. [4]

On January 31, 1816, Calhoun gave a major speech, urging continued military preparedness. He expected more wars with Great Britain. The navy would defend us. Calhoun declared for internal improvements with roads like the Romans, not for subjugation like those of the Romans, but for defense and connecting the interests of the various parts of the nation. He was in favor of domestic industry and national encouragement for defense and clothing manufacture, because it was wise and politic.

The Difficult War: The Era of the War of 1812

During this time he joined the advocates for a national bank. He was not alarmed by the constitutional question in his early career. To him, the bank was a good idea. Because he wanted the United States to be industrially independent, he promoted the idea of protective tariffs in the national interest. Calhoun took the lead in the nationalistic movement and was its earliest spokesman. He was to be followed by Clay and John Quincy Adams in the same interest. [5]

During wartime, every bank south of New England had discontinued paying gold and silver on demand for banknotes. This resulted in a flood of banknotes through the nation. The banks were unreliable and their notes were paid at a great discount, with its effect on commerce. This was hard on all classes. Since the discount was the most in the area of the Chesapeake, it was there that the imports were most concentrated. Those in power in the land decided that they must act to correct the situation. The obvious decision was to create a new national bank. This was done and those with the most discounted banknotes had a big windfall when they turned in their banknotes for the full value in specie.

Since Calhoun had been the major speaker in this debate in the war years, he was made chairman of the Committee on National Currency. He drew up a charter for the Second Bank of the United States. In his speeches, Calhoun argued that such an institution was the most practical means for the rehabilitation of the currency. The Federal government would compel the state banks to redeem their banknotes or fail. Calhoun worked out the details with Secretary of the Treasury Alexander J. Dallas with Madison's approval. John Randolph and Daniel Webster opposed the bank way to resolve the currency difficulty. The vote was a close 80 to 71 in favor in the Houses. Calhoun was later to correctly say that had it not been for him the bank would have never been chartered. The bank did not solve all of the problems and there were troubles ahead, but without it America would have been racked with severe consequence. It was the best solution at hand, and when it was closed down two decades later, the results were harmful. [6]

America came out of the war years most intent upon protectionism and a strong economy. They had been troubled by unpreparedness when the war began and when it was over, the British had flooded the market with cheap goods. Northern states had an interest in high tariffs, but got Southern support for patriotic reasons. All Americans were in favor of a stronger country in order to meet British hostility. At the time it looked like there would be still another war with Great Britain. Southerners were prosperous and felt they could sacrifice for a stronger economy in the North and use a limited high tariff for revenues from cotton and woolen goods. Northerners promised not to levy a tax on other goods. This agreement made the way easier for Calhoun.

Calhoun was also interested in the protective tariff and supported it in Congress. When it ran into some difficulty, he spoke out in it favor. He used the usual arguments in its behalf. Webster and Randolph once again opposed a forward looking measure. Randolph was to say that the import duty bear upon poor men and on slaveholders, a view that Calhoun was later to use when he changed his views. Calhoun made a persuasive speech near the end of the debate on April 4, 1816, about the necessity to have agriculture, manufacturing, and commerce together. He argued that a protective tariff act was required for prosperity for every class. The Southern spoke out also for internal improvements and a strong navy to protect American coastal trade.

The House voted for the bill 85 to 54. It was passed by large votes from the middle states and western states and help from most New Englanders and some from the South. Previous duties were doubled and added to in extent. The tariff was to protect capitalists and jobs alike, but it did make things more expensive for those who relied upon foreign goods especially. It was only partially successful in protecting American industry. The free trade idea had, however, received a set back and although the tariff was not raised as hoped in 1820, it was increased in 1824. Some manufacturers wanted still higher rates.

At this time, they also gained better appropriation for the army and the navy, another nationalistic movement platform plank. Of greater difficulty than the tariff to achieve were internal improvements. Calhoun and other eminent legislators suggested that the bonus paid by the Bank of a million and a half dollars be used for internal improvements. He chaired the committee for doing just that. Calhoun suggested a main artery from Maine to Louisiana. There were a number of connections and with most of the South opposed, two thirds of the South Carolinians supported the bill. The nationalistic movement was strong in South Carolina. This bill passed by a bare 86 to 84. Calhoun made the difference by gaining South Carolina. People in the state liked Calhoun and supported him unswervingly. However, Madison vetoed the bill because he believed it unconstitutional. There was no way the veto could be overridden and an idea of what would have been a great benefit to the nation was lost. [7]

The caucus system with its emphasis on selection of candidates by a few politicians was not suitable to a democracy and sooner or later was to be attacked by the people for its inadequate nature. On March 16, 1816, one hundred and nineteen Democratic-Republican congressmen met and voted for a presidential candidate. Because Monroe only won by a few votes and the candidate of many congressmen did not have public backing, the people were alarmed. Crawford had almost won against their wishes. There was an uproar of protest against the caucus and concurrently against other aspects of government which minority groups could broadcast. The masses were angry. Newspapers took up the hue and cry.

One of Lancaster's newspapers spoke out against congressmen in Washington. The American people were no longer anyone in politics. Nobody in this famous land of liberty was. They are oxen bartered away at market. Sixty-five members of Congress had ignored the wishes of the country. Congress made the presidents the editor said. Whether in caucus or in Congress directly in case of a undecided election. It was the right of the American people to select their presidents. The present situation was not American. Congress had the say and this system was called a democracy. [8]

At this time, a weak banking system was a problem in Virginia as it was elsewhere. The East could not understand the dire situation of credit in Virginia and Kentucky. In the western counties of Virginia, specie had become scarce. Money was needed for operation of businesses and farms. In order to gain credit, the westerners resorted to illegal banks in small towns, which emitted bills which proved worthless. But the people were desperate. When the Virginia banks stopped specie payments, the legislature thought that they could force the banks to resume. It was actually outside the hand of anybody. The system could not work that way. If they issued their gold and silver it would leave the state and the banks would have to stop again.

Thomas Ritchie stepped in and opposed the new law. He said a national bank was unconstitutional. To allow westerners to have their way would endanger the banking monopoly of Richmond, which his cousin Dr. Brockenbrough had built up. Kentucky had followed western theories on banking and faced a great crisis. New banks should not be incorporated as long as the old ones could not pay gold and silver. They would not be able to do it at all. He called upon Thomas Jefferson to publish his idea of banking and currency. Ritchie was influential and single-handedly got the Assembly to meet in emergency session and repeal the act of forcing banks to pay specie. However, the legislature incorporated two more banks in western Virginia. Also, illegal sound practices prevailed. Ritchie compromised on the questions of grievances of the western counties. He arranged for more representation for them in the state senate in exchanged for paying more equitable land taxes in those counties. [9]

Capital in the Second Bank of the United States was put on sale in twenty locations throughout the state for twenty days in each locale in July of 1816. There was no rush to take the stock, but most of it managed to be sold. Only three million dollars was left unsubscribed. Stephen Girard came to the rescue of the sale and subscribed the last three million dollars.

President Madison named all the government directors from his party. Stockholders named ten Republicans and ten Federalists directors of the Bank. Madison was able to have William Jones elected president of the Bank. He had been secretary of the navy and secretary of treasury pro tempore in the Madison administration. [10]

An intriguing Andrew Jackson ordered Brigadier General Edmund Pendleton Gaines to build a fort just north of the boundary with Spanish Florida with ulterior aims. Called Fort Scott, it needed supply routes. The best route was up the Apalachicola. Now upon that river was Fort Negro, built by British Lieutenant Colonel Edward Nicolls, and occupied by free Negroes. Jackson thought he would provoke the blacks to fire upon an American supply ship and gain a reason to destroy the fort and allow supply ships to sail up the river and supply Fort Scott.

In the summer, Jackson ordered a supply ship followed by naval vessels to travel the river. It was fired upon and some men were wounded. Jackson ordered Gaines to destroy the fort. A naval ship fired upon the fort and a hot cannon ball hit the power magazine on July 27, 1816, and blew the place to the skies. Casualties were heavy amounting to 300 blacks. American Lieutenant Colonel Duncan L. Clinch took his Creek friends and they salvaged 2,500 muskets, 50 carbines, 400 pistols, and 500 swords for the Creeks as promised by Clinch. His use of Creeks divided the Creeks and the Seminole hostiles for a political gain.[11]

John Pintard was very engrossed in his promotion of the New York Historical Society in the city. He used his free time for the development of the society. The efforts were voluntary, he wrote his daughter. It was, he wrote, his own child. He hoped it would transmit some worthy information of a useful existence. He did all the work in arranging the society library. Some members looked in to see him at work. Every organization needs someone to do the work, and Pintard was happy. He was content to surmount his task. The books were more numerous and valuable than his expectations of them. At the meeting of the society, he was assured that he would receive credit for his work. The room was neatly fitted up and papered over, with a convenient library room at hand. [12]

In the field of 1816 diplomacy, at St. Petersburg, Alexander I was contemplating expanding the tripartite treaty, recently concluded between Russia, Austria, and Prussia or Holy Alliance to include the United States. On August 4, 1816, the Czar had his foreign secretary inform Levitt Harris, in charge of the American ministry in Russia that he wished to know American sentiments on the alliance. To offset the concerns over the motives felt by the Americans, the ruler emphasized the object of the alliance to be peace in Europe. Noting the previous use of the United States to counter Great Britain's power and the hostility toward England in Russian circles, Harris was cautious and said he would have to await the arrival of envoy William Pinkney. Word of the friendly approach of Alexander to the United States led Castlereagh to work for good will with America some fifteen months later. [13]

It was a long way from the palaces of St. Petersburg to the backwoods of America. Neither knew about the other. Like other kids Lincoln loved the water. This could be a danger. In the autumn of 1816, Abe went into the water of Knob Creek at age seven. His friend Austin Gollaher had to save him from drowning. This was the most dangerous of Abraham's adventures. He and his playmates took delight in climbing high trees and the hills. Young Abe excelled in the activities of his childhood. They would shoot fish in puddles and once killed a fawn. [14]

At the close of the War of 1812, people were swarming into Kentucky so much so that the state had a half of a million people in 1816. The Kentucky in which Abe roamed was less wilderness and more civilization now and Hardin County had over eight thousand inhabitants. Schools and libraries were opening up and there were some paved streets in Kentucky towns. [15]

Thomas Lincoln sought better land than Kentucky land in the fall of 1816. He had heard about fine land in Indiana and he determined to gain land there. Building a flatboat, he loaded it with tools and four hundred gallons of whisky for sale. Thomas set out on Rolling Fork and let the current take him down to Salt Creek, which flowed into the Ohio River where his boat capsized. The whiskey kegs and tools went overboard and Thomas had to dive into the waters to recover his goods. He righted his boat and floated with the current to Thompson's Ferry in Perry County, Indiana. He left his goods in safekeeping and set out to seek land. He went sixteen miles, found the land he wanted, marked it off, and went to Vincennes to purchase the land for two dollars and acre. Then he headed for Kentucky to pick up his little family. They traveled to Indiana with two horses and settled on the land.

Thomas built a shelter with one open wall. It was a half-faced camp shelter to protect them against the cold weather which came early to Indiana. He placed a pole from branch to branch of two trees. A few feet from the trees, two stout saplings forked at the top, with sharpened bottom ends to be driven into the ground. In these forked poles were placed, parallel with the first, a pole and on the two ends. On the three closed sides, Thomas piled up poles. For his roof he added poles, brush, and leaves. On the open side was a campfire. It was at once started by steel and tinder for cooking and heat. The floor was covered by leaves and skins were used for bedding in the typical pioneer fashion. This would have to serve for the season. During that winter they ate mostly meat, melted the snow, and carried water from the distant spring. He turned it over after a year to Thomas and Betsy Sparrow, who had come to the state with Denis Hanks. He then built for his family a cabin enclosed on all sides.

Herndon described the Lincoln cabin: "it was of hewed logs, and was eighteen feet square. It was high enough to admit of a loft, where Abe slept, and to which he ascended each night by means of pegs driven in the wall. The rude furniture was in keeping with the surroundings. Three-legged stools answered for chairs. The bedstead, made of poles fastened in the cracks on one side, and supported by a crotched stick driven in the ground on the other, was covered with skins, leaves, and old clothes. A table was of the same finish as the stools, a few pewter dishes, a Dutch oven, and a skillet completed the household outfit." Then, early in October of 1818, Abe Lincoln's mother died. In 1819, Thomas went to Elizabethtown, Kentucky, where he married Sally Bush, the widow of Daniel Johnston. She went with him to Indiana and made him put a floor in the cabin and windows in the walls.

The Difficult War: The Era of the War of 1812   275

As Abe Lincoln later wrote, Thomas Lincoln "settled in an unbroken forest, and the clearing away of surplus wood was the great task ahead. Abraham, though very young, was large for his age, and had an ax put into his hands at once; and from that till while in his twenty-third year he was almost constantly handling that most useful instrument--less, of course, in plowing and harvesting seasons." Corn was the major crop, but some wheat was raised. A few cattle and sheep were raised. Hunting was often resorted to for meat. Lincoln wrote, "It was a wild region, with many bears and other wild animals still in the wood." Abe shot wild turkey and deer, but he did not like hunting, and soon foreswore hunting.

His enjoyment was to go to the mill, seven miles away. In his eleventh year he began to grow rapidly. David Turnham, a boyhood friend, related, "As he shot up, he seemed to change in appearance and action. Although quick-witted and ready with an answer, he began to exhibit deep thoughtfulness, and was so often lost in studied reflection we could not help noticing the strange turn in his actions. He disclosed rare timidity and sensitiveness. especially in the presence of men and women, and although cheerful enough in the presence of boys, he did not appear to seek our company as earnestly as before. His step mother had been a widow with kids. The boy Abraham worked well with her, in perfect harmony together at indoor and outdoor chores. It was a good relationship. "[16]

When Thomas Lincoln had reached Indiana, he found forests only partially cleared by the half-farmers half-hunters. It was populated by large trees. There was a variety including sycamore, oak, elm, willow, hackberry, poplar, sugar-maple, ash, sweet-gum, hickory, beech, and walnut. It was dark under the trees and populated by raccoon, squirrel, opossum, skunk, deer, bear, wolf, wildcat, and panther, by wild turkey, grouse and quail under the trees, and by pigeons, wild duck, geese, mosquitoes, and flies in the air. There were plenty of hogs breaking the silence of the forests. Indiana had a human population of sixty-four thousand persons, enough to be in the last stage of entering statehood status. Indianapolis, in the center of Indiana, was a mere village. [17]

Abraham Lincoln himself explained the motive of the Lincoln move from Kentucky to Indiana in 1816. He wrote in 1860, that it was partly the issue of slavery, but mostly the difficulty of land titles in Kentucky. In Indiana all titles were clear of mistakes. In Kentucky on three occasions, Thomas lost land he had claimed. This problem was true of many of his neighbors. Historians have blamed this situation on an antiquated system of meter and bounds surveying. Things were regularized in Indiana in rectangular fashion and land was originally owned by the federal government. [18]

At the time that Lincoln was moving with his family to Indiana, James K. Polk was entering college at Chapel Hill. Unlike the wiry Abraham, James had been a weakening and made the best of matters by excelling academically to his father's joy and encouragement. He saw to it that his oldest son got the best education available. Because of his superior learning, Polk was admitted to the sophomore class. The University of North Carolina had the bare essentials in faculty, but an impressive outlay of buildings. [19]

His father sent William Henry Seward to be educated at Union College of Schenectady, New York, as a new sophomore. This all-male college was one of a collection of liberal arts schools two decades or so earlier. Several Protestant churches backed the college. Presbyterian minister Eliphalet Nott headed the school and stamped his impact on it for half-a-century plus. Nott was a reformer who effectively spoke for anti-slavery and temperance. He was a liberal for his day and was not afraid of innovation. Although clerical opinion of his time was adamantly opposed to gambling of any kind, Nott raised a lottery to finance his college. Seward felt that he was able, smart, and good. He was clever, but strict. He educated a lot of men, but Seward was his best product. The two became life long friends.

Seward' stay was pleasant although the pace was rigorous and demanding with hours of work which modern college students would have found too strong. There was a heavy schedule of classes, recitations, and prayers. Rote learning which was particularly important at the time was unsuited to Seward's concept of education and he wrote he had been "hurried mechanically through the miserable rudiments of an American collegiate education." [20]

He had an easy time adapting and soon was very self-confident and with an ease of manners that impressed a visiting family friend. He was congenial and had a good circle of friends. However, he was under peer pressure which led to rebellion against his demanding father. His allowances were small and the upperclassmen chided him as a country bumpkin, so he spent the money he did not have on clothes. His father refused to pay the bill.

In 1819, on New Year's Day, he and a fellow student left college and headed for the South, where the other guy had been promised a teaching job. They reached the South and when the fellow decided to take another job instead of the one promised, Seward took that job and taught school for two months. He made friends with the farmers and others and got along well. However, his antislavery view hardened while there. He could see slavery close at hand. The Southerners praised him and a newspaper advertisement about him reached his father, who wanted him to return home. The elder Seward threatened to sue the school if William stayed and his mother wrote letters to him. Seaward left and returned home, where he studied law and then returned to college to finish his courses and graduate. [21]

The Pottowatomie chief, Gomo, told his story to Black Hawk who related it in his autobiography. He stated that the war chief at Peoria was a very good man and treated his people well. He always spoke the truth. Sending for Gomo one day, he said he was almost out of provisions and wished the chief to send his men out on a hunt to supply the fort. They went hunting and came back with twenty dead deer. The Americans could now eat. Days later this was again repeated, and the American officer gave him some powder and lead for the purpose.

A warrior named Ma'-ta-tah' agreed to go beyond the Illinois with eight hunters and his wife and several squaws. After mid-day they saw a party of white men with a drove of cattle. Since the Indians felt no danger, the Indian leader decided to go speak with the whites. The whites saw them and headed their way at full speed. Ma'-ta-tah' gave up his gun and explained his mission. The whites did not respect this and fired and wounded him. He immediately leaped to a tree to keep from being run over by the horses. The sorry white cattle drivers fired again and wounded the friendly Indian again. He had to take measures of self-defense. He sprung at a white and killed him with the man's gun. The white fell dead.

The eight hunters were in the rear and saw everything. They tried to escape, but they were pursued and murdered,, excepting one wounded brave. He returned to the village and reported to Gomo. He said the whites had abandoned their cattle and gone back to the settlement. Gomo and his Indians mourned the dead. Gomo blackened his face and went to the white officer. He told him what had happened and read the sorry on the Americans face. The officer said the men would be punished. Gomo said he would seek his revenge

The Difficult War: The Era of the War of 1812   277

at the settlement. He and a party of hunters killed several deer and left them at the fort gate on the way to the American town. [22]

---

[1]Griffin, pp. 69-78; Pintard, John, *Letters from John Pintard to his Daughter Eliza Noel Pintard Davidson, 1816-1833*, 4 vols., New York: New-York Historical Society, 1940, I, 2-3.

[2]Bowen, *Yankee*, pp. 30-31.

[3]Duffs, *Santa Fe*, pp. 61-64.

[4]Davis, John H., *The Bouviers: From Waterloo to the Kennedy's and Beyond*, Washington DC.: National Press Books, 1993, pp. 21, 24.

[5]Von Holst, *Calhoun*, pp. 26-37.

[6]Capers, *Calhoun*, pp. 52-53. Quote on p. 52.

[7]*Ibid.*, pp. 53-55; Bancroft, Frederic, *Calhoun and the South Carolina Nullification Movement*, Baltimore: John Hopkins Press, 1928, Reprint, Gloucester, Mass: Peter Smith, 1966, pp. 1-15; Preyer, Norris W.," Southern Support of the Tariff of 1816: A Reappraisal," Gatell, Frank Otto, (ed.). *Essays on Jacksonian America*, New York: Holt, Rinehart & Winston, 1970, pp. 12-20.

[8]Klein, Philip Shriller, *Pennsylvania Politics, 1817-1832: A Game Without Rules*, Philadelphia: 1940.

[9]Ambler, *Thomas Ritchie*, pp. 66-68.

[10]Catterall, pp. 22-23.

[11]Mahon, J.K., *History*, 1967, pp. 22-24.

[12]Pintard, *Letters*, I, 18-19.

[13]Thomas, Benjamin Platt, *Russo-American Relations, 1815-1867*, Baltimore: Johns Hopkins Press, 1930, pp. 17-20.

[14]Pratt, H.E., *Lincoln 1809-1839*, 1941, p. 3; Beveridge, I, 29-30.

[15]Beveridge, I, 32-33.

[16]Herndon, William H. and Jesse W. Weik, *Herndon's Life of Lincoln*, New York: Albert & Charles Boni, 1936; Beveridge, I, 42-44, Booth, E.T., *Country*, 1947, pp. 200-203.

[17]Beveridge, *Lincoln*, I, 38.

[18]Barfelt, William E., "The Land Dealings of Spencer County, Indiana, Pioneer Thomas Lincoln," *Indiana Magazine of History*, LXXXVII, No. 3 (September 1991), 211.

[19]Sellers, *Polk*, 39-51.

[20]Taylor, *Seward*, p. 15. Quote on p. 15.

[21]*Ibid.*, pp. 16-17.

[22]Black Hawk, *Autobiography*, pp. 84-86.

CHAPTER XXXIV

MATTERS OF PEACE

Congress was in trouble with the electorate. Congressmen had almost universally voted themselves a pay raise from six dollars per day to fifteen hundred dollars in annual salaries. They believed their representatives in House and Senate were lazy and that they could always find those who were willing to take six dollar a day each day sessions were held. Many of the representatives and senators up for re-election were afraid to run. Most of those who did were defeated in November. An abashed Webster moved to Massachusetts to run and won his election. Clay had to do some quick stumping to convince his constituents to reelect him. Calhoun had to explain not only his vote for increased pay but also his vote for the tariff which South Carolinians at the grass roots opposed. Calhoun returned to his state to back down and campaign successfully. He returned to Washington to vote to make the pay raise, because he said that workmen were worth their hire. Good salaries brought in able men who remained although they could make more money elsewhere. [1]

The public good was very much the question in these year. Ever eager for the public good on all levels, John Pintard wrote on December 4, 1816, in an interest for a saving bank for New York City. He wrote his daughter of a bank for one in the *Herald*. He was promoting one for laying up the earnings of domestics and laboring people. He was one of the directors. Having upper class motives for the venture, he stated that it would remove the need for charity and charges on his class, because the lower classes would have their own funds to draw on in bad times and in retirement. Pintard trusted that a savings bank would be eminently beneficial to society. It would excite "thrift, frugality, a pride of character and independence which will be productive of moral and religious habits. It is an experiment, the utility of which has been proved in Great Britain but will require time, perhaps years, before it can reach any great extent in the United States. A similar plan is going on in Boston and Philadelphia and it is assumed would be adopted in every city and principal town in the Union." He would do his share of benevolence and had he been independently wealthy, he would have devoted all of his life to good causes.[2]

This new appointment would prevent, for lack of time, his becoming an active member of the American Bible Society. In that same letter, he noticed several cross currents of his social endeavors.. His friend Mr. Bayard wanted him to become an officer in the Bible Society, but he did not have the time, and could work for the benefit of the society without holding office. He sincerely regretted that Bishop Hobart opposed it. He thought Hobart's apprehensions of danger to his Episcopal interests were groundless. And his zeal misguided his judgment. He would not hold office in the society also to not offend his bishop. Pintard's job precluded much effort and he did not have time to do all he wished. Because of his age of 57, he felt he must curtail some of his public efforts. When he ended some associations, he would retain others until his last day. [3]

Earlier in 1808, David Barron took what was for the times a radical stand on slavery. He refused to recognize that slavery was lawful or that compensation was just. He wanted freedom for slaves without paying any money for what the owners considered their property. Americans must end slavery if they did not want God to punish America. To him slavery was a sin. Four years before Lincoln's birth, Thomas Branagan suggested that freed African Americans should be colonized in the West. Slaves should be freed and settled in Indian lands. He did not say what would the Indians do if blacks took their place. Branagan believed that slavery would collapse and God would not send an apocalyptic racial war as divine judgment.

Later, in 1817, John Kendrick wanted the immediate abolition of slavery and African American settlement in the West. No one was listening except for the few. Immigrant George Bourne who was to influence William Lloyd Garrison condemned Christians who would not support total and immediate abolition. That was the only cure of a corrupt system of religion developed in the United States. Churches must be purged of the sin of slavery. The chief concern of most of these early abolitionists was the punishment of God upon a nation of such a great sin as slaver. Another important thread was colonization of blacks in western lands on the frontier. [4]

Several Americans met in Washington DC, on December 16, 1816, to discuss the black problem. Their solution was to colonize African Americans in Africa. The basic idea was to return free blacks to Africa, because they considered free African Americans to be a problem. However, they wanted slaveholders to emancipate slaves and send them to Africa also. To the Southerner free blacks were a source of danger. Bushrod Washington presided and Henry Clay and John Randolph of Roanoke spoke at this first meeting of the American Colonization Society. They requested Congress to give aid in procuring territory in Africa or elsewhere for their black colony. The founders were interested in the welfare of the African Americans.

A member from the South, William H. Fitzhugh of Virginia was to free his slaves by his will and promised special inducements if they would go to Liberia, the colony decided upon. They embarked upon this course, suffering criticism from South Carolina and New England, the colonization movement was a middle state moderate solution to the problem of African Americans in the United States and met opposition from the immoderate and many African Americans too. The latter wanted to stay in the United States, their home. [5]

There was a census in the Territory of Mississippi which included Alabama in 1816. This was taken under the act of the legislature. Census workers counted 45,085 free white persons and 30,061 slaves. Also counted were 366 freedmen. The census fell short of the 60,000 inhabitants it would take to make a state in the agreement between the United States and Georgia. However, there was a clause that it could occur at an earlier if Congress should consider it expedient. It was hoped that a state should be established from this territory upon a liberal congressional policy. The House had already passed three bills at different times for its admission when numbers were much lower.

The territory was too large to be admitted as one state, and it was settled generally in three areas only. One area was on the Tennessee River in the north, on the Mississippi River in the west, and around Mobile in the south. In the areas between it was wilderness, but the Indian titles had been generally extinguished in the territory. There was no commerce between the three areas, but it was hoped that trade would be established once the intervening countryside was settled and its intervening fine navigation streams explored and improved. The parts were too widely separated to make it into a single state and indeed, in time, it was made into two different states, Alabama and Mississippi. Land sales were good. West of the Pearl River, in 1816, 295 thousand acres were sold. The war had impeded sales, but now the gates were open with the territory peaceful at last. [6]

Calhoun's goal in those days was nationalistic. He felt the Union was threatened by "selfish instincts" of the individual and the "rival jealousies" of the States. Union was second only to liberty. He saw diversity and clashing interests of the sections to be dangerous. If sectional interest became pronounced, the Union would fall. His prophecy proved true. Interests must be reconciled and minority sections protected. Growth was "our pride and our danger, our weakness and our strength." Distance would break sympathies, hence his emphasis on building roads and canals. The founding fathers believed that if the United States expanded too far, it would endanger the country. Calhoun followed this view. "The mail and the press are the nerves of the body politic. By then the slightest impression made on the remote parts, is communicated to the whole system." He realized that it was necessary for the common good that may work for the common good. He opposed agitation and legislation on slavery. [7]

At first, states such as Calhoun's South Carolina believed themselves headed for industrialization in the cloth or textile trade. This state and others in the South had plenty of water power necessary in textile mill operation. As far as it went there were few Southerners interested in going into the textile business. All for the worst of the state. It was more genteel to become planters. This class were looked up to and had less work to do and more display and good living to do. However, they had oft times voted for protective tariffs because they had thought that mills would be established in their section. Now they were against the tariff which added to the cost of goods they imported from England. In time they were to feel these restraints upon themselves and react strongly. John C. Calhoun used the idea of nullification to force the Northerners to lower the tariff in a compromise. However, this was to come in the future. [8]

Although Henry Clay was one of the largest slaveowners in Kentucky, he considered slavery to be morally wrong. He was kind to his slaves, formed friendships with his body servants, emancipated several of his slaves, tried to keep slave families together, and encouraged them to learn useful trades. They were human beings to Clay and he expected they would eventually be freed. Even so, he could use his energies in hunting down the few slaves who ran away and was to support fugitive slave acts. Wishing the blacks to be settled back in Africa, he supported the organizations wishing to settle freed slaves in the nation in their original homeland. Philanthropic agencies would shoulder the cost of this. Freed slaves would earn and save the money to pay for their transportation to Africa and be emancipated and sent on ships from border states. The Federal government would emancipate deep South slaves of those slaveowners who were willing and a Federal agency would pay for their transportation.

From 1816 to 1830, Clay was very active in the American Colonization Society and took a more moderate course between the Southerners who thought slavery was good and the Northerners who argued for abolition. Caught in the middle in the thirties, Clay suffered from both sides in the slave question. He upheld the right of abolitionists to petition for abolition, the power of Congress to legislate against slavery in the District of Columbia, and the right of abolitionists to send their literature through the mails. However, Clay was to hold that petitions could be sent to committee to die, anti-slavery in the district was inexpedient, and the mails, once they left the Post Office, could be confiscated. These views pleased no one and hurt Clay in his bid for the presidency in 1840. In all this, it should be remembered that Clay was a slaveholder. [9]

Educated at Harvard, Boston entrepreneur Francis Cabot Lowell made his mark in the business and industrial world by steeping out on new ventures. After Harvard, Lowell worked in the import-export business with his uncle, William Cabot for seventeen years. Then in 1810, he beset by bad health, he journeyed to the British Isles. While touring, he was struck by the importance of manufacturing and the development of textile machinery in Lancashire. The area was at the front of the industrial revolution in the world. He returned to Boston in 1812, determined to establish a cotton textile factory in New England. Since commerce was at a low ebb due to the war, he had plenty of time to work on his project. He talked with his brother-in-law, Patrick Tracy Jackson and Patrick became interested in the plan. Jackson had been a sea captain and had become a merchant with capital saved while he was a captain. He specialized with trade with the East and West Indies. Although his way led him to near bankruptcy in 1811, by the time Lowell told him his idea, he was going well in business and was quickly won over to Lowell's project. [10]

Lowell formed the Boston Manufacturing Company, purchased land at Waltham, and in the winter of 1812-1813 supervised the creation of the textile mill machinery in the factory he built there. His chief engineer was mechanical genius Paul Moody, who learned about machinery from his years of work in various industries. After marriage in 1800 Paul entered into a partnership with Ezra Worthen in a cotton mill in Amesburg. Working for Lowell, he made several inventions and served to turn Lowell's ideas into reality. Using his memory, Lowell made sketches of British machinery and improved them by inventing the double speeder, which Moody later improved and the method of spinning the thread directly through the quill. It was another year before the manufacturing process was ready and production began. It was believed to be the first mill in the world which combined all operations from the raw product into finished cloth in the same facility. Leading stockholder Nathan Appleton said, that although Jackson and Moody had the greatest talent and energy in the industry, it was Lowell who was the forming soul. It was he who gave them direction and from to the entire proceeding. [11]

The operation was turning out cloth when the War of 1812 ended. Commerce with England was reopened and cloth flooded the country from England. The British manufacturers did not mind selling to the Americans at a loss if it would drive the American manufacturers out of business and insure them a future profitable captive market. Some seventy-five percent of American factory owners were soon out of business. A once twelve million dollar woolen business was devastated. The flood of British broadcloth products gravely hurt that business also. [12]

Faced with this unfair competition, Lowell felt that his plant was threatened, so he and others went to Washington DC where they convinced Lowndes and Calhoun that American industry should be protected. The congressional leaders included a substantial duty on foreign cotton cloth in the tariff of 1816 and a policy of protectionism was established. This protectionism was a product of increased industrialization and the flood of complaints arising from English goods entering the country after the war. Lowell and his friends were not the only ones interested in protectionism. [13]

The Republicans under Jefferson lead had early been opposed to industrialization. On the other hand, Hamilton had believed that every nation must endeavor to develop for itself national supply or manufacture. The event of the War of 1812 changed the beliefs of the Jeffersonians. In war, a country had to be able to have his own sources. Jefferson then favored production so that the comforts of life were fabricated by the people who used them. Now, those who were against national manufacturing would reduced the nation to dependence on such as England, or to be clothed in skins. Such would mean Americans would be reduced to living like beasts in caves. He prided himself in saying that he was not one of these. Domestic production, he had learned from experience, was necessary as much for American independence as for American comfort. That same year Jefferson wrote this to Benjamin Austin of Boston, the Congress adopted protectionism. Their fear that the industrial progress would make slaves out of men did not then come into being. Labor was too scarce and there was too much farmland for the worker to allow that to happen. The growing American population provided a market for New England cotton goods. A weakness in commerce provided capital for industrialization which would have gone into commerce, as we have seen in the case of Lowell.

The merchants of New York City were not happy with the tariff. The events before the tariff deadline saw a variety of actions on the seafront. On June 30, 1816, the day before the tariff went into effect the men worked overtime, to bring in as many goods duty free as possible. Captain Benjamin Wood, the boarding officer at Quarantine Ground boarded inward bound vessels and endorse their manifests until midnight. This saved the merchants large sums of money, which would have had been paid for duties if it were delayed until the next morning. This was praised by New York's *Evening Post* which wrote editorially that this fine generosity and conduct deserved the commendation and thanks of everyone, except the woolen manufacturers." [14]

In 1816, Daniel Webster was already a Federalist of high standing in Boston and was listening to when he wrote an article for *North American Review* deploring the party strife that drove men of merit out of public life. Their virtue had been attacked and the issues they fought for had been distorted by Republican party leaders and their editors and by other Federalist no doubt too. Party labels were deplored of course since Webster would have rather have had men of merit, notably himself, decide the questions of the day without party divisions.

Citizens were forgetting rational independent appraisal of men and issues. This was leading, Webster feared, to professional politicians and licentious (the word was his) editors. Men of merit must gain regain control and bring the press under control, forget party strife, and return character and ability to power. He wanted a meritocracy. He looked to the past generation when Washingtons, Adams, Franklins, Hamiltons, and Jeffersons ruled. This was common enough for the time. The giants of the pass were no longer in power. They had died or retired. The giants of the present were Clay, Calhoun, and Webster and none were to gain the presidency. Men of talent in both parties could prove to the world that "character is power."

Webster called upon both parties, but the weaker Federalists had the most to gain. There were men of merit in both parties, but those of the Republican were in control. Webster did not see it that way. A later president, Truman, would have told him that if he could not stand the heat, stay out of the kitchen, but Webster wanted a higher law and did not like the party strife. Although the people were not interested, there were many thinkers who were concerned. [15]

The antiparty feeling of Webster was inherent in the evangelical brand of Puritanism in the North. Man conscience, it was thought, could not bow to party compromise and abandon his principles. The organization of parties was alien to the highly moral stance and beliefs of many men in the Federalist party. This attitude weakened the party and was one of the reasons it failed. Weakness in politics due to inflexible principle was dangerous to party success. Many Federalists suffered for it when it came to winning and keeping political control. It also led to a disdain for leadership of the masses through organization. In this way, the Federalists were forfeiting political power and success. This view, typified by Webster led to weakness in politics. [16]

Meanwhile, Samuel Davis believed that the school his son Jeff was attending was not good enough. The planter wanted the best education for his son. He had reports of the excellence of a Springfield (Kentucky) boy's school run by Dominican friars. Although he was a Baptist, he preferred the Catholic school to his alternatives for Jeff. The boy was seven and his mother felt he was too young to be away from home, but the father's decision was law. Jane Davis never consented to this action, but Samuel was sure of what he wanted to do and sent Jefferson Davis with Major Hinds and his family and their two African American servants over the wilderness trail to Kentucky. It was an exciting trip for the boy and he had the Hinds boy in the party who was also seven. They passed through Nashville and met the courteous Andrew Jackson. Hinds and Jackson had fought against the British at New Orleans not too many months before. The wide-eyed boy saw his first hero outside his family and their friends. He found Rachel Jackson amiable and affectionate.

They reached Springfield and the young Davis began the second stage of his education, almost becoming a Catholic in the process. After two years, his mother demanded he return and Samuel had Jeff brought back downriver by steamboat, newly in operation on the Ohio and Mississippi. Once home, he continued his education at another boys' school, Jefferson College, near Natchez, where his older brother Joseph lived. The next year, the people opened an academy at Woodville and Samuel transferred him there. Once ready for higher education, Jefferson Davis entered Transylvania University of Lexington, Kentucky, one of the best colleges in the nation. He learned religious tolerance from Horace Holley and excelled in collegiate subjects. [17]

There was a clubfooted youth, born in Vermont on April 4, 1792, soon after the installation of the new American government. The pain of that youth over his physical deformity was such that it was evident throughout his life, molded his character, and helped shape history. His name was Thaddeus Stevens, the fourth and last child of a shoemaker who was more interested in exhibiting his skill as a wrestler in the nearby villages and further afield than tending to his family. He drank, was in debt constantly, and was a failure as a father. The father did not mold the child fortunately. As it was Thaddeus needed help. Of more importance to Stevens, than his fathers periodic desertion, was his belief that his clubfoot was an unjust punishment. The result was a life long bitterness and a sensitivity toward the oppressed. Coming from the poor class, he opposed unwarranted privilege and preference.

Sarah Stevens knew that there was a way open for her clubfoot son and so she encouraged him to read and learn where he could not play with the taunting boys of the neighborhood who in childlike fashion minced the unfortunate boy and rejected his difference. Thaddeus began with the family Bible and the few books of commentary and then walked to neighbors to borrow other books, while his mother expressed her hope that he would become a minister.

In 1797, neighboring Peacham built the county academy and Mrs. Stevens moved so her son could enjoy the benefits of education. The building was small filled with benches, a handful of classics, some texts, and a globe but for Thaddeus it was a opportunity. There he could mix some with the children and exceeded them in school studies. He did

The Difficult War: The Era of the War of 1812

find companionship in his last year when he participated in staging a forbidden tragedy at night by candlelight. Stevens signed a paper of apology admitting his mistake and promising to abide by the rules in the future. The Puritanical men of the Board of Trustees were satisfied. This was in 1811. The young man's studies led to attendance at Dartmouth College and the University of Vermont for a short time. He was at the last when the government took over buildings to house soldiers.

The war turmoil on the northern frontier was reflected circumstantially in Sevens' difficulties at Dartmouth. Bad behavior got him into trouble, a common occurrence. He studied with a minister, Mr. Carpenter, who told Thaddeus he would give him testimonials of good behavior. He had another friend teacher, a Samuel Merrill who had moved to York, Pennsylvania. Stevens thought secret societies provided sycophantic opportunities for unearned position. He was against fraternities especially.

After graduating, Stevens spent year and a half studying law under Judge John Battocks in Vermont. Then he got a teaching job at York with the aid of Merrill. He studied law while teaching and he kept away from friendships. In the Indian summer of 1816, he became a lawyer. He went to Lancaster to live and practice. This was to remain his home. Winning his first case, he entered a period of near poverty. Then he gained a substantial fee as he defendant's lawyer in a murder case. He lost. However, he was now known for ability and a proclivity for accepting unpopular cases and it was common knowledge that he would also take the cases of those who had little or no funds. Still considered an outsider, the people did now know him better, but respected him. He grew prosperous and bought land and a house, and was a city councilman of the Borough. [18]

---

[1]Coit, *Calhoun*, pp. 117-119.

[2]Pintard, *Letters*, I, 38-39. Quote on p. 38-39.

[3]*Ibid.*, I, 39-40. See 44.

[4]Davis, David Brion, "The Emergence of Immediatism in British and American Antislavery Thought," *Mississippi Valley Historical Review*, pp. 222-224.

[5]Fox, Early Lee, *The American Colonization Society, 1817-1840*, Baltimore, Johns Hopkins University Press, 1919, Reprint, New York: AMS Press, 1971, pp. 13-50.

[6]Carter, Clarence Edwin, *The Territorial Papers of the United States*, vol XVIII: The Territory of Alabama, 1817-1819, Washington DC: Government Publishing Office, 1962, pp. 3-10, 23.

[7]Coit, *Calhoun*, pp. 114-115. Quotes on p. 115.

[8]Current, Richard H., John C. Calhoun, *New York: Washington Square Press, 1966, pp.10-19.*

[9]Seager, Robert II, "Henry Clay and the Politics of Compromise and Non-Compromise," *The Register of the Kentucky Historical Society, LXXXV No. 1 (Winter 1987), 15-18.*

[10]*Dictionary of American Biography* VI 1, 456, V 1, 552.

[11]*Ibid.*, VI 1, 456, VII 1, 106-107.

[12]*Ibid.*, VI 1, 456; Mack, Edward C., *Peter Cooper: Citizen of New York*, 1949, p. 56.

[13]*Dictionary of American Biography*, VI 1, 456-457, IV, 365.

[14]Albion, p. 62. Quote on p. 62. See Bagnall, William R., *The Textile Industry of the United States*, Cambridge, Mass: Riverside Press, 1893, Reprint, 1971, vol. I, for information on this American industry, where it tells on pp. 218-219 that the tariff of 1816 raised the price of British cloth and the use of the power loom lowered the price of American cloth, making the American product more competitive.

[15]Nathans, Sydney, *Daniel Webster and Jacksonian Democracy*, Baltimore: The Johns Hopkins University Press, 1973, pp. 15-16.

[16]Formisano, Ronald P., "Political Character, Antipartyism, and the Second Party System," *American Quarterly*, 21 (Winter 1969), 683-709.

[17]Strode, *Davis*, pp. 11-25.

[18]Woodley, Thomas Frederick, *Great Leveler: The Life of Thaddeus Stevens, pp. 5-32.*

A

Abolitionism, 36
Adams, John, 8, 10, 25, 30, 31, 34, 38, 40, 43, 44, 46, 50, 70, 85, 91, 93, 95, 97, 105, 113, 116, 136, 137, 153, 154, 172, 175, 199, 202, 221, 223, 224, 226, 232, 244, 249, 250, 251, 255, 262, 264, 267, 269, 271, 283
African Americans, 36, 50, 63, 214, 223, 230, 233, 236, 238, 247, 249, 265, 266, 267, 280
agrarian interests, 5
Albert Gallatin, 3, 23, 171, 172, 176, 214, 232, 264
Alexander Cochrane, 215, 239
Alexander Contee Hanson, 119
Alexander I, 31, 38, 43, 269, 273
American army, 48, 133, 175, 182, 204, 205, 213, 214, 217, 225, 259
American exports, 5
American industry, 272, 282, 285
American Revolution, 15, 16, 48, 75, 77, 246, 262
American ships, 4, 5, 9, 11, 12, 13, 14, 24, 25, 28, 39, 49, 58, 94, 126, 128, 149, 153, 164, 174, 180, 183, 199, 222, 236, 240, 241
American soldiers, 111, 139, 141, 148, 169, 192, 193, 198, 206, 219
American trade, 12, 23, 24, 38, 39, 76, 102, 137
Andrew Jackson, 73, 80, 81, 82, 85, 88, 91, 95, 167, 168, 184, 193, 197, 200, 203, 228, 229, 238, 239, 241, 263, 266, 273, 284

B

Baltimoreans, 97, 207, 214
Bank of the United States, 24, 25, 35, 53, 60, 77, 103, 171, 271, 273
banking system, 272
Battle of Fallen Timbers, 46
Battle of Lake Erie, 187, 189, 193
Battle of Raisin, 167
Battle of the Thames, 192, 242
Black Hawk, 51, 193, 219, 225, 276, 277
Black Hawk War, 51
British army, 84, 112, 173, 190, 192, 211, 213, 215, 217, 222, 241, 242, 243
British forces, 99, 205, 228
British impressments, 14
British navy, 8, 9, 125, 153, 163, 195, 235
British Navy, 12, 108
British ships, 9, 13, 14, 23, 25, 31, 107, 109, 110, 139, 143, 145, 146, 163, 206, 220, 221, 225, 230, 247, 248
British trade, 11, 58

British troops, 111, 137, 198, 199, 211, 213, 227, 233, 235, 239
British victory, 214
British West Indies, 14, 165, 231
British-Canadian army, 174

C

Canada, 13, 19, 33, 38, 45, 48, 57, 58, 60, 66, 67, 69, 71, 73, 74, 75, 78, 79, 80, 84, 85, 87, 90, 93, 94, 95, 99, 102, 103, 104, 105, 110, 113, 117, 124, 126, 127, 128, 137, 139, 140, 142, 143, 149, 155, 157, 158, 165, 168, 173, 175, 179, 187, 191, 193, 195, 199, 205, 207, 215, 217, 223, 224, 225, 228, 237
Canadian defenses, 195
Cherokee, 17, 18, 28, 37, 79, 84, 85, 88, 89, 168, 169, 188, 193, 197, 205, 228, 229, 259, 260, 261
Chesapeake, 5, 12, 13, 14, 24, 25, 36, 83, 100, 116, 131, 134, 144, 153, 158, 161, 163, 164, 165, 176, 181, 208, 209, 271
Chickasaws, 27, 62, 228
Clay, Henry, 25, 35, 38, 43, 47, 68, 74, 76, 86, 87, 91, 104, 123, 127, 128, 133, 148, 199, 202, 223, 262, 267, 280, 281, 285
cloth, 113, 156, 219, 248, 264, 281, 282, 285
coastal trade, 112, 142, 165, 271
Codore letter, 39
colonization, 50, 109, 223, 280
conservatives, 15
Contraband, 4, 12
Creeks, 63, 65, 88, 89, 147, 148, 167, 168, 183, 184, 188, 191, 193, 197, 203, 204, 228, 229, 259, 261, 273
custom agents, 15, 102

D

Daniel Webster, 51, 172, 178, 181, 236, 255, 256, 257, 271, 283, 285
Davy Crockett, 191
Declaration of Independence, 4, 35, 59, 222
declaration of war, 67, 83, 94, 96, 97, 102, 110, 112, 113, 116, 117
defenses, 5, 59, 87, 99, 103, 140, 149, 157, 165, 181, 183, 185, 205, 207, 208, 213, 215, 216, 223, 227, 231, 236, 241
defensive policy, 96
depression, 14, 75, 112
Detroit, 28, 57, 58, 59, 60, 65, 84, 94, 99, 100, 107, 110, 111, 113, 123, 124, 127, 128, 133, 135, 136, 137, 139, 140, 166, 171, 191, 192, 250, 263
Duels, 200

E

economic sanctions, 8
Elbridge Gerry, 80, 85
election day, 265
emancipationist, 74
embargo, 13, 14, 15, 19, 24, 25, 28, 31, 35, 36,
    39, 54, 69, 79, 86, 97, 104, 112, 167, 244, 256
Embargo Act, 5
English goods, 282
Essex, 109, 125, 130, 144, 145, 146
European thinkers, 15
European war, 14, 265
excise tax, 3

F

Federal Club, 255
Federalism, 4, 266
Federalists, 4, 6, 7, 8, 14, 24, 43, 45, 49, 54, 57,
    74, 75, 78, 79, 80, 86, 87, 89, 90, 95, 97, 103,
    115, 119, 120, 150, 155, 156, 205, 206, 232,
    233, 243, 244, 248, 256, 273, 283, 284
foreign policy, 8, 86, 103
Fort Barrancas, 235
Fort Bowyer, 173, 230
Fort Crawford, 251, 253, 254
Fort Dearborn, 66, 111, 123, 128, 253, 254
Fort George, 128, 136, 140, 141, 149, 168, 173,
    174, 175, 179, 180, 198, 215
Fort Harrison, 95, 111, 131, 132, 147, 148
Fort Jackson, 229
Fort McHenry, 215, 216
Fort Meigs, 171, 176, 184
Fort Mims, 184, 188, 190
Fort Pickering, 131
Fort Scott, 273
Fort Stephenson, 185, 187
Fort Strother, 167, 169, 191, 196, 197, 203, 228
Fort Strothers, 228
Fort Wayne, 55, 123, 127, 128, 129, 132, 135,
    139
Fort Wayne Treaty, 55
Fort Winnebago, 254
Francis Scott Key, 216
Freemasons, 223
Frenchmen, 15, 39, 99, 118, 166
Frenchtown, 163, 166, 170

G

General Brock, 99, 128, 135, 140
General Protor, 185
General Stephen Van Rensselaer, 139, 140
George Armistead, 215
George Cockburn, 163, 183, 215

George McClure, 198
George Prevost, 84, 99, 128, 175, 224, 225, 227,
    237
George Washington, 9, 36, 46, 48, 58, 61, 64, 69,
    102, 158, 184, 255, 262

H

Hamilton, Alexander, 15, 19, 175
Harriet Beecher Stowe, 59
Hartford Convention, 32, 218, 236, 243, 244
Henry Dearborn, 18, 27, 84, 104, 112, 173
Henry Winder, 208, 215
Hezehiah Niles, 62
Hispanic America, 43, 77, 181, 240, 269
Holmes, Oliver Wendall, 31
Horace Greeley, 55, 60
House of Representatives, 13, 31, 39, 53, 68, 79,
    89, 95, 97, 150, 242
Hundred Days, 264
Hurons, 65

I

impressment, 8, 11, 12, 66, 75, 78, 86, 94, 115,
    224, 237
Indian attacks, 28, 75, 104, 133
Indian lands, 19, 65, 133, 254, 280
Indian policy, 58, 251
Indians, 17, 18, 19, 21, 25, 28, 29, 33, 37, 38, 41,
    42, 45, 46, 51, 54, 55, 57, 58, 59, 62, 63, 64,
    65, 66, 67, 69, 70, 78, 79, 84, 85, 86, 88, 89,
    94, 95, 99, 103, 104, 109, 110, 111, 117, 123,
    124, 127, 128, 129, 130, 131, 132, 133, 135,
    136, 139, 140, 142, 147, 148, 150, 152, 158,
    166, 167, 168, 169, 171, 172, 173, 175, 176,
    177, 181, 182, 184, 185, 187, 188, 190, 191,
    192, 195, 197, 198, 199, 203, 204, 205, 206,
    217, 219, 224, 229, 235, 236, 237, 238, 244,
    250, 251, 253, 254, 259, 260, 261, 263, 265,
    270, 276, 280
industrialization, 77, 281, 282
Isaac Brock, 66, 84, 99, 111, 141
Isaac Hull, 115, 120, 124, 126, 149

J

James Madison, 11, 16, 25, 27, 34, 50, 73, 86,
    155, 158, 261
James Monroe, 8, 9, 24, 35, 58, 75, 127, 133,
    153, 172, 209, 211, 212, 249, 250, 256
Jay Treaty, 232, 256
Jefferson Davis, 20, 25, 199, 284
Jefferson, Thomas, 3, 14, 15, 17, 34, 35, 50, 62,
    67, 222, 272
Jeffersonians, 3, 8, 148, 151, 266, 283

John Abbot, 51
John C. Calhoun, 7, 10, 59, 68, 70, 71, 76, 103, 104, 156, 253, 281, 285
John Harvey, 175
John Henry, 80
John Jacob Astor, 19, 264, 267
John Marshall, 34, 35, 50, 69, 266
John Quincy Adams, 31, 34, 38, 137, 153, 154, 172, 199, 224, 250, 262, 264, 271
John Randolph, 93
Johns Hopkins, 25, 214, 218, 245, 246, 251, 277, 285
Joseph Bonaparte, 118, 270
Joseph LaFollette, 206

K

Kentuckians, 13, 28, 29, 32, 82, 96, 104, 110, 123, 127, 133, 139, 156, 166, 167, 171, 172, 243
Kickapoo, 46, 87, 123, 148, 200, 219

L

Lewis and Clark Expedition, 19
Lewis Cass, 51, 111, 133
liberals, 8, 15, 115, 187, 269
Lincoln, Abraham, 3, 25, 29, 35, 42, 74, 261, 266, 275
Louisiana Purchase, 3, 18, 19, 73, 158, 269

M

Madison, James, 11, 16, 25, 27, 34, 50, 73, 86, 155, 158, 261
Madisonians, 155
manufacturing, 5, 29, 50, 68, 167, 271, 282, 283
Martin Van Buren, 5, 6, 155
Mexico, 20, 33, 41, 42, 44, 70, 78, 109, 158, 187, 193, 240, 260
militia system, 83, 149
militiamen, 12, 55, 59, 66, 112, 115, 120, 129, 130, 133, 139, 141, 142, 148, 150, 151, 160, 171, 172, 174, 175, 180, 184, 187, 198, 204, 207, 208, 209, 215, 217, 224, 243, 247
Missouri Fur Trade Company, 19
Missouri Territory, 19
monopolies, 29, 50

N

Napoleon, 8, 11, 12, 15, 16, 38, 39, 43, 48, 49, 56, 58, 76, 82, 85, 87, 93, 108, 109, 112, 115, 117, 118, 119, 137, 156, 174, 205, 206, 208, 214, 237, 240, 249, 255, 256, 264, 270

Napoleonic wars, 28, 206, 256
Napoleonic Wars, 49
national debt, 199
nationalists, 74
naval force, 7, 54, 57, 127, 139, 169, 236, 237
New England militia, 100
New England., 5, 54, 109, 159, 224, 227, 233, 265, 280, 282
Niagara, 16, 66, 90, 94, 99, 100, 102, 111, 112, 123, 127, 129, 133, 134, 136, 139, 140, 149, 174, 189, 191, 198, 216
Nonimportation Act, 108
Northwest, 46, 52, 65, 84, 100, 111, 123, 124, 139, 156, 171, 191, 192, 237, 251, 253, 257, 264
Northwestern army, 123

O

Old Ironsides, 116, 120, 251
Old Northwest, 253
Oliver Wendell Holmes, 270
Osage, 263

P

peace treaty, 173, 206, 228, 237, 250
Pennsylvanians, 139
post-war period, 253
Potawatomi, 46, 55, 87, 263
Potawwatomi, 139
privateer *Yankee*, 124
privateering, 105, 109, 126, 215, 244
Proctor, Henry, 166, 171, 172, 179, 185, 187, 191, 192
proslavery, 36, 50
protectionism, 29, 271, 282, 283
Prussian king, 206, 224

Q

quartermaster, 84, 151, 152, 193
Queenston, 136, 139, 140, 141, 174, 175, 181

R

Republican party, 53, 56, 67, 94, 283
Republican Party, 4, 27
Republicans, 4, 5, 7, 8, 12, 43, 45, 53, 74, 75, 78, 79, 86, 87, 89, 97, 103, 115, 119, 120, 125, 142, 150, 155, 156, 205, 232, 233, 243, 248, 273, 282
Revolutionary War, 20, 39, 58, 59, 79, 84, 97, 100, 116, 193, 200, 216, 220, 223
Richard Byron, 101

Russia, 31, 34, 38, 76, 137, 153, 154, 172, 199, 256, 264, 273
Russian czar, 172, 224

S

Sac, 29, 167, 219, 250, 263
Santa Anna, 42, 187
schooner *Atlas*, 124
schooner *Saratoga*, 153
Seminole, 86, 135, 137, 150, 273
Senate, 13, 31, 38, 48, 53, 56, 89, 94, 95, 148, 236, 256, 279
Senecas, 129
separationism, 20
Shawnee, 33, 46, 62, 89, 95, 132
Shenandoah Valley, 21, 103
slaveholders, 49, 50, 51, 63, 271, 280
slavery, 5, 6, 33, 36, 47, 49, 50, 59, 64, 68, 74, 118, 130, 135, 147, 150, 156, 222, 231, 245, 250, 262, 265, 275, 276, 280, 281
slaves, 5, 6, 7, 21, 29, 33, 35, 36, 47, 49, 50, 51, 63, 64, 67, 81, 85, 135, 150, 159, 163, 174, 184, 197, 222, 223, 230, 238, 241, 245, 249, 250, 280, 281, 283
smuggling, 5, 11, 14, 54, 102
Spanish army, 187, 240
Spanish colonies, 43
Steven Van Rensselaer, 136
Supreme Court, 24, 25, 34, 50, 51, 52, 59, 71

T

Tammany Hall, 223
tariff barriers, 29
Tecumseh, 33, 45, 46, 51, 55, 62, 63, 65, 89, 147, 148, 169, 183, 184, 187, 191, 192
Thomas Lincoln, 21, 22, 74, 133, 206, 261, 274, 275, 277
Timothy Pickering, 43, 233
Tippecanoe, 46, 65, 66, 68, 70, 79, 110, 130, 154, 162, 167, 170, 178, 193
Treaty of Fort Wayne, 46
Treaty of Ghent, 224, 250, 263

U

United States Navy, 9, 143

V

Van Buren, Martin, 5, 6, 155, 162, 262
Venezuelan revolution, 43

W

Walter Scott, 246, 251
war declaration, 237
war effort, 115, 134, 150, 152, 155, 157, 169, 171, 236
War Hawks, 36, 45, 49, 56, 59, 67, 68, 75, 79, 86, 93, 94, 96, 104, 112, 125, 163
Waterloo, 249, 255, 256, 270, 277
West Indies, 14, 84, 87, 95, 96, 108, 116, 134, 143, 144, 152, 153, 181, 196, 220, 221, 282
westerners, 32, 38, 66, 75, 78, 151, 158, 165, 272
Whiskey Rebellion, 3, 232
William Blount, 85
William Danridge Claiborne. See Claiborne, William Danridge
William Eustis, 30, 57, 65, 87, 90, 111, 151
William Henry Harrison, 19, 46, 63, 70, 95, 123, 128, 139, 165, 168, 263
William Henry Seward, 6, 275
William Hull, 33, 57, 58, 94, 100, 110, 123, 128, 158, 169
William Pitt, 8
Winfield Scott, 13, 16, 98, 136, 137, 141, 168, 173, 216, 222
Winnebagoes, 65, 95
Winnebagos, 254
working class, 266
Wyandots, 59, 65

Z

Zachery Taylor, 111, 131